The Complete Idiot's Refe

Wine Store Evaluation C

- ❑ Does the store carry a large selection of win...
- ❑ Are the wines organized well on the shelves?
- ❑ Are the wine clerks knowledgeable?
- ❑ Do they provide courteous and patient service?
- ❑ Are the prices competitive?
- ❑ Is the store display area cool?
- ❑ Is the wine storage area air conditioned?
- ❑ Are the better wines stored on their sides?
- ❑ Does the store feature many wines on special or discount?
- ❑ Does the store feature private labels or direct imports to provide savings?

Restaurant Wine Service Evaluation Checklist

- ❑ Does the restaurant have a well-rounded wine list or is it a limited one made up by its supplier?
- ❑ Does the wine list offer overaged and potentially dead famous wines at astronomical prices?
- ❑ Does the restaurant have a sommelier? If not, are the waiters knowledgeable about the wine?
- ❑ Are the wine glasses large enough?
- ❑ Are there different-shaped wine glasses for different kinds of wine?
- ❑ Are the wines stored in a refrigerated wine cellar?
- ❑ Are the white wines pre-chilled? If so, ask for a bottle to be chilled especially for you.
- ❑ Are the wine prices more than double retail?
- ❑ Can you bring your own bottle for a reasonable corkage fee?
- ❑ Can you take home what's left in the bottle?
- ❑ Does the restaurant offer several premium wines by the glass?
- ❑ Does the wine list feature half-bottles?

ALPHA

Vintage Chart

	97	96	95	94	93	92	91	90	89	88	87	86	85	84	83	82	81	80	79	78	77	76
Bordeaux Red	8a	8a	8a	7a	7a	6b	6b	9b	10b	7b	8c	8b	9b	6c	7b	10b	7c	6c	7c	7c	6d	7c
Bordeaux White	8a	8b	8a	7a	7b	6b	5c	10c	10d	6c	*	8d	8d	*	6d	6d	6d	5d	8d	8d	6d	7c
Bordeaux White Sweet (Sauternes)	8a	8a	8a	7a	7b	6b	5b	10b	10b	9b	*	8b	6c	5c	7b	7c	7c	7c	9c	8c	*	8c
Burgundy Red	9a	9a	8a	6a	8b	6b	6b	10b	8b	9b	7c	6d	7c	6d	8b	6d	7d	7d	7d	9c	5d	9c
Burgundy White	9a	9a	8b	9b	6c	8b	6c	8c	8c	7d	7d	8d	7c	6d	8d	8d	7d	7d	*	8d	*	8c
Alsace	9a	8b	8a	7a	7c	7c	7b	9c	10d	7d	7d	8d	8d	6d	10d	8d	8d	7d	10d	10d	*	10d
Rhone Red	–	–	8a	7a	4c	6b	7b	9b	9b	8c	5c	7c	9c	6d	8d	8d	7d	6d	7d	10d	*	7d
Champagne	8a	9a	8a	8b	7c	7c	5c	10b	10c	8c	NV	7c	10c	NV	8d	8d	8c	NV	8c	9b	NV	8c
German Rheingau	8a	8b	7b	8b	7c	6c	6c	9c	8c	7c	*	6c	7c	*	8d	*	*	*	*	*	*	10d
German Mosel Saar-Ruwer	-9a	8b	7c	9c	7c	6c	6c	9c	9d	7d	*	*	7d	*	*	*	*	*	*	*	*	10d
Italy-Piedmont	9a	9a	8a	7c	8b	6c	6c	9b	8c	9c	6c	8c	9c	5d	7c	9c	6c	7c	8c	9c	*	*
Italy-Tuscany	9a	8a	8a	7c	8c	7c	7d	9b	6c	7d	6c	8c	8c	5d	8c	9c	7d	7d	8c	9c	*	*
Portugal–Vintage Porto	–	–	–	10a	NV	9a	9b	NV	NV	NV	NV	NV	9a	NV	8b	7b	NV	7b	NV	9b	NV	NV
California Red (Napa/Sonoma Cabernet Sauvignon)	9a	9a	8a	9b	8b	8b	8b	9b	7c	6c	8c	8c	8c	7c	8d	8c	8c	9c	8c	9b	7c	8c
California White (Napa/Sonoma Chardonnay)	8a	8b	8b	9b	6c	8b	8b	8c	6d	7c	8d	8d	9d	8d	9d	8d	9d	8d	7d	8d	8d	8d

Key

10 – Exceptional	a – Too young to drink now
9 – Outstanding	b – Can be consumed now but will improve with aging
7-8 – Very Good	c – Ready to drink now
6 – Good	d – May be too old
5 – Average	NV – Non-vintage
4 – Poor	
1-3 – Very Poor	

*Try it, you'll probably pour it out, but you may be surprised

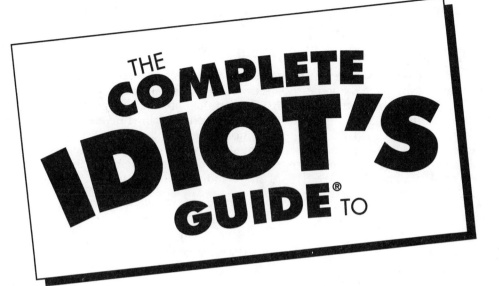

Wine
Second Edition

by Philip Seldon

alpha books

A Pearson Education Company

This book is dedicated to Pretty Lady and Sir Hillary, and to the memory of Princess, Dustbin, Gus, and Ginger Snap, all fabulous felines.

Copyright © 2000 by Philip Seldon

Publisher
Marie Butler-Knight

Product Manager
Phil Kitchel

Associate Managing Editor
Cari Luna

Acquisitions Editors
Gary M. Krebs
Amy Zavatto

Development Editor
Joan D. Paterson

Production Editor
JoAnna Kremer

Copy Editor
Carla Hall

Illustrator
Jody P. Schaeffer

Cover Designers
Mike Freeland
Kevin Spear

Book Designers
Scott Cook and Amy Adams of DesignLab

Indexer
Angie Bess

Layout/Proofreading
Fran Blauw
Darin Crone
Terri Edwards
Mary Hunt
Liz Johnston
Jeannette McKay
Louis Porter Jr.

Contents at a Glance

Appendixes

Contents

ix

xiii

Foreword

When I first started my winery in 1966, there were only 16 wineries in Napa Valley and a hundred or so wineries in all of California. Today there are 1,000 wineries in California, and over 250 in Napa Valley alone. Wine country is on the map as a popular tourist destination. Indeed, over four million persons visit Napa Valley every year. Over the past three decades, interest in wine has grown dramatically as American consumers have discovered the delicious taste of wine and how it adds to the quality of life, including its beneficial effect on health. And with the advent of new wine-making technology, affordable, quality wines are getting better and better with each passing year.

There are more than 30,000 wines available in the United States. While it is wonderful to have such choice, new wine consumers often feel like they are in a foreign country when visiting a wine store. There is a compelling need for a wine book that demystifies wine and explains wine in a straightforward language all consumers can understand. The *Complete Idiot's Guide to Wine* fills that need. Philip Seldon has written a marvelous book in direct, down-to-earth language, ideal for introducing wine to novice wine enthusiasts.

This second edition expands on the first with advanced chapters on Bordeaux and Burgundy and new chapters on everyday wines, organic wines, kosher wines, cooking with wine, and attending a winetasting. It is one of the best introductory books ever written; it demystifies wine and debunks notions that fine wine is something to be reserved only for special occasions and celebrations. It encourages individuals who are new to wine to take pleasure in a glass of wine with every meal as part of a rich and rewarding lifestyle. Furthermore, it emphasizes that wine is the beverage of moderation.

Philip Seldon touches on a subject that has been very close to my heart for more than six decades; specifically, the fact that moderate consumption of wine is beneficial to most people's health. He correctly points out that regular consumption of wine reduces the incidence of heart attack and stroke. Wine has the potential to add years to one's life, as well as enhance one's pleasure in living.

Philip Seldon is a leading figure on the international wine scene. I recall his early visits to my winery when he first founded *Vintage Magazine.* His questions were astute and to the point. He never left a stone unturned in his quest for knowledge about the wine industry and its numerous diverse products. He is to be commended for writing *The Complete Idiot's Guide to Wine* and bringing to the bookshelf a much-needed introduction to the complex subject of wine.

Robert Mondavi

Founder, Robert Mondavi Winery

Introduction

I love wine! Wine has been both my vocation and avocation for more years than I am willing to admit. And like most people who love something, I want to share the experience with others.

Wine offers many rich and wonderful adventures. But wine has baggage, a mystique, that keeps many people from opening its treasure chest of pleasures. Simply, wine scares people!

How about that wine list in the fancy restaurant? All those words in French, Italian, and German (some of them probably misspelled)! Or what about that wine shop, with bins and bottles and labels—and the clerk who wants to know what kind of wine you are seeking? And those prices—all over the map! Which are the values, and which the rip-offs?

I want to dispel all these uncertainties and fears, and I want you to have fun in the process. This is not an initiation into some ancient and mystical order! It's just a few simple basics. And some more simple things that build on those. And a few more.

The fact is this: Anybody can be a wine expert. It doesn't require some inborn gift or a graduate education. Don't get me wrong: The world of wine is a big one. No one person ever can assimilate it all. But that first 1 percent of wine knowledge will get you through 99 percent of your wine situations—at home, in a restaurant, in a wine shop.

That's why I wrote the two editions of this book. I want to make it easy for you, and fun. I like to know I've helped increase the world's population of savvy wine drinkers. I've tried to keep it simple as I distill my own rich experiences of the world of wine.

I'm not some armchair wine theorist. As founder of *Vintage Magazine*, I have developed a keen sense of what someone new to wine needs to know. I've been inside the wineries, the wine cellars, and the warehouses of distributors and major retailers. I've asked questions and gotten answers (not always the right ones!). I've tasted more than 200,000 wines and experienced first-hand the improvements in quality and consistency gained from modern winemaking technology throughout the world.

With this new, second edition, I've revised and updated the material and written eight new chapters:

➤ Two in-depth chapters about the noblest Bordeaux and Burgundies
➤ Canadian wines, very much worth your attention
➤ Organic wines
➤ Kosher wines
➤ Everyday wines, better than ever
➤ Attending winetastings
➤ Cooking with wine

New appendixes will help you discover more information about wine through the Internet; select wines for special occasions and be able to offer an appropriate toast; and choose accessories that complement your growing appreciation for wine.

I hope you enjoy reading this book as much as I've enjoyed writing it. More important, I hope you'll put your new knowledge to good use. Believe me: Wine is much better in your glass than it is on the printed page!

Extras

Throughout the book, you'll find helpful boxes that provide you with extra information. Here's what you'll find in each type of box:

The Sommelier Says

The advice of your own personal sommelier cautions you about practices in the wine world that can prevent the development of your own perceptions of wine.

Vino Vocab

Definitions of wine terms ensure you'll pick up the right lingo.

Tasting Tip

The information in these boxes helps you recognize and appreciate the qualities of wine.

Heard It Through the Grapevine

These boxes highlight historical and technological things you should know about wine.

Acknowledgments

First I would like to acknowledge my thousands of friends in the world of wine who helped me acquire the in-depth knowledge of wine necessary to write this book. They answered intrusive questions honestly and helped me learn how to taste a wine like a professional—an education that could not be obtained in any school, and one that would have required decades of experience in the wine trade to learn by assimilation. I would like to acknowledge my dear friend, Astrid Herren, whose company makes imbibing wine such a pleasure. Lastly, to all my readers of *Vintage Magazine,* who inspire me to write about wine.

Many thanks to my able colleague, Tony Moats, who provided invaluable assistance and moral support in writing this book. I would also like to acknowledge the guidance and patience of my editors, Amy Zavatto and Joan Paterson, who devoted timeless hours poring over the material for this book. Peter Slupski, webmaster of vine2wine.com, provided invaluable assistance with the Internet. Above all, I would like to honor the memory of the late Alexis Lichine, a good friend whose classic and monumental book, Alexis Lichine's *Encyclopedia of Wine,* was my ready reference whenever I needed specific information or statistics about a particular wine or wine region.

Trademarks

All terms mentioned in this book that are known to be or are suspected of being trademarks or service marks have been appropriately capitalized. Alpha Books and Pearson Education cannot attest to the accuracy of this information. Use of a term in this book should not be regarded as affecting the validity of any trademark or service mark.

Part 1
Let's Toast Wine!

Wine is older than history. Humans didn't invent wine. We discovered it—a natural process involving fruit and yeasts. Wine is as natural as milk and honey. But (if I may say so) far more interesting, far more complex, and firmly wedded with human tradition, both sacred and profane.

You can devote a lifetime to the study and appreciation of wine and fail to grasp it all, but a simple sip of the most unassuming vintage can provide pleasures accessible to anyone. You don't need a Ph.D. in oenology (the study of wine) to enjoy wine. But a gustatory education can be a valuable start toward getting the most out of your wine experiences. That's what this section is about.

You're going to learn what wine is, how it's made, and how it's served. Most important, we're going to banish any mysteries that might linger in your imagination about wine culture.

More specifically, you'll learn about the different grades of wine, from the everyday to the noble. We'll explore the wine color chart, from the palest gold to the deepest garnet. And we'll talk you through that very first glass, from pulling the cork through evaluating the aftertaste.

Here's where we discuss swirling and gurgling, but also, we'll cover the more mundane (though necessary) aspects of the wine experience—glassware, corkscrews, and storage. This section will be your introduction, not only to wine, but to the remainder of this book.

Chapter 1

The Wonders of Wine

In This Chapter

➤ The benefits of wine knowledge

➤ What *is* wine?

➤ Types of wine

➤ Quality categories

In this chapter you'll discover that wine is more than an ordinary beverage. But let's start with the most basic fact: Wine is the fermented juice of grapes or other fruit. (In this book we'll deal only with grapes.)

Grapes! Through a marriage of ancient tradition and modern technology, these unassuming fruits can be turned into just about anything—ranging from a simple and enjoyable drink to a complex and noble tribute to the winemaker's art.

Wine comes in many types and qualities, and in this chapter I'll provide an introduction to the awesome but thoroughly accessible world of wine.

The Road to Savvy Sipping

Okay. Just drink it, if you like. Imagine that wine is just a thirst-quenching beverage with a little bit of a kick. Imagine that one bottle is about as good as any other—or maybe you might say that one wine is a little flat, another a little sweet. Believe me, you'll have some good experiences, but it's doubtful any would be what you might call great.

To be sure, a glass of wine can augment the pleasure of a good meal. Wine enhances most any social gathering. And there's nothing quite like a contemplative glass or two during a quiet evening at home.

Let's compare drinking wine with listening to a great piece of music. Sure, you can listen while you're dressing for work, paying your bills, or microwaving popcorn. But can these ever equal the joy of sitting back, attuning your mind, and savoring the intricate melodies and harmonies that separate style, composer, and interpreter?

Those of us who know wine—and that can include you—know that a glass of wine can reward us with many variations of style and taste.

Honing Your Palate

If you're serious about tasting wine and increasing your knowledge of wine, you've probably got a lot of questions. For example, you want to know what distinguishes a mediocre wine from a great wine, right? Okay. Let me further develop my music analogy:

Imagine you're hearing, say, Beethoven's Fifth Symphony played by a community symphony orchestra. The orchestra has rehearsed. Everyone's playing the right notes at the right time. Sure, the listening experience is pleasant. But if this is your very first exposure to Beethoven, you may wonder why so many generations have been so awed by the scowling, shaggy-haired maestro.

On the other hand, if you'd heard the same work played by one of the world's great orchestras, you would have experienced all those things that community orchestras seldom deliver: subtlety, style, and flavor. Only a great conductor can reveal the most subtle nuances of orchestration by drawing on the talents of each musician.

Heard It Through the Grapevine

You may know that every major orchestra has its own unique style: the bite of the strings, the color of the woodwinds, the sonority of the brass, and the overall balance. Sometimes orchestra, conductor, and composition all come together in your listening presence, and you know you are in the middle of a very big experience. At the end, you simply have to find release for all that accumulated feeling—joy, pathos, humor. A little polite applause simply won't do. You are up out of your seat crying, "Bravo! Bravo!"

Please indulge me as I milk this music analogy a little further. Here's an exercise you can do that may bring my point home:

1. Go through your CD collection. Anything: classical, jazz, rock, whatever.

2. Pick out a really superlative recording—one where all the elements add up to produce nothing less than what you would call the best. Then pick out another one that is so-so. Your choice.

3. After listening to both of them, get paper and pencil and make a list of all the things that make the super recording stand out and all the things that the mediocre version lacks.

Chances are that with only a few slight modifications, you'll be able to apply this very list to tasting wine.

Complexity Builds Confidence

Learning about wine isn't easy. There's a lot more to it than, say, remembering which foods go with red wine and which with white. The first thing you must do is to free yourself from the constraints of other people's decisions. We live in a fluid society where rigid ideas of how things should be done aren't acceptable anymore.

Think of learning about wine as a tool of empowerment. Imagine some know-it-all insisting that red wine has no place with seafood. Imagine, now, you disagreeing heartily, knowing you can back up your own stance with vigor and confidence. You'll feel good on two counts: You'll have the pleasure that comes from the fullest appreciation of the qualities of a good wine, and you'll have defended your own taste, rather than having bowed meekly to some bully's passé assertion.

The Sommelier Says

Pay no attention to wine snobs. These are people who take more pleasure in being correct than they do in wine. Your wine experiences are for your own pleasure, not to deal with the hang-ups of others.

Wine Defined

Wine is fermented fruit juice. *Fermentation* is the conversion of sugar—in the case of wine, grape sugar—into alcohol by the action of yeast. (If we go too far, the process continues all the way to acetic acid, or vinegar.) Wine can be made from a number of fruits—from apples to pomegranates—but the scope of this book is limited to wine made from grapes. (Whew!)

The complexity of wine lies in the fact that good wine does not just appear naturally, although grapes will ferment into wine on their own and then turn into vinegar.

Vino Vocab

Fermentation is a biochemical process that turns sugars into alcohol and carbon dioxide. It takes place inside one-celled fungi called yeasts.

Three factors interact to determine the character of a wine:

1. The grape variety and how it's grown
2. The climate and soil where it is grown
3. The vintner's (winemaker's) creative or commercial objective and winemaking skills

The odds do not favor the winemaker. In an ideal world, a superior grape planted in a favorable environment will automatically produce a great wine. But in the real world of winemaking, it is surprisingly easy to turn a potentially great wine into an expensive bottle of mediocrity, if not some awful-tasting microbiological disaster.

The vintner has the dual role of scientist and artist. Europeans tend to favor the artistic element, while New World winemakers accent the scientific. This distinction may not be surprising in light of the fact that we live in a society where Microsoft is more of a household word than Michelangelo. It may also have to do with the fact that the growth of the American wine industry has coincided with the technological advances of the past 30 years.

Winemakers today have sophisticated technology that enables them to make good quality wine at low prices (a good thing to know when you feel like telling off snobbish acquaintances). Technology serves as the background for artistry, enabling winemakers to infuse their wines with the subtle differences in flavor and style that distinguish the products of one vintner from another, grapes and environment being the same.

Heard It Through the Grapevine

Research studies suggest that drinking wine in moderation is good for your health. That does not mean that you should cancel your health insurance and buy more wine with the money you save! A glass or two of red wine each day will reduce both your cholesterol and your risk of heart disease. One or two glasses of any kind of wine a day will reduce the risk of heart attack from other causes. However, keep in mind that drinking any alcoholic beverage in excess can cause serious health problems. (See Chapter 34, "To Your Health!" for more on wine and your health.)

What's My Wine?

An appreciation of harmony and subtlety is essential to the experience of fine wines. But it takes more than that to discriminate between a superb wine and one that is simply good—or the good from the merely mediocre. We need to understand why some German Rieslings stand head-and-shoulders above those wines made from the same grape variety in California. Or how a Napa Valley Cabernet Sauvignon may run circles around an Italian Chianti Classico.

Believe me, there is nothing inherently better or worse about European or New World wines. A number of factors are involved, and the quality of the end product depends on the interaction among them.

To help you understand what to expect from a particular wine, you first need to understand what kind of wine it is. So let's examine the basic types of wine:

➤ Table wines

➤ Sparkling wines

➤ Fortified wines

➤ Apéritif wines

Red, White, and You!

If the term *table wine* evokes an image of a bottle or carafe sitting on a red-and-white checkered tablecloth, you have the right idea! Table wines, simply, are reds, whites, and rosés produced to accompany a meal. Most of the wines we drink (and will discuss in this book) fall into this basic category.

Wineries are required to state alcohol content on the label. But this rule is a little lax: The stated amount may be off by as much as 1.5 percentage points! That is, a wine designated as 12 percent alcohol could fall anywhere between 10.5 and 13.5 percent. Despite this legal laxity, some labels are very accurate. When you see a number like 11.2 percent or 12.6 percent, chances are the winemaker is giving you a more precise reading. I mean, would you make up a number like 11.2 percent?

Tasting Tip

Table wines range in alcohol content from 9 to 14 percent (by volume). Wines with more than 14 percent alcohol (that is, fortified wines) are subject to higher taxation and are classified separately. Ports, Sherries, Marsalas, and Madeiras are examples of fortified wines.

Varietals Are the Spice of Life

Varietal wines are named for the primary grape used to make the wine. Some varietal wines use one grape exclusively, while others blend the dominant grape with other grape types. When more than one grape is used, the minimum percentage of the designated grape is regulated by law. There's considerable variety in the regulatory codes.

Here are a few examples:

➤ In California and Washington, the minimum percentage of the named grape is 75 percent.

➤ In Oregon, it's 90 percent (with the exception of Cabernet, which may be only 75 percent, like its northern and southern neighbors).

➤ In Australia and the countries of the European Union, the required content is 85 percent.

Drinking Stars

Sparkling wine is wine with bubbles—like soda, but not artificially carbonated. Sparkling wine was first perfected in Champagne, France, in the early 1700s by the Benedictine monk and cellarmaster Dom Perignon. (So that's who he was!) Upon seeing the bubbles in his glass, the good brother eloquently captured the essence of his discovery with the words, "I am drinking stars!"

In the United States, the terms *champagne* (that's a lowercase *c*!) and *sparkling wine* often are used interchangeably. Legally, winemakers in the U.S., Canada, and Australia are allowed to use the name champagne for their sparkling wines with one catch: The bubbles must be produced naturally during the fermentation process and not added through artificial carbonation. Within that requirement, the choice of grape varieties is up to the producer, and champagne can be made by several methods (not necessarily those used by the French).

In France, the home of the real (capital *C*) Champagne district (or *appellation*), the story is entirely different. Understandably, the proud French are not amused that others use the name of their fine and cherished creation for just any effervescent wine.

In France, only sparkling wines made from grapes grown in the Champagne region may bear the name Champagne (or anything resembling it). This rule is law, also, in all the member nations of the European Union.

Strong, But Sweet

Fortified wines are those in which the alcohol content has been increased by the addition of brandy or neutral spirits. They usually range from 17–21 percent alcohol, by volume. Ports, Sherries, Marsalas, and Madeiras all are fortified wines. In the U.S., many look on these as a matter of acquired taste.

Dessert wines are almost always fortified wines. Most, though not all, are quite sweet. They are best suited to drinking by themselves or after a meal. The terms *fortified wines* and *dessert wines* often are used interchangeably.

More Than Mixers

Technically, *apéritif* (appetizer) wines are white or red wines flavored with herbs and spices to give them a unique flavor (and often, a unique color). Vermouth falls into this category. Lillet is another example. Lillet is a lot more popular in Europe than in the U.S.

Vino Vocab

Appellation is a fancy English word (and a perfectly good French one) meaning name, title, or designation. In the world of wine, it's commonly applied geographically.

Heard It Through the Grapevine

The word **apéritif** seems to be a fancy way of saying "appetizer," but originally it meant something very different—a purgative, literally something that opens you up. Traditionally, mixtures of bitter herbs did the job. Some milder concentrations of these happen to taste good and remain with us today in such popular forms as vermouth.

Subtle Shades of Wine

The three basic colors of wine are white, red, and pink (rosé). Within each color category, there are countless gradations. Sometimes, these can provide clues to the wine's taste quality (such as lightness, fullness, clarity, brilliance) and age. More important, the appearance of the wine can reveal flaws that should place you on guard when you take that tasting sip.

From Straw to Gold

To say a wine is white essentially means it lacks red pigment. If wine shops had swatch books for customers like paint emporiums, white wines would present a rich palette from pale straw, through light green-yellow, through yellow, to a deep golden color.

White wines attain their color (or lack of color, depending on your perspective) in one of two ways. Most frequently, they are made from white grapes. (Of course, white grapes actually are green or yellow or a combination of the two.)

Now here's a surprise for you: White wine can also be made from the juice of red grapes! In fact, the red pigment resides only in the grape's skin, not in the juice. Therefore, when wine is fermented without the skins, the wine will remain white regardless of the grape variety.

White wine comes in a number of styles, such as "light-bodied and refreshing," "soft and mild," "full-bodied," or "oaked and complex." We will go into greater detail on wine styles and qualities later in this book.

Tasting Tip

Like people, wines look best in natural or incandescent lighting. Unless you're drinking your wine at the office party, avoid fluorescent lights because they give the wine a false color. Fluorescent light is missing parts of the spectrum, and it will distort the colors of red wines, giving them the brownish appearance of wines that have aged past their prime.

Red and Rich

Red wine is easily identified by—you guessed it—its deep red color. Without even making the association, you may have, at some time or another, used the name of the most famous red wine region—Burgundy—to describe the color of a scarf or sofa or dress or the upholstery of the car with the six-figure price tag. To many people, the very color of red wine denotes richness.

Heard It Through the Grapevine

In a decorator's swatch book, red wines would range in color from pale brick, through deep ruby, through purple, to inky-dark burgundy. In winemaker's language, the grapes from which red wines are made are black grapes (although here I will continue to refer to them as red). During the fermentation process, the dark skins remain in contact with the colorless juice, and voilà!—red wine.

Tannic or Tart

The skins of red grapes contain *tannin*, which is the key to the major taste distinction between red and white wines. The longer the juice is left in contact with the skins, the higher the tannin content, which gives the wine an astringent and tart character.

If you're not used to the taste of a strong red wine, you may find yourself puckering up. You may have had a similar sensation the first time you tasted strong tea (which, like wine, contains tannic acid) or even lemonade (citric acid). Once you become used to the taste of tannin, you'll miss it when it's not there.

In wine language, tannins produce the firmness of a red wine. A wine with a high tannin content may taste bitter to even the most seasoned wine lover. This is one reason why red wines are matched carefully with a meal. A wine that tastes unpleasantly bitter on its own may be the perfect complement to a steak or roast beef dinner.

Vino Vocab

Tannin is an astringent acid derived from the skins and seeds of grapes that causes a puckering sensation in the mouth.

A Bit of Blush

The third shade (type) of wine is recognized by its pink color—and no, it is not made by mixing red and white wine together! Rosé wines are made from red grapes that are left in contact with the skins for only a few hours—just long enough to absorb a tinge of color and very little tannin.

Light and Rosy

Because the skin contact in rosés is minimal, their tannin content is low. No puckering up. Like white wines, rosés are served chilled and go better with lighter foods. They make a refreshing summer drink and a good party beverage.

Quality Control

Wine comes in several qualities, but the wine industry and many authors differentiate only two categories—everyday (or jug wine) and *premium wine*, with the premium category encompassing wines ranging from a low of $7 a bottle to wines selling for several hundred dollars a bottle.

This broad premium category is meaningless for describing all these wines! For the purpose of explaining wine quality, I've devised a scheme of wine categories that divides the old premium category into three: simple, mid-premium, and super-premium. And I have added a new category, noble wines, for those rare wines that evolve into magnificent works of art when fully mature.

The wine industry uses the term "fine wine" to denote, simply, wines that are bottled in glass and closed with a cork (as opposed to a screw cap, plastic bottles, or boxes). Now that many everyday wines are bottled with corks rather than screw caps, this term should refer only to wines that are in the mid-premium quality category or better.

Good Ol' Wines

What does the term "jug wine" invoke? A dorm party? A big ol' jug on the floor of the car or pickup when you were just barely old enough to drink (or, yikes, drive)?

Actually, jug wines don't always come in jugs. Many now come in *magnums* (double-sized bottles). Over the years, they've gotten a lot of bad press. Jug wines are simple wines made for immediate consumption. They're not really bad—just ordinary. Like the community orchestra playing Beethoven, it's still Beethoven. Just don't look for a lot of complexity or finesse.

Premium and Super-Premium

Premium wines have more character and finesse. They have texture and complexity. They evoke the flavors and aromas of the grape variety (or varieties) of the region of origin. Unlike jug wines, which have a short after-taste, the taste of premium wines lingers on the palate, which adds another dimension to the wine-tasting experience: Frequently, new flavors appear in the aftertaste.

Premium wines span a price range from $7 to $35 per bottle, with a similar range in quality. I'll use the term "super-premium" frequently in this book to describe the higher-quality end of the premium category with the hope that the wine industry adopts it. It should. It's a very useful descriptive term for wines that are close to noble quality but not quite there.

Tasting Tip

Good jug and everyday wines can be tasty, pleasant, and refreshing. They offer vinous (grape-like) flavor, along with body, balance, and straightfor-ward appeal.

Nobility and Breeding

In my scheme of wine quality categories, *noble wines* are the best-of-the-best among fine wines. Simply to call them "fine wines" would be like calling Japan's prized Kobi beef "steak" or a Triple Crown-winning racehorse a "nag."

The producers of noble wines spare no expense or effort in producing them, and the result is a wine of breathtaking beauty. Noble wines have distinctive characteristics that set them apart from all other libations. "Breeding" is a good word to describe them, and it's not meant for snob appeal.

These wines are like a performance on the cello by YoYo Ma or a flawless operatic per-formance in Vienna. It's the nature of these rare wines to be complex, leading us to such assessments as "delicate, yet assertive." These wines are multifaceted, like dia-monds. In the world of wine, noble wines are truly the greatest works of art.

Heard It Through the Grapevine

The unique qualities of noble wines are most apparent after prolonged aging. Just as with the world's greatest artists, their performance gains in stature as they mature. We may find our noble wines cloistered in climate-controlled cellars, developing their maximum potential as great works of art. When aged, lesser wines may not develop better qualities and may actually deteriorate.

Estate Bottling: Doing It All

An *estate* is a wine plantation where the grapes are grown, fermented, and ultimately, bottled. This all-in-one approach to winemaking is a good way to ensure quality. In the world of business, this is called "vertical integration."

Vino Vocab

Estate bottling means that no part of the winemaking operation is farmed out to someone who might be content to give less than an all-out effort.

With estate bottling, there are no gaps in the chain of accountability. The winery controlling the vineyards is responsible for the whole deal, from the raw materials through the end product. Winemakers take pride in their operations and strive toward products that satisfy customer tastes. Most estate-bottled wines say so on the bottle, but not always. While in days gone by, the term *estate bottling* was used only on the finest of wines, today many inexpensive and sometimes inferior wines use the term estate bottled as they legally qualify.

Nothing but the Best

As noted before, wine is the midpoint between grape juice and vinegar. Noble wines like Chateau Lafite-Rothschild don't just happen by accident, and there's not much market for noble vinaigrette.

The more expensive wines are the product of superior grapes, technical expertise, artistic indulgence, and loving care. A lot of personal involvement goes into the process, along with skill, flair, and finesse.

Harmony, symmetry, complexity, finesse, and elegance are some of the words defining the unique character of a noble wine. Close your eyes and see what images those words invoke. Now you know why some wines cost so much.

Simple, but Satisfying

Barring some strange disaster, any winemaker can produce a decent jug wine. There's no need for split-second timing in harvesting, no subtle blending, no anxious nail biting during fermentation. The result is simple and pleasant and virtually guaranteed.

Producing a wine that's merely competent is less labor-intensive, less chancy, and consequently less expensive than producing an extraordinary wine. They cost less to make, so they cost less to buy. Pretty simple, huh?

The Least You Need to Know

➤ A little knowledge—not easy, but worthwhile—will make wine-drinking more enjoyable.

➤ Wine is the fermented juice of grapes or other fruit.

➤ Wine comes in several varieties—table wine, apéritif wine, dessert or fortified wine, and sparkling wine. It also comes in three basic colors—white, red, and rosé.

➤ Wines range in quality from ordinary to rare and wonderful works of art—jug wines, premium wines, and noble wines.

➤ Better wines cost more because they are more expensive to make.

Savvy Serving

In this chapter you'll become acquainted with those strange gadgets called corkscrews and those crystalline bowls on stilts, called wineglasses. In addition to all the special accessories, serving wine requires a bit of special knowledge.

Here, you'll learn the best temperatures for serving red and white wines, and you can join the debate over breathing versus nonbreathing (that is, letting wine stand before serving or pouring immediately). You'll learn that a decanter is more than a decorative item.

Finally, you'll find out how to keep an open bottle of wine without having to use it as salad dressing. Opening and serving wine may not be as simple as pouring a soda, but it is not the arcane task you might have thought.

Conquering the Cork

Wine bottles don't come with pop tops. Yes, some do come with screw caps (and a negative image).

It's possible that part of the cork's elite image is due to the trouble it takes to open a corked bottle. You figure that with all the effort involved, there has to be something worthwhile inside. That's one good reason to increase your wine know-how. It increases the chances that the beverage inside this sealed bottle really will be worth opening.

There is one practical reason for the traditional association of corks with good wine: Only a cork provides the permanent seal necessary for prolonged aging. Corks used for noble wines are longer (two inches) and less porous than those used for many premium wines.

The Sommelier Says

Many people insist on corked bottles, disdaining screw caps. They believe the bottle closure is an indicator of quality. It isn't.

Heard It Through the Grapevine

The reason for using a cork seal is not to make wine lovers feel like klutzes. Cork has some very special properties. This lightweight wonder is made of millions of hollow cells, each separated by a strong, impermeable membrane. A cork can be compressed for insertion, and once in place, it expands to create a tight fit. Most wine producers prefer a straight, untapered cork at least one and one-half inches long.

Most corks used throughout the wine world come from Spain or Portugal—they provide close to 90 percent of the world's total supply. The tree used for cork is the cork oak, *Quercus suber*, which grows in warm climates.

If a cork is dry or crumbles when you try to remove it, it is a sign that the wine has not been stored on its side to keep the cork moist. Most of the time, the wine still will be okay, but if it isn't you have a good reason to reject it in a restaurant. Sniff the cork to see if it smells like wine. If it smells of vinegar or mold (or anything else), you know the wine is spoiled.

First the Foil

Before you even get to the cork, you will need to deal with the foil (called the *capsule*). You can remove it in any of three ways:

➤ Cut through it with a knife below the lip area at the top of the bottle.

➤ Slice through the foil around the neck and rip the whole thing off in one motion.

➤ Use the foil cutter on your wine-opening tool, which makes cutting the foil a breeze.

I prefer to remove the foil entirely. That way you can see the length of the cork and the chateau name or trademark printed on it before you open the bottle. Sometimes the vintage date or even the brand may be different from what is on the label. In this case, go with the cork!

You Need a Good Gadget ...

Removing a cork requires neither the brain of Albert Einstein nor the brawn of Arnold Schwarzenegger. It takes just a little practiced skill and an instrument of some sort.

For years, our choice in corkscrews was very limited. Today, there are a variety on the market. Some are great, some not so good. Select the corkscrew that best suits your own wine-opening style.

The most popular corkscrew is the waiter's corkscrew, which looks like a shiny, scaled-down Swiss Army knife (without the red handle). The waiter's corkscrew has a *helix*-type worm (spiral screw) that works well because it grips the cork firmly, allowing for easy removal. Avoid the *augur* type, with its point set dead-center. With this, the cork is more likely to emerge in pieces.

The waiter's corkscrew has a fold-out piece for a fulcrum and a knife for cutting the foil. It takes some practice to use it efficiently, but once you acquire the skill you will appreciate its traditional simplicity. Here's how: You screw the corkscrew into the cork. Then you place the little fulcrum arm on the lip of the bottle. Finally, you use the body of the instrument as a lever to pull the cork.

Vino Vocab

A **helix** is what you'd get if you wound a wire several turns around a pencil and then stretched it out a bit. An **auger** is similar, but shaped more like a spiral staircase.

Waiter's corkscrew.

The "Ah-So" pronged corkpuller (you can invent your own reason for this unusual name) is not a corkscrew at all, but a two-pronged device developed in Germany.

To use it, you insert one slender steel leg, the longer one, a little way alongside the cork. Then you insert the other prong along the other side. Then you use a rocking motion to get the prongs fully inserted around the cork. (Be very careful you don't push the cork into the bottle!) Finally, you remove the cork by twisting gently and pulling.

I think the Ah-So is a difficult gadget. Not only does it demand a tender touch, but it does not work on all corks. When it does work, the Ah-So has two major advantages. The first is the reasonable ease and speed of operation. The second is that the cork is removed intact and can be reinserted easily.

The drawbacks are that the Ah-So requires much more skill than most corkscrews, and it's severely challenged by a dried-out cork. If the cork is at all loose, the Ah-So pushes it into the wine before it can be gripped. This is the nightmare of many wine novices (and non-novices). If the thought of it makes you sweat, try another device.

Tasting Tip

For all the trouble the Ah-So corkpuller can be, I recommend you get one. Here's why: Once your corkscrew has drilled a big hole through the cork, and the cork remains in the bottle, the Ah-So is your only hope.

Ah-So corkpuller.

At first glance, the twin-lever and twin-screw corkscrews look like Rube Goldberg inventions. They are somewhat clumsy in size, but both are simple to use. Both gadgets rely on the principle of mechanical advantage to make removing the cork easier.

The twin-lever works by twisting the screw into the cork and then using another lever to pull it out. If the device is made well, it really will be effortless. To use the twin-lever corkscrew, follow these simple steps:

1. Place the instrument over the wine bottle.
2. Turn the handle attached to the screw to get the worm into the cork.
3. Turn the second handle attached to the cylinder. The cork glides out of the bottle.

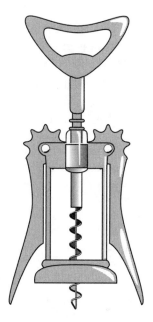

Twin-lever corkscrew.

Depending on the manufacturer, these devices can range from excellent to awful. Twin-levers come in either wood or metal. Look for a sharp point and a wide-helix worm.

But Not a Trendy One!

It was all the rage a decade ago—the device with a needle, which pumped air to force out the cork. It seemed to be a clever gadget, but in the end, it wasn't very smart. It should have disappeared. Instead, it seems to have proliferated! Pick up any wine accessories catalog and I'm sure you'll see one.

This horrible instrument is all wrong for wine in nearly every respect. First, it pumps air into the wine, which can stir up the sediment, especially in an older wine. Second, the needle simply may push a loose cork in. Third, if a cork is no longer airtight, the air simply escapes and the cork stays put. The last drawback can be disastrous. In a case where the cork is tight and the bottle defective, the pressure can cause the bottle to shatter.

Simply the Best Corkscrew

The Screwpull is the patented name of a sculptural-looking item that minimizes finger pressure and offers great strength and durability for long-term use. This nifty piece of design comes with a long, powerful worm and a strong plastic design for the needed support. Its self-centering action removes corks with minimal effort.

The Screwpull makes it easy for even the most inept person to extract any cork like a pro, using the following steps:

The Sommelier Says...

Unfortunately, the worm of the Screwpull can come out of its housing and present a serious hazard to children (and adults as well), as it is extremely sharp. Keep the Screwpull in a place safe from children.

1. Simply put the Screwpull over the bottle's top, centering the worm over the cork, and turn the handle on the top counterclockwise.

2. After the worm is in the cork, keep turning and the cork moves out of the bottle.

3. After the cork is out of the bottle, hold on to the cork and turn the handle counterclockwise some more—the cork will pop right off the worm.

The Screwpull also comes in a completely automatic lever version, which is my favorite. It makes pulling the cork a breeze in a two-step process. You place this gadget over the bottle and pull the lever—the screw goes in and the cork comes out in one simple operation. Then you pull the lever again, and the cork slips off the screw. Really neat!

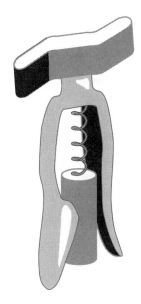

The Screwpull.

Glass Act

Does it make a difference what kind of glass you drink your wine in? Indeed it does! Let me give you a few simple guidelines for choosing the right glass (once you've chosen the right wine, that is).

Crystal glasses are ideal but not necessary. Their beauty and clarity make the wine sparkle with a true radiance. However, ordinary glass vessels are fine and less likely to break in a dishwasher. I have experienced some crystal stemware that was so delicate it shattered even when I gave it a gentle bump. Serious wine service needs something a bit hardier.

You can find good, ordinary glass wine glasses for about $50 to $75 a dozen. Crystal wine glasses start at around $75 a dozen, and the sky is the limit—$40 a stem is not unusual, and the best sell for upwards of $100.

Red Wine, Not Green Glasses!

Colorful Art Deco glasses are not what you should choose for your wine. After all, the wine's color is a clue to its body, richness, and quality. You'll

The Sommelier Says

Beware of lead crystal. Studies have determined that the lead in the glass leaches out into the wine in as short a period as a half hour. Wine, particularly Ports and other high-alcohol wines, should not be stored in lead-crystal decanters. Many crystal glass manufacturers are using ingredients other than lead to harden their glass—look for crystal that does not use lead.

never be able to weed out wines with imperfections when viewing them through some colored glass. Any glass that masks or changes the wine's true color certainly will not enhance your sensory experience.

Of course, if you insist on using blue, red, or green glasses, you may come up with new phrases for wine tasting: "Ah yes, the color of Mississippi mud, this is no doubt a fine vintage Lafite Rothschild ...."

Stick with the old rule of clear, colorless glasses.

Shape and Stem

Some are fatter and rounder and some are elliptical. Is there really a reason, you ask? And why do they all have that long stem that makes breakage so easy, if not inevitable?

There is a reason why wine glasses have a long stem (and it's not to make glassmakers rich as you keep replacing them). The stem is there to keep you from touching the bowl, which can result in a temperature change of the wine from the heat of your hand. It also keeps fingerprints off the bowl. Remember, enjoying wine is a pan-sensory experience. Do you really want to be looking at thumb whorls as you examine the deep, rich color of a tawny Port?

The capacity of the glass should be ample. This is hardly surprising when you consider that your nose is going to dive in.

The actual shape of the glass is less important. But there is one rule to follow: The rim of the bowl should curve in slightly to help capture the aroma you generate by swirling.

An All-Purpose Vessel

If you don't want to splurge on five or six types of glasses, or you don't have the room to store them, you're in the company of most wine drinkers. The usual all-purpose glass is a round-stemmed glass with an 8- or 12-ounce capacity.

Tasting Tip

Either the classic Bordeaux or Burgundy glass makes a fine all-purpose wine glass. One exception is Champagne, which needs its own glass. Get these two types of glasses, and you'll be set!

The Burgundy Bowl

The Burgundy glass is a large, round-stemmed wine glass with a large, curved bowl and a width approximately the same dimension as its height. It has a large opening and is particularly suitable for capturing the exquisite perfume and bouquet of a fine Burgundy. A typical size will be 12 or 16 ounces (although many come 24 ounces or larger). Of course, it's good for any kind of wine, and it is ideal for wine with very complex aromas.

The Burgundy glass.

The Oblong Bordeaux

The Bordeaux glass is quite different from the Burgundy glass in that its height is much greater than its width. Generally, it has a smaller opening than the Burgundy glass to capture the vinous quality of a fine Bordeaux. It is also a good choice if you can select only one wine glass.

The Bordeaux glass.

The Magic Flute

To fully appreciate the bubbles, pour your Champagne only into glasses with a high, narrow, tapering bowl—like the traditional Champagne *flute*. These usually come in a six- to eight-ounce size that can be filled to the top.

25

Champagne flutes.

You mustn't swirl your Champagne (see Chapter 3, "Sensory Sipping and Sensible Storage," for more about swirling). Its forceful bubbles exude the wine's flavor, so you don't need to have a large space above the wine, as with most other table wines.

Hocks, Snifters, and Balloons

If you're a white wine enthusiast, you might want to try the tall, slender Hock glass, originally intended for Rhine wines. If your choice is red, a big Burgundy balloon glass can add some variety to your table, although some wine drinkers find it too unwieldy.

No doubt you've seen the oversized Cognac or Brandy snifters. Their large size enables devotees to capture the wine's essence, slowly funneling it to the nose. Snifters add an elegant touch to your table, and this is one case where bigger is definitely better.

Note: A 16-ounce snifter is actually meant to hold no more than one or two ounces!

Keeping 'Em Clean

Regardless of whether you opt for the basics or set aside room for a wine connoisseur's collection of glassware, caring for wine glasses requires special attention. Not only do you want to avoid breaking any, but you want to keep your wines looking and tasting their very best.

The Sommelier Says

Avoid the typical wedding glass—that flat saucer with the hollow stem. Otherwise, you'll watch in dismay as those costly bubbles fade quickly from sight.

Tasting Tip

There's a special Sherry glass, called a *copita*. It's a small glass with a narrow taper and a small opening. The Sherry glass is made to capture the wine's aroma, and it's also perfect for enjoying other cordials.

Wine glasses must be absolutely clean. This is especially true if they've been resting in the cabinet for a while and have picked up dust or musty off-odors. Always wash your glasses prior to use. Choose a good dishwashing detergent, and be sure to rinse them thoroughly several times to remove all detergent residue. You don't want to hear a guest saying, "This is a fine Burgundy with just a hint of lemon."

The best way to be sure your glass is really clean is to exhale gently into the glass and then smell it. Any residual odors that remain will reveal themselves. You don't want these to spoil your experience after you pour the wine into the glass.

Practice Perfect Pouring

Well, you've practiced with your corkscrew and foil cutter. Now what? What's the best way to pour?

Believe it or not, there's no standard technique for pouring wine in your home, except to get the contents into the glass. Hold the bottle any way you feel comfortable. If you feel insecure holding it from the bottom, no problem. Just be sure your fingers are far away from the lip.

Aim for the center of the glass and pour slowly, keeping alert for that invisible one-third to one-half full zone. (Wine glasses should never be filled to the top.) When you've poured the right amount, give the bottle a slight twist as you raise it to avoid drips.

Tasting Tip

Don't be afraid to smell the glass when dining out. Even some of the best restaurants are notorious for stale glasses. You're paying enough for your wine; the least you deserve is a clean, unadulterated glass.

Serving at Seventy

The rule of "room temperature" for serving red wines originated long before central heating. When you're talking about wine, room temperature means about 70 degrees. (Some wine devotees prefer 65 degrees.)

If you're taking your bottle from a controlled-environment wine storage area, chances are it's ready for serving as-is. If your home or apartment is overheated, or if you've just brought a bottle home on a hot day, don't be afraid to put your red wine in the fridge. A short layover there will bring it down to the 70-degree mark without damaging its contents.

The Sommelier Says

Some restaurateurs insist their staff pour wine by holding the bottle at the bottom with the thumb in the indentation. This isn't always practical. First, not all bottles have indentations. And second, a heavy bottle could mean an embarrassing (and costly) accident.

Tasting Tip

Did you leave that bottle of red too long in the cooler? Use your microwave on low power for 20–30 seconds. Repeat, if needed. (But make sure the glass is microwave safe—no lead crystal or wine bottle foil!)

Avoiding a Cold Chill

White wines taste best when served chilled, but too much cold can interfere with the flavor. Quite a few restaurants are guilty of over-refrigeration. This goes for rosé wines as well as whites. If the glass feels like a snow cone, let it stand a little while before drinking.

To Stand or Not

How long should your wine stand before pouring? It's tempting to say, "Until you're ready to drink it, of course." However, there is some debate on this issue, and it's been going on for years. Read on ....

Breathers vs. Nonbreathers

The debate over when to open the bottle rages between the breathers and nonbreathers. The breathers insist that exposure to air makes the wine come to life because the aromas are unleashed. They may be right. First, certain flavor components in the wine may erupt with exposure to air. Second, some odors that block our perception of more delicate smells may dissipate with airing, allowing the more subtle odors to come through.

Vino Vocab

Breathing is the process of exposing wine to air (by opening the bottle) for a few minutes to a few hours before drinking it.

While it's true that *breathing* allows some off-odors to dissipate, the nonbreathers maintain we can accomplish the same thing by swirling. Breathers also argue that standing time enhances the flavor of young (recently vinted) wines, although I'm not quite convinced.

I don't want to take sides here, though I admit I'm more of a nonbreather. There are no hard-and-fast rules. Try it both ways and see which you like better. Perhaps you'll find your breathing time varies with the type of wine, the vintage, or even the particular bottle.

If you opt for breathing, I suggest you open the wine bottle 15 to 20 minutes before serving. Then pour some into glasses a few minutes before you and your guests are seated. If breathing really brings improvements, they will be more likely to come along in good-sized wine glasses than in the bottle with its tiny opening.

Decanter de Rigeur?

Decanters can be beautiful, decorative objects, but are they necessary? Decanting does have a purpose, and that purpose is not just to impress your friends with your elegant taste in cut glass. Decanters are made for old wines, which collect sediment during the aging process.

Bottle-aging wines for 10 or more years (sometimes even less) can build up a deposit. When this sediment is mixed with the wine, the taste is bitter and unpleasant. In its mildest form, the sediment will mask the subtle nuances that have been developing over the years. The last thing you want is a bottle of very expensive sludge.

Not all aged wines have deposits. The ones that do were usually made with minimal filtering, so the flavors become more intricate and complex during aging. All the more reason to get rid of the sediment before drinking.

Incidentally, decanting also aerates the wine (lets the wine breathe). While the decanters sold in wine shops and catalogs are sure to get compliments from your friends, you actually can use any vessel as a decanter. Just be sure it's absolutely clean and free of any off-aromas.

During decanting, you should have good, bright light illuminating the bottle's neck so you can see when the sediment is close to being poured. Once any sediment is near the neck, stop! If your decanter has a stopper, replace it until you are ready to serve the wine. Bring the bottle with you to the table. It's an impressive touch, and your guests will want to know the wine they are enjoying.

Tasting Tip

Wine, properly stored on its side, will collect sediment on the side. So a few days before you serve, stand the bottle upright, allowing the sediment to fall to the bottom before you decant it.

Aerating for Aroma

If you decide that you want to aerate your wine, there are several ways to do it. The traditional method is simply to open the wine an hour or so before you plan to drink it. Or you can decant it and leave the stopper off the decanter. Some wine drinkers like to aerate their wines in the glass, but if the wine needs several hours or more of aeration (some wines may benefit from prolonged aeration), this is not practicable. Depending on the circumstances, all methods have their benefits.

Will It Keep?

Theoretically, wine begins to deteriorate from oxidation immediately upon opening, and even breathers will admit a bottle of wine is best consumed within a few hours. (Isn't that a great excuse to have more than one glass?) But if you're enjoying your wine by yourself, or the two of you really don't want half a bottle each, there are good ways to keep wine for several weeks without losing too much flavor.

Here's a general rule: The more ordinary the wine, the better it will keep. Jug wines, made with thoroughly modern techniques, have no microorganisms in the wine to culture and spoil, and they usually come with screw caps, anyway. Finer wines are more of a risk.

Chill Out

Like any perishable food, wine will keep longer if it's chilled. However, unlike your cottage cheese or orange juice, wine does lose some of its flavor in cold storage, but in a decade of experiments, I have found that there is very little flavor deterioration even with fine wines if it is well-chilled in the refrigerator for as long as three weeks. Be sure to cork the bottle. It's the oxidation of the wine that impairs the flavor in most cases. Also, chilling the wine prevents the formation of vinegar, the natural by-product of wine.

Tasting Tip

The best way to keep a wine after it is open is to cork the bottle and put it into a cold refrigerator. This will prevent the air (that was absorbed by the wine after it was opened) from oxidizing the wine.

Freeze Frame

Believe it or not, wine can be frozen for prolonged storage after it has been opened! In one experiment, I froze some of the finest grand cru Bordeaux and Burgundies after a really big winetasting of premier cru wines.

That was 18 years ago! This wine retained its character from the time it was frozen. I still have a few bottles in the freezer and will let you know in a decade or so how long a wine can be kept frozen. Incidentally, the wine can be thawed out and re-frozen with little flavor impairment.

Under Pressure

There are systems that dispense wine by using CO_2 (carbon dioxide gas) under pressure. I approve!

Because the gadget is inserted into the bottle immediately after opening, there is less risk of oxidation. The wine will keep for several days. This is an excellent method of always having a bottle available for a glass or two without having to keep it in the refrigerator. Some of the units are highly attractive and make a fine addition to a bar or dining room.

Forget Gadgets!

There are gadgets that purport to preserve the wine by removing the air from the bottle or to prevent oxidation by squirting CO_2 into the bottle after it has been opened. In my experiments, I have found these methods to be useless. Once the bottle is opened, the wine begins absorbing the air and the damage has already been done.

What will preserve the wine is not a vacuum or CO_2 in the bottle, but a procedure that will prevent the absorbed oxygen from acting on the wine. As iron does not rust much in the winter, you can similarly impede the oxidation of the wine by keeping it chilled. Forget these gadgets! Simply refrigerate your wine for future drinking.

No Rebottling Necessary

Some wine experts advise that you pour the leftover wine into a smaller bottle. Or do this when first opening the wine. This serves no useful purpose, as the wine already has absorbed air and will oxidize if not refrigerated. As I said before, if you want to preserve a bottle after it has been opened, keep it in the refrigerator or freezer.

The Least You Need to Know

➤ Wine bottles are sealed with screw caps or corks. Only the least expensive wines use screw caps, but a cork is not a guarantee of quality.

➤ Corks can be tricky to remove, but the right gadget and a little practice can make it easy and fun.

➤ You only need one or two wine glass styles. Choose only clear glasses so you can assess the wine's color and clarity.

➤ Red wine should be served slightly below most room temperatures. White wines should be served chilled, but not overchilled.

➤ You can keep an open bottle of wine in the refrigerator for several weeks without losing much flavor.

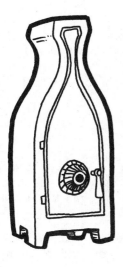

Chapter 3

Sensory Sipping and Sensible Storage

In This Chapter

➤ Becoming a good wine taster

➤ Evaluating wines

➤ Why vintage dating?

➤ Choosing a wine rack

➤ Cellaring your wines

I'm sure this is what you've been waiting for—how to taste your wine. In this chapter you'll learn what to look for when you bring the glass to your lips, and why your nose is as important as your taste buds. You'll learn how to tell a great wine from one that merely is competent and what all those vintage dates really mean. Also, we'll cover the basics of matching wine with food to enhance your tasting experiences.

Here we're going to discuss a few things you can do when you savor your wine. It doesn't matter if you're tasting different wines to become familiar with them, or if you're enjoying a bottle you've just opened for dinner.

We'll also consider your needs for a wine cellar. Many enthusiasts consider home-cellaring an important part of serving and enjoying wine at home. We'll cover the various ways to store wine in your own home.

More Than a Beverage

Yes, it's wine, but it's more than just a beverage. It's something wonderful to behold, to smell, to taste, to swallow! So let's learn some preliminary techniques before we move to the next chapter. That's where we'll cover what's in the glass and how to spot different wine attributes.

The Art of the Swirl

Now that you've chosen an uncorking gadget and you're ready to try out your skills, it's time to get down to some basics of tasting. The first step in this venture is swirling. Before you actually get down to tasting wines, you should practice swirling just to become comfortable with the act.

Here is where the shape of the traditional wine glass makes a real difference. Swirling wine in your glass helps bring the aroma and flavors up to the surface, where they are trapped by the curved design of the glass.

Just for practice, try swirling with water. Fill the glass roughly one-third of the way. Slightly more is fine, but be sure it's no more than half-full. Keep the rim of the glass parallel to the floor, and use your wrist to make a subtle, circular motion. The trick is to keep the motion minimal and the glass straight rather than tilted.

Heard It Through the Grapevine

After you swirl the wine, you may notice rivulets of wine clinging to the side of the glass. These are called *legs* or *tears* and are a sign of a wine with a full body or high alcohol. These occur because the different components of wine evaporate at different rates. Sometimes the legs are caused by glycerin in the wine as well. Legs are a clue that the wine is a superior wine, but as with most other things in wine, this is not always the case.

One way to perfect your swirling technique is to try it first with the glass still on the table. When you feel secure, try it at waist level. (Now you know why I suggested water.) When you graduate to the real thing, try it this way: pale white wines first, deep red wines last.

Light, Color, Wine!

Have you ever watched a wine-lover examining a fresh glass of wine? What can we learn from just looking?

For one thing, examining appearance will reveal obvious flaws. For example:

➤ Brown color in either a white or red wine is a sign of overoxidation.

➤ Cloudiness is a sign that the wine is spoiled.

But let's not get too hung up on appearance. This custom of visual checking comes from the old days when wines often were neither clean nor clear because of poor winemaking techniques. Today, with improved techniques and quality standards, there's little chance of this.

Remember what we said earlier about lighting? It's important. Natural or incandescent lighting allows you to see how the wine really looks. Soft lighting is fine, especially if you're enjoying your wine as part of a romantic dinner. But avoid fluorescent lighting, especially when you are drinking red wines. To view a glass of wine of rich color and gem-like brilliance in natural lighting is a sublime experience.

Trust Your Nose

You've diligently practiced your swirling. You've mastered whites, rosés, and reds, and you're even keeping the tablecloth on the table clean. The question now is "What do you learn when you place your nose into a wine glass?"

Wine is the only natural beverage that offers a complete and complex palette of aromas, fragrances (there is a difference between the two; I'll get to that in a moment), and flavors. Orange juice always smells like orange juice; milk, like milk. Oh, and vodka—despite what the advertisers would like us to believe—is purely one-dimensional unless it is flavored.

The Sommelier Says

Check for clarity. Haziness usually is a sign of a biological instability or a bacterial or chemical taint, usually from faulty winemaking. Of course, tasting will reveal this for sure.

Inhaling a fine wine is like the opening of an artist's retrospective at a metropolitan art museum. When you enter the gallery, you will be confronted with a variety of canvases, large and small, and many colors, textures, and designs. And yet, there is a unity of vision that informs you that these are all works by Monet, Picasso, or Chagall.

You might call wine a sensory art gallery. Or a symphony. Or an elaborate ballet. The range of smells and fragrances is almost unlimited. Wines can be vinous, wine-like, and grapey; they can be like nesting Russian dolls, with layers upon layers upon .... You get the picture.

The scent of a wine is referred to as its *nose. Aroma* is used to describe the scent of a young, undeveloped wine. For an older, more complex wine, the term we use is *bouquet*. This distinction is easy when you think of the image that goes with each word.

➤ When you think of aroma, you tend to think of a single item like coffee.

➤ A bouquet, in contrast, is an intricate arrangement with a fragrance that results from the delicate interaction of its components.

Before I discuss what you want to smell, let me say a little about what your nose doesn't want to find. Some of these less-pleasant odors are so powerful your nose won't even get near the rim of the glass before you know something's wrong. Other odors are more subtle, so it's even more important you know what they are to tell a good wine from a flawed one.

➤ Vinegar is an obvious one, indicating your wine bottle has been open too long or something has gone wrong in the winemaking.

➤ The smell of raisins or cooked or baked qualities are also indications that something is wrong, usually that the wine is too old. (Have you ever heard anyone describing a fine wine as "raisiny"?)

There are a number of faults that are signs of microbiological contamination. The most frequently encountered ones are

➤ Sulfur dioxide (think of the smell of a just-struck match).

➤ Hydrogen sulfide (rotten eggs).

➤ Dekkara (the smell of rancid corn chips).

➤ Volatile acidity (vinegar).

➤ Ethyl acetate (nail polish remover).

➤ Mercaptins (range in smell from garlic and onion to skunk).

➤ Smells of decay (wilted lettuce, dead leaves, mucus, manure, vomit).

➤ Petrochemical smells (diesel fuel, Vaseline).

➤ Geraniums (from bacterial spoilage).

➤ Potassium sorbate. (Believe it or not, this one smells like bubble gum.)

➤ Corky (actually, the scent of a particular mold that grows in corks; wines with this flaw are said to be *corked*).

Heard It Through the Grapevine

Most wines contain sulfur dioxide, a preservative. Sulfur dioxide is sort of a wine wonder drug (which works as an antibacterial antioxidant) and anti-yeast agent (which keeps sweet wines from refermenting in the bottle). Winemakers are required by law to put the words "Contains Sulfites" on the labels of all wines with sulfur dioxide that are sold for U.S. consumption to caution those rare persons who are hypersensitive to sulfites. Pru-dently, winemakers opt for minimal levels of this additive, and any residual smell should dissipate with airing. Occasionally, wines get an overdose and airing the wine won't help. In this case (as with all of the flaws mentioned above), you're justified in returning the wine.

The nose of a wine can be nonexistent, weak, moderate, or intense. *Closed-in* refers to a nose that is weak because it has not had the chance to develop. The other taste components provide the clues to whether the nose is closed-in or simply weak. It takes some experience to interpret these clues, but it's not hard to pick up.

Wines that display an array of flavors both on the nose and on the palate, usually with subtle or supple undertones, are complex. When the various elements work in harmony, the wine is said to be balanced. When one element dominates all the rest, the wine is unbalanced. The balance is described in relative terms that resemble a ratings quiz. For starters, here are a few terms that experts use, grouped accordingly:

Superlative	Adequate	Inadequate
harmonious	good	poor
excellent	normal	acidic
perfect	average	unbalanced

Many wine scents may seem strange at first:

➤ The scent of a fine Burgundy frequently resembles wild violets, tar, or truffles.

➤ An aged Bordeaux smells pleasantly roasted, like a pot roast.

➤ A Late Harvest Riesling smells nutty and honeyed.

➤ A young Riesling or a Muscat resembles pine oil.

➤ American labrusca varieties, referred to as foxy, have a pungent odor all their own.

Some wine smells require getting used to. Others require getting used to the fact that they're just plain unusual.

Taste Will Tell

Now that your nose is out of your glass and you've uttered all your adjectives, it's time to take a sip.

1. Take a sizable sip, filling your mouth with wine.

2. Roll the wine over your tongue and palate to get the feel, or the body, of the wine.

3. Savor and evaluate the wine.

Body is determined by the wine's alcohol, glycerin, and extract. Either it's light, moderate, or full, and may or may not be in balance with the flavor and other components. The body will appear firm when there's sufficient acidity, but it may be flabby when acidity is lacking.

Many other words may come to mind to describe what you experience as body. It may feel heavy from residual sugar. Or body can seem harsh, rough, coarse, silky, velvety, smooth, or creamy, depending on its structure. Trust your palate here.

The tannins in red wines frequently add a necessary and pleasing astringency to fine wines. This may not seem so pleasing at first pucker, but as your wine experience progresses, certain wines will begin to seem flat and dull without it.

Purse Your Lips and Gurgle

Okay. You've swirled and sniffed and mouthed. Now it's time to gurgle. (The wine's still in your mouth, right?) Just purse your lips and draw air into your mouth, slightly gurgling the wine to vaporize it. The result is a whooshing sound that identifies experienced wine tasters. This isn't really bad manners, though I wouldn't suggest it for quiet, formal gatherings.

Gurgling the wine permits the full flavor of the wine, warmed by the mouth, to flow through the nasal canal to the olfactory bulb. In short, it's tasting and sniffing rolled into one. It does have a purpose (other than startling your guests). It enables you to experience fully every nuance of flavor.

It's really simple: Purse your lips as if you are going to whistle; then suck in the air over the wine.

From Swirl to Finish

Continuity is the sign of a well-structured wine. There should be no conflict between what you taste and what you smell. The flavor in your mouth should confirm your initial olfactory impression.

After you swallow the wine, you usually will notice a lingering aftertaste, known as the *finish*. The finish may be described as long, lingering, fleeting, or nonexistent. Accompanying these temporal adjectives are complex, acidic, sharp, or dull. Often, the wine's finish will be a taste experience in itself, adding new dimensions and flavors. Professionals evaluate the finish in terms of the time (usually in seconds) that the flavor lingers.

The Sommelier Says

You can tell when a wine is beginning to pass the peak of maturity by its finish. There may be a hint of dead leaves, or a lack of vinous flavor, which is called dried out.

Heard It Through the Grapevine

Scents, flavors, body, alcohol, acidity, and astringency provide the total impression of a wine, all of which make up its structure. Here are a few adjectives you may use when describing a wine's structure:

➤ Well-defined
➤ Firm
➤ Broad
➤ Tightly knit

➤ Good backbone
➤ One-dimensional
➤ Multifaceted

When all the elements of structure, flavor, and complexity attain a perfect harmony (this is really hard to describe), the result is *breed* or *finesse*. These are terms we use frequently to describe classic noble wines.

Vintages: Quality or Hype?

The structure of a high-quality wine often is related to its *vintage* (year it was produced). A famous wine property might produce one-dimensional wines in a poor vintage but glorious, multifaceted wines in a superb vintage. For that reason, it is important to know what vintage your wine comes from.

The Sommelier Says

American consumers have been led to believe that a vintage date means quality, and that only inferior or inexpensive wines are not vintaged. In reality, having a vintage date on a bottle has little bearing on the quality of its contents. (However, knowing the vintage still is important with high-quality wines.)

Tasting Tip

There are factors that make one vintage better or worse than another. The grapes, climate, and winemaker are all important, and they're all interrelated. The one factor determining the quality of the finished product is ultimately the climate.

We've all seen it in the movies. One way to show that the hero or heroine is elegant and sophisticated, the party is chic, or the occasion momentous is to have someone hold up a bottle announcing, "Lafite '61." (Or '45 or '72 or '59.)

A declaration of vintage on a label merely indicates when the grapes were harvested and when the wine was made.

➤ California law requires at least 95 percent of the grapes be picked that year.

➤ In France, the minimum generally is 80 percent, and in Germany, 75 percent.

➤ Each country or region establishes its own standards for determining vintage.

A vintage date declares when the wine was made, but not how or under what conditions. In short, if you're not familiar with the reputation of an individual producer or vintage, all the label reveals is the wine's age or freshness. Most wines—probably at least 80 percent—do not improve with *cellaring* (prolonged aging). They were meant to be enjoyed two to three years after the vintage date.

An ideal vintage means that certain weather conditions were met the entire year. The perfect winter has ample rainfall and enough cold (to let the vines have the grapes' equivalent of REM sleep). The spring is mild and free from frosts, rains, or other assaults. The midseason begins cool and heats up slowly, without any environmental mood swings. The ripening period is neither too hot nor too rainy.

The gradual heat over the late mid-ripening period increases the grapes' natural sugars. Incremental warming with cool evenings lets them retain high acidity. The absence of rain in the mid- or late season keeps the berries from becoming diluted, or swollen with water.

No matter how skilled or experienced, the vintner's role always includes some high-stakes gambling.

➤ For those with conservative leanings, when the vines are pruned in midwinter to control vine growth, they can be pruned to produce a small crop of guaranteed high-quality fruit. In doing so, there is always the risk that the crop will be smaller than desired.

➤ Growers (vineyardists) can bet that the vintage will bring warm (but not hot) and dry conditions so they'll get equal quality from a larger crop. If the vintage is not optimal, there is the risk that the larger crop will be of lesser quality.

The better growers understand the unique capabilities of each grape variety they work with. If they hold out for both quantity and quality, unpredictable climates can cost them both. If they play it conservative and prune drastically for a small crop, a spell of bad weather can mean a complete wipeout.

Harvesting is always a crucial decision. Vineyardists are more likely to harvest too early rather than too late. Picking too late carries many risks: rains, hail, unwanted molds from high humidity. Sometimes an early-harvest decision is a wise one, based on experience. Sometimes it's just loss of nerve.

Heard It Through the Grapevine

One decisive factor in vintage quality is whether a vineyard, variety, or the whole crop is picked in a short time, or whether the process is staggered, based on the peak ripeness of the vineyard, row, or even a single vine.

For example, the vine's age makes a big difference. Young vines typically ripen early, producing a *light* (small) crop. Really old vines also produce light crops, but they take much longer to ripen. Average-age vines (7 to 25 years), not surprisingly, yield average-size crops.

All of this barely touches a few of the intricate mechanisms involved in coming up with a great vintage (or not). Even in so-called great vintages, producers can make a mistake or two, and the quality will be below par. Fortunately, all you have to do is read a label.

The Vino Vault

Vaults are not just for rich people who live in castles. You really don't need a deep dark hillside cavern (although if you should have one, you'll no doubt be the envy of your wine-loving friends). All you really need is a place that's away from direct sunlight, free of vibration, and with temperatures that don't change quickly.

Wine racks or wine closets make your storage task easier to manage. A beautiful assemblage of wine racks or a fine-furniture wine closet has aesthetic value beyond its utility. This section introduces you to the best methods for keeping your wines in good condition.

Vino Vocab

Cellaring means putting wine away for months or years. But you don't need an actual cellar to cellar your wines.

Tasting Tip

If you're in the stage of short-term storage, the cardboard boxes or wooden cases wines come in will serve nicely. Tilt the cases so that the wine bottles are lying on their side. Beware: These are not made for stacking. If you try to stack them too high, the bottom row can collapse. (Do you really want a stream of deep crimson leading a path from your living room?)

Side by Side

Whether you need a wine rack depends on your cellaring needs. Remember, we store wine bottles on their sides to keep the cork from drying out. This makes it difficult to keep your wine on a shelf or on top of a cabinet, because they like to roll.

If you prefer to keep only a few cases or a few bottles on hand for occasional use, there's no need to invest in elaborate storage units or racks. Many people keep a few bottles of wine on hand just so they won't have to go running to the local wine shop at the penultimate moment.

You might begin that way, until one day you realize that wine bottles have taken over the bookcase and dresser. Then, if you find yourself sliding carefully from your bed to avoid a protruding wine bottle, you know it's time for a special storage unit.

Wine Racks; Wine Walls

Wine racks will hold your bottles in the perfect lying-down orientation. They come in a variety of sizes structures, and materials. There are inexpensive materials, like white pine, and expensive ones, like clear Lucite or polished brass. Some designer-decorated homes boast a wine wall, a built-in rack that can cost up to several thousand dollars.

The type of rack you choose will depend on your needs, taste, and budget. If you're thinking of going for glitter, remember this: Assuming you have located your collection away from bright light and heat, your wine rack rarely will be on public display.

Where to Find It

You can find wine racks in most department or houseware stores. In states where wine dealers may sell merchandise in addition to beverages, many offer their own fine selection. There also are several wine accessory catalog companies that sell wine racks, wine rack wall units, and wine storage furniture by mail order. (Refer to Chapter 26, "Swimming in the Wine Market," for more information.)

The Right Rack

Wine racks come in two basic configurations—the 12-bottle shelf and the much larger bookcase style. Unless you're thinking of getting serious fast, and you've got a lot of extra space, the bookcase style may be a bit much.

Many small racks are very well-designed and easily stacked without danger of toppling. They fit easily into closets, on bookshelves, or in other convenient nooks, and they allow you to add as needed. But however small your rack might be, make sure the bins are large enough to accommodate Champagne bottles!

Bookshelf-style wine racks come either with openings for single bottles or with square or diamond-shaped ports that hold from six to a dozen bottles. You can find attractive models in fine-furniture hardwoods, wrought iron, brass, chrome, or Lucite. The single-bottle models generally are more expensive. It's not necessary to splurge, but if you decide to pull out all the stops ... well, why not?

The Monk's Cellar at Home

If you really want to go all out, there are completely self-contained, temperature-regulated wine cabinets. Your own private storage vault, the urban equivalent of a monk's cellar!

These storage vaults are available as fine furniture and come in a variety of styles, woods, and finishes. Prices range from several hundred dollars to several thousand. If you seek an impressive and attractive way to show off your wine collection, consider investing in one of these units.

Different models make use of different types of cooling units. Some use ordinary refrigerator units or air conditioners. These are unsuitable. You're better off using devices intended specifically for wine cooling. Vibration is a serious enemy because it can prematurely age your wine; make sure the manufacturer guarantees the unit is vibration-free.

The Sommelier Says

Firms that make self-contained wine storage range from reputable to fly-by-night. Some years ago, a leading mail-order wine storage company simply disappeared, along with hundreds of thousands of dollars of wine lovers' money. Beware. Always consider the age of the firm, its reputation, its warranty, and whether it has local service agents in case of trouble.

Another factor to consider is how to arrange your bottles. In some models, you have to remove the front bottles first to get to the others. You may find this a real nuisance. Or you may not.

I recommend buying one of these more expensive units only from a local department store, a reputable furniture store, a decorator with a high profile, or one of the mail-order companies mentioned in Chapter 26, but only if it has arrangements for on-site guarantee service. Buying from someone you trust guarantees that your wine cellar stays user friendly.

The Three Fs: Fifty-Five Fahrenheit

Some experts will tell you that a wine-storage temperature of 55 degrees is essential. It isn't. Temperature uniformity is more important. Ideally, the temperature should not change by more than 10 Fahrenheit degrees, in either direction, over the course of a week.

You can store your wines at temperatures of up to 65 or even 70 degrees without damage. However, fine wines do not develop to their fullest potential if stored at too high a temperature. If your home has a fruit cellar, this might work well for storing your wine.

Keep It Steady

As I noted, many experts believe your cellar should be kept at a constant 55 degrees. By all means, strive for this! But if it's not practical for you, don't despair. As long as the changes in temperature are gradual and there are no extremes of heat and cold, your wines won't suffer. If your storage conditions vary from, say 50 degrees in winter to a high of about 70 degrees in summer, you don't have to worry.

The Least You Need to Know

➤ The aroma of a wine will give you a good idea of its taste; the color of a wine can give you a clue about its condition.

➤ For high-quality wines, the vintage year is a sign of the wine's quality in that vintage; for most other wines (mid-premium and below), the vintage date merely is a sign of freshness and drinkability.

➤ Wine racks should have holes large enough to accommodate Champagne bottles.

➤ Wine should be stored at a cool temperature (55 degrees Fahrenheit or so), with the bottle lying on its side.

➤ Freedom from light, vibration, and rapid temperature changes is most important in cellaring your wines.

Chapter 4

Talking Wine Talk

In This Chapter

➤ Describe your taste sensations

➤ The role of oak in fine wine

➤ The complex flavors of wine

➤ Aroma, taste, and finish

Ever peek at a wine taster's notes? "Subtle yet assertive, with just a hint of violets and a trace of truffles." Oh yes, and maybe with "a touch of tar." Sounds pretty neat, doesn't it? Being able to say something that sounds like nonsense to most people while being taken for an expert seems pretty cool.

The idea is not to confuse or bamboozle. It's to provide some order to our own recollections of our own impressions of the wines we experience. Of course, tasting is subjective. Indeed, you might read someone else's notes at a winetasting and wonder if he or she had sampled the same wine as you did.

Winetasting and state funerals are the two areas where society accepts, even encourages, purple prose. In the case of wines, this is not unreasonable. Wines do have the scents of flowers, herbs, fruits, and a host of other evocative elements. We may describe them as robust or flabby, silky or coarse, with a fleeting or lingering finish.

As wine allows you to expand your sensory experiences and awareness, it must engage your vocabulary as well. You no longer will think "astringent" refers only to your mouthwash or facial cleanser.

Speaking the Language

You've noticed by now that some words seem to crop up repeatedly. Just as English, French, Italian, and German (four languages that may appear on labels of fine wines) have their parts of speech, wine jargon has its categories for classification. The following three adjectives fit into the category of winetasting:

➤ Complex

➤ Acidic

➤ Herbaceous

Someday some over-enthusiastic wine writer might proclaim, "This wine has a triangular structure with a diminished-seventh harmony, an Olympic balance, and a nose reminiscent of wild mushrooms, rose hips, and comfrey, with just a soupçon of Dijon mustard. Oh, and a bracing but irresolute aftertaste." (Of course, only the writer will understand what this means!)

Yes, you can be creative. But where you can, stick with the terms you see in this book and in the wine magazines and newsletters. In general, it's better to use common terms than to make up your own. Try to evoke comparisons with scents and flavors that you already know, such as violets, truffles, chocolate, berries of all sorts, and the like. (Of course, it is perfectly acceptable to say that a wine tastes like a Bordeaux, a Cabernet Sauvignon, or Chardonnay.)

Tasting Tip

These days, oaky wines are very much in favor. Chardonnay, for example, is at the peak of popularity, while the non-oaked Riesling is considered by some to be slightly outré. (Remember, all this is subjective; there's no reason why you should not prefer a non-oaky wine.)

Oaky, Not from Muskogee

In wine jargon, the term *oaky* has nothing to do with the song by Merle Haggard or the novel by John Steinbeck. We say a wine is oaky if it exhibits oak flavors from being in contact with oak. Look for a woody or oaky scent and taste.

How does wine come into contact with oak? Oaken barrels. These (typically) 62-gallon containers house the wine during both fermentation and aging. The most expensive wines reach maturity in brand-new barrels with full-power oakiness. (Barrels lose their oakiness with use.)

Contact with oak imparts special flavors and aromas. Oaking also acts as a catalyst for chemical changes in the wine, although most wine lovers would consider this secondary (or tertiary) to the distinctive quality of an oaked wine.

The term *barrel-fermented* refers to those white wines that went into barrels (usually oak) as grape juice and emerged as wine. The term *barrel-aged* refers to wine put in barrels after fermentation. Because they are fermented with their skins, red wines are fermented in stainless steel containers or large wooden vats and then aged in small oak barrels after the skins have been removed from the liquid. Some fruity wines (red or white) are not aged in oak at all.

Brix

Brix refers to a measure of potential alcohol, based on the sugar content of the grape. The more sugar, the higher the potential level of alcohol. Frequently you will see this term on the back labels of wines (California in particular) and in the wine literature.

The Sommelier Says

Some lesser wines are made by immersing oak chips or shavings in the maturing liquid or even by adding liquid oak essence (illegal in some places; legal in others). The best wines, however, are allowed to sleep happily in those wonderful oaken casks.

Recipe for a Fine Wine

Actually, we're not adding any ingredients here. It's just that we may detect a vanilla flavor with our oaked wines. And this is not a trick of our imagination. New oak barrels contain *vanillin*, the organic substance that gives vanilla beans their flavor. Wines aged in these barrels take on a vanilla flavor as part of their oaky charm. As an ice cream flavor, vanilla may be simple; in a wine, it adds complexity and smoothness. The process of the second fermentation, known as malolactic fermentation, produces the flavor of butter, which adds a flavorful note to wine.

Vino Vocab

The **Brix** scale is named for Alfred F. Brix, a nineteenth century German wine chemist, who developed this method of determining sugar content through measuring specific gravity.

Terms of the Taste and Trade

Our wine vocabulary has very few terms unique to it. Instead, it features dozens of everyday words in special senses. If you've looked through wine magazines or newsletters, you will have seen these, perhaps puzzled over them.

Here are a few of the most useful terms, enough to let you get the sense of almost anything you might read about wine.

Heard It Through the Grapevine

Butter gets its characteristic taste from diacetyl compounds, which are a by-product of the malolactic fermentation (see Chapter 8, "Hot Off the Vine"). Some winemakers make a point of putting their wines through a malolactic fermentation to impart this taste to their wines. The buttery taste adds character and complexity to wine, particularly to Chardonnay.

Bouquet

Bouquet is the smell of a wine after it has lost its grapey fragrances (something like losing baby fat). A genuine bouquet may develop only after years of aging and continue as the wine matures in the bottle. The result is a complexity of flavor nuances that did not previously exist. It's very much like smelling a floral arrangement of many different flowers.

Backbone

Our backbones are built of vertebrae, which anchor the most important parts of our skeleton. A wine's *backbone* also is the structure on which its character is built: the wine's alcohol, acids, and tannins.

What do you think of when you hear that a person has backbone? Quiet strength. And a wine with a firm backbone is well structured and provides a pleasing mouthfeel. However, a wine that lacks acidity, tannins, or flavor has the undesirable character of flabbiness.

Finish

Finish is the aftertaste once you have swallowed the wine. The quality of the wine determines the finish. Simple wines have a short finish—or no finish at all. Premium wines generally have a finish that lingers on the palate for several seconds or more and mirrors the taste of the wine. With noble wines, the finish can linger and linger on the palate as it takes you through a kaleidoscope of flavors. It's this kind of sensory experience that makes wine appreciation so fascinating.

Aged

An *aged wine* is one that has had a chance to mature in the bottle for a number of years to acquire complex scents and flavors different from what it displayed in its youth. A wine aged to maturity is said to be at its peak. And a wine that has become tired or lost its flavors from being aged too long is said to be over-the-hill (just as with people).

Bottle-Sick

After a wine is bottled, it suffers from the shock of the process. For some period of time, it may be deficient in aroma and taste. When this occurs, the wine is described as being *bottle-sick*—most usually recover after a few months.

Cru Classé

We find this term frequently on French wine bottles and in the wine literature. *Cru Classé* refers to the classification system in which French wines are defined specifically under French wine law. (I will discuss this at some length in the chapters on French wines.)

Elegance

Like people, some wines show *elegance* and others do not. It's like being well dressed and perfectly coifed. An elegant wine is one that provides a sense of grace, harmony, delicate balance, and beauty. It is a characteristic that is found only in the finest of wines.

Éleveur

You will find the French term *éleveur* (or its equivalent in other languages) on some wine labels. This refers to a wine company that buys finished wines and cares for them in its barrel aging and refining procedures. Often, this firm will be a wine distributor or shipper.

Négociant

You may see the term *négociant* on some French wine labels. It refers to the winebroker or shipper responsible for the wine. Some buy bottled wines from the wine producers, and others buy finished wine and produce blends under their own name. A number of these firms have acquired a reputation for fine wines; their names are worth looking for.

Extract

Extract refers to the nonsugar solids in a wine that are frequently dissolved in alcohol. A wine with a lot of extract will feel fuller on the palate.

Goût de Terroir

No, *goût de terroir* has nothing to do with Ivan the Terrible! Think "territory." This term is a little hard to define, but translates into the flavor that comes from the specific vineyard or wine area, embracing soil, microclimate, drainage, and other territorial characteristics.

Herbaceous

You will find that the term *herbaceous* appears frequently in winetasting notes. It refers to an aroma and flavor evocative of herbs that are frequently found in wines made from Cabernet Sauvignon, Sauvignon Blanc, or Pinot Noir. Sometimes this is desirable, and sometimes not.

Legs

No, I'm not referring to Betty Grable or Marlene Dietrich! The *legs* of a wine are the *tears*, or streams, of wine that cling to the glass after a wine is swirled. The legs are a result of different evaporation rates of alcohol and other liquids, such as glycerin, in the wine. Usually good legs are a sign of a wine with body and quality, and something wine lovers look for. Besides being a sign of a good wine, legs are pretty to look at as they develop, stream down the side of the glass, and then disappear.

Maître de Chai

A wine cellar in France is called a Chai; so the cellarmaster is the *Maître de Chai*. He is responsible for tending the maturing casks of wine. Frequently, he may be the winemaker, too. This is the position of highest importance in a French winery.

Mis en Bouteilles sur lie

The term *Mis en Bouteilles sur lie* indicates wines that were bottled off the *lees*, directly from the barrel, without *racking*. That is, the wine was removed from the solid matter (lees) without undergoing aeration during fermentation (racking).

Wine bottled this way retains a fresh, lively, zany quality, often with a slight effervescence (prickly sensation) due to carbon dioxide absorbed during fermentation that did not have the time to dissipate before being bottled.

Middle-Body

You will find the term *middle-body* in wine writers' tasting notes frequently published in wine magazines and newsletters. This refers to that part of the taste sensation that you experience after the initial taste impact on your palate. Middle-body provides the core of the taste on which you usually base your assessments. The first taste, or *entry*, and the last, *finish*, will harmonize with the middle-body in a well-structured wine.

Round

Round is a winetasting term that describes the smooth, gentle feel of a wine with a particular alcohol/acid balance that smoothes the sharpness of the acidity and makes a wine feel round in the mouth rather than sharp-cornered.

The Sommelier Says

A slight effervescence in a wine may be the sign of a wine bottled *sur lie*, or it might be an indication that the wine had a second fermentation in the bottle, which can lead to un-pleasant flavors. When a wine tastes fresh, the slight effervescence enhances the wine. When a wine has off-flavors, the effervescence is a sign of a spoiled wine.

Unresolved

Unresolved is a negative term you might apply to an impression that the wine has not yet harmonized its various components to create a smooth or balanced whole, a result of aging.

Charm

Like people, a wine can display *charm*. Wines that have a lovely scent and taste and are generous with their attributes frequently are characterized as having charm. This characteristic transcends quality categories and is frequently found in young and fruity wines like those from Beaujolais or Provence.

Fighting Varietal

In my opinion, this is a very stupid term devised by some clever wine industry writer to describe how the less popular varietal wines fight to gain market share. Thus, wines such as Chenin Blanc and Johannisburg Riesling are described as fighting varitals. You will see this term in wine magazines and newsletters. But I do wish they'd stop using it, because it does not describe the wine at all (just its marketing)!

Off-Dry

A wine that contains a slight amount of residual sugar—from 0.5–2 percent—is said to be *off-dry*. When the residual sugar is low, it tempers the acidity of the wine and gives the impression of a wine that is softer and easier to drink. At the higher end, the wine is slightly but pleasingly sweet.

Blind Tasting

No, you need not use a blindfold! The term refers to the important practice of hiding the identity of the wine from the wine taster so that the impression will not be influenced by the label. All you need to do is conceal the bottles in rumpled brown bags when you do a tasting (see Chapter 30, "Attending a Winetasting").

Heard It Through the Grapevine

Blind tasting is fun at home, but it is *de rigueur* when judging at wine competitions worldwide. It's human nature: Wine judges don't want to award a low score to some famous vintage, lest it be a reflection on their tasting ability. Tasting "blind" protects the integrity of the wine judge.

Some experienced professional tasters in the wine trade point out that they do not need to taste blind when they have confidence in their palates. Frequently, famous wines are flawed or not up to snuff in a particular vintage, and it's up to these professionals to determine this so that these wines do not reach the marketplace.

The Least You Need to Know

➤ With some wines, part of their character derives from their contact with wood.

➤ The use of common wine terms affords better communication and understanding.

➤ A wine has a bouquet, middle-body, and finish.

➤ Many winetasting impressions are subjective, not absolute.

Part 2

Wine Doesn't Grow on Trees

Bouquet and taste. Varietals and variety. Art and science. They all are here in this section. We'll begin by analyzing the wine experience, identifying those diverse parts that comprise a single sip of a single wine. And that wine will be the right one, with our tips for matching wines with food.

Then we'll sample grapes, grapes, and more grapes—white and red, the varieties we associate with the finest wines from around the world (and with the most ordinary).

Finally, we'll explore the art and science of oenology (winemaking). Climate, grapes, and harvest—only the beginning. Then pressing, fermentation, clarifying, aging, bottling—and maybe even more fermentation. Oh, and barrels and casks, large and small, oaken or stainless.

Chapter 5

Tune Up Your Taste Buds

In This Chapter

➤ Why wine tastes good

➤ Characteristics of wine

➤ Wine-with-food basics

Wine is just grape juice and alcohol, right? Wrong! Grape juice is made up of simple flavors that stay simple, regardless of what you add. It's the process of fermentation that makes wine a multidimensional product, intriguing and intricate. This chapter will help you train your own taste buds to these wine wonders.

Many of the scents and flavors created by the transformation of grape juice into wine cannot be found anywhere else in nature. Wine writers try to describe wines by evoking comparisons with various berries, bell peppers, leather (think fine leather glove), chocolate, and so forth.

These descriptions are far from exact. The flavors they seek to characterize are unique to wine. Describing a wine is kind of like telling a friend what a banana tastes like. Your friend just will have to eat a banana to know.

Scent and Sensibility

Very often, what we call taste really is our perception of a scent or scents that enter the olfactory canal through the mouth. In fact, we experience most flavors through our sense of smell. Think how food tastes when you have a cold. With a stuffed-up nose, there's not much difference between your favorite cookie and the cardboard box it came in.

That's why I advised you (Chapter 2, "Savvy Serving") to allow enough room in your wine glass to stick your nose halfway in while drinking. Scientists have identified more than 300 chemical components in wine, and they believe at least 200 are odor-producing.

We detect smells through a complex of nerve endings called the olfactory bulb, which is located in the upper part of the nose. This little bulb is a very acute sensor. Sometimes only a few molecules of a substance are enough. These nerve endings become particularly sharp when we inhale, which is why we sniff to experience wine's full flavor.

Heard It Through the Grapevine

Although there are some excellent theories, scientists have yet to tell us what mechanism allows us to discriminate among this vast catalog of aromas we sense. We do know we can detect certain weak scents despite the presence of a dominating one, or that certain substances can mask the smell of others. And we know the olfactory sense may become accustomed to a scent after it's been experienced. After a short time, it may lose its impact.

Premium and noble wines contain numerous aromatic and flavor compounds. Many of these compounds will not be present in jug or ordinary wines. These contribute to the wine's character by providing its bouquet—an aromatic or perfumed scent. These finest wines contain myriad delicate nuances of flavor, making them comparable to fine works of art or music.

Coaching Your Taste Buds

You've known since grade school that taste resides in the tongue. Our tongues have four specific areas that correspond to the four basic tastes: sweet, salt, bitter, and sour. The sweet sensation is strongest on the tip of the tongue, saltiness and sourness on the sides, and bitterness on the back. These tastes reach our brain through receptor cells inside the taste buds.

The taste buds themselves are contained within the papillae, those tiny cell-like structures that seem to pave our tongues. Sensations pass through the pores of these sensitive little cells and travel via nerve endings to the cortex of the brain. Not surprisingly, these nerves end very close to where the smelling nerves end. It's not difficult to see how the two processes of taste and smell are intertwined.

Two things govern the way our senses work when confronted with taste and aroma. The first, of course, is the character of the taste and scent. The second is our individual ability to perceive the taste and scent.

In wine circles, we have debated for years about whether tasters are made or born. I believe the answer is something of both. Some people do smell and taste more acutely than others. For the most part, though, tasters are made.

It's like learning to appreciate any art. If you're not familiar with modern art and you see a Picasso for the first time, you may wonder why the eyes are in such a weird place or why those funny lines go through somebody's cheekbone. You may miss the subtleties of color and form entirely. But once you learn what to look for in a painting—how to really see what is on the canvas—it's like having a new pair of eyes (although maybe not eyes quite like Picasso's version).

You've probably noticed that your abilities to taste or smell aren't always the same. The most obvious block to full flavor is a cold or active allergy. Mood and mental state are two other factors. If you're even mildly fatigued, familiar objects like your briefcase or gym bag can feel a lot heavier. Images start swimming across the page or computer screen. It's the same with taste and smell, although you may not be as aware of it.

Have you ever felt a bit blue and said, "Food doesn't taste the same anymore?" It's not just a figure of speech. Your taste buds are just feeling like the rest of you. Even the stress of breaking bread with people you don't like can diminish your food pleasure.

On the bright side, the whole idea of tasting wine is going to put you in a good mood. That will rouse your taste buds to peak condition, and surely you will enjoy the company of your tasting partners.

The Sommelier Says

One recent wine book suggests that because different receptors are concentrated in the front or back of the tongue, you should taste the various components in some orderly progression. This is nonsense! Wine stimulates all your taste and scent receptors at once. Wine doesn't glide slowly through your mouth like lava. Your perception of a wine is immediate.

Heard It Through the Grapevine

Taste is an individual thing. If you read the tasting notes of three wine experts, you may think they've sampled different bottles. So just because someone waves a glass at you, saying, "Ah! The outdoors! This wine tastes of fresh leaves and wildflowers!" doesn't mean you're a philistine because you don't taste a single daisy.

Fresh leaves and wildflowers are often associated with wine. So are raspberries, ripe cherries, cinnamon, sage, and roses. When the flavor is less distinct, you might just say it tastes fruity. It's a positive quality, although not particularly well defined.

So let's do it! First, I want you to clear your mind of ideas, beliefs, and expectations. This tasting business is an individual experience, though it's not an exercise in free association. Those flavor adjectives wine lovers use don't emerge only from the imagination. The comments of an experienced taster actually can help you discover more of your own tasting capacity.

Continuity

A good wine is characterized by *continuity*. Your taste buds confirm what your nose has promised, and you experience a lingering aftertaste after you swallow. The aftertaste or finish may be fleeting, barely perceptible, or it may evoke a whole new vocabulary of adjectives.

Most often, the aftertaste will add new perceptions of taste that didn't seem to be there when the wine was still in your mouth. The following are some qualities you can seek when savoring a wine.

Body

The *body* is the fullness (or lack of) that you feel when you roll the wine over your tongue and palate. Body is the product of the wine's alcohol, glycerin, and extract. It may be light, moderate, or full. It may or may not be in balance with the flavor and other constituents.

Viscosity

No, we are not talking about motor oil. A wine characterized by *viscosity* is thicker, fuller, and has a heavier body than the average wine. A full-bodied wine high in alcohol and glycerin, and with more flavor than acidity, is said to be fat. A wine with viscosity frequently will display legs, formed by wine clinging to the side of the glass.

Acidity

Acidity refers to the acids in wine, which are principally tartaric, malic, and citric. These acids provide the wine with a sense of freshness and (we hope) balance.

Sufficient acidity gives a wine firm body, while lack of acidity may make it feel flabby. (And no, despite what you'd like to believe, drinking acidic wines will not tone up flabby thighs and abdomens.)

Balance

Balance refers to the proportion of the various elements of a wine in relation to one another. For example, acid against sweetness; fruit flavors against wood; and tannic alcohol against acid and flavor.

When all the components are working together, like the colors and fabrics in a decorated home, the wine is balanced. Harmonious is the adjective of choice. When wines are unbalanced, they may be acetic, cloying, flat or flabby, or even awkward. Ever wonder why negative descriptions always outweigh the good ones? I think it's because many wine writers compare wines with their ideas of utter perfection, noting what they lack while neglecting what they afford. Too bad for them!

Backbone

We defined this in Chapter 4, "Talking Wine Talk," The *backbone* is the structural framework of a wine provided by the alcohol, acids, and tannins. A wine with good backbone leaves a positive impression on the taste buds and olfactory sense.

Mouthfeel

The *mouthfeel* of the wine is its texture. Don't confuse this with body, which is the wine's weight or viscosity. Never neglect to savor the wine fully, rolling it over your mouth. And if the tasting environment permits, don't forget your gurgling. The texture and feel of the wine in the mouth is part of the beauty that makes wine so exciting.

Overall, the adjectives used to describe mouthfeel are tactile (the same ones we use to describe textures): silky, velvety, rough, coarse, or smooth. The one exception to this rule is the pucker of tannic red wines. The puckering quality may seem strange at first, but as your winetasting experience progresses, certain wines will seem flat or dull without it.

Harmony

Harmony refers to the interplay of the wine's constituents. Harmony means smooth, flowing, and compatible. When everything is in sync, the result is a balanced wine.

Finesse and Breed

Finesse and *breed* are two descriptors that speak for themselves, like Cary Grant and Eva Marie Saint emerging from your wine cellar. (If you can't think of contemporary stars who measure up, don't worry about it. Hollywood has changed.)

Heard It Through the Grapevine

Wines with breed and finesse are the loveliest, most harmonious, most refined wines. The classics. These are the wines that age gracefully and wondrously. We don't find these qualities in mid-premium or lesser wines.

Wines with breed and finesse are those rare noble wines in which all elements of structure, flavor, and complexity combine to a peak of almost indescribable perfection. For these noble beauties, fermentation merely is the beginning of a long life, culminating in an artwork of the highest standard.

It's hard to speak of finesse and breed without throwing in at least a touch of romanticism. Technically, finesse is the quality of elegance that separates a fine wine from one that simply is good.

Breed goes up even higher. Breed is the term we use to describe wines that achieve classical proportions. It's star quality at its utmost. The quality is usually elusive to describe, but you'll know it the moment you experience it. Noble wines such as Chateau Lafite-Rothschild, Chateau d'Yquem, or the legendary Burgundy, Romanée-Conti, have finesse and breed.

Making a Perfect Match

Now that you know what to look for in a wine, the next step is to know how to match wine with food. The following is a first look. For a more complete discussion, see Chapter 32, "The Match Game."

Say it with Rosés

When it comes to matching food with rosés, there are two extremes of the advice spectrum. There are the marketing experts who claim that rosé goes with everything. Then there are the snobs who claim that rosé goes with nothing, that it's passé. Don't listen to either of them.

Because the grape-skin contact in making rosés is minimal, they don't have the tannic quality that makes red wines heavier and harder to match with foods (and sometimes harder to drink on their own) than whites. Like white wines, rosés are served chilled and make a good summer beverage. They can be great for barbecues and outdoor parties.

Most rosé fans recommend them with the same dishes you usually pair up with light white wines. Things like fish or seafood or vegetarian favorites go well with rosés. A good dry rosé, like a French Tavel, goes beautifully with ham, white meat, and poultry dishes as well as Asian foods.

Delicate to Dominant Whites

Contrary to assumption, white wines actually are a varied lot. They range from pale and delicate young wines (in danger of being overpowered if your chef salad has too much Roquefort dressing) to tawny grandes dames (grands hommes?) that can give any red a run for its vintage.

Traditional But Tricky Reds

Let me come right out and say it: The best way to impress people with your wine expertise is the tried-and-true method of showing them how well you can choose the perfect red wine for dinner. With their influence on the tannic taste buds, red wines can be tricky critters. The finest red wine without a proper pairing can make your cheeks hollow in seconds.

Tasting Tip

Rosés are light wines in taste as well as in color. They're thoroughly overpowered by steaks, chops, and roasts. They may not be the best match for very sweet or salted tidbits, or anything too assertive in taste. Think of the foods you tend to enjoy in warmer weather, and chances are that you'll be able to come up with some good matches for rosé.

Heard It Through the Grapevine

Light young reds, like Beaujolais Nouveau (serve this one chilled), are a good choice with the same type of foods you'd usually pair with white wine. This is a handy thing to know if you have a guest with an allergy to white wines. (White wines contain more sulfites than reds.) And some guests simply may prefer reds.

Reds that are high in tannins are perfect with high-protein foods like beef or cheese. A well-chosen red wine is a superb complement to a cheese platter (equally well-chosen). In general, you'll want to avoid sweet or excessively salty foods, which tend to make tannic wines taste even more tannic. Remember, most red wines are best served slightly cooler than room temperature.

The Least You Need to Know

➤ Wine's unique flavors are a by-product of fermentation.

➤ The important characteristics of wine include body, viscosity, acidity, balance, backbone, and mouthfeel.

➤ Some foods go best with white wines; others go best with reds.

➤ Rosé wines do not go with everything.

Chapter 6

The Vine—Then Wine

In This Chapter

➤ Not all grapevines produce good wine

➤ Growing conditions for grapevines

➤ Anatomy of a grape

➤ Vine diseases you can taste

There are approximately 8,000 varieties of grapes. Since all grapes contain at least some sugar, we could make each and every one into some sort of wine. But we wouldn't want to!

During Prohibition in the United States, people made wines from all sorts of grapes (and other fruits); in fact, from anything they could grow in their backyards or window boxes! That's how we know that most grape varieties are unsuitable for wine. But wine has been legal in the U.S. since 1933, and we can buy any wine we like (assuming we can afford it).

Only about a hundred grape varieties can make wines we might enjoy drinking, and of these, only about a dozen will yield a wine we would call great.

A Vine Is a Vine

Vino Vocab

Vitis vinifera, genus and species, are two Latin words. Vitis means vine, and vinifera means wine-bearing. We see these Latin roots in the words **viticulture** (grape-growing) and **vinification** (wine-making).

The *Vitis vinifera* grape species is the worldwide favorite for commercial winemaking. This grape species has a long history. We believe *Vitis vinifera* originated in the region near the Caspian Sea, where people cultivated it more than 5,000 years ago. It thrived in the Mediterranean Basin. Greeks and Romans planted it widely through Europe and the Middle East. Today, this wonderful wine grape legacy is planted throughout the world, Old and New.

When European wine grapes arrived in the New World, there already was a native grape, *Vitis lambrusca*. This species is indigenous to the Mid-Atlantic states. The best-known lambrusca grape is the *Concord*, which is widely planted in New York state and used to make very sweet wines. *Concord* is also widely used for grape juice, jellies, and jams.

All the world's finest wines, especially the great ones, are made from one or more members of *Vitis vinifera*. Most varieties yield wines that are *vinous*, or wine-like. (That word makes sense, doesn't it?) A certain few are capable of giving their product an elegant and distinctive identity. These are the noble grapes. The noble red grapes include: *Cabernet Sauvignon, Pinot Noir, Merlot,* and *Zinfandel*. Among noble white grapes we have *Chardonnay, Riesling, Sauvignon Blanc, Semillon,* and *Gewürztraminer*.

Heard It Through the Grapevine

When planted from seed, grapevines don't grow true to type. Most vines are propagated from cuttings or from cuttings grafted onto an already-grown vine root called *rootstock*. Either way, the new vine will spend most of its first year developing its root system. During the second year, the vine will show top-growth through branches and leaves. By the third year (or third leaf), a healthy vine will produce grapes for wine production.

Vines bear fruit into a comfortable old age. Like Picasso, Martha Graham, and George Burns, some vines keep their a creative edge at 80, 90, or 100 years. With age, however, production decreases. The average lives of most commercially productive vines are 20 to 30 years.

Grape-growing (or *viticulture*) is an art and a science, exacting in both senses. Grape vines are tended individually and carefully throughout their lives. In their second year, after planting, the viticulturist begins training or trellising the vine. This marks the start of the annual regime of pruning to control the quantity of fruit the vine will produce. Growers practice *quality* control through *quantity* control. The fewer grapes per vine, the better their flavor and character. Pruning is essential to the production of well-balanced mature grapes.

Growers do their pruning in midwinter. This involves removal of old growth in order to regulate the coming year's new growth. Careful pruning keeps a wine from wasting its energy on branches and shoots and keeps it focused on producing rich fruit.

There's an old viticulturist's saying that the vine has to "struggle." (It's the vinous equivalent to "no pain no gain.") Vines that have it too easy—that is, those planted in fertile soils—may produce enormous foliage but grapes weak in character. However, vines planted in poor soils (but in the right climate!) yield grapes that are fragrant, balanced, and suitable for making fine wine. (I know there's a moral in there somewhere.)

Training, trellising, and pruning can compensate somewhat for a less-than-ideal environment or climate. In hot regions, growers train their vines so that the foliage provides a canopy to shade the grapes (much like a parasol). In cool areas, the vines are stretched out to afford the grapes better exposure to the limited sunlight, to facilitate the photosynthesis needed for ripening.

Heard It Through the Grapevine

The trunk of the vine bears the branches and shoots that display the flower-clusters that ultimately become grapes. The root system and the leaves are the most critical determinants in growing quality wine grapes. Depending on the vine's age and the soil, the root system extends six to ten feet beneath the surface (and 30 feet is not unusual in certain soils) to seek out underground water and mineral nutrients. Think of these as vitamins for grapes.

Just as we are at out best when we obtain good nutrition, grapes only develop their most subtle flavors when they are well-fed. The vines that struggle to root themselves deep in the earth produce the best wines.

Although native American grapes cannot make superior wines, American rootstock plays an important role in most vine regions today. New vines are grafted onto American rootstock in order to avoid the devastating root disease, *phylloxera*. (This is short for the *Phylloxera vasatrix*, a plant louse that arrived in Europe in the nineteenth century with native American vines that were imported.)

You may have heard some claims that grafted vines produce wines inferior to those grown on their own roots. These assertions are unsubstantiated. And if true, the wine industry worldwide would be reduced to a fraction of its size. Even more of a problem to viticulturists than phylloxera are the viruses that attack the leaf nodes of the vines early in the season, depriving the vines of the working foliage they need for the grapes to mature fully. Once infected, a vine cannot be cured. The only solution to this problem is to propagate virus-free vines, an exacting task that begins in vine nurseries under controlled, sterile conditions. Fortunately for us wine lovers, grapevine propagation has developed into a fine art, and the bright scarlet leaves of a virus-infected vineyard have faded into the past.

The vine's leaves play the most important role in determining a grape's quality. Through the process of photosynthesis, they form and store carbohydrates, enabling the plants to produce the sugars, which are stored in the leaves. As the ripening period gets nearer, the leaves send their sugars to the berries.

If the leaves are diseased or if heavy rains, frosts, hailstorms, or any of the many other possible blights (you can see how the deck is stacked) destroy the leaves, the grapes can't mature properly. Then even the most noble grapes will be inadequate to yield great wine. It's a precarious process at best. Carefully tended vines contribute to the quality of the grape and with the winemaker's skill, to the ultimate quality of the wine.

Tasting Tip

By pruning and trellising, growers encourage their vines to push leaf development early in the season. Once the leaves are developed, they can concentrate on the slow and gradual development of the grape sugar, necessary for winemaking.

Climate and Soil

The quintessential grape may be the prerequisite for quality, but it requires support from both the climate and the soil. *Vitis vinifera* grapes are temperamental creatures, characterized by their sensitivity to both.

Pinot Noir grown on the upper slopes of Burgundy, where the soil is rich in chalk and limestone and the climate is very cool, can yield extraordinary wines. Those coming from tiny vineyards like the famed La Tache or Romanée Conti have qualities that defy description. The *Pinot Noir* wines that emerge from the fertile floor soil of the Napa Valley with hot, late-season weather, simply are not the same. The *Cabernet Sauvignon* grown in the hot climate and fertile soil of

Fresno, California bears little resemblance to wines made in the small commune of Pauillac in the Bordeaux region of France.

I'm not trying to support the purists' contention that Old World wines are superior to the home-grown item! It's just that some grape varieties tend to prefer "La Marseillaise" to "California, Here I Come." When it comes to wines labeled with the name of a grape variety (varietal wines), *where* the grapes were grown really is of great importance.

Grape Riviera

Like humans, grapes feel invigorated when the weather is just right, and they feel down when it's out of kilter. They like to bask in the sun, but they can't run indoors from a downpour or slather themselves in lotion to keep from baking. Unfortunately, even their human sponsors, the vintners, can't control the weather conditions under which the grapes luxuriate or decline.

The Sommelier Says

The relationship of soil and climate to the quality of the grape is crucial to successful winemaking. It's virtually impossible to isolate one element from another. As you become familiar with the intricacies of the wine-making process, the pieces of the winemaking puzzle all fall into place.

When climate is less than optimum, grapes will develop out of balance. The sugar will be either too low or too high. This determines how much alcohol will develop on fermentation. Also, acidity may be too high or too low, resulting in a wine that's either too sharp or too dull. The grape's flavor can wind up either undeveloped or overcooked by the summer's sun *(raisined)*. And excess rain and humidity can cause rot or mold.

The ideal climatic conditions (Riviera conditions, if you want to be picturesque) that produce happy, thriving wine grapes include

➤ Cold, but not freezing, winter months (for dormancy of the vine) and rainy winters to build up water tables

➤ Mild frost-free spring weather

➤ Gradual warm, sunny, long, dry summer months

➤ Mild "Indian summer" in the fall

Generally, the only places on earth where these conditions can be met lie between 34 and 49 degrees latitude, north or south. But yes, there are exceptions.

Germany's fine Rieslings actually grow at 51 degrees latitude, but growers can deal with the colder temperatures by limiting their plantings to south- or west-facing slopes for maximum sun exposure, and usually near a river, which has a moderating effect on temperature.

At the other extreme, in parts of Napa, the intense heat of the days is compensated for by cool evenings and early mornings (aided by the famed California mist), which allow the grapes to recover.

The Growing Season

The growing season of a vine depends on the specific variety and the climate. The average ripening period is 105 days. However, grapes are finicky. Some grapes need only 90 days from budding to maturity, while others may require as many as 190 days! A normal pattern looks like this:

April 1st	Buds break
May 15th	Flowering or blooming
June 1st	Berries set
July 15th	Berries begin ripening
September 15th	Maturity at last

Mother Nature, of course, ensures this pattern often is purely hypothetical. Spring frosts can ruin the flowers by stunting or destroying them. Excessive rains during the flowering and before the berry set create irregular-sized berries which will not ripen at the same time—if at all. Rains occurring in the midst of maturity can swell the berries, diluting their sugar and acids, even splitting their skins and rotting the grapes!

If rains are severe enough or accompanied by winds, they can blow off or destroy the leaves before the grapes are fully developed, inhibiting any further ripening. The first late fall rainstorm may ruin the bold and adventurous gamble of a winemaker shooting for the greatest possible maturity. And even without rain, high humidity encourages mold and mildew.

To avoid killing frosts, growers light oil-burning heaters in their vineyards. And they may even use giant fans to move the air.

California growers use overhead-sprinkler irrigation in a novel way to prevent frost. When temperatures fall, they turn on the sprinklers, which coat the vines and berries with a fine mist. The mist freezes, and acts to protect from freezing. How, you might wonder? Well, when water freezes it liberates heat, some of which

The Sommelier Says

Unseasonable weather can destroy any vintner's best efforts. Today, however, the world's grape growers apply various technologies to avert most normal climatic disasters.

goes into the grapes. Then the thin layer of ice serves to insulate the parts of the vine. Pretty resourceful! Who knows. Maybe someone got the idea while sitting out in a hot tub in a frigid, outdoor breeze.

Temperature is the climate factor that's most difficult to control. Without enough sunshine, grapes simply don't ripen. With too much, they ripen too fast, and too much of the wine ends up tasting "baked." Heat in the early season can sunburn the grapes. Long-term heat waves bake the acid out of the grapes. And of course, prolonged warm spells in the winter months prevent the vine from going into needed dormancy.

Heard It Through the Grapevine

Unfortunately, there's no vineyard thermostat that adjusts the weather automatically. However, clever vineyard managers have figured out that they can control the effect of the sun by how they prune the leaves of the vine and the orientation of the vines to the sun. This has brought tremendous improvements in grape quality, which is ultimately displayed in the wine in bottle.

Perfect climate conditions rarely occur. The quality of a vintage simply depends on the vagaries of nature during the growing season. A frost when the vines are in bud or flower can cause the vine to lose its grapes or for the grape bunches to ripen unevenly. Cold temperatures during the late summer can cause the vines to slow down, and the grapes will not mature. Rain during the harvest, the winemakers worst dream, dilutes the grapes with water and the wine will be thin and watery. But there are many tricks winegrowers can apply to less-than-perfect harvests. So today, even in relatively poor vintages we can enjoy good and drinkable wines.

Acids

Early in their development, grapes are very acidic. (Try one. Bet you pucker!) With maturation, sugars increase and acids diminish. Sound all right, so far? Like sugar added to lemonade, right? No. Not quite. This is wine we're talking about! Acidity is the backbone of the wine's balance. Too little acid, and you might as well be drinking Snapple.

The Sommelier Says

In addition to blending with a low-acid wine to correct too-high acidity, some vintners adjust hyperacidity through ion exchange. (This is how a water softener works.) If this sounds a bit too chemical, it may be. The resulting wines often taste flat.

Tasting Tip

Wines with a small amount of residual sugar (from one-half to two percent) are called "off-dry." These wines are perfect for those who consider a dry wine too austere.

So sometimes, a wine's acidity is less than sufficient to provide a good balance. Or else, the acidity may decrease during fermentation and may require a little adjustment. Under these circumstances, winemakers add natural acids. This practice is permitted, legal, and universally used for even the finest wines.

Various types of acid are used depending on the style and quality of the wine:

➤ **Tartaric acid** The natural acid in wines is the most expensive to use; tartaric acid has no distinct flavor of its own and blends perfectly with wine flavors.

➤ **Citric acid** The acid of lemons is relatively inexpensive and is used for many inexpensive wines.

➤ **Blending high-acid wines with acid-deficient wines** Another way of correcting acid balance; careful selection of the blending wines is essential to avoid clashing flavors.

Sugar

In general, dry wines tend to be more popular than sweet wines. To some people, sweet wines are an acquired taste or associated only with fortified or dessert wines. Others like their wine with a touch (or more) of sweetness.

In what we call "dry" wines, all of the grape's natural sugar is converted into alcohol. For sweeter wines, some of the natural sugar must remain. There are many methods and styles.

For instance, we have the low-alcohol, sweet, late-harvest German wines, renowned the world over. And we have those wines we call "fortified wines" (See Chapter 22, "Fortified Wine".) To stop fermentation, vintners may chill the fermenting must and then remove the yeast cells by filtering. Or they may add alcohol (in the form of brandy, perhaps) to the fermenting wine to kill the yeast and stop fermentation.

Balance

When we're talking wine grapes, balance refers to the proportions of several related pairs of the taste elements that eventually will become wine. In the finished product, there are

➤ Acid against sweetness

➤ Fruit flavors against wood

➤ Tannic alcohol against acid and flavor

Understanding how the flavors of harvested grapes will change over the course of fermentation (and aging) is an art that you could never learn from a book. How the vintner manages fermentation is critical to the quality of the bottled product.

Harmony

Harmony is the interplay of the wine's constituents. Harmony means smooth, flowing, and compatible. When everything complements everything else, the result is a pleasing wine.

Breed

I feel this one is the utmost characteristic. Wines with breed are the loveliest, most harmonious and refined wines. The classics. These are the wines that age gracefully and wondrously. For these noble beauties, fermentation is merely the beginning of a long life.

Vine Diseases Make Wine Diseases

The mere mention of the tiny plant louse phylloxera is enough to make any grower shudder in horror. Mention noble rot, however, and the expression instantly changes. It's like the difference between the mildew on your shower curtain and the very expensive fungi in your grocery's gourmet section. Some vine diseases destroy the crop entirely, while others yield grapes that seem to say, "Even when I'm bad, I'm pretty good!"

Noble Rot

The technical term is *Botrytis cinerea*; the popular appellation is noble rot. On red grapes and most white varieties it is devastating and can destroy a crop in a matter of days. (This is the mold you find on strawberries and raspberries.) However, this is one little organism that some wine growers actually encourage when they want to produce late-harvest wines of distinction. Noble rot concentrates the sugars in sweet wines. It attacks the grapes right at the moment of maturity, concentrates their essences by dehydrating the berries, and leaves the infected grapes with a unique and luscious flavor.

Heard It Through the Grapevine

Within the Graves district, south of the city of Bordeaux, are the Sauternes and Barsac districts that produce only sweet wines and rely on Botrytis as their *raison d'être*. The climate there is ideal for the growth of Botrytis.

Actually, it's a risky procedure. This is in case when it's the lack of infection that results in a poor wine instead of the reverse. As a result, Sauternes grapes are picked by hand on a bunch-by-bunch or even a berry-by-berry basis! There may be several of these small, select harvests. If you wonder why not harvest all at once, the answer is that not every berry will be infected, and the wines will be less concentrated, less honeyed, and consequently, less flavorful.

Mold

High humidity during the late growing season can result in the growth of mold and mildew. (Well, yes, Botrytis is a mold, but that's a special case.) The molds we're talking about here are the bad guys.

When you sniff your wine, the smell of mold will be obvious. Think of the smell of a moldy berry or peach or apricot. If the wine was made from grapes that were not totally fresh or healthy, you'll notice it immediately. The bottle should be discarded (or returned).

Tasting Tip

Botrytis (what the Germans call Edelfaule) also is the darling of German winemakers. The finest German sweet wines are made from grapes that simply stay on the vine to rot. The quality of their flavor is unrivaled—and they usually carry a price tag to prove it.

Phylloxera

Phylloxera vasatrix is a pesky root louse, indigenous to North America, that thrives on vine roots. Native American vines have thick-skinned roots that are more resistant to the burrowing insect. By contrast, the European vines, with their delicate root systems, quickly succumb. During the 1870s, following the importation of American vines abroad, a sizable portion of Europe's most important vineyard districts were devastated. This nasty plague raged through the finest French vineyards for a full decade until Phylloxera was identified as the cause.

The Europeans saved their grapevines by grafting the *Vitus vinifera* vine to the American rootstock. The practice continues today throughout the wine-growing world. Fortunately, the alien rootstock has no influence on the character of the grape.

The Sommelier Says

A "corked" wine is one infected with a peculiar type of mold that grows in corks. This is another odor you'll notice as soon as you sniff.

Virus

Viruses are nasty creatures that can attack the leaf nodes of the wines early in the growing season. When this happens, the vines may not enjoy adequate working foliage, and may never reach full maturity. A vine once infected cannot be cured. The only solution to this problem is to propagate virus-free vines. This exacting, meticulous task is begun in vine nurseries under the most sterile, scientific conditions. Through modern technology, grapevine propagation has developed into a fine art, and virus-infected leaves rapidly are becoming obsolete.

Odium

Odium is a nasty mold that attacks and kills grapevines, and was responsible for killing vines all over Europe at the turn of the century. It makes an occasional reappearance, but for the most part this scourge has been stamped out.

The Least You Need to Know

➤ Only certain species of grape vines are suitable for wine.

➤ Grapes are complex, with many flavor components and other characteristics.

➤ Modern winegrowers have learned how to deal with many of the natural problems that once meant death to wine crops.

Chapter 7

D'Vine Diversity

In This Chapter

➤ Differences among varieties of white grapes

➤ Range of red grape varieties

Botanists have identified more than 8,000 varieties of grape. But don't panic! Only a select few of these are on display at your local wine shop. You don't need to learn thousands of varieties, but the number used for fine wines still is large. Knowing the characteristics of these grapes will reward you the next time you shop.

In this chapter, we will list white first, then red—for no particular reason.

White Wines: The Favorites

Most (but not all) white wines are made from white grapes. There are hundreds of white grape varieties that are made into wine, but only a handful are seen on wine labels as varietal wines. Here are some of the most popular.

Chardonnay

Chardonnay is the haute varietal among white wine grapes. It is known as the king of white grape varieties. Power and finesse are two qualities of this white *vinifera*, which yields the world's finest white wines.

In northern Burgundy, the Chardonnay grape is responsible for Chablis. Some people call Chardonnay the Champagne grape. This is correct on two levels: Chardonnay is the primary grape variety in the finest Champagnes, and both Chardonnay and Champagne are names that evoke images of high quality.

In California, the styles of Chardonnay vary widely. Some made from ripe grapes are fermented and aged in French oak barrels to yield round, rich wines—flavorful, powerful, and oily in texture. Others approximate this style, but to a lesser degree. A few non-oaked versions capture the direct fruitiness of the Chardonnay in a crisp style. Most California Chardonnays are fuller in body and higher in alcohol than their French cousins.

It's impossible to discuss Chardonnay without mentioning oak. Most Chardonnay receives a restful yet invigorating treatment in an oak bath. The best Chardonnays get their spa treatment inside the traditional French oak barrel. Less expensive wines have to be content with soaking in oak chips or even with the addition of a liquid essence of oak.

The flavors imparted by oak have a vanilla, smoky, spicy, or nutty character. That's easy to associate—they're all woodsy qualities. The Chardonnay flavors and scents are rich and fruity. You can name any fruit you like, from apples to mangoes, and chances are you'll taste at least a hint of it in a cool glass of Chardonnay.

Pinot Grigio (Pinot Gris)

Pinot Grigio, or Pinot Gris, is a white vinifera, related to the Pinot Noir. It's known as the Tokay in Alsace, and the Rulander in Germany.

Northeastern Italy is the most characteristic locale for this grape. It's grown in small quantities in the U.S., mainly in Oregon, although it's becoming more popular in California.

Heard It Through the Grapevine

The skin of Pinot Grigio is strikingly dark for a white variety, and some of its wines are unusually deep in color. They're medium- to full-bodied, somewhat neutral in flavor, and low in acidity when well made.

Picked before fully ripe, these grapes can be high in acidity and undistinguished. Often dismissed as without distinction, some Pinot Grigios from Italy are beginning to take center stage. Pinot Grigio wines are inexpensive and, when well made, easy to drink.

Sauvignon Blanc

Sauvignon Blanc is an adaptive white vinifera. It's a fairly productive grape that ripens in midseason. Harvested at full maturity, it offers wines with a characteristic herbaceous, sometimes peppery aroma. Picked early, the grape is intensely grassy (and yes, that can be a compliment, though not always).

In France, Sauvignon Blanc is the important grape of the Loire Valley wines from Sancerre to Pouilly-Fumé, and a major component in Sauternes from southern Bordeaux. The grape provides backbone and flavor to the luscious, sweet wines of Sauternes and Barsac.

White Graves and Pessac-Leognan wines of Bordeaux are primarily Sauvignon Blanc. They range in style from dry to semisweet and are usually ordinary in quality, although some are of exceptional quality. As the Bordeaulais learn to make better white wines, you will see more and more good wines from this region.

Sauvignon Blanc is higher in acidity than Chardonnay. Some wine lovers savor its crispness; others prefer Chardonnay. Sauvignon Blanc wines are light- to medium-bodied and generally dry. The European varieties are largely unoaked. The California versions usually are oaked. Maybe Californians just like to experiment. California Sauvignon Blancs range from dry to slightly sweet. "Fumé Blanc" is a popular varietal label.

Riesling

If Chardonnay is the king of white grape varieties, *Riesling* is its queen. Riesling is a white vinifera variety that gained its ranking among noble grapes through the great

The Sommelier Says

The noble grape is the Johannisberg Riesling. Gray Riesling and Silvaner Riesling wines actually are made from lesser grapes. To add additional insult, vast quantities of simple jug wines from South Africa and Australia are designated Rieslings, although they bear little resemblance to the fine wines of the Rhine.

Riesling wines of Germany. Unfortunately, the name has suffered a lot of misuse on wine labels.

Riesling does thrive in a few places outside of Germany, notably Alsace in northeastern France (near Germany), Washington state, and the Finger Lakes district of New York. Quality varies, so be sure to use caution here as well.

Riesling wines have dropped off the popularity charts, but they often are good values, and I urge you to try them. Oaky is in these days, but Rieslings refuse to be oaked. (An oaked Riesling would taste awful!) They're lighter in body than Chardonnay, but light can be refreshing and quite satisfying to the palate. Overall, Rieslings are high in acidity, low to medium in alcohol content, and have a fruity or flowery taste and scent that is distinctive.

German Rieslings come in a variety of styles, all with their own levels of dryness, aromas, and flavors. If you're looking for a top-quality dessert wine, a fine German late-harvest Riesling is the perfect choice.

Gewürztraminer

Gewürztraminer (guh-VERTZ-tra-MEE-ner) wines are a lot easier to drink than pronounce. The grape is a clonal selection of the once widely planted traminer white vinifera. Its name means, literally, "spicy grape from Traminer."

Gewürztraminer wines recently have gained in stature because of their distinctive appearance and taste. The wines are deep gold in color, with the spicy aroma of roses and lychee fruit. They're exotic and intriguing. The scent is spicy, floral, and fruity, the flavor surprisingly dry.

The most distinctive examples of Gewürztraminer come from Alsace. U.S. styles tend to be lighter and sweeter than their Alsatian counterparts, but dry Gewürztraminers now are produced in California and Oregon.

Chenin Blanc

Chenin Blanc is a fruity wine ranging from bone dry to slightly, or even very, sweet. The best sweet versions come from the Côteaux du Layon and Vouvray in France, and occasionally rise to legendary quality. Wines of the highest quality have high acidity and an unusual oily texture, age to a beautiful deep gold color, and can last for 50 years or more! The aroma typically is reminiscent of apples, quince, and honey; when harvested early, it's slightly grassy and herbaceous.

Heard It Through the Grapevine

The Gewürztraminer grape tends to be high sugar, low acid. The result is a soft wine with a high alcohol content. However, Gewürztraminer wines also have high extract (essentially, the solid matter of the wine left after you boil off the water and alcohol), which counteracts the feeling of softness. In short, the high extract adds substance and verve and keeps the wine from being flabby.

This noble white grape originally hails from the Loire Valley in France, where it is used both for still wine and vin mousseux (sparkling wines). It's also popular in California, Australia, South Africa, and South America.

Müller-Thurgau

Müller-Thurgau is Germany's most often planted white vinifera, although its ancestry is uncertain. It may be a cross between Riesling and Sylvaner or between two clones of Riesling. It ripens earlier than the Rieslings, which gives it an edge in cool climates. The wine is fragrant, soft, round, and may lack character.

Muscat

The *Muscat* family includes Muscat Blanc, Moscato, Muscadelle, and Muscat of Alexandria. All are white grape varieties with a unique, easily recognizable aroma—pungent, musky, piney, and spicy. The Muscat Blanc offers the best potential for winemakers, although all varieties have been made into table, sparkling, and fortified wines. Muscat is used for Italy's sparkling Asti, which tastes just like the ripe grape itself.

The Sommelier Says

Do not confuse the Muscat family with Muscatel, a cheap fortified wine usually consumed for its high alcohol content. Most of the Muscats you'll find in your wine shop bear little resemblance to this nefarious brew. Muscat wines are low in acidity and have a perfumed, floral aroma ranging from spicy to evergreen, and an inherent bitterness often countered by sweetness.

Vino Vocab

Blender, in this context, refers to a grape variety that is used primarily for blending with other varieties to make a wine, as opposed to a variety used to make a varietal wine.

The Muscat character ranges from subtle to overpowering, depending on growing conditions and winemaking. The styles range from dry to very sweet. Alsatian Muscat is a light, dry, pleasant wine, and California produces some appealing semisweet table wines.

Pinot Blanc

Pinot Blanc, the white variant of the noble Pinot Noir, is grown in many regions. Its main production is in Burgundy, Alsace, Italy, Germany, Austria, and California. In Germany, it's Weissburgunder (White Burgundy), and in Italy it goes by Pinot Bianco or Pinot d'Alba.

The better versions present a spicy fruit, hard, high acid, almost tart profile that demands some cellaring. In California, it is used by many wineries as a sparkling wine blender. As an early ripener and very shy bearer, the grape has lost out in competition with Chardonnay.

Semillon

Semillon is the blending partner of Sauvignon Blanc in the sweet wines from Sauternes. Grown throughout the wine world, it is always the bridesmaid; its main role is as a *blender.*

Semillon is relatively low in acid and has appealing but subtle aromas. It can have the scent of lanolin or smell mildly herbaceous when young. It yields Sauternes-like wines in South Africa and pleasant, dry wines in South American countries. The Australian versions range from dry to semisweet and often are labeled "Rieslings." In California, the wines are finished sweet and are blended into generics.

Trebbiano

Trebbiano is a white vinifera that's grown widely in Central Italy. It ripens late, is very productive, and derives its importance from its role in making Soave, Orvieto, and other popular Italian white wines. In France it is called Ugni Blanc or St. Emilion, and it's favored for Cognac production. Characteristics are high acidity, low sugar, light body, and neutral aromas.

Viognier

Native to the Rhône Valley of France, the *Viognier* grape is a shy bearer, which limits its production. The wines are marked by a spicy, floral aroma, similar to melons, apricots, and peaches. It is medium- to full-bodied with low acidity. Viognier grapes recently have interested California winemakers, but so far quantities have been limited.

Red Wines: The A List

As with white wines, there are a large number of red wine grape varieties. Similarly, only a handful appear on wine labels as varietal names. This section will introduce you to the most popular red grape varieties.

Cabernet Sauvignon

Cabernet Sauvignon is the red counterpart to the royal Chardonnay. It's the reigning monarch of the red viniferas. Ideally, Cabernet Sauvignon wines offer great depth of flavor and intensity of color, and develop finesse and breed with bottle aging.

Heard It Through the Grapevine

The red, royal Cabernet Sauvignon grows well in many wine regions, yielding wines that range from outstanding to mediocre in quality. (After all, it takes more than just a grape for success.) In France, this distinguished grape takes the credit for the grand reputation of Bordeaux red wines. It's the prime element in many of the finest bottlings.

In northern Italy, this grape yields a reasonable facsimile of Bordeaux. Cabernet also grows in many eastern European countries, where it is made into pleasant, light-style wines.

Cabernet is one émigré that thrives in the California sunshine. Some of its California bottlings actually are on par with Bordeaux, with a few even attaining noble quality. Other California Cabernets run the entire quality gamut. South American countries, particularly Chile and Argentina, produce Cabernet in vast quantities, but quality can be shaky.

Cabernet Sauvignon wines are high in tannin and medium- to full-bodied. Their distinctive varietal character is a spicy, bell pepper aroma and flavor with high astringency. Deeply colored wines made from very ripe grapes are often minty and cedary, with a black currant or cassis character.

Tasting Tip

Cabernet wines are at their best and longest-lived when made with close to 100-percent Cabernet grapes. However, this versatile vinifera blends well with other wines. A few of its favored companions are Cabernet Franc, Merlot, Malbec, and Petit Verdot in the Médoc; Merlot and sometimes Zinfandel in California; and Shiraz in Australia.

Merlot

Merlot is a French variety of red vinifera that's grown in many wine regions. It is an early-ripening, medium-colored red grape. As a varietal, it makes wines that are soft and subtle, yet substantial. (Say that very fast while swooshing the wine in your mouth!) The finest Merlots possess great depth, complexity, and longevity.

Merlot has a distinctive, herbaceous aroma quite different from the bell pepper quality of the Cabernet. It is softer in tannins and usually lower in acidity, producing a rounder, fatter, and earlier-maturing wine.

The very qualities that make Merlot less powerful than Cabernet Sauvignon make it more palatable for some wine drinkers. Don't be intimidated by wine snobs. Merlot is easier to drink by itself, and it goes well with lighter foods.

Pinot Noir

Pinot Noir is one of the noblest of all wine grapes. It is grown throughout the wine world, but success varies because of its sensitivity to soil, climate, and the clonal variant of the vine. This is one temperamental vinifera!

Pinot Noir grows best in well-drained, chalky, or clay soils and cool climates. Happily ensconced in clay, it produces wines that often go on to a long aging process, replete with complex fragrances resembling violets, roses, truffles, or other intricate scents. Under less ideal conditions, its wines have a distinctive grapiness, which still is appealing. Under poor conditions, it produces coarse, undistinguished wines, frequently thin and acidic, and unworthy of varietal bottling. (I said it was temperamental!)

Until fairly recently, winemakers believed that Pinot Noir would remain a true French patriot, giving its best only under the tricolor banner. However, a handful of wineries in the U.S. (California, Oregon, Washington, and New York), Australia, South Africa, and Italy have shown that with the proper selection of the vine's clones, exacting care in the vineyards, and appropriate winemaking techniques, the variety can be grown to rival its French counterparts.

Tasting Tip

In France, Pinot Noir is the principal red grape of the Côte d'Or region of Burgundy, where it produces some of the world's most celebrated and costly wines. This grape is used as a base for all Champagnes except Blanc de Blanc and is admired for its body and elegance.

In Switzerland, Pinot Noir is grown in Valais and produces a wine called Dole, which is full-bodied and rich, with some aging potential. In Germany, it is known as Spätburgunder or Rotclevner and yields only thin and acidic red wines of little distinction. (Maybe it doesn't like these German names.)

In northern Italy, Pinot Noir produces wines with verve and aging potential. In Hungary, Romania, and South America, it yields medium- to full-bodied wines, simple and direct for jug wine consumption.

Heard It Through the Grapevine

In the Médoc and other regions of Bordeaux, Merlot is used as an elegant and mellowing component in Cabernet Sauvignon. In the St. Emilion and Pomerol regions of Bordeaux, Merlot is the star, usually making up 60–80 percent of the blend and producing complex, velvety, and sometimes frightfully expensive wines. In California, Italy, Chile, and elsewhere, an increasing number of wineries now produce varietal Merlots, but Merlot is used primarily as a blending agent with the more powerful Cabernet. In Hollywood terms, Merlot is the best supporting actor, while Cabernet Sauvignon remains the big draw.

Zinfandel

Zinfandel is a red vinifera that is grown commercially only in California (an interesting sort of status). It's related to an Italian grape, but boasts no French heritage whatsoever, so it's exempt from the unfair comparisons many fine California wines have to endure.

Even more popular than a full-bodied red Zinfandel in today's market is the blush wine known as White Zinfandel. Grape-skin contact for these Zinfandels is minimal. (In contrast, Zinfandel reds exhibit the richest, deepest colors.)

Syrah/Shiraz

Syrah traces its origin to the days of the Roman and Greek Empires. Its ancestral home is the northern part of the Rhône Valley, where it is used to make the full-bodied, deeply-colored, powerful, long-lived wines from the Côte Rôtie, Chateauneuf-du-Pape, and Hermitage regions.

Heard It Through the Grapevine

Although not as finicky as Pinot Noir, Zinfandel is sensitive to climate and location. It tends to raisin in hot climates and overproduce in others. (Quantity and quality go in inverse proportion.) The wines range from thin, jug wine quality to wines intensely rich in flavor, heavy-bodied with tannins and extract. The typical character is berry-like—blackberry or raspberry—with a hint of spiciness. Styles vary from light and young to heavy and syrupy. The current trend favors heady wines that are warm, tannic, and rich in flavor, which call out for some cellaring.

In Australia, where it's known as the Shiraz or Hermitage grape, it yields potent wines that often are blended with Cabernet. The Syrah also is responsible for South Africa's finest red wines.

Syrah's firm and full-bodied wines have aromas and flavors that suggest roasted peppers (à la Cabernet Sauvignon), smoked meat, tar, and even burnt rubber. (Did I tell you that some wine scents are just plain strange?) Some of the Australian varieties are softer, less full-bodied, and more berry-like than the arche-type Syrah.

The Sommelier Says

The Syrah is one grape variety where California lags behind. So far, it has had only moderate success with this shy-bearing, midseason ripener.

Nebbiolo

Nebbiolo is the pride of Italy's Piedmont region. This pride is well-earned! This red vinifera is sensitive to subtle changes in climate and soil and grows well in few places. It reaches its peak in the rich, aged wines of Barolo, Barbaresco, and Gattinara (in some districts it is known as Spanna).

Most Piedmont versions share a deep color and full body. They have a distinctive fragrance of violets, truffles, or earthiness, sometimes with a hint of tar. Some are herbaceous, and the young wines have a fruity aroma.

Sangiovese

Sangiovese is the principal grape variety used to make Chianti and several other red wines from Tuscany. A small-berry variant called Brunello is used in Brunello di Montalcino wines.

The wines have moderate to high acidity and are moderately tannic. They can be light- to full-bodied, depending on the exact location of origin and the winemaking style. The aromas and flavors are fruity, particularly cherry, with a subtle hint of violets. Sometimes they have a slight nuttiness. Basically, their style is direct and simple, but Chianti Riservas and Brunello di Montalcino can be complex and ageworthy.

Tempranillo

Tempranillo is a Spanish vinifera. Its wines have low acidity and moderate alcohol. The grape itself has a deep color, but this is often masked by long wood aging and blending with lighter varieties like Grenache, as in many Rioja wines.

Aglianico

Indigenous to southern Italy, the *Aglianico* is a little-known grape used to make Taurasi and other powerful red wines that demand cellaring.

Barbera

Barbera is grown primarily in Italy and California. In many Italian districts it is bottled as a varietal identified by a place name (for example, Barbera d'Asti). Depending on the growing conditions and the location, the Italian versions range from pleasantly fruity to slightly rich and tart in flavor.

In California, the plantings are primarily in warm to hot regions, with the resulting wines fruity and soft. They usually are intended for blending into jug wines, but every now and then a robust, rough, rich wine emerges. The current trend is to age the wine in new oak to increase the tannin level and enhance crispness.

Gamay

Gamay reaches its peak in the Beaujolais district of France. It's also grown in California, where it is known as Napa Gamay. (There is a Gamay Beaujolais grown in California, but this is believed to be a clone of Pinot Noir.)

Traditionally, Gamay has been banned in most of Burgundy by a royal edict from centuries ago, but it thrives in Beaujolais, where it produces light, delightfully fresh

and fruity wines for immediate consumption. In its nouveau style, it yields a fresh, fruity wine with strawberry or raspberry flavors. Check out the wine shops in late fall; you'll see signs announcing the arrival of Beaujolais Nouveau on November 15.

Grenache

Grenache is Spanish by heritage but most often identified with France's Rhône Valley, where it yields full-bodied rosés and fruity reds ranging from simple Côtes-du-Rhône to magnificent Châteauneuf-du-Pape. In Spain, it is known as Garnacha and is one of the many varieties blended to make Rioja.

Grenache is used as a blending variety in Châteauneuf-du-Pape, Gigondas, and Côtes du Rhône, the well-known reds of the Rhône. It also produces some full-bodied, fruity reds and stylish rosés in the Languedoc and Provence regions. It thrives in hot climates and is found in many wine regions throughout the world, where it is blended into generic reds and rosés.

> **Tasting Tip**
>
> The Grenache grape has a distinctive orange color and a fruity, strawberry flavor that makes it ideal for rosés and blending. A prime example is Tavel, a rosé produced in the Rhône Valley. At its best, it is full-bodied, assertive, dry, and a deeper red/pink color.

The Least You Need to Know

➤ The most popular white grape varieties are Chardonnay, Sauvignon Blanc, and Riesling.

➤ The most popular red grape varieties are Cabernet Sauvignon, Pinot Noir, Merlot, and Zinfandel.

Chapter 8

Hot Off the Vine

In This Chapter

➤ How wine is made

➤ How winemakers adjust the taste

➤ Wine flaws you can spot

Unless you plan to read wine magazines or advanced books on wine, you really don't need to know how wine is made. But aren't you just a bit curious?

Do you imagine vineyard folk taking off their shoes, hiking up their pant legs or skirts, and climbing into a vat of grapes? If so, you'll be disappointed. Winemaking today is like any other modern manufacturing process—with clean environments and rigorous quality control.

Let's review: The three factors that interact to determine the character of a wine are

1. The grape variety and how it is grown.
2. The climate and soil in which it is grown.
3. The vintner's (winemaker's) intent and expertise in making the wine.

In this chapter you'll see the tricky relationships among the grape, the climate, and the soil. And you'll learn a little about the humans who must deal with these factors.

Grapes Rule!

Each grape variety has its own exacting requirements. Once these are met, the trick lies in picking the grapes when they have developed the target level of sugar, acidity, and flavor for the type of wine being made.

As grapes head toward maturity, these three components undergo rapid change. In warm winegrowing regions, a big concern is the changing sugar/acidity ratio. The vintner wants good sugar without losing the necessary acidity. In the coolest wine-growing regions, the growers concern themselves with achieving the desired sugar and flavor ripeness. Too often, grapes grown in cool climates will ripen with inadequate sugar levels. Fortunately, this can be corrected, as you'll see.

Grapes signal their ripeness by changes in composition, with sugar levels increasing and acidity falling when the grape is ready. A few varieties, such as Gewürztraminer and Sauvignon Blanc, are flavor-mature within a narrow range of sugar development. When picked too late or too early, the grapes lack their distinctive character. This can occur within a matter of hours, so the winemaker has to be very attentive!

Heard It Through the Grapevine

Even within the same vineyard, grapes may vary in maturity for many reasons. Differences in the direction of the slope in relation to the sun, soil type, depth, fertility, and water penetration are some factors. That's why vintners test their grapes in every part of the vineyard.

Winemakers use an instrument called a refractometer. With this handy gadget, the vintner walks through the vineyard and measures the sugar content of the grapes on the vine. Today's sugar is tomorrow's alcohol. The sugar is expressed in terms of degrees Brix, which may range from 17 to 25 degrees Brix, depending on the desired outcome.

The grape *cluster* (bunch) consists of three parts, each of which contributes to the quality of the wine:

1. *Stems* make up 2 to 6 percent of the cluster's weight. These are rich in wood tannins, but they also can leave the wines with a bitter flavor. For most wines, the stems are removed prior to fermentation, but they may be left in some wines to augment the tannins, adding complexity to the flavor.

2. *Skin* represents about 5 to 16 percent of the grape's weight. When mature, the skin is covered with a bloom of wild yeast that sometimes is used for fermentation. The skin and the layers just below it contain most of the aroma and flavor constituents of the grape. They also contain the grape tannins. In this case, there's a distinction between tannins: The ones found in the skin tend to be softer and less bitter than the ones in the stems and pits. Grape tannins are the essential element of red wines intended for aging.

3. *Pulp,* which contains the juice in a fibrous membrane, makes up most of the grape's weight. The juice consists of the ever-changing proportions of water, sugar, and acid. Within the pulp, the membrane responds to the changing needs of the juice. It gets filled or depleted as the grapevine responds to its environment.

The pulp also contains a number of complex fruit acids that undergo chemical changes—along with glycerins, proteins, and other elements that may or may not be desired by the winemaker. In the end, the pulp presents the winemaker with a serious concern. All of it must be removed to get only clear, clean wine.

Thanks to advances in technology, grapes can be harvested and transported to the winery with a minimum of damage. Hand-picking still is practiced by the very best producers. Generally, giant machines resembling praying mantises work night and day in the vineyards to harvest grapes at their peak. (Not a bad idea for a sci-fi flick, actually; they really do look like giant insects!)

The Sommelier Says

The sugar in the grape can drop drastically if it is needed to support the vine. It may end up being diluted if the vine receives too much moisture. This is where soil and climatic conditions are critical.

The machines sometimes work in tandem with portable crushers. The juice, crushed in the vineyard, is sent to the winery protected by an atmosphere of carbon dioxide to prevent premature fermentation and oxidation. Whichever way the grapes are harvested, the trick is to transport them to the winery as quickly as possible. Those quirky wine-bearers begin to deteriorate as soon as they leave the vine.

Artist, Scientist, Winemaker

The winemakers set to work as soon as they have the grapes in their hands. When the grapes are picked, they go into a crusher/stemmer, where the stems are removed. In the case of a white wine, the harvest goes directly into a wine press, where the juice is extracted and the skins separated.

The vintners pump the juice into a tank or vat. There it ferments in its own wild yeast. Or more likely, the winemaker will inoculate it with a selected yeast strain. That's because each yeast strain has particular characteristics of fermentation and flavors it leaves behind.

Heard It Through the Grapevine

Yeast enzymes react with the sugar, producing alcohol and carbon dioxide. The process may also yield minute quantities of certain organic compounds that may or may not be pleasing. That's why modern vintners don't like to leave anything to chance.

During fermentation, the liquid in the vats is called *must*. After fermentation, the transformed juice has become wine. The winemaker stores the product in either casks or tanks. The last steps are clarification, stabilization, and bottling. (Winemakers wish it were all that simple!)

Tasting Tip

Dark-skinned grapes are used to make full-bodied Champagnes and the still (no bubbles) white table wines called Blanc de Noirs. The vintner can moderate the color by separating the must from the skins at first blush.

Stems and Skins

The juice of most grapes is white, which is why we can make white wine even from red grapes. Red wine gets its color from the pigmentation of the skins during contact with the must.

With most white wines, the must is separated from the skins immediately after crushing. However, the skins can add bitterness (not necessarily a bad thing!) or tannins to a white wine. Depending on the type of wine being made, the winemaker may allow some skin contact prior to fermentation.

For red wines, the skins remain with the juice and go with it into the fermentation vessel. During the fermentation process, both color and tannins are leached from the skins. Sometimes the winemaker will allow the stems to remain with the must. Some may even add a quantity of stems to the wine. This enhances the firmness and complexity of certain red wines.

Rosé wines remain with their skins just long enough to pick up the required tinge. Then they're vinified in much the same way as white wines.

Fermentation: Take One

During fermentation, winemakers perform both as scientists and creative artists. (Actually, in the case of jug wines, the vintners basically are hands-off manufacturers.) But for distinctive, high-quality wines, they work rather like film directors, molding their characters and shooting their scenes until they have a full-scale artistic work. (Unfortunately, they don't get to reshoot the bad scenes, and they often make it to market.)

The skillful winemaker directs the wine, molds its structure, flavors, nuances, and character to correspond to some personal vision. The result: a vinous work of art. Maybe. The process of fermentation can be as fickle as a movie audience.

Heard It Through the Grapevine

Alcoholic fermentation is the reaction between yeast and sugar that creates alcohol and carbon dioxide. It's a complex chemical reaction involving numerous stages. In its simplest form, the chemical equation looks like this:

$$C_6H_{12}O_6 \quad = \quad 2C_2H_5OH \quad + \quad 2CO_2 \quad + \quad HEAT$$

natural grape sugar	ethyl alcohol (ethanol)	carbon dioxide (a gas)	

The vintner's greatest concern is a healthy fermentation. Certain yeasts are good for wine, while others can turn a wine straight into vinegar or leave it with some very unpleasant flavors. The idea is to create a vigorous population of the appropriate yeast before some alien yeast can take over.

Bordeaux vintners harvest some of their grapes early to develop a starter vat. Once that early fermentation is underway, they add the actual full harvest.

Once started, fermentation continues slowly, but soon picks up speed. As the yeast cells multiply, fermentation proceeds, usually until all the sugar is transformed into alcohol or until the vintner deliberately calls a halt. For most table wines, this means something between 11 and 14 percent. Should the alcohol level reach 15 or 16 percent, fermentation will stop in any case. Few yeasts can survive in a high-alcohol environment.

Tasting Tip

When ingredients are labeled in percentages, it's usually by weight. One exception is ethanol (the kind of alcohol in fermented beverages), which always is denoted by volume.

The traditional fermentation vessel is a wooden vat or cement-lined tank. Many modern vintners, however, use a temperature-controlled stainless steel tank. Stainless steel, of course, adds no flavor, and these tanks are easy to clean. Also, it's easy to equip these with cooling coils and a thermostatic, temperature-controlled refrigeration unit to control the temperature of fermentation.

Climate Control

Fermentation temperature is an essential consideration. Each grape variety or strain of yeast reacts differently to various temperatures, affording a whole universe of winemaking possibilities. The winemaker's ability to control temperature to produce individual flavors, nuances of character, and harmony of structure is like having a magic wand. And the magic spell becomes the vintner's unique signature.

Temperature control seems to be a simple thing. It's not. Fermentation, you see, produces heat as a by-product of transforming sugar into alcohol. Too much heat can be a real problem. For example, higher temperatures cause fermentation to proceed at an irregular rate, often too rapidly. This can oxidize or break down certain flavor compounds, resulting in a baked flavor, or it can spur the growth of undesirable organisms.

Since reds are fermented with both their skins and seeds, the mass of solids, called the *cap*, rises to the surface. To extract maximum flavors and tannins, as well as to allow for the release of heat, the cap must be broken from time to time. Winemakers do this in a number of ways:

➤ Pumping the must up over the cap

➤ Punching the cap down several times a day

➤ Adding a false top to force the cap into the must

Heard It Through the Grapevine

The rate and length of fermentation influence the fruity fragrance, or complexity, of a wine. At cooler temperatures, fermentation proceeds slowly, frequently over weeks. With white wines, this leisurely process retains the aromatic flavors of the grape and provides flowery, pleasing wines. It even enhances the flavor of wines made from the lesser grape varieties. In fact, cold fermentation has been responsible for the vast improvement in most American jug wines.

Fermentation temperatures for most white wines range between 45 and 55 degrees Fahrenheit. Reds generally ferment in the 55–75 degree range. The character of many red wines is determined by the rate of fermentation at specific stages of the process, regulated under the winemaker's meticulous control.

During the growing season, the winemaker—however skilled and experienced—is a gambler. During the fermentation process, science replaces chance. In contemporary winemaking, winemakers act on knowledge rather than on gut.

The vintner monitors the fermentation frequently by checking the sugar, alcohol, acid, and balance—both through tasting and laboratory analysis. Tasting is critical; no matter how advanced and elaborate the machinery, there's nothing that equals the knowledge and discrimination of human taste buds.

Many winemakers taste each of their wines at least once a day during crucial periods. That way, they can make any needed adjustments or corrections. Where needed, they can alter the process, applying new techniques to their quest for a balanced wine.

Microbes: Good, Bad, and Noble

Yeasts are minuscule one-celled organisms (fungi, actually) that are entirely responsible for the fermentation process. They reproduce by growing buds that break off when they get large.

Without yeasts, we'd have grape juice instead of wine (and breakfast cereal instead of beer and whiskey). Yeasts produce enzymes that convert sugars into ethanol (the kind of alcohol in wine) and carbon dioxide. When their work is complete, voilà! Vino!

Certain microorganisms, which may come along with the grape itself or be present in the wine casks, can survive both the fermentation process and its development of alcohol. (Some bacteria even survive at the bottom on the seas where hot sulfuric acid is vented from the earth.) Two bacteria we are concerned about here are *Acetobacter xylinium* and *Lactobacillus*.

Acetobacter xylinium always is present in small amounts in fermenting wines. It produces small, though acceptable, levels of acetic acid (vinegar). This reacts with the alcohol to make ethyl acetate, which smells a little like nail polish remover. But as long as these exist in very small quantities, these compounds actually add to the complexity of a wine.

Now add a little oxygen, and these bacteria become a real threat. *Acetobacter xylinium* thrives on fermented wine and, in the presence of oxygen, quickly turns the wine into vinegar by converting its alcohol into acetic acid. Winemakers have to stay on their toes to prevent air and *Acetobacter* from becoming an evil wrestling tag team determined to ruin their product.

Lactobacillus is the most common variety of lactic acid bacteria, and it's essentially harmless. During fermentation, it produces by-products that add to the complexity of the wine. But occasionally, *Lactobacilli* run out of control, producing the peculiarly pungent and offensive odor of geraniums, which can be corrected only by stripping the wine of all its flavors.

Not Too Sweet!

Many styles of wine require that some of the grape's natural sugar remain unfermented. Among these are the low alcohol, sweet, late harvest wines for which Germany is renowned. So sometimes, vintners must arrest the action of yeast once the desired level of alcohol or sweetness is achieved.

One way to accomplish this is by chilling the fermenting must and removing the yeast cells by filtering. In the case of fortified sweet wines, the winemaker adds alcohol to the fermenting wine. This extra alcohol kills the yeast, and fermentation stops.

Many styles of white wines retain a slight sweetness, usually around 2 percent. Chilling will not always give the winemaker enough control over the balance needed for these wines. A modern technique is to ferment the wine completely. Then the vintner adds a small amount of the grape juice, which has been set aside to sweeten the wine. The sweetness of the resulting wine can be adjusted with great precision and makes it easy for the winemaker to stabilize the wine to prevent it from refermenting in the bottle.

This technique is known as sweet reserve or sweet must. It's widely used in the U.S. and Germany, where fine, well-balanced, fragrant, slightly sweet table wines are a favored commodity.

Fermentation: Take Two

Sometimes it's desirable to put wine through a second fermentation, using bacteria rather than yeast. Malolactic fermentation transforms the wine's malic acid, which tastes hard, into the softer, less acid-tasting lactic acid. The transformation takes place with only a slight decrease in the actual measured acidity of the wine.

This second fermentation also produces certain by-products that may or may not be desirable for a particular kind of wine. It's up to the winemaker to decide whether to encourage or prevent malolactic fermentation.

With most whites, this process is decidedly undesirable. It reduces the wine's sense of crisp freshness. One notable exception is Chardonnay. When Chardonnay undergoes a malolactic fermentation, it produces diacetyl compounds, the major flavor components of butter. As a result, the wine develops a buttery complexity, which marries well with the flavors of the Chardonnay grape.

For noble reds like Cabernet Sauvignon and Pinot Noir, the malolactic fermentation is favored to soften the acid taste. It also enhances the wine by adding considerable complexity, flavor nuances, and suppleness.

Heard It Through the Grapevine

Some wines undergo a spontaneous second fermentation when temperatures warm up in the spring after the harvest. Winemakers can choose to let this happen naturally by leaving the wine in barrels or tanks that will warm with the weather. Or they can induce it by introducing a malolactic strain of bacteria.

The vintner must take scrupulous care that malolactic fermentation is complete before bottling. Complex red wines cannot be preserved the same way many simpler wines can. A malolactic fermentation that continues after the wine is bottled causes the wine to become fizzy, with stinky flavors that will not dissipate after the wine is poured.

On the Rack

The fermentation is done, and it's time to clarify the wine. Vintners use gravity in a process we call *racking*. This traditional method is still the best one for fine wines.

To rack, the winemaker puts the wine into small casks to allow the suspended solids to settle. Then the clear wine or juice is pumped or siphoned from the lees (sediment—old yeast, grape skins and solids, and potassium bitartrate) and into a clean, fresh tank or cask.

The racking schedule is frequent within the first year, often five times or more. It requires considerable labor and includes cleaning the previous casks. It's sort of like those hourly feeding schedules for newborns. A lot of loving care goes into making a noble wine!

The Sommelier Says

Frequent rackings aerate the wine, ridding it of natural by-products of winemaking such as foul-smelling hydrogen sulfide that can impair its healthy development. But racking must be done with extreme caution. Excessive contact with air, and you're left with a cask of noble vinegar!

Wine Ailments You Can Taste in the Glass: A Close Look

Winemaking is fraught with potential disaster, either from the microbes that float in the air looking for wine to ruin or from less-than-perfect care in the winery. Here are some of the wine ailments that can affect the wine you buy. When you spot these, return the wine to the store where you bought it, or reject any such wine served in a restaurant.

Pediococcus

This is a peculiarly pungent bacterial strain of bacterium. It gives your wine the ripe smell of sweaty socks. Under no circumstances should your wine have the aroma of your gym bag or any of its contents!

Sulfur Compounds

One natural by-product that must be removed from wine is hydrogen sulfide. This gives off the smell of rotten eggs. Hydrogen sulfide occurs naturally during yeast fermentation (more or less, depending on the strain of yeast) and usually is dissipated early in the clarifying process. If not, you'll know it immediately.

Vintners use sulfur dioxide, a pungent gas, as a preservative. Used properly, it's very effective and leaves nothing behind to interfere with your pleasure, but too heavy a dose can. If your wine smells or tastes like a newly struck match, you've got a bad bottle.

Mercaptan

If hydrogen sulfide is left in the cask or tank during fermentation, it rapidly combines with the alcohol to form ethyl mercaptan. Mercaptan is the most odorous of all chemicals, similar to the stuff they put in natural gas to alert you to leaks.

Its odors range from onions to children's clay to garlic to skunk! Once it has completely bound with the alcohol, there is no getting it out. Careful winemakers make sure that all the hydrogen sulfide has been aired out of the wine. Still, the mercaptan odors do occur—a mark of sloppy winemaking.

Dekkara

Dekkara is a bacteria that creates the aroma and taste of rancid corn chips. If you don't see a pile of stale Fritos on the table, chances are your wine's been infected.

Corkiness

Corked wines have the scent of a mold that likes to grow on wine corks. (I can't say I blame the mold for its choice of habitat, but it's not something that enhances the wine's appeal.) This makes your wine smell and taste moldy. But until we find a better way to seal a bottle, even the most costly wines may succumb to this blight.

Old World Charm

The traditional Old World winery may lack modern equipment, such as stainless steel fermentation tanks, filtration, centrifuges, and sterile bottling. All these are important innovations, essential to modern viniculture (winemaking).

Some of the world's finest wines still are produced the old-fashioned way. The trend, however, especially in California and increasingly in Bordeaux and elsewhere, is to invest in modern equipment to avoid the pitfalls of the traditional winery.

Heard It Through the Grapevine

When white wine is made by the traditional method, the grapes, either white or red, are crushed, destemmed, and pumped directly into the wine press. The wine is pressed quickly to prevent it from picking up color or tannins from the skins. Following pressing, the wine may settle or be pumped directly into fermentation tanks.

Some wines are aged in oak following fermentation; some are not. Most wines are clarified (solid particles removed) with egg white. Egg whites remove the solid particles in the wine and do not form crystals. The crystals are formed when the wine is chilled, thus removing the tartaric acid in the wine. Following clarification, the wine may be pumped into a "cold room" or into refrigeration tanks to precipitate any tartrate crystals. This allows for removal of crystals before the wine enters the bottle. However, some traditional wineries leave out this step, which explains why some wines' bottles may have these crystals in the bottle and on the cork.

Traditionally, red wine grapes pass through a crusher/destemmer and are pumped into wooden or concrete vats (cuves). There, the wine ferments with its skins, pulp, pits, and (sometimes) stems. Following fermentation, the *free-run juice* is removed for the best wine. (The wine that flows freely, without heavy pressure from the wine press, is called free-run juice.) It is the cleanest and usually most distinctive wine.

Red wines are aged in small oak barrels or in larger upright casks. The aged wine is clarified by *fining* (removing solid particles dispersed in the wine), usually with egg white. After clarification, the wine is bottled. Occasionally, bottling is still done by hand, although rarely in the U.S.

Once the first fermentation is complete, the wine is drawn off the lees (solids in the bottom of the barrel) and placed in tanks or large casks. This allows the remaining solids suspended in the wine to settle.

For wines fermented with their skins, the remaining juicy pulp is pressed, leaving behind a cake-like mass of solids called pomice. This wine is called press wine. It varies from light press to heavy press, depending on the pressure exerted.

Often, each press batch is handled and aged separately. Later on, it may be combined with another wine in some proportion. Or not.

High-Tech

The modern winery uses advanced technology, which makes for better control of the winemaking process. This technology actually gives the winemaker more artistic control over the winemaking process, resulting in a product closer to the vintner's vision.

White wine grapes are brought to the winery in gondolas or special tank trucks blanketed with inert carbon dioxide or nitrogen gases to prevent oxidation. Machines may do the harvesting and field crushing. The grapes are crushed in a special horizontal press— gently, to avoid harsh tannins.

Tasting Tip

Frequently, the wine is separated into different vats as the pressing proceeds. The heavier the press, the darker the color, the fuller and coarser the flavor, and the more bitter and tannic the wine will be.

Prior to fermentation, the winemaker may use a centrifuge to remove solid matter from the juice. Sometimes after fermentation, and sometimes both before and after. As you remember, these wines will be cold-fermented to preserve their freshness and fruitiness. Some may be aged in wooden casks, large or small.

If the fermented wine has not been centrifuged, it will be filtered. Then it will be cold-stabilized to precipitate tartrate crystals. Finally, the vintner bottles the wine on a sterile line to prevent air and other contaminants from entering the bottle.

The modern vintner pumps red wine's crushed grapes into concrete or stainless steel fermentation vats. Ordinary or everyday wines may be heated first to extract color and flavor rapidly without tannin. Next the wine is aged in small or large wooden casks. The desired quality of the wine determines the type of cask: new oak for most super-premium or noble wines, used oak or redwood for lesser wines, or even no wood for everyday wines.

The Centrifuge

Some vintners call the centrifuge "God's gift to the winemaker." Those who have one swear by it. Most of those who do not swear at their bad luck. But there are a few odd ones who believe centrifuges strip their wine of its flavor.

The centrifuge is a little like a giant Cuisinart. This nifty device has a vast and varied usefulness in the winemaking process. How's it work? It whirls the wine at high speed, using centrifugal forces to separate heavier components from lighter ones. Unwanted items like yeast cells, pulp, dirt, and dust are discarded, leaving behind a clear, clean liquid.

Heard It Through the Grapevine

Many winemakers find that centrifuged juice ferments more easily and produces a cleaner wine than batches that were cleaned in other ways. That's why they use the centrifuge to clean white wine must before fermentation. Both white and simple reds may be centrifuged instead of racked or filtered.

Wines with certain off-flavors may receive a heavy centrifuging. (Sounds like a punishment, doesn't it?) This can strip a wine of all character but salvage an otherwise unusable wine. For jug wines, subtle character isn't a consideration. The centrifuge is widely used to clean jug-quality wines prior to bottling.

Chaptalization

Chaptalization is the addition of beet or cane sugar to the fermenting wine. This type of "cheating" compensates for the insufficiently ripe grapes from a cool vintage. It increases both body and alcohol level, enabling the wine to meet quality standards.

Vino Vocab

No, **chaptalization** was not named for some Chaptal region in France! It was named after Jean Chaptal, the French Minister of Agriculture who invented the process.

There are legal standards, national and regional, that limit the amount of sugar vintners may add. (Few winemakers, of course, would choose to go sky-high on sweetness.) Chaptalization is permitted in France, Germany, and most other European countries. And it's allowed in the winemaking states of the U.S., except for California (where it isn't needed anyway).

When used to increase the alcohol level of a wine by a small amount, say 1 percent, and applied carefully, the process is virtually undetectable to even the most discerning wine expert. The amount of sugar needed is meticulously computed. No guessing!

Some purists decry the process, claiming it affects the quality of the wine. But I'll bet they've drunk chaptalized wine themselves, blissfully ignorant. Only when the process is ineptly applied or used to excess is the character of the wine adversely affected.

With excess chaptalization (although within legal limits), wine can become alcohol-unbalanced, tasting hot and harsh. Also, such wines will taste thin or diluted in flavor or character. However, this is unusual. The vast majority of winemakers value their product and reputation too highly to abuse their technology.

The Least You Need to Know

➤ A knowledge of winemaking can enhance your appreciation of fine wines.

➤ The grape, the vineyard, and the winemaker play equally important roles in making fine wine.

➤ Simple wines are not expensive to make.

➤ Expensive wines are more costly because the winemaker uses expensive grapes, oak barrels, and more human labor.

➤ Careless winemaking and accidents of nature can result in wines that taste bad.

Part 3

Bottle of Red, Bottle of White

Get out your Frequent-Flyer card! You're going to use it in this section as we take a world tour, beginning in France. (We'll linger long in that land of the noblest wine traditions.) Then on to Italy, Spain, and Portugal. And then a hop over the Atlantic on the Concorde to get our passports stamped in Chile and Argentina. Just in time to return to Europe for a whirl through Germany, Austria, Hungary, and Greece. And once more to the New World, as we travel through the U.S. and Canada on chartered buses. And airborne again, as we travel around the vast world south of the equator—Australia, New Zealand, and South Africa.

Whew! Are we done yet? No, we're not! Back to a little bit of France to learn all about Champagne, the real thing, and elsewhere to sample sparkling wines. And then, commencing on the Iberian Peninsula, a survey of fortified wines. No. We're not done yet! We want to look into organic wines from Europe, Australia, and North America. And kosher wines, also from Europe and the U.S. It's a big world we live in, and wine has made it even bigger.

Chapter 9

C'est Magnifique!

In This Chapter

➤ Understanding French wine laws

➤ Regions of origin

➤ Are French wines better?

Before Louis XIV, before Joan of Arc, before Charlemagne, even ... France was a wine country. When the seafaring Greeks founded Marseilles, France's oldest city (around 600 B.C.E.), they brought wine. When Julius Caesar took over in 49 B.C.E., Romans diffused knowledge of wine throughout Gaul. And France has been a big-time wine producer ever since.

Wine was most important to the ancient world. Until modern times, very little water was safe to drink. And people had to drink something, right?

Those ancient wines had little in common with those we enjoy today. But after centuries of practice, the French have made winemaking into an art. French wine knowledge became their gift to the world. In this chapter we'll explore France and its venerable winemaking culture.

Regulations and More Regulations

The French seem to regulate everything: their language, distribution of safety matches, even names new parents may choose for their children! In the case of wine, though, this is a good thing.

French wine laws ensure that what's printed on the label is clear, correct, and informative. Taken individually, these wine regulations are simple and logical. But when they appear in one place—as on a wine label—they can be intimidating, especially in the case of France's very finest wines. So I'd like to give you some essential background knowledge.

Every Wine Knows Its Place

The French system of identifying and regulating wine regions is known as the *Appellation d'Origine Contrôlée* (AOC or AC), translated simply as "regulated place name." Most French wines are named for places, not grapes.

Here's where things get messy. Each wine district has its own organization for enforcing the Appellation Contrôlée regulations that are specific to that region. These controlling bodies determine and implement criteria that may vary from place to place. These systems guarantee minimum quality levels. They also provide classification schemes that denominate the various quality levels.

French culture is very conscious of hierarchical standing. This is true particularly in the case of French wines. Under French laws, a wine can aspire to one of four status levels. One of these descriptions must appear on the label of every bottle of wine:

> ➤ Appellation d'Origine Contrôlée (AOC) is the highest tier. Most labels give the actual place name in place of "d'Origine." For example: Appellation Bordeaux Contrôlée indicates a wine from the Bordeaux region. These wines range from mid-premium to *noble* in quality.

> ➤ Vin Délimité de Qualité Supérieur (VDQS), the second-highest level, translates as "demarcated wine of superior quality." These wines range from simple-premium to premium in quality.

> ➤ Vins de Pays means, literally, "country wine." On the label, you'll see this written with a place name. But this place will encompass a much larger area than the places named in the two higher grades. These wines resemble the jug and magnum wines you might find from California, Chile, or Italy—simple-premium wines.

> ➤ Finally, we have Vin de Table, or ordinary table wine. These wines have neither a region nor a grape on their labels. Wines of this quality rarely come into the United States. In France, these are sold in plastic bottles. At best, they are jug quality, sometimes not even.

Vino Vocab

Remember my scheme of dividing the premium wine category into three subdivisions? Simple-premium, mid-premium, and super-premium. And one new category, **noble**, for wines that approach magnificence when mature.

Heard It Through the Grapevine

Until recently, few of the wines from the two lower classifications were sold in the U.S. Now, however, wines labeled "Vins de Pays D'Oc" (or some other region) have become available as some wine regions now make fine varietal and blended wines, above their traditional quality level. This is an example of the continuing progress made in French winemaking. Many French winemakers provide good value and pleasing, flavorful wines at this level.

VDQS wines, despite the "superior quality" designation, are relatively ordinary, though some display extra flavor and distinction. You will see some of these in your wine shop. However, most French wines consumed in the U.S. are AOC wines. And when we select from this top level, we find it's broken down into its own hierarchy of quality. (Just when you thought you understood it all!)

Many French wines are named for the places they come from in France.

At the bottom of the AOC ladder we have a category that refers only to the broadest regions, whose wines meet certain standards. Moving upward, the designations get tighter in geography and higher in quality. At the very top, some of the greatest vineyards have their own appellation.

You can think of these classifications as concentric circles, with the smallest denoting the best. Let's begin with the largest circle and work inward (and upward) :

➤ **An entire region, say Bordeaux or Burgundy**   Simple-premium to premium quality. The label will designate simply Bordeaux, Bordeaux Supérieur, or other.

➤ **A district within a region, such as Haut-Médoc or Côte de Beaune**   Somewhat higher in quality, but still ranging from simple-premium to premium, with a few better wines. Within this tier may be subdistricts that produce somewhat better wine—for example, Côte de Beaune Villages, Beaujolais villages.

➤ **A village or commune within a district—Pauillac or Meursault, for example**   These wines may be considerably better than those of the previous appellation, depending on the producer. When wines are blended from several vineyards within the commune or district, they are known as Regional or Village wines, depending on the custom of the locality. These wines range from mid- to super-premium quality and noble.

➤ **A single vineyard, such as Le Montrachet**   In Burgundy and (rarely) other districts, a wine of extraordinary distinction and fame is honored with its own appellation. These wines are designated as a *Grand Cru* and are the equivalent of a *First Growth (Premier Cru Classé)* of Bordeaux.

Tasting Tip

Within a village or commune appellation, some wines can be much better than others. (You really need to know the château or vineyard names.) In Bordeaux, a number of the commune wines are classified as growths or Cru Classé, which are immediate indicators of, respectively, higher or highest quality. Some of these wines are equal to those designated by vineyard.

There's more to French wine regulation than appellations. Much more. For instance, the government stipulates the quantity of grapes that can be produced in any hectare (about 2.5 acres) in each AOC district. And there are several specific quality regulations as well, such as the designation of *crus* (growths). As the wines go up the quality tier, these regulations grow more stringent.

In many AOC regions, the wine actually has to pass a government tasting test in order to get its AOC designation for that vintage. Sometimes a vineyard making wine from a higher classification will allow some of its wine to be labeled under a broader designation. For instance, wine from younger plantings may be declassified and sold under a second label or in bulk to a négociant or éleveur (see the section in Chapter 4, "Terms of the Taste and Trade") to be used in their blends.

Heard It Through the Grapevine

French labeling requires little more than the correct appellation. To assess the quality of wine by its appellation alone, you'll need to do some homework. In general, the more specific the appellation, the costlier the contents. But cost alone does not ensure quality.

But do look for the word "Cru" on the label. Within certain appellations, wines classified into Crus have legal standing. The Cru designation can assure you the quality of the wine is quite high.

Yes, the French wine label looks fairly simple. And what you've learned so far can help you shop for quality or value. Up to a point. You still need some more specific knowledge of French wines to better know what's in that bottle.

Does Français Mean Supérieur?

Before the 1960s, wine lovers considered French wines *de rigueur*. Simply, they were the only wines one drank! With those legendary vineyards and all, everybody knew the best wines came from France. End of story.

California wine? Oh, yeah … before the '60s, jugs of plonk (cheap wine) with the name of a huge producer on them! Italian wine? Cheap bottles of thin and acidic Chiantis; you threw away the wine to use the bottle as a candle holder.

But things happened in the 1960s. Kennedy, The Beatles, Woodstock—and new attitudes toward wine. Scientific winemaking with modern equipment put many countries on the winemaking map. The U.S. and Italy, for instance, began to produce wines that rivaled the best French wines. And bear in mind, the lesser French wines never were much better than those from other countries.

Tasting Tip

So why buy French wines? For one thing, France offers a very wide variety among its very best wines. For another, many of these wines are unique, found nowhere else. Finally, when you go shopping for fine wines, France offers many excellent bargains.

As you gain confidence in your skills as a wine enthusiast, you'll do your own taste comparisons. You'll answer for yourself whether French wines really are the best of their kind. Never forget, the most important opinion is your own.

The Least You Need to Know

➤ There are four quality tiers in the French appellation system: Appellation d'Origine Contrôlée (AOC), Vin Délimité de Qualité Supérieur (VDQS), Vins de Pays, and Vin de Table.

➤ AOC wines are the best quality. Within this category are subcategories of increasing quality.

➤ French wines are the role model for most other wines, but they're not necessarily better just because they're French.

Bordeaux—
Le Roi du Vin

The Bordeaux wine region is named for the Atlantic seacoast city (population approximately 220,000) in southwestern France. The Bordeaux winegrowing districts lie on slopes near the seacoast, through the valleys of the Garonne and Dordogne rivers, and along the Gironde estuary these rivers flow into. It is by far the largest and most prolific producer of famous and high-quality wines. Bordeaux itself is a major commercial port. Many top wine brokers and shippers maintain their offices along the port's Quai de Chartrons.

In this chapter we'll tour this renowned wine region. Bordeaux is the stuff of legends—home to such famous names as Château Lafite-Rothschild, Château Latour, and Châteaux Margaux. Not all the region's exports are in this rarefied category (fortunately for most of us). Bordeaux winemakers are known also for many high-quality, enjoyable, and affordable wines.

With its appellations, *communes* (jurisdictions), and *crus* (growths), it's easy to get a bit lost in Bordeaux. This chapter will unravel the mysteries of the region we call "the King of Wine." We'll cover the inner appellations and vineyards that make up Bordeaux, and the different wines, grapes (they're not all Cabernet Sauvignon), and price tags.

The wine regions of Bordeaux have districts within districts as the wines get better.

A Legend is Born

In the Bordeaux region, several hundred *châteaux* (vineyards) produce the outstanding wines that have made Bordeaux a legend. They send their liquid treasures to brokers and shippers in Bordeaux.

A few names—Château Lafite-Rothschild, Château Mouton-Rothschild, Château Latour, and Château Margaux—have come to mean "superlative wine" throughout the world. These names have endowed Bordeaux with a certain mystique. But let's not get carried away. The region also makes prodigious quantities of ordinary wines for local consumption. But few of these lesser wines ever appear on our shelves or tables, so the Bordeaux legend remains intact.

Heard It Through the Grapevine

Bordeaux produces 10 percent of all French wine and an astounding 26 percent of all AOC wine. Most Bordeaux wines are dry reds. About 15 percent are dry white wines, and 2 percent are sweet white wines, most notably the Sauternes.

Bordeaux wines range in price from cheap to outrageous. Some noble wines from great vintages have sold for $500 or more. But don't worry: You needn't be Donald Trump to enjoy a fine Bordeaux! Many good-quality Bordeaux, both red and white, begin at about $10 a bottle when they are young.

Many of the Bordeaux you will hear about are of super-premium or noble quality. These are the wines vintners aspire to imitate. When they are young, the typical Bordeaux classified growth will have a deep ruby hue with aromas of black currants, spice, cedar, fine leather, chocolate, and cassis, the French apéritif.

For the first five to 10 years, these finest wines can be very vinous and austere, with puckering tannins. As they age, their colors change to garnet, with a gem-like brilliance. These will develop an extraordinarily complex bouquet and flavor with more agreeable tannins. On rare occasions, the very best will develop an unusual scent that is almost devoid of flavor, like the air after a rainstorm. The subtle nuances of bouquet will be delicate and beautiful. I call this marvelous quality "vaporous."

The greatest classified red Bordeaux wines may take 20 years or more to reach maturity. (Some continue to improve even after 50 years in the bottle!) As you may expect, the greatest of these wines, from extraordinary vintages, command a king's ransom. Not too long ago a bottle of 1797 Château Lafite-Rothschild alleged to have belonged to Thomas Jefferson sold at auction for more than $150,000!

Tasting Tip

The greatest Bordeaux châteaux develop wines of power, yet that exhibit the softest nuances of flavor, like the piccolo coming through the orchestral *tutti* at the end of Beethoven's Fifth. The very best also develop an extraordinary refinement, one we have described as finesse and breed.

The Best Come from Médoc

The Médoc is a district—our second tier of wine quality within the larger AOC of Bordeaux. The most famous—and definitely the best—red-wine vineyards of the Bordeaux district lie within the Médoc, north of the city along the Gironde estuary.

The best vineyards are situated along a narrow strip of gravely soil, about 10 miles long and no more than seven miles wide. In this small area, extraordinary conditions of climate and soil meet centuries of winemaking tradition and dedication. Here thrives the noble Cabernet Sauvignon grape.

The wines of the four major communes of Médoc have distinct characteristics and subtle nuances, described in the following table, as do the red wines of Graves, a district to the south, known also for its high-quality wines.

The Four Major Communes of Médoc and Graves

Commune	Example	Distinct Characteristics
Margaux	Château Lascombes	Moderately tannic; medium-bodied; fragrant, perfumed aromas; complex, generous, elegant, and long-lived.
Saint-Julien	Château Léoville- Poyferré	Softer tannins; rich, flavorful; medium- /full-bodied; sometimes fruity; earlier maturing; elegance and finesse.
Pauillac	Château Lafite-Rothschild	Firm tannins; rich, powerful, yet with delicate nuances of flavor; firm backbone; full-bodied; extraordinary finesse and elegance (First Growths) black currants and cedar aromas; extremely long-lived.
Saint-Estèphe	Château d'Estournel	Tannic hard, firm; full-bodied earthy and vinous; rarely elegant but pleasingly masculine; slow to mature.
Graves	Château Haut-Brion	Moderately tannic; vinous with (ironically) a gravelly mouthfeel; earthy; early to mature.

The 1855 Overture

I'll bet you're still wondering about that word "Cru" on the label! I think I can help out, but you have to indulge me as I give a brief history lesson. We need to go back to 1855, the year of Napoléon III's Exposition Universelle de Paris. France was about to put itself on display for the whole world. And Bordeaux wines would be featured. (Mais naturellement!)

So the organizers of this exposition asked the Gironde Chamber of Commerce to create a classification of the region's wines to accompany their display. The Chamber assigned the job to the wine brokers of Bordeaux, who selected 61 superior red wines, dividing them into five categories or crus (the cru, or growth, refers to the wine estate) based on price.

Price? Well, in those days, price really was a sound indicator of quality. While the classification was supposed to be limited to the districts of the Médoc, one wine of the Graves, Château Haut-Brion, also was listed because of its excellence and fame.

Heard It Through the Grapevine

If you are confused about our four tiers and the crus of the top one, you are not alone. A cru is a separate classification within an appellation or district in our quality-ranking system. Some appellations have classifications; others, not so worthy, do not.

Actually, some less-deserving appellations do have their own classifications now. It's very political and confusing. But all you need to know is that crus are classifications within a district in Bordeaux. Thus a classified wine has both an appellation and a designation that reflects the fact that within a particular district, some wines are better than others.

Here's what's amazing: In the nearly 150 years since that 1855 Classification of the Médoc, they have made only one change! A decree of June 21, 1973, upgraded Chateau Mouton-Rothschild from deuxieme (second) cru to premier (first) cru. The following table shows the châteaux of the first and second crus.

The First Two Growths of Bordeaux

Château	Commune
First Growths	
Château Lafite-Rothschild	Pauillac
Château Latour	Pauillac
Château Margaux	Margaux
Château Haut-Brion	Graves (Pessac)
Château Mouton-Rothschild[*]	Pauillac
Second Growths	
Château Rausan-Ségla	Margaux
Château Rauzan-Gassies	Margaux
Château Léoville-Las Cases	Saint-Julien
Château Léoville-Poyferré	Saint-Julien
Château Léoville-Barton	Saint-Julien
Château Durfort-Vivens	Margaux
Château Lascombes	Margaux
Château Gruaud-Larose	Saint-Julien
Château Brane-Cantenac	Margaux
Château Pichon-Longueville Baron	Pauillac
Château Pichon-Lalande	Pauillac
Château Ducru-Beaucaillou	Saint-Julien
Château Cos d'Estournel	Saint-Estèphe
Château Montrose	Saint-Estèphe

Elevated from Second Growth in 1973

For a listing of the third, fourth, and fifth crus, see Appendix A, "Recommended Wines."

The 61 ranked wines also are known as *Grands Crus Classés*. While some vineyards have deteriorated or been incorporated into others, these rankings seem firmly set in stone, with only one growth, Château Mouton-Rothschild, ever changing its status. Today there are rumblings about this rigidity as several châteaux have upgraded through big-dollar investments both in wineries and vineyards. Now they are politicking for elevation to a higher status.

As you may expect, there is considerable controversy over the 1855 classification. Many lesser-classified growths in this classification scheme feel worthy of promotion. To fully understand the honor of being one of the 61 Grands Crus Classés, remember, even in 1855, there were thousands of wine producers in Bordeaux.

Also, you've noticed that with the exception of Château Haut-Brion, all of the wines listed are from the Médoc region. Château Haut-Brion was included because in 1855 it was considered one of the finest wines of Bordeaux (as well as one of the most expensive). No one dared ignore it.

Only two regions were classified in 1855: the Médoc and Sauternes (a sweet wine area in southern Graves). Over the years, other Bordeaux regions, such as Saint-Emilion and Pomerol, have been classified. But with the exception of Château Pétrus and a few others, none measures up to the first growths of the 1855 Médoc classification.

Sit and Sip in Saint-Emilion and Pomerol

The districts of Saint-Emilion and Pomerol lie to the east of the city of Bordeaux. Picturesque Saint-Emilion has many cafés that look out over the vineyards. There, you can sip your wine and watch it grow at the same time.

Thousands of small châteaux cover the district, although only a few enjoy the best soils and microclimates for producing great wines. Saint-Emilion produces many fine wines from a variety of conditions that differ from those of the Médoc and Graves. The district does have its classified first growths now. However, with few exceptions, these first growths do not measure up to the first growths of the 1855 Médoc classification. I count at least 40 excellent estates here.

In the Pomerol district, several estates rival those of the 1855 Médoc classification, and many others produce very fine wines. The soil here contains large amounts of clay in which Merlot grapes grow merrily. This gives the wines of Pomerol a distinct character from their Cabernet Sauvignon-producing neighbors.

Tasting Tip

Smaller and lesser known, Pomerol has gained recognition from wine connoisseurs over the past two decades. Rightly so, as its best wine, Chateau Pétrus, commands the highest price in Bordeaux!

The Sommelier Says

Despite the fact that it offers some of the world's greatest white wines, Graves still ships a quantity of mediocre, overly sulfured product. You have to be careful when buying white wines from this district, choosing only from those producers who make the better wines.

Tasting Tip

The principal white-wine grape varieties of Graves are Sauvignon Blanc and Semillon. As a blend, they are well matched. The Sauvignon Blanc grape offers immediate flavor and charm, while the Semillon adds body and depth to the wine.

The Gravelly Soil of Graves

The district of Graves, located along the southern limits of the city of Bordeaux, gets its name from its gravelly soil. (I'm not making this up!) I find it interesting that the wines of this district also seem to present a gravelly sense on my palate.

Graves produces both red and white wines, but it's most renowned for its fine whites. Dry and sweet wines are divided pretty much into north and south parts, respectively. Northern Graves—specifically, the district of Pessac-Léognan—is home to some of the world's most prestigious dry white wines. The best dry white Graves are refreshing, crisp, and delightful when young. With age they become mellow, developing complexity and richness.

Sauternes—Sweet and Noble Rot

Within the larger Graves district south of Bordeaux are the Sauternes and Barsac districts. (Yes, there are districts within districts!) These produce sweet wines, mostly thanks to a particular family of *fungi*.

Fungi of the genus *Botrytis* are responsible for much disease in vegetables and fruits. But on the skins of grapes, under loving attention and control, they create wonders—what vintners call "the noble rot." And nowhere is this rot nobler (nor more prolific) than in the Sauternes and Barsac districts of Graves!

The best Sauternes wines owe their unique and luscious flavor to *Botrytis*—and to the labor of vineyard workers who hand-pick the grapes. Grape by grape! Each berry is selected and harvested by hand, only the fully mature berries being chosen. At the best châteaux, a vineyard may be harvested 10 times or more.

This is one reason why the best Sauternes—like its most famous, Château d'Yquem—are so expensive. And (you've heard it from me before) this is where it pays to know your vineyards. Some properties are more meticulous and obsessive with these procedures than others. The most outstanding (and expensive) Sauternes are produced by only a few in the district.

Cru Bourgeois: Pleasant and Cheap

If you're looking for a good buy in a Bordeaux wine, here's a tip: Stay away from the classified crus. Demand for these wines has driven prices high, sometimes out-of-sight high. Believe me, you don't need a wine from the 1855 classification to enjoy Bordeaux. In fact, you can drink the non-classified wines long before you can their classified cousins. And often they're nearly as good.

There is a newer classification just below that of 1855. This is the *Cru Bourgeois*, with roughly 400 red wines to choose from. Generally, these sell for less than $20 (sometimes less than $10!), and several can be comparable to or even better than the lower-end classified growths of the 1855 classification!

To Cellar or to Sip?

Think about it: You might have to wait a lifetime to drink a Premier Cru, unless you pay a fortune for an aged bottle. But many fine Bordeaux mature much sooner. Many lesser 1855 Cru Classé wines will be ready in five or 10 years, though others can take longer. Most petit châteaux, commune wines, and négociant blends are made for early consumption.

Generally, you can tell from the price of your wine and its classification (or lack of classification) whether it is made for early consumption or yearns for solitude in your wine cellar. A wine that needs aging will taste unpleasantly tannic if you drink it too soon. Drinking such a wine before its time is a form of wine infanticide. Any wine that needs long cellaring will not display its extraordinary qualities too young. In fact, it can be rather unpleasant.

Vino Vocab

Fungi refers to the family of organisms that includes mushrooms and mold.

Tasting Tip

There are several red and white Bordeaux called "petits châteaux" that have no formal classification. Selling for $10 or less, these are light-bodied wines that you can enjoy immediately. They're perfectly fine for any informal dinner at home.

The Least You Need to Know

➤ Bordeaux wines come in varying qualities, from average to exceptional.

➤ You can judge the quality of a Bordeaux wine from its appellation.

➤ The best Bordeaux wines are classified into "growths" or "crus."

➤ Sauternes from the Bordeaux region are revered for their unique flavors.

➤ The Bordeaux region offers many great bargains.

The Noble Wines of Bordeaux

In This Chapter

➤ Shopping for a good Bordeaux

➤ Classifications of Bordeaux

➤ Discovering the châteaux

➤ Where to find values

In the last chapter we discussed the Bordeaux region in general. In this chapter we're going to take a very close look at the Bordeaux region's most distinguished districts and châteaux—those capable of producing wines that belong to that rarefied class that I call "noble."

In this chapter I've provided many lists and tables. You'll find these useful when you go shopping for a great, noble Bordeaux.

The Classiest Classifications

In Chapter 10, we looked at the 1855 Classification of the wines of the Haut-Médoc, which considered the wines of the Médoc (and one of Graves, Château Haut-Brion). At that time, these rankings represented a local consensus (as reflected in price). In all those years, only one change has been made.

The 1855 Classification was, by far, the most prestigious. But it was not the only such ranking of Bordeaux wines. There have been others, including another from the year 1855. While the Médoc classification looked only at red wines, the 1855 classification of the châteaux of Sauternes-Barsac ranked this region's unique sweet white wines.

Tasting Tip

There's a good reason a quality ranking from 1855 might remain useful, even today. The conditions of soil and microclimate that distinguished these chateaux back then still exist. Very few wines from the 1855 classification have fallen in quality. But many others from outside that classification have improved and now compare favorably with their honored cousins.

The 1855 Classification of Sauternes-Barsac set Château d'Yquem above all the rest. The other 23 châteaux then were divided among Premiers Crus (First Growths) and Deuxièmes Crus (Second Growths).

First Growths of Sauternes-Barsac are

➤ Château Guiraud

➤ Château La Tour Blanche

➤ Château Lafaurie-Peyraguey

➤ Château de Rayne-Vigneau

➤ Château Sigalas-Rabaud

➤ Château Rabaud-Promis

➤ Château Haut-Peyraguey

➤ Château Coutet

➤ Château Climens

➤ Château Suduiraut

➤ Château Rieussec

Second Growths of Sauternes-Barsac are

➤ Château d'Arche

➤ Château Filhot

➤ Château Lamothe

➤ Château de Myrat

➤ Château Doisy-Védrines

➤ Château Doisy-Daëne

➤ Château Suau

➤ Château Broustet

➤ Château Caillou

➤ Château Nairac

➤ Château de Malle

➤ Château Romer

Wine label of Château d'Yquem.

As with the 1855 Médoc classification, these remain fairly reliable, though not perfect.

A hundred years passed before any other Bordeaux regions were classified. In 1955, the production of Saint-Emilion was put into two classifications: Premiers Grands Crus Classés (First Great Growths) and Grands Crus Classés (Great Growths). These were corrected in 1959 and revised in 1969 and 1996. We will look at the very best of these later this chapter.

Graves lies due south of the city of Bordeaux. Under the 1959 classification of this region, 13 châteaux that produce red wines achieved Cru Classé (Classified Growth) status. These were joined by eight châteaux that produce white wines.

The Sommelier Says

The market value of a high classification is enormous. So you can imagine the pressures on those who are responsible for wine rankings! Though a few classified wines may not be worthy of their official status, it's more likely there are several unclassified wines that are. This is where you look for bargains, if you are more interested in wine than prestige.

Graves Classified Growths of 1959, Red Wine

Estate	Commune
Château Haut-Brion	Pessac
Château Bouscaut	Cadaujac
Château Carbonnieux	Léognan
Domaine de Chevalier	Léognan
Château de Fieuzal	Léognan
Château Haut-Bailly	Léognan
Château La Mission-Haut-Brion	Pessac
Château La Tour-Haut-Brion	Talence
Château La Tour-Martillac	Martillac
Château Malartic-Lagraviére	Léognan
Château Olivier	Léognan
Château Pape-Clément	Pessac
Château Smith-Haut-Lafitte	Martillac

Graves Classified Growths of 1959, White Wine

Estate	Commune
Château Bouscaut	Cadaujac
Château Carbonnieux	Léognan
Domaine de Chevalier	Léognan
Château Couhins	Villaneve-d'Ornon
Château Laville-Haut-Brion	Talence
Château Malartic-Lagraviére	Léognan
Château Olivier	Léognan
Château La Tour-Martillac	Martillac

Haut-Médoc on High

The northern third of the Médoc Peninsula is called, simply, Médoc (sometimes Bas-Médoc). The southern two thirds is called Haut-Médoc (Upper Médoc), ending in the south at the city of Bordeaux. This is geography, though, not wine! The AOC appellations don't follow that scheme exactly.

Heard It Through the Grapevine

In the Médoc, there are two regional appellations, Médoc and Haut-Médoc. And there are six communal appellations: Saint-Estèphe, Pauillac, Saint-Julien, Moulis, Listrac, and Margaux. These communal appellations, geographically, are part of the Haut-Médoc. However, the appellation Haut-Médoc applies only to those parts of that region that are not part of those six communal appellations.

Four communal appellations of the Haut-Médoc (geographic, not appellation)—Pauillac, Margaux, Saint-Julien, and Saint-Estèphe—account for all the *First* and *Second Growths* of the 1855 Classification (except for that one from Graves). However, five châteaux from three communes within the regional appellation Haut-Médoc appear in the 1855 Classification among the *Third, Fourth,* and *Fifth Growths*:

➤ Château La Lagune, in Ludon (Third Growth)

➤ Château La Tour Carnet, in Saint-Laurent (Fourth Growth)

➤ Château Belgrave, in Saint-Laurent (Fifth Growth)

➤ Château de Camensac, in Saint-Laurent (Fifth Growth)

➤ Château Cantemerle, in Macau (Fifth Growth)

The AOC Haut-Médoc region is enormous, with more than 10,000 acres of grapes in 15 communes. The soils here are sandy-gravelly, but with considerable local variation. Principal grapes are Cabernet Sauvignon, Merlot, and Cabernet Franc, with Merlot increasing its share in the mix.

Vino Vocab

Let's review French ordinal numbers. The 1855 classification ranked wines into five growths:

Premiers Crus, **First Growths**

Deuxièmes Crus, **Second Growths**

Troisièmes Crus, **Third Growths**

Quatrièmes Crus, **Fourth Growths**

Cinquièmes Crus, **Fifth Growths**

125

Saint-Emilion Superiority

This large district lies along the right bank of the Dordogne River, almost due east of Bordeaux. The Saint-Emilion appellation is centered on the picturesque medieval town of the same name. The Saint-Emilion region is divided into two parts: Côtes and Graves ("slopes" and "gravel").

Heard It Through the Grapevine

The Côtes region of Saint-Emilion comprises the slopes south of the town and the plateau beyond. A thin layer of clay and limestone soils sits on a bed of limestone. This is perfect for the Merlot and Cabernet Franc grapes.

The Graves region lies west of the town. Here the soils are deeper and gravelly, with some clay and sand, which allows some planting in Cabernet Sauvignon.

Tasting Tip

One thing that distinguishes the wines of Pomerol from those of the other great Bordeaux appellations is that they are made mostly from the Merlot grape, sometimes entirely. Most Bordeaux wines are based on the Cabernet Sauvignon grape, with Merlot and other permitted grapes blended. But Pomerol's soils favor Merlot, and they can favor you, too, with their remarkable difference.

The wines from the Côtes are nicely colored, perfumed, and medium-bodied. Yet they can display a strong tannic complexity. They age well, but you can drink them earlier than those from the Médoc or Graves appellations.

Wines grown in the Graves region of Saint-Emilion resemble those of the nearby Pomerol appellation, featuring a distinct fruitiness. You can drink these quite young, but aging doesn't harm them.

Praise for Pomerol

The Pomerol appellation lies just north of Saint-Emilion. It's the smallest of the Bordeaux appellations, but wine lovers treasure the wines from this district's many small vintners. Winemaking standards here are very high, and it's remarkable that Pomerol's wines never have undergone classification.

Styles vary greatly among the châteaux of Pomerol—from the powerful flavor presence favored by Château Pétrus to the silk-textured subtlety sought by Château l'Evangile.

Haut-Médoc Premiers Crus

Let's look now at Bordeaux's noblest (and most desired) wines: the Premiers Crus of the 1855 Classification.

Château Lafite-Rothschild

Wine label of Château Lafite Rothschild.

This famous estate is in Pauillac. (Actually, a tiny bit lies in Saint-Estèphe, but for AOC purposes, it's all in Pauillac.)

If you are traveling in France, you haven't seen Bordeaux until you've visited Château Lafite-Rothschild! This is the home of Bordeaux's noblest wine.

The estate is large, with about 225 acres in production. (If you're talking soybeans, that's tiny. But for fine vinifera, it's huge!) Cabernet Sauvignon accounts for two thirds of the planting, with Merlot and Cabernet Franc at one-sixth each. The vines are quite old, averaging nearly 40 years.

The complexity and stature of this wine are impossible to describe. It is considered the best of the Premiers Crus. All I will say is take one sip, and you'll know forever the meaning of the word "finesse." You can drink this 10 years after vintage, or set it aside for 35.

Château Margaux

Wine label of Château Margaux.

Château Margaux is guess where? Margaux! What a pretty name! (And a pretty wine to go with it.) Even if you weren't a wine lover, you might want to visit this distinguished Château for its splendid architecture and its classical beauty. The village is self-sustaining, with Old World artisans capable of any task—even barrel cooperage.

The estate's 170 producing acres are planted three quarters in Cabernet Sauvignon and a quarter in Merlot. Like its name, Margaux's wine is delicate and refined when fully mature (minimum 10 years old), like a rare china teacup. The floral scents add to the impression. Despite that delicacy, this wine ages very well. Yes, it's great young (although not delicate), but it only gets better!

Château Latour

Château Latour is another first growth estate in Pauillac, not as famous as Lafite-Rothschild but most worthy of its Premier Cru status.

Latour is not the same château as it was in 1855! Since 1963, it's been (mostly) in the hands of British investors, who have put large sums of money into its modernization. For one thing, the large and ancient oaken fermenting casks were replaced by stainless steel. But this wine is no stranger to wood. After fermentation, it's transferred gently into new, small, oak casks where it rests peacefully for two years before being bottled.

Heard It Through the Grapevine

When it comes to fermenting a fine wine, why replace oak with stainless steel? There are two good reasons. First, clean, nonabsorbent stainless neither adds nor takes anything away from the wine. This ensures consistent quality year after year. Second, the thin, strong walls of stainless steel casks permit precise temperature control during fermentation, another important quality consideration.

About 150 acres are in vine, and about 120 of these acres are covered with older vines. Three fourths is planted in Cabernet Sauvignon, 15 percent in Cabernet Franc, 8 percent in Merlot, and 2 percent in Petit Verdot.

This wine "rests on its skins" for a week or more after fermentation, allowing the fullest development of color and tannins. You definitely do not want to drink this one young! But do consider buying some from a vintage year for your grandchildren. Age brings out this wine's breeding and authority.

Château Haut-Brion

Château Haut-Brion is in Graves. What's wrong with this picture? Graves is not part of the Médoc region. The appellation lies just southwest of Bordeaux, near the left bank of the Garonne. It's the only non-Médoc wine in the 1855 classification. (Its fame was so great, they didn't dare exclude it.)

What makes Haut-Brion great? Its soil—unique to the region—is gravel covered with sand. And perfect for Médoc-style wines.

The estate's 100 producing acres are planted 55 percent in Cabernet Sauvignon, 25 percent in Cabernet Franc, and 20 percent in Merlot. (Actually, a little plot is dedicated to Sauvignon Blanc and Sémillon for this estate's dry white Haut-Brion Blanc.)

In flavor, this wine shows a strength and depth, with no harshness. And, of course, it improves greatly with age (it takes eight to 10 years to mature before drinking).

Château Mouton-Rothschild

Château Mouton-Rothschild, the third First Growth from Pauillac, may be remembered best as the only estate to have been upgraded in the 1855 Classification. That was in 1973, and with the consent of the other four Premier Crus.

This change only formalized what had been a de facto classification since the 1920s. Château Mouton-Rothschild readily commanded the same market prices as the then four First Growths.

The estate has about 150 acres in production. Cabernet Sauvignon accounts for 90 percent, with 7 percent Cabernet Franc and 3 percent Merlot.

Distinguished Districts

Four communes produce wines of such distinctions that they are appellations separate from the remainder of the Haut-Médoc regional appellation. These distinguished districts—Margaux, Saint-Julien, Pauillac, and Saint-Estèphe—lie south to north along the western shore of the Gironde estuary, north of Bordeaux.

Generally, the slopes face the morning sun, but innumerable east-flowing streams provide small slopes with southern exposure. The soils here are deep and very permeable, being sand, gravel, and limestone. For most agriculture, these are very poor soils. But for the wine grapes grown in the Médoc, they're perfect.

The soils hold the day's heat very well, moderating nighttime temperatures. Daytime doesn't become excessively hot, either, because of the estuary and the nearby Atlantic.

Cool days; temperate nights; clear, sunny skies; long summer days; and thick, porous soils conspire to create wine growing conditions found nowhere else on earth.

The Graves district sits apart, adjoining Bordeaux to the southwest. Its gravelly soils and similar microclimate provide an environment like that of the four districts along the Gironde.

Margaux

Margaux has the honor of supplying 21 growths to the 1855 classification. As we move up the wide Gironde (toward the south), the wines become supple, smooth, and elegant. Ruby in color, they are full without being overpowering.

The soils here have a high portion of white gravel, with some chalk. Subsoils vary from sandy to gravelly, accounting for some of the variety we observe within the châteaux.

Saint-Julien

Saint-Julien is the smallest producer among the four Haut-Médoc communes. In addition to the 11 wines this region contributes to the 1855 Classification, you will find several châteaux represented in the Cru Bourgeois classification.

These wines are similar to those of Pauillac but lack their power. You can drink these young, yet they do age well.

The terrain is very gravelly, with subsoils of sandstone and clay. Most of the châteaux lie close to the Gironde estuary. With its excellent drainage, Saint-Julien can produce excellent wines even in wetter years.

Pauillac

Pauillac means prestige! Three of Médoc's four First Growths come from here (along with 15 other classified wines)! But prestige comes at a price: The three Premiers Crus—Latour, Lafite-Rothschild, and Mouton-Rothschild—can put a strain on your wallet. But don't despair. This commune seems incapable of producing a poor wine.

To the three Premiers Crus I would add Chateau Pichon-Longueville, for unique flavors and excellent aging potential.

Saint-Estèphe

Of the communal appellations of the Haut-Médoc (geographically), Saint-Estèphe is the largest producer. This district lies closest to the mouth of the Gironde. Its soils have less gravel and more clay than those further south. These heavier soils drain slowly, leading to very robust wines. Some might say too robust. And indeed, there has been a trend since the 1960s to grow and blend more Merlot, which is fruitier and less tannic than the Cabernet Sauvignon.

Tasting Tip

It's hard to generalize about the noble wines of Pauillac. Subtle differences in soil, drainage, and sunlight bring about wonderful differences you will have no trouble distinguishing.

Although only five Saint-Estèphe wines made the 1855 Classification, you will find several worthy rivals among the Crus Grands Bourgeois Exceptionnels.

Saint-Estèphe lacks the prestige of Margaux, Saint-Julien, and Pauillac. That's good for you, because with careful shopping, you can get some great values from here. While it's true that the commune earned only five places in the 1855 Classification, several wines from the lesser Cru Bourgeois classification have achieved genuine greatness in recent years.

The commune's vineyards, with over 2,800 acres planted, have been slow to mature, developing lots of tannins and an overall toughness. This has been less of a problem since growers switched much of their production from Cabernet Sauvignon to the juicier Merlot.

Graves

The wines of Graves were the first of Bordeaux to be exported, going back to the twelfth century! And Thomas Jefferson was no stranger to these wines.

Heard It Through the Grapevine

The Graves region takes its name from its gravelly soil, overlaid with a fine sand. In the southern part, there's a bit more clay and limestone. The drainage is excellent, so drought years can present quality problems. However, in wet years, these wines can be sublime!

The best white wines of this region are among the best in France. But it's the red wines that have made Graves famous. The Premier Cru Haut-Brion has been famous for centuries.

Deuxièmes Crus

Remember that old Avis slogan, "When you're Number Two, you try harder."? The Deuxièmes Crus (second growths) from the 1855 Classification of the Médoc are no slouches when it comes to careful winemaking. Here are some of the most popular:

➤ **Château Rauzan-Ségla** Formerly known as Rausan-Ségla, this 121-acre estate is located in Margaux. It's planted about two-thirds Cabernet Sauvignon, a third Merlot, with small amounts of Petit Verdot and Cabernet Franc. Set this aside seven to 30 years.

➤ **Château Léoville-Las Cases** This estate is in Saint-Julien. Its 240 acres are planted 65 percent Cabernet Sauvignon, 19 percent Merlot, 13 percent Cabernet Franc, and 3 percent Petit Verdot. Age it eight to 30 years to do it justice.

➤ **Château Léoville-Poyferré**   Also in Saint-Julien, this estate is planted over about 200 acres. The grapes are 52 percent Cabernet Sauvignon, 28 percent Merlot, 12 percent Cabernet Franc, and 8 percent Petit Verdot. Keep this eight to 20 years after vintage.

➤ **Château Lascombes**   The 125 acres of this Margaux estate are planted 50 percent Cabernet Sauvignon, 40 percent Merlot, and 5 percent, each, in Cabernet Franc and Petit Verdot. Good for drinking six to 20 years after vintage.

➤ **Château Gruaud-Larose**   About 200 acres of this large Saint-Julien estate are in vine, with an average vine age of 45 years! The grapes are 57 percent Cabernet Sauvignon, 30 percent Merlot, 7 percent Cabernet Franc, 4 percent Petit Verdot, and 2 percent Malbec. (Yep. It adds up to 100.) You should age this 10 to 35 years.

➤ **Château Brane-Cantenac**   Here, in Cantenac-Margaux, 210 acres are planted in 70 percent Cabernet Sauvignon, 15 percent Merlot, 13 percent Cabernet Franc, and 2 percent Petit Verdot. You can drink this relatively young, about five years after vintage.

➤ **Château Pichon-Longueville-Baron**   (This also is known as Pichon-Baron.) This Pauillac estate is planted 70 percent Cabernet Sauvignon, 25 percent Merlot, and 5 percent Cabernet Franc. Drink it in eight years, or let it age for 25.

➤ **Château Ducru-Beaucaillou**   These 125 acres in Saint-Julien are planted 65 percent Cabernet Sauvignon, 25 percent Merlot, 5 percent Cabernet Franc, and 5 percent Petit Verdot. Age this 10 to 30 years.

➤ **Château Cos d'Estournel**   These 158 acres in Saint-Estèphe are planted 60 percent Cabernet Sauvignon and 40 percent Merlot. You can age this eight to 30 years.

Most of the Deuxièmes Crus produce wines close to the quality of the Premiere Crus but sell for considerably less money. Although they are still expensive, they provide good relative value next to the Premiere Crus, which are almost always overpriced due to demand.

Autres Crus

What about the Autres Crus (other growths): third, fourth, and fifth? Some of these are quite well known and very highly regarded. They represent a fine way to add wines from the Haut-Médoc to your collection at affordable prices. Here are some I would recommend.

Wine label of Château Langoa Barton.

CRU CLASSÉ EN 1855

1993

CHATEAU
LANGOA BARTON

SAINT-JULIEN
APPELLATION SAINT-JULIEN CONTRÔLÉE

S.A. DES CHATEAUX LANGOA ET LEOVILLE-BARTON
A SAINT-JULIEN-BEYCHEVELLE — GIRONDE

MIS EN BOUTEILLE AU CHATEAU

12,5 % vol.   PRODUCE OF FRANCE   750 ml

L. 001293

There are 14 Troisièmes Crus (third growths), from which I recommend the following (communes in parentheses):

➤ Château Giscours (Labarde-Margaux)

➤ Château Langoa-Barton (Saint-Julien)

➤ Château Palmer (Cantenac-Margaux)

➤ Château Calon-Ségur (Saint-Estèphe)

Of the 10 Quatrièmes Crus (fourth growths), you can't go wrong with these:

➤ Château Talbot (Saint-Julien)

➤ Château Duhart-Milon-Rothschild (Pauillac)

➤ Château Beychevelle (Saint-Julien)

➤ Château Prieuré-Lichine (Cantenac-Margaux)

And finally, don't neglect these from among the 18 Cinquièmes Crus (fifth growths):

➤ Château Pontet-Canet (Pauillac)

➤ Château Grand-Puy-Lacoste (Pauillac)

➤ Château Haut-Batailley (Pauillac)

➤ Château Lynch-Bages (Pauillac)

Saint-Emilion

Although the classified wines of Saint-Emilion do not meet the lofty standard set by those of the Haut-Médoc (with a few notable exceptions), they are very highly regarded. The district is planted mainly in Merlot, and this is reflected in the grape blends of its wines. These are round and fruity and a little more alcoholic than those from the Médoc.

Premiers Grands Crus Classés

The 1996 classification of Saint-Emilion lists 13 Premiers Grands Crus Classés (First Great Growths). Of these, I feel the noblest are

➤ **Château Ausone**   This estate's 17 acres are planted in vines 40 to 50 years old! The grapes are Cabernet Sauvignon and Merlot, half and half. You can put these away as long as 50 years, but don't drink them younger than 15.

➤ **Château Cheval Blanc**   The vines average 40 years in age on this 90-acre estate. It's planted two-thirds Cabernet Franc and one third Merlot. You can drink this superb wine as young as five years after vintage. (Or cellar it for 20 years.)

➤ **Château Canon**   Here we have 45 acres planted with 55 percent Merlot and 45 percent Cabernet Sauvignon. Age this seven to 25 years.

➤ **Château Figeac**   Large by Saint-Emilion standards, this estate plants its 100 acres about equally in Cabernet Sauvignon, Cabernet Franc, and Merlot. You can drink this as young as three years, but after 15 it may have passed its peak.

➤ **Château Trottevielle**   The vines average 40 years old on this estate's 25 acres. The grapes are half Merlot, with 45 percent Cabernet Franc and 5 percent Cabernet Sauvignon. Age this five to 20 years.

While a Premiere Grand Cru of Saint-Emilion may not rival a Premiere Cru from the Medoc, they are excellent wines and provide good relative value.

Grands Crus Classés

There are 57 Grands Crus Classés (Great Growths) in Saint-Emilion. Often a lesser classification means a greater value for you. The following wines will satisfy your desire to sample from among the best Bordeaux without too much damage to your bank account:

➤ Château Bellevue

➤ Château Canon-La-Gaff

➤ Château Dassault

➤ Château Cadet-Piola

➤ Château Clos de Jabob

➤ Château Soutard

Pomerol

The wines of Pomerol are 80 to 100 percent Merlot. Their fruitiness is plummy, and they are as smooth as velvet. Their rich, ruby colors provide further joys. You can drink these much younger than those made predominantly from the Cabernet Sauvignon grape.

Best of the Best

Here are some wines I recommend without hesitation:

➤ **Château Pétrus**   This is the best of the best of the best! Some wine experts rate this wine alongside the great Château Lafite-Rothschild, at the top of the first-growth list in the Haut-Médoc 1855 Classification (and that's reflected in its sky-high price). This small (28 acres) estate is the only one that features a clay topsoil. That and its very old vines account for this wine's noble attributes. It's planted 95 percent Merlot and 5 percent Cabernet Franc. Set this one aside 10 to 30 years.

➤ **Château La Conseillante**   This 30-acre estate is planted 70 percent Merlot, 25 percent Cabernet Sauvignon, and 5 percent Malbec/Pressac.

➤ **Château La Fleur de Gay**   The small (10 acres) estate is planted 100 percent Merlot, with a 40-year average age of the vines, the same as at Château Pétrus.

➤ **Château Lafleur**   This cozy estate (11 acres) is planted equally in Merlot and Cabernet Franc.

➤ **Château Le Pin**   Here, the grapes (92 percent Merlot, 8 percent Cabernet Franc) are grown on a minuscule 5-acre plot. Drink four to 12 years after vintage.

➤ **Château Trotanoy**   The 22 acres of this estate are planted 80 percent Merlot, 10 percent Cabernet Franc, and 10 percent mixed.

Second Best

The wines from these Pomerol châteaux will not disappoint you:

➤ Château Clinet   ➤ Château l'Eglise-Clinet

➤ Château l'Evangile   ➤ Château Certan de May

➤ Château Latour á Pomerol   ➤ Château Petit Village

➤ Château Vieux-Châteaux-Certan

Petrus is frequently the highest-priced wine of Bordeaux, although many of the other wines of Pomerol are excellent values.

The Least You Need to Know

➤ The great 1855 Classification of the Médoc was not the only one in Bordeaux.

➤ Many wines from other classifications rival those of the famed 1855 Classification.

➤ Pomerol, which never has been classified, offers some of Bordeaux's finest wines.

➤ Careful selection among the lesser classifications can provide excellent value.

Burgundy—La Reine du Vin

Burgundy wines can be very frustrating. To be sure, your wine-seller stocks many good, if not exceptional, Burgundies. But price isn't a reliable guide. Some of the most expensive Burgundies can be downright awful when produced by low-quality négociants or careless estates.

So why bother? Because Burgundy's very best wines truly are *vins extraordinaires*. They stand among the most fascinating and interesting of all wines. Unfortunately for the consumer, they also bear price tags displaying their stratospheric status, and many importers and wine merchants refuse to handle such expensive wares in small lots.

Unless you happen to be touring Burgundy or you've hit that lottery number, the ultimate Burgundies may be beyond your grasp. But don't be dismayed. It just happens you can enjoy some very pleasant red and white Burgundy wines without much outlay.

In this chapter, we'll visit Burgundy's five wine districts, each home to a number of small estates. You'll find out how the *terroir* effects the grapes grown on each estate, producing distinctively different wines. And you'll learn the characteristics of fine red and white Burgundies. Also, you'll learn about a very refreshing Burgundy bargain— Beaujolais, the inexpensive, refreshing, light-bodied red wine that you serve chilled, like a white.

Part of the problem with selecting fine Burgundies lies in the fact that the Burgundy region produces much less than Bordeaux, only about a quarter. And of that smaller yield, the selection of superior wines is disturbingly meager. (We hardly can count the Beaujolais district. Though, technically, part of Burgundy, it produces a very different type of wine.)

The Domain of the Domaine

The vineyards of Burgundy are much smaller than those of Bordeaux. An estate or *domaine* of 50 or 60 acres represents a very large holding, and such a vineyard owned by only one proprietor is an exception. Here's an example: Clos de Vougeot consists of 165 acres, but it's owned by more than 80 individuals! This can make it somewhat complicated to judge the quality of a wine by reading its label. More on that later.

The *citoyens* of the French Revolution had a hand in this vineyard fragmentation. Before the Revolution, the majority of vineyards were owned by the First and Second Estates (nobility and clergy). After the revolution, these vineyards were distributed among the peasants. With the institution of the *Code civil des Françaises (1804)*, which required that land be divided equally among all heirs, vineyard ownership was divided even further.

Vino Vocab

There's another difference between vineyard holdings in Burgundy and in Bordeaux. A Burgundian estate is called a **domaine**, while in Bordeaux, we have the majestic **château**.

Burgundy comprises five districts, all of which produce distinctive wines:

➤ Mâconnais

➤ Beaujolais

➤ Chablis

➤ the Côte Chalonnaise

➤ the Côte d'Or—literally "golden coast" or "river bank"—is again divided into two parts: the Côte de Nuits and the Côte de Beaune.)

Burgundy's climate is marked by hot summers and cold winters, but is not subject to hailstorms that can damage delicate grapes. Limestone and clay are the prevalent soil types.

The prime varietals of this region are Pinot Noir for red Burgundies, and Chardonnay for white. Burgundy is where that fussy vinifera, Pinot Noir, is on its best behavior, displaying its most regal and charming character. As you head south into the Beaujolais district, the soil becomes granitic. This is where we find the red Gamay grape.

The *terroir* of Burgundy (location, soils, climate, topography) is highly variable. Soils vary from one site to the next. Within one vineyard, two plots of the same varietal growing only a short distance from each other may yield two distinctively different wines. This is where knowledge of the Burgundy label becomes important. Owners, even within the same small vineyard, will not necessarily produce the same qualities or styles of wines.

The AOC structure for Burgundy takes *terroir* into consideration. There are AOC Burgundy appellations for individual vineyard sites that are of exceptional quality.

In Burgundy, the terms *Premier cru* (first growth) and *Grand cru* (great growth, the very highest quality) are official designations under AOC law. This is in contrast to Bordeaux, where the same terms designate status imparted outside of AOC legislation.

The following table provides examples of AOC names in Burgundy from the most general to the most specific, the individual vineyard. The two broadest categories—regional and district—account for about 63 percent of all Burgundy wines. These run from $7 to $15 per bottle. Commune or village wines, such as Gevrey-Chambertin, make up 25 percent of Burgundy's production, and they retail for $15 to $30 per bottle. There are 53 communes in Burgundy with their own appellation.

Getting more distinguished, we have the Premier Crus, such as Puligny-Montrachet Les Pucelles. These make up approximately 11 percent of total production; 561 vineyards carry the Premier Cru appellation. These wines sell for $25 to $80 per bottle.

At the rarest level, we have the 32 Grand Crus, such as Corton-Charlemagne or Le Montrachet. These account for a mere 1 percent of Burgundy's production. Grand Cru prices begin around $40, and they can soar to upward of $500 a bottle for, say, Romanée-Conti. (Or how about $3,000 for a bottle of the same in a mature great vintage?)

Vino Vocab

It's very easy to confuse the Bordeaux term **Grand Cru Classé** with the Burgundian **Grand cru**. The first, not part of the AOC system, applies to all 61 classified wines of Bordeaux. The second, AOC official, is awarded only to Burgundy's very finest wines. (It's almost as though the French wanted to confuse us.)

The classification of your Burgundy wine may not even appear! Grand Cru Burgundies with their own appellation may choose to display only the vineyard name, with the term *"appellation controlée"* below, without the esteemed *Grand Cru*. I suppose this is because they are very snooty about their reputations, figuring that those who appreciate their product will know exactly who they are.

The Structure of Burgundy AOC Names

Specificity of Site	Example
Region	Bourgogne Rouge
District	Côte de Nuits Villages; Mâcon-Villages
Village or Commune	Nuits-St.-Georges; Gevrey-Chambertin; Fixin
Premier Cru	Puligny-Montrachet Les Pucelles; Beaune Clos-des-Ursules; Nuits-St.-Georges; Les Perriéres
Grand Cru	Le Chambertin; La Romanée; Le Montrachet

The last two classifications refer to specific vineyards.

Heard It Through the Grapevine

You may have read in some wine books that the labels for Premier Cru wines bear the name of the commune plus the name of the vineyard in the same-size type, and that if the vineyard name appears in smaller lettering than the commune name, the wine is not a Premier Cru. Not true!

In practice, most Premier Cru labels actually do display the vineyard name in smaller type than the commune name. But not always. The vineyard name may appear in the same size or even larger type. Just remember: If there is a vineyard name on the label of a Burgundy wine, it's either a Premier or Grand Cru.

So how do you tell these quiet Grands Crus from lesser "village wines" with commune appellations (for example, "appellation Meursault controlée")? The best way is to know your cru domaines, or consult a wine encyclopedia or Burgundy book. But there's a simpler way: If it's cheap, it's not a Grand Cru.

Some vintners will blend the grapes from two or more Premier Cru vineyards in the same commune. These wines still are Premier Crus, but the label will not have the name of a specific Premier cru vineyard. Instead, the label will have a commune name with the words "Premier Cru" or "1er Cru." These wines generally come from *négociants* (winebrokers who buy wine and sell it under their own name). However, some growers with several tiny, lesser-known vineyards may blend their product and sell it simply as Premier Cru. Good marketing, I suppose.

Ne Plus Ultra White

White Burgundy combines a silky mouthfeel and fullness of flavor with lively acidity. The better appellations have a touch of oak. These develop complexity and finesse with age. Grand Crus may require up to 10 years in the bottle, but most white Burgundies are ready to drink after two or three years.

Is It Burgundy or Bordeaux?

A fine red Burgundy is as different from its Bordeaux counterpart as night and day. Since they are made from the Pinot Noir grape, Burgundies are lighter in color. They are medium-to full-bodied, and they are relatively low in tannins, often silky or velvety on the palate.

The Burgundy aroma is unique, with flavors that may defy description. Not uncommon are flavors resembling cherries and ripe berries, or moss and woodsy mushroom scents. With age, a superior Burgundy develops great complexity with subtle nuances of flavor and finesse that can be memorable. A red Burgundy requires seven to 10 years to mature, and the greatest can continue to improve for decades.

> **Tasting Tip**
>
> White Burgundies often delight us with an aftertaste that's a lingering kaleidoscope of flavors—both from the taste of the wine and some that are new. The world offers us some great Chardonnays, but there's nothing like a great white Burgundy (except a great red Burgundy).

Navigating the Export Maze

Let's look at the principal wine districts of Burgundy. Wines from these districts are the ones that you most likely will find in the U.S.

Mâcon-Villages

The Mâconnais district lies directly south of the Chalonnaise and north of Beaujolais. The overall climate is sunny and mild, and the winemaking center is the city of Mâcon. The hills surrounding this area are replete with the chalky limestone loved by Chardonnay grapes.

Mâcon-Villages wines are whites of excellent value at $5 to $10 a bottle. To be sure, they lack the complexity and distinction of the more expensive Pouilly-Fuissé wines. But these wines are lively and crisp, meant to be enjoyed young. Most are soft, round, and fruity. Made from 100 percent Chardonnay grapes, their unoaked freshness contrasts with the oaked majority of Chardonnay wines.

The label will read "Mâcon" or "Mâcon-Villages." Mâcon-Villages is a cut above mere Mâcon, and the best wines are those that come from a specific village. You can tell by the name of the village added to the appellation (for example, Mâcon-Viré, Mâcon-Lugny).

Pouilly-Fuissé

Pouilly-Fuissé and Saint-Véran are two inner appellations within the Mâcon district made from Chardonnay grapes grown on rolling hills with a soil that imbues them with a unique quality. Both wines are similar to Chablis, but softer and less steely.

Pouilly-Fuissé wines are mid-premium quality, usually selling for $15 to $25 a bottle. They are distinctly Chardonnay and have a crisp apple aroma, with a smooth texture and slight depth of flavor. Unlike the simple Mâcon wines, they often are oaked, rendering them richer and fuller in body. The best of these wines come from the villages of Solutré-Pouilly, Davayé, and Fuisse. They display more fruitiness and depth than Chablis, and the finish reveals a clean, earthy flavor. After three or four years' aging, Pouilly-Fuissés develop a subtle degree of finesse. Saint-Véran wines are an excellent value at $7 to $14 a bottle.

The Sommelier Says

Pouilly-Fuissé became the darling of wine importers during the 1960s. This meteoric fame was matched by meteoric prices. But that's no concern to us today. Priced way beyond its worth during its 15 minutes of fame, Pouilly-Fuissé has returned to being a pleasant, unpretentious, and reasonably priced white wine.

Beaujolais

Every year around Thanksgiving, you will see the signs in wine shop windows: "Beaujolais Nouveau is here!" This has nothing to do, actually, with our American holiday. It's just fortuitous timing.

Beaujolais wine, nouveau or not, is made from the red Gamay vinifera, not Pinot Noir. The Gamay thrives in Beaujolais, though it does poorly elsewhere in France. In fact, there once was a royal decree that banned this grape from vineyards outside Beaujolais.

Beaujolais and Beaujolais Supérieur (which has 1 percent more alcohol) are districtwide AOC appellations. These wines come from the southern area of Beaujolais. The clay soil in this district produces simple, light-bodied, fruity wines that sell for less than $8 a bottle and are best served no more than a year or two after their vintage. Unlike most other red wines, they go well with light foods and are great to drink in warm weather.

Several communes in the north of Beaujolais produce wines with potential mid-premium quality. These are the crus Beaujolais, which are distinctly better than Beaujolais-Villages. Only the name of the cru appears on the label, so you have to know the names of crus to know that they are Beaujolais wines. Here they are: Brouilly, Chénas, Chiroubles, Côte-de-Brouilly, Fleurie, Juliénas, Morgon, Moulin-a-Vent, Regnié, and Saint-Amour.

Wines from Brouilly and Fleurie tend to be elegant in style and very fragrant. Those from Moulin-a-Vent and Morgon offer rich flavor and style and are capable of longer aging. Over time, the best may resemble a village red Burgundy. The following table reviews the crus of Beaujolais.

Tasting Tip

Beaujolais nouveau is only six weeks old when it appears on Thanksgiving tables. Its vinous and fruity quality (very low in tannins) makes it a refreshing beverage by itself or with your favorite snacks. Don't even think of storing it! It's meant to be enjoyed within six months of its vintage.

The Crus of Beaujolais

Cru	Description
Brouilly	The lightest and fruitiest of the cru. Drink within two years.
Côte de Brouilly	A step better than Brouilly, fuller with more concentration; drink within three years.
Regnié	This is the newest addition to the Beaujolais crus. It is very similar to Brouilly in style and flavor.
Morgon	This cru resembles a red Burgundy more than a Beaujolais. It is full, rich, and earthy. It can age up to five to eight years.
Chiroubles	Very delicate, flavorful, and perfumed. They are often super-premium wines. Drink within four years.
Fleurie	Rich and flavorful with a medium body and velvety mouth-feel. Drink within four years.
Moulin-a-Vent	The richest and most concentrated of the cru. Powerful, with the capacity to age up to 10 years or more.

continues

145

The Cru of Beaujolais   (continued)

Cru	Description
Chénas	Rich and flavorful. Similar to a Moulin-a-Vent. Drink within four years.
Juliénas	Rich, full-bodied, and full-flavored. One of the best of the crus. Drink within four years.
Saint-Amour	Light to medium body, soft and delicate. Drink within two years.

Beaujolais generally are sold by large négociants—companies that buy grapes and wines from growers to blend, bottle, and sell under their own labels. Two premier négociants are Georges Duboeuf and Louis Jadot. These names on the label are reliable indicators of quality, as they do more than just buy finished wine. They work with the growers and set high standards for what they will buy. There also are some better estate-bottled Beaujolais available, primarily imported by Alain Junguenet and Louis/Dresner Selections.

Chablis

As luck would have it, the village of Chablis shares its name with the best-known generic jug wine labeled "Chablis" from the U.S. (This is where your new wine knowledge comes in very handy.) The vineyards of Chablis are the northernmost in Burgundy, situated on the hills of the Serein River valley. The locale's limestone soil imparts a special character to the Chardonnay grape and combines with the cooler climate to give Chablis Chardonnay a distinctive quality.

Heard It Through the Grapevine

Chablis wines undergo a somewhat different processing than do other Burgundy whites. While the white wines of the Côte d'Or generally are fermented and aged in oak barrels, most Chablis winemakers have switched to stainless steel.

The best Chablis wines come from a relatively small vineyard area. Chablis wines are light, austere, crisp wines with a characteristic bouquet and a steely taste resembling gunflint. The finest Chablis, ranked as Grand Crus, develop a degree of elegance and style, although many feel they are no match for their cousins of the Côte d'Or.

The Côte Chalonnaise

The Côte Chalonnaise is a Burgundy lover's dream. These lovely wines are both enjoyable and reasonably priced. They lack the refinement of the Côte d'Or wines, being somewhat coarser and earthier and with less perfume, but they are perfectly drinkable. (Moreover, you won't have to skimp on your meal to pay for it.)

The district lies to the south of the Côte d'Or and has five appellations that produce good wines for $8 to $20 per bottle.

➤ **Mercurey**   These wines are mostly reds, some whites. This is the home of the best Chalonnaise wines ($15 to $20).

➤ **Rully**   About evenly divided between reds and whites. The earthy white wines are far superior to the reds.

➤ **Givry**   Mostly red, some white. Here the reds are superior, although quite earthy.

➤ **Montagny**   All white wines, which are pleasant and enjoyable.

➤ **Bouzeron**   Wines from this district frequently are labeled "Bourgogne Rouge," "Bourgogne Blanc," or "Bourgogne Aligote" (the only other white grape permitted in Burgundy).

The Great Wines of the Côte d'Or

Without question, wines from the Côte d'Or are the most costly. Alas, this fact too often is a reflection of pricing zeal rather than of outstanding quality.

When they are on target, Côte d'Or wines are superb. When they miss, they can be very bad, even dreadful, suffering from indifferent winemaking or an overly ambitious quest for big production. These should be subtle, replete with nuances, supple in texture, and unique in style.

The Sommelier Says

The Côte d'Or quality depends on the skill and integrity of the grower. The temperamental Pinot Noir grape tolerates no error. One mistake and good-bye, Charlie! So sometimes the result can be very disappointing. One way to avoid surprises is to acquaint yourself with the best growers and producers. For a list of the most reliable producers and négociants, see Chapter 13, "The Noble Wines of Burgundy," and Appendix A, "Recommended Wines."

The Côte d'Or, where wine legends are made, is a narrow 40-mile strip consisting of two main subdivisions. The northern part is the Côte de Nuits, named for its commercial center, the city of Nuits-Saint-Georges. This is the origin of some of the finest red Burgundies. The southern part is the Côte de Beaune, named for its most important city, Beaune. The Côte de Beaune is famous for both red and white wines, but its white Burgundies are especially celebrated.

You'll find mid-premium Burgundies from the Côte d'Or have two general appellations. Those from the larger place names will either be called Côte de Nuits or Côte de Nuits-Villages, or Côte de Beaune or Côte de Beaune-Villages. Wines with village names usually are of higher quality, although all fall within the same general range.

The red wines have a recognizably fruity, vinous aroma of Pinot Noir with the regional character of red Burgundies. With experience, you'll come to recognize this distinctive flair and aroma. The wines are straightforward, simple, and reasonably well-balanced, with soft tannins and a lingering finish. Though sometimes coarse and lacking in finesse, they amply exhibit the character of the Burgundy region.

Côte de Nuits

The red wines from the Côte de Nuits tend to be fuller-bodied, firmer, and more sharply defined than their southern counterparts from the Côte de Beaune.

Each wine district of the Côte de Nuits produces a unique wine.

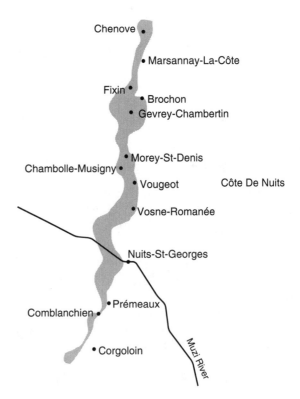

Let's look at the wines of the Côte de Nuits:

➤ The village of **Gevrey-Chambertin** in the Côte de Nuits is rightfully famous. Its Premier Cru wines are super-premium quality, offering great intensity of flavor with balance. The Grand Crus (of which there are eight) are labeled "Chambertin," sometimes hyphenated with a vineyard name.

Chambertin and Chambertin-Clos de Beze, its neighbor, are outstanding examples. Complex, rich, harmonious, and beautifully structured, they combine power with finesse as they age. The other Grand crus vineyards of Chambertin don't offer quite as much complexity, but they still rank highly in quality.

➤ **Chambolle-Musigny** lies further south. Its wines tend to be delicate, feminine, soft, and elegant, possessing great finesse. This area is typified by the Grand Cru vineyard, Le Musigny, a noble wine of uncommon breed. Unlike most of the vineyards of the Côte de Nuits, Le Musigny is noted for its superb white as well as red Burgundy.

➤ **Vougeot** is the home of the immense Grand Cru vineyard (by Burgundy standards) Clos de Vougeot. Although quality varies (remember, this one domaine has beaucoup owners), Clos de Vougeot wines are enormously aromatic, sturdy, and complex. They are medium-bodied, not as muscular as those of Chambertin. The finest offerings of the vineyard have unquestionably noble bearing.

➤ **Flagey-Echézeaux** is the name of a commune, but it's not used as an appellation. It contains two Grand Cru wines, Grand Echézeaux and Echézeaux, each of which has several owners. These are super-premium wines—aromatic, with a slightly more refined style than their Vougeot cousins.

➤ **Vosne-Romanée** is a village associated with many of Burgundy's most famous and revered wines. Its Grand Crus—La Romanée-Conti, La Romanée, La Tache, Richebourg, and Romanée-Saint-Vivant—are giants in the world of wine. These rich, velvety wines combine a depth and complexity of flavor from truffles, herbs, and berries in a style that epitomizes finesse and rare breed.

The Grand Crus—with the exception of Saint-Vivant, which is slightly lighter—usually achieve noble-quality status. Their aging potential is tremendous. Bottle-aging accentuates these wines' harmonious character and finish.

➤ **Nuits-Saint-Georges** contains no Grand Cru vineyards at all, though it has many Premier Crus. Stylistically, these wines are strongly aromatic, earthy, and often more tannic than the wines of other communes. They possess a sturdy, full-bodied, very vinous flavor that comes into full harmony with long aging. If they are not noble wines, they are not far off the mark.

➤ **Fixin** is the northernmost district in the Côte de Nuits. It produces sturdy, earthy red wines that do not develop finesse.

➤ **Morey-Saint-Denis** produces full-bodied, sturdy, rich red wines. Grand Crus include part of Bonnes Mares, Clos des Lambrays, Clos de la Roche, Clos Saint-Denis, and Clos de Tart. These wines provide good value for the high quality they offer.

Côte de Beaune

The Côte de Beaune produces fewer Grand Cru wines, but it gives us numerous Premier Crus and super-premium red wines. The red wines from the northern part of the Côte de Beaune, around Aloxe-Corton, are softer, fuller-bodied, and richer in flavor than the wines from the Côte de Nuits.

Like the Côte de Nuits, each wine district of the Côte de Beaune produces a unique wine.

The following is a list of the wines of the Côte de Beaune:

➤ **Aloxe-Corton** produces full-bodied, sturdy, mid-premium wines labeled under the simple "Corton" appellation. The better, Premier Cru Le Corton, Corton-Clos du Roi, and Corton-Bressandes are super-premium wines.

Heard It Through the Grapevine

Aloxe-Corton offers two superlative white Grand Cru vineyards—Corton-Charlemagne and Charlemagne. These Chardonnay wines are of noble quality. Stylistically, they offer a rich, perfumed aroma of complex fruit and butter with classical proportion. The texture is oily, like butterscotch, but with fine acid balance for structure and longevity.

➤ **Savigny-les-Beaune** wines offer good value. Five of the wines are Premier Cru appellations. The wines labeled under the Savigny-lès-Beaune appellation are mid-premium quality. The Premier Crus possess superior delicacy and finesse.

➤ Beaune, Côte de Beaune, and Côte de Beaune Villages are wines from the village of **Beaune**, which is entitled to use one of these appellations, depending on the quality of the vineyards. Beaune wines are medium-bodied, gentle reds and whites.

➤ **Chorey-les-Beaune** has red wines, similar to the Côte de Beaune wines. These offer good value.

➤ **Pommard** is a village that produces many mid-premium wines under its appellation. These can be village bottlings or from specific vineyard sites. The Premier Crus are fairly rich in aroma and body, with a typical earthy characteristic finish. They age reasonably well and may aspire to super-premium status. Three recommended Grand Crus are Les Grands Epenots, Clos Blanc, and Les Rugiens.

➤ **Volnay** wines are the lightest in style of all the Côte de Beaune wines, almost to the point of being fragile. Delicate and early maturing, the Volnay Premier Crus are soft and elegant red wines with delicacy and finesse that place them in the super-premium division.

Tasting Tip

Côte de Beaune Villages wines generally are mid-premium quality, with some finesse and moderate aging potential. The Premier Crus are complex wines, capable of combining great depth with a distinctive aroma and lightness of body with a firm structure.

151

➤ **Auxey-Duresses, Monthélie, Saint-Romain,** and **Saint-Aubin** are little-known villages producing mostly red with some good white wines; they provide good value as they are not in much demand.

➤ **Pernand-Vergelesses** is another little-known district that provides good value in red and white wines.

➤ **Santenay,** in the south of the Côte de Beaune, produces lighter and more delicate wines that have less aging potential in the bottle.

➤ The **Meursault** place name offers some red wines. However, it's better regarded for its white wines, which range from mid- to super-premium. Those labeled simply "Meursault" are the mid-premiums—floral in character and streamlined in body, with high, crisp acidity. The Premier Crus of Meursault are the super-premiums, which display a silky texture, full body, assertive aroma, and complex flavors.

➤ **Puligny-Montrachet** white Burgundies are wine perfection! The Grand Crus—Le Montrachet, Bâtard-Montrachet, Chevalier-Montrachet, and Bienvenue-Bâtard-Montrachet—are legendary single-vineyard appellations capable of noble quality. Some of the vineyards, namely Le Montrachet and Bâtard-Montrachet, cross over into Chassagne-Montrachet. The wines have a rich, complex, fruity aroma, often buttery in character, and combine depth of flavor with a hard veneer that is intense yet austere. They achieve unusual power and finesse for white wines and require upward of 10 years of cellaring before they reach their peak.

Heard It Through the Grapevine

The Premier Crus of both Puligny and Chassagne tend to be super-premium wines. Some, such as Les Combettes and Les Pucelles, have, on occasion, rivaled the Grand Crus in noble quality. However, as the vineyards are owned by so many different proprietors and these appellations are used by so many shippers, the names of owners and shippers become your crucial quality determinants.

➤ **Chassagne-Montrachet** offers some red wines, but it's most famed for its stylish white wines, particularly the Premier Crus, which are full and firm in structure, with a distinct earthy flavor and character. Often they are super-premium wines. Chassagne-Montrachet are somewhat sturdier than Puligny, but with less finesse.

Value? It's All Relative

In Burgundy, value is a relative term. Value-priced wines such as the village and lesser-known appellations offer good value, but these do not display the qualities and subtleties that make Burgundian wines so revered.

When it comes to the Premier Crus and Grand Crus, you should look to the vineyards and growers that currently are less fashionable among collectors. Finding the best values requires a familiarity with the numerous growers, their properties, and reputation. (Did I ever say learning about wine would be easy?) Burgundy presents the greatest challenge for the wine lover.

The Intricate Ages of Burgundy

While there are guidelines for aging Burgundy, there also are exceptions to these. The techniques of the different growers in any quality tier can make for either early- or late-maturing wines.

The Sommelier Says

Eager, no-credit-limit wine hobbyists have driven the price of the most desired wines into the stratosphere. Wines from the best growers, as well as most revered vineyard sites, command such a high price that they offer little value relative to their costs.

Generally, you can consume red or white wines labeled from the Bourgogne or village appellations three to five years from their vintage. Red wines from Premier Cru vineyards mature five to 10 years from their vintage, with notable exceptions that can age for decades.

You should drink the Premier Cru whites three to seven years from their vintage. But make sure you cellar Grand Cru reds at least seven years, because it takes time for them to develop their noble qualities. These peak, generally, in 10 to 15 years, with some having an aging potential of decades. Grand Cru whites should have a minimum of three years of aging, preferably five years. Many even improve for 10 years or more.

The Least You Need to Know

➤ Burgundy is the most complex and confusing wine region in the world.

➤ Burgundy produces both red and white wines, many of which are among the finest wines in the world.

➤ You can fine good values in the village appellations and in wines from the lesser-known producers.

Chapter 13

The Noble Wines of Burgundy

In This Chapter

➤ Burgundy's unique terminology

➤ A tour of the Côte d'Or

➤ Selected growers and producers

As you learned from the previous chapter, the Burgundy wine region comprises five districts: Mâconnais, Beaujolais, Chablis, the Côte Chalonnaise, and the Côte d'Or. In this chapter we'll explore genuine nobility, which takes us through only one of these five, the Côte d'Or.

Burgundy and Bordeaux might as well be from different planets as from two wine regions from the same country. They have very little in common. The languages of their classifications differ, as do their bottles, their characteristics, and their aging qualities.

These also differ in prices. Some of the noblest Burgundies are produced in extremely small quantities, sometimes as few as 50 cases a year! And some connoisseurs (or collectors) want one of everything, so prices go through the roof sometimes.

Fortunately, not all noble Burgundies are rare. This chapter will point you to some good values.

Burgundian Classifications

In a sense, Burgundy has been an official wine region since 1415, when Charles VI (Charles the Mad) issued an edict delimiting what rightly could be called "Bourgogne." The first modern classification of the wine-growing regions of Côte d'Or was in 1905, amended after World War I in 1919.

Heard It Through the Grapevine

Many people know the name Côtes d'Or means "golden slopes." And any traveler who has viewed these picturesque hillsides in the autumn cannot deny that they are golden indeed! But according to a négociant of that region, the name actually is shortened from Côte d'Orient, so called after its many east-facing slopes (the most desirable).

This classification looked at individual crops, usually single vineyards, called *climats*. These have been assembled into appellations such as Beaune and Meursault.

Grand Cru

Only 32 climats (vineyards) were declared Grand Cru, or Great Growth. Of these, 25 are in the northern Côte de Nuits and seven in the southern Côte de Beaune.

Look on the labels, and you'll see only the name of the vineyard. (And the Appellation Contrôlée, of course.) That's how you know it's a *Grand Cru*.

Vino Vocab

What we call **Grand Cru** formerly had been called **Tête de Cuvée**, literally "head of the class."

Premier Cru

From among thousands of climats, about 600 were designated as Premier Cru, or First Growth. (Note the distinction between the same designation in Bordeaux!)

On the labels of these bottles, you will read the name of the commune, followed by the name of the vineyard in lettering of the same size, color, and style. (And also the Appellation Contrôlée assurance.)

Village Appellations

The vast numbers of vineyards of the Côte d'Or are neither Grands Crus nor Premiers Crus. These account for the largest share of the region's production. On the label, you will read the village name but no vineyard designation. Though none of these is anywhere near noble in quality, many of these are quite good and fairly priced.

Visit Côte de Nuits and See

Named for the small but important village of Nuits-Saint-Georges, this is the part of the Côte d'Or that's responsible for the color Burgundy—because of its red wines. Twelve miles long and one mile wide, this magical wine kingdom features some of the most famous vineyards of France.

Nuits-Saint-Georges

The largest town between Dijon and Beaune has barely 5,000 people. (They are called *Nuitons.*) Yet it gives its name to this northern part of the Côte d'Or. Like the larger Beaune, Nuits-Saint-Georges is an important commercial wine center, home to many important négociants and cellars. Six of this village's vineyards are Premier Cru. None are Grand Cru.

The following Premiers Crus come from vineyards 12 to 21 acres in size:

➤ Les Damodes   ➤ Aux Boudots

➤ La Richemone   ➤ Aux Murgers

➤ Les Saint-Greorges ➤ Les Vaucrains

If you're lucky enough to find one of these excellent wines representing good value, buy it.

Gevrey-Chambertin

Here near its northern limit is the flagship commune of the Côte de Nuits. About 1,300 acres are under vine, including nine Grands Crus (215 acres) and 26 Premiers Crus (210 acres).

The nine Grands Crus are

➤ Mazis-Chambertin   ➤ Ruchottes-Chambertin

➤ Chambertin   ➤ Chapelle-
Clos-de-Bèze   Chambertin

➤ Griotte-Chambertin   ➤ Charmes-Chambertin

➤ Le Chambertin   ➤ Latricières-Chambertin

➤ Mazoyères-Chambertin

Tasting Tip

Although there are no Grand Cru climats here, some of the commune's 40 Premiers Cru compare favorably with those of the upper classification. The better vineyards here are very small, though, and you'll have trouble finding some of the tannic, full-bodied, and strong wines that are characteristic of this commune.

The soils here exhibit wide variety, with further variety of slope and sunlight. These famous wines are highly regarded for their earthy, meaty style. The Emperor Napoleon liked these wines especially, which played no small part in the development of their reputation.

Chambolle-Musigny

This commune lies between Gevrey-Chambertin and Nuits-Saint-Georges. Of its 550 acres, 64 are dedicated to two Grands Crus, and 150 to 24 Premiers Crus. The two Grands Crus are

➤ Bonnes Mares

➤ Le Musigny

Of the 24 Premiers Crus, the most respected are

➤ Les Amoureuses

➤ Les Charmes

These are the lightest, most delicate reds of the Côte de Nuits. You can attribute this to the commune's limestone soils.

Vosne-Romanée

This commune lies just north of Nuits-Saint-Georges. Together with tiny, adjacent Flagey-Echézeaux to the east, we have seven Grands Crus and 14 Premiers Crus. The two communes total only 465 acres. In the Vosne-Remanée commune lie the finest of Burgundy's vineyards; tiny Romanée-Conti is considered probably the very finest wine produced on earth, followed by La Tâche, Richebourg, and La Romanée. Naturally, they command a king's ransom for a bottle.

Heard It Through the Grapevine

The miniature village of Flagey-Echézeaux, associated with Vosne-Romanée, literally is on the "wrong side of the tracks." Separated by the north–south running railroad, its slopes lie to the east of its larger sibling.

The Grand Crus from here are the most expensive, being praised for their finesse:

- ➤ Romanée-Conti
- ➤ La Romanée
- ➤ La Tâche
- ➤ Romanée-Saint-Vivant
- ➤ Grand Echézeaux
- ➤ Richebourg
- ➤ Echézeaux

These wines are the most expensive because they are of extraordinary quality and character and are produced in minuscule quantities. They are also very expensive to produce as the production standards are so high.

Vougeot

The walled, 124-acre Clos de Vougeot vineyard sits on a steep hillside a mile south of town. This Grand Cru climat dominates this commune's total acreage, which is only 163.

Grand Cru red Burgundy.

Nearly 80 proprietors make wine from this single vineyard! Who's to say that any one is characteristic? I recommend Alain Hudelot-Noëllat as an excellent and affordable example from this property. Some others you might consider are

- ➤ Chopin-Groffier
- ➤ Gros Frère et Soeur
- ➤ Leroy
- ➤ Mongeard-Mugneret
- ➤ Jean Tardy
- ➤ J. Confuron-Contidot
- ➤ Haegelen-Jayer
- ➤ Méo-Camuzet
- ➤ Georges Roumier

While the vineyard can produce wines of excellent quality, mediocre wines can result from poor winemaking and grape growing. Use caution when buying Clos Vougeot—you must know your grower or négociant.

Morey-Saint-Denis

Just southeast of Gevrey-Chambertin is this tiny village surrounded by 674 acres of vineyards. These include five Grands Crus:

➤ Clos de la Roche   ➤   Clos Saint-Denis

➤ Clos des Lambrays   ➤   Clos de Tart

➤ Bonnes Mares

These are among the very finest Grand Cru Burgundies, and yet they sell for something less than those of the more famous neighboring communes. These wines are firm, rich, and fragrant.

Now for Côte de Beaune

What a difference a few miles to the south makes! Well, it's not the latitude, actually, but differences in soils, slope, and drainage. This southern part of the Côte d'Or is where we find most of the White Burgundies, which many wine lovers consider to be the best white wines on earth. This 15-mile strip presents a kaleidoscope of vinous color.

Tasting Tip

The colors match! The soils of the Côte de Beaune are lighter in color than the reddish earth of the Côte de Nuits, having more limestone and less iron. This favors the Chardonnay grape, which has made the Côte de Beaune famous for its White Burgundies.

Corton

About 4 miles north of Beaune sits the village of Corton, at the base of an imposing south- and east-facing hill, one covered with viticulture. The Grand Cru Corton covers 396 acres, some in two adjacent communes. These are planted mostly in the Pinot Noir grape. This gigantic Grand Cru property actually is made up of 21 individual vineyards. You'll recognize them on the labels, as each vineyard name is attached to the name "Corton."

Adjacent to this large collection of red-wine property, on the southwest, is the Corton-Charlemagne vineyard, an additional 177 acres. It's a separate Grand Cru called Corton-Charlemagne, and this is the Chardonnay you simply must drink—White Burgundy at its very best!

Beaune

Beaune is the capital of Burgundy—and its winemaking heart and soul. This medieval walled city of about 20,000 is a popular tourist destination. Though it gives its name to the Côte de Beaune and though it's headquarters to much of the Côte d'Or's wine trade, it offers no Grand Cru climats of its own.

Premier Cru red Burgundy.

Beaune does feature 40 Premiers Crus planted over 765 acres. Three of my favorite producers are Louis Latour, Joseph Drouhin, and Maison Louis Jadot, which I write about later. About 95 percent of the commune's production is red wine. These wines are not gigantic in flavor, but their smoothness, fruitiness, and harmony make up for this amply.

Pommard

This well-known commune just south of Beaune has 1,650 acres, all Pinot Noir. Although it has no Grand Cru vineyards, its 27 Premiers Crus (310 acres) offer some of the fullest wines of the Côte de Beaune. Its wines are not very tannic, and they are concentrated and perfumy—what I call breed.

Here are some producers you might look for:

- ➤ Comte Armand
- ➤ Courcel
- ➤ Jean Garaudet
- ➤ Machard de Gramont
- ➤ Louis Jadot

- ➤ Ballot-Millot
- ➤ Joseph Drouhin
- ➤ Armand Girardin
- ➤ Jaboulet-Vercherre
- ➤ Leroy

Volnay

Moving south from Pommard, we come to Volnay. It has no Grands Crus, but its 35 Premiers Crus are worth your attention. They differ substantially from those of Pommard, being light, delicate, and subtle, what I call elegant.

I am especially fond of Marquis d'Angerville, with its Premier Cru Clos des Ducs, which I mention later in this chapter. Other growers you might look for are

➤ J. M. Bouley

➤ Comte Lafon

➤ Hubert de Montille

➤ Domaine de la Pousse d'Or

Meursault

This village lies a mile or so due south of Pommard. The gentle slopes to the south of the town all are planted in Chardonnay. These White Burgundies are big and exhilarating.

Premier Cru white Burgundy.

Domaine Darnat

CLOS RICHEMONT
MEURSAULT 1er CRU MONOPOLE
APPELLATION MEURSAULT 1er CRU LES CRAS CONTROLÉE

WHITE BURGUNDY WINE
MIS EN BOUTEILLE AU DOMAINE DARNAT
PROPRIÉTAIRE A MEURSAULT (COTE - D'OR)

PRODUCE OF FRANCE

IMPORTED BY (CHATEAU & ESTATE) NEW YORK, N. Y.
— SEAGRAM —
— WINES CO —
Alc. 13% by vol. - White Burgundy Wine - CONTAINS SULFITES - Net Contents 750 ML

There are no Grands Crus, but there are 13 Premiers Crus. Some producers you might consider are

➤ Robert Ampeau

➤ Bitouzet-Prieur

➤ Coche-Debord

➤ Ballot-Minot

Heard It Through the Grapevine

Don't write off a commune like Meursault because it lacks Grand Cru vineyards. It takes more than a great grape to make a great wine. Many of Burgundy's domaines have produced Premier Cru wines that approach or reach nobility. Considering the prices Burgundy's Grands Crus fetch, it's worthwhile getting to know a few of the Premiers Crus. But most important, as always: Know your grower!

Puligny-Montrachet

This tiny village 6 miles south of Beaune features four Grands Crus. Its name nearly is synonymous with White Burgundy. Subtle differences in soil, drainage, and slope provide considerable variation, but not in overall quality, which is quite high.

The four Grands Crus of Puligny-Montrachet are

➤ Montrachet

➤ Chevalier-Montrachet

➤ Bâtard-Montrachet

➤ Bienvenues-Bâtard-Montrachet

The total acreage for these Grands Crus is only 76, so these can be hard to find—and very expensive.

Chassagne-Montrachet

This tiny hamlet, near the southern limit of the Côte de Beaune, features three Grands Crus. Unfortunately, these cover only 28 acres of the 1,100 acres of vineyards in the commune.

About half of Chassagne-Montrachet's output is red wine, and these fine wines tend to go for moderate prices. The Grands Crus all are white wines:

➤ Le Montrachet

➤ Bâtard-Montrachet

➤ Criots-Bâtard-Montrachet

The last named Grand Cru is only 3.9 acres!

These white wines are big, opulent, and with lots of fruit.

163

Santenay

Santenay lies at the southernmost part of the Côte de Beaune, but it's still only half an hour by car from Beaune. Surprisingly, this is a red-wine commune, producing white wine in minuscule quantities only.

There are no Grands Crus here, but eight Premiers Crus occupy about half of the commune's 630 acres of vines:

- ➤ La Comme
- ➤ Clos de Tavannes
- ➤ Les Gravières
- ➤ Passetemps
- ➤ La Maladière
- ➤ Grand Clos Rousseau
- ➤ Clos de Mouches
- ➤ Beauregard

The Sommelier Says

Why do Burgundies cost so much? Considering the scarcity of some Grands Crus, sometimes only a few dozen cases a year, you might wonder why some don't cost more.

But with a little knowledge and a little experience, it is possible to get some pretty good Burgundies for reasonable (though never cheap) prices. But you have to know your domaines!

Growers and Producers

The Grands Crus and the Premiers Crus of the Côte d'Or generally are apportioned over large numbers of growers. A single vineyard can yield a number of rather different wines. It all depends on the grower! (Well, not all. Sometimes small differences in soils and other growing conditions account for some of the variability.)

Here is a list of growers I like. Not all their grapes come from Grand Cru climats, and some Burgundy drinkers will argue whether this one or that one belongs on this small list. But as I have said many times, the appreciation of wine is an individual experience. Once you have begun sipping Burgundies—red, white, or both—you're sure to develop your own list of favorites.

The Very Best

These growers are at the top of my list:

➤ **Philippe Leclerc (Gevrey-Chambertin)**   Here 20 acres are planted with vines 40 to 60 years old. The domaine produces red wines from eight holdings, including four Premier Crus. These are Champonnets, Les Champeaux, Les Cazetiers, and La Combe Aux Moines.

➤ **Dujac (Morey-Saint-Denis)**   With holdings spanning 30 acres, this domaine harvests from 13 vineyards. Five have Grand Cru status: Clos de la Roche, Clos-Saint-Denis, Bonnes Mares, Charmes-Chambertin, and Echézeaux. Four are Premier Crus: Clos de la Roche, Clos-Saint-Denis, Bonnes Mares, and Charmes-Chambertin.

➤ **Georges Roumier (Chambolle-Musigny)**   These nine holdings, about 30 acres of Pinot Noir, feature four of Grand Cru status: Bonnes-Mares, Musigny, Corton-Charlemagne, and Clos Vougeot.

➤ **Jean Gros (Vosne-Romanée)**   A dozen tiny holdings over 22 acres, with the smallest amount of Chardonnay (about a half acre). The two Grands Crus are Richebourg and Clos de Vougeot.

➤ **Domaine de la Romanée-Conti (Vosne-Romanée)**   This remarkable domaine has 60 acres of holdings in seven Grand Cru climats: Romanée-Conti, La Tâche, Richebourg, Romanée-Saint-Vivant, Grands-Echézeaux, Echézeaux, and Montrachet. A fine selection of red Burgundies!

➤ **Faiveley (Nuits-Saint-Georges)**   This giant domaine spans 120 acres, with nearly 30 holdings, all red wines. Eight have Grand Cru status: Chambertin Clos de Bèze, Mazis-Chambertin, Latricières-Chambertin, Musigny, Clos de Vougeot, Echézeaux, Rougnet et Corton, and Corton-Charlemagne.

➤ **Domaine des Comtes Lafon (Meursault)**   This great White Burgundy domaine of about 30 acres is predominantly Premier Cru, with the exception of a holding, less than an acre, in Montrachet. But don't neglect the Premiers Crus Les Charmes and Les Perrières, which should be a little easier to find and a lot less expensive.

➤ **Leflaive (Puligny-Montrachet)**   This 55-acre domaine has four distinguished Grand Cru holdings: Montrachet, Chevalier-Montrachet, Bâtard-Montrachet, and Bienvenues-Bâtard-Montrachet. The first of these is a minuscule one-fifth acre! Leflaive produces one red Premier Cru, Sous le Dos d'Ane.

➤ **Ramonet (Chassagne-Montrachet)**   This distinguished domaine has three Grand Cru holdings among its 33 acres of vineyards: Le Montrachet, Bâtard-Montrachet, and Bienvenues-Bâtard-Montrachet. They all are Chardonnays, of course.

➤ **Comte Georges de Vogüé (Chambolle-Musigny)**   This domaine has about 30 acres from five holdings, three of which are Grand Crus: Musigny, Bonnes-Mares, and Musigny (blanc). That last, the white wine, yields only 160 cases a year, a rare Chardonnay grown on Côte de Nuits soil.

The Next Best

These producers do not have the reputation of the preceding list for any number of factors, including not having or controlling the best vineyards, not being the best wine producer, or not gaining acclaim from wine critics. Still, they produce excellent wines and frequently represent good value.

➤ **Bruno Clair (Marsannay)**   With 20 holdings totaling 58 acres, this domaine produces both red and white wines—and a distinguished rosé. One small plot has vines that are more than 90 years old! The two Grands Crus are Clos de Bèze, red, and Le Charlemagne, white. Six vineyards hold Premier Cru status.

➤ **Armand Rousseau (Gevrey-Chambertin)**   This remarkable domaine of 34 acres produces its distinguished red wines from 11 vineyards, six of which are Grand Crus: Mazis-Chambertin, Charmes-Mazoyères, Clos de Bèze, Chambertin, Ruchottes Chambertin, and Clos de la Roche. Four other vineyards are Premier Crus.

➤ **Ponsot (Morey-Saint-Denis)**   Here we have 10 holdings totaling about 22 acres. These are red wines, except for the output of the tiny Clos des Monts-Luisants, which is planted in a blend of Chardonnay and the rare Aligoté, from vines planted in 1911! The Grand Cru holdings are Griotte-Chambertin, Chambertin, Chapelle-Chambertin, Clos de la Roche, and Clos Saint-Denis.

➤ **Barthod-Noëllat (Chambolle-Musigny)**   This domaine has nine holdings totaling only 14 acres. Seven are Premier Crus. Perhaps the finest, and rarest, is the one from Les Charmes, a holding of less than an acre.

➤ **Michel Chevillon (Nuits-Saint-Georges)**   About 20 acres over nine holdings are all planted in Pinot Noir. Four wines are Premier Crus: Les Saint-Georges, Les Porets, Champs Perdrix, and Crots Bousselots.

➤ **Robert Chevillon (Nuits-Saint-Georges)**   This domaine has 13 holdings totaling 30 acres, nine of which are Premiers Crus. Two that you might find are Les Vaucrains and Les Chaignots.

➤ **Jean Grivot (Vosne-Romanée)**   Here we have 17 holdings over only 35 acres, including three Grands Crus: Echézeaux, Clos de Vougeot, and Richebourg. All are red wines, from vines averaging more than 50 years old.

➤ **Joseph Drouhin (Beaune)**   This large domaine, 62 acres, has 10 Grands Crus among its holdings, all reds, except for a small amount of white from the

Clos des Mouches, a Premier Cru. Most of the Grand Cru holdings are very small, the largest being a 2-acre parcel in Clos de Vougeot.

➤ **Maison Louis Jadot (Beaune)**   This 65-acre domaine has two dozen holdings, including five Grands Crus. These are Chambertin Clos de Bèze, Chapelle Chambertin, Bonnes-Mares, Musigny, and Clos de Vougeot. Jadot produces one village-appellation rosé and a few regional whites.

➤ **Leroy (Auxey-Duresses)**   In this 65-acre domaine we span the full range, from the ordinary to the exquisite. Along with regional and village appellations and several Premiers Crus, Leroy produces red wines from nine distinguished Grands Crus: Corton-Charlemagne, Corton Renardes, Romanée-Saint-Vivant, Richebourg, Clos de Vougeot, Musigny, Clos de la Roche, Latricières Chambertin, and Chambertin.

➤ **Colin Deleger (Chassagne-Montrachet)**   Except for some regional and village reds, this 47-acre domaine produces White Burgundies, predominantly from Premier Cru vineyards. One notable white, though, is the Grand Cru Chevalier Montrachet "Les Demoiselles," from a holding of less than one acre.

➤ **Jean-Marc Morey (Chassagne-Montrachet)**   This 20-acre domaine has no Grand Cru holdings but produces both reds and whites from 10 Premiers Crus. Jean-Marc Morey is proudest of his Les Champs Gains red and his Les Caillerets white.

➤ **Bernard Morey (Chassagne-Montrachet)**   Bernard Morey produces both reds and whites from Premiers Crus over his 28 acres of holdings. I recommend the Les Charmois white.

Good and Reliable

The following producers make very good wine but have not gained the fame or reputation of the better growers. Since their wines are not in extreme demand, they frequently can represent good relative value and won't let you down.

➤ **Louis Trapet (Gevrey-Chambertin)**   The domaine produces red wines over 30 acres from seven holdings, a few with vines more than 80 years old. Three vineyards are Grand Crus: Chambertin, Chapelle-Chambertin, and Latricières-Chambertin. One is Premier Cru.

➤ **Domaine des Lambres (Morey-Saint-Denis)**   These holdings comprise 32 acres, all red wines, with two Grand Cru and 4 Premier Cru vineyards. The Grands Crus are Clos de Lambrays and Corton, Clos des Maréchaudes. The Premiers Crus are Le Village-La Riotte, Corton, Clos des Maréchaudes, Les Maillerets, and Les Folatières.

➤ **Alain Hudelot-Noëllat (Vougeot)** Here we have 22 acres over 11 holdings, all red. Three of these are Grand Crus: Clos de Vougeot, Romanée-Saint-Vivant, and Richebourg.

➤ **Henri Gouges (Nuits-Saint-Georges)** This domaine has 34 acres over nine holdings. Six are Premier Crus, including La Perrière, which is planted in Chardonnay. Another white Burgundy is grown on a regional appellation vineyard. The rest are reds.

➤ **Louis Latour (Beaune)** This large (115 acres) domaine has 20 holdings, including seven Grands Crus, both red and white Burgundies. The reds are Corton Bressandes, Chevalier-Montrachat, Chambertin, and Romanée-Saint-Vivant. The whites are Le Charlemagne, Les Languettes, and Le Corton.

➤ **Marquis d'Angerville (Volnay)** Yes, he's a real marquis! And his domaine of 33 acres includes nine Premiers Crus and one village appellation, all planted in Pinot Noir. Of special note is the Clos des Ducs.

➤ **Jacques Prieur (Meursault)** This domain, about 34 acres, features both reds and whites from eight small Grand Cru holdings. The whites are Montrachet and Chevalier Montrachet. The reds are Corton Bressandes, Corton Charlemagne, Clos de Vougeot, Le Musigny, Chambertin, and Chambertin Clos de Bèze.

While many Burgundies are virtually impossible to find due to the very small production, you can find the wines in this list in most of the better wine stores.

The Least You Need to Know

➤ Individual holdings in Burgundy's best vineyards often are very small, resulting in a scarcity of many excellent wines.

➤ The Côte de Nuits produces mainly red wines.

➤ The Côte de Beaune is the source of most White Burgundies.

➤ The grower and producer are as important as the vineyard in determining quality.

Chapter 14

The Tour de France

In This Chapter

➤ The Loire Valley: fresh and fruity

➤ The Rhône Valley: wines of substance

➤ Alsace: German wines of France

➤ Provence: land of sunshine

➤ Champagne: where the bubbles sparkle

➤ Pays D'Oc: simple wines for everyday

We've lingered long in the Bordeaux and Burgundy regions. In Chapter 21, "A Bit of Bubbly," we'll call on France's Champagne region, as well. But in this chapter we'll visit all the rest of France.

The French grow their wine grapes simply everywhere. We'll begin with the Loire River Valley. In that wine-growing region the longest in the world, grapes, flavors, and styles vary with the scenery. They offer us many distinctive, enjoyable, and affordable wines.

Then we'll explore the Rhône Valley, with its hearty, full-bodied wines. Then on to Alsace, where three centuries of contention between France and Germany have left us a French wine region with a decidedly German flair. This is where the noble Riesling varietal shares its fame with the spicy Gewürztraminer.

Next we'll travel south near the Riviera to sunny Provence. There we'll find large quantities of straightforward, refreshing wines.

Finally, you'll learn how modern technology has transformed the once-inferior wines of Pays D'Oc, in south-central France, into table wines of excellent value.

The Loire River Valley

In its winding path, the Loire River extends nearly 650 miles. Along its lower reaches, this river nurtures the world's longest viticultural region. The area is rich in picturesque vineyards, pleasant and agreeable wines, and magnificent castles and châteaux.

The Loire is France's longest river. It rises in the Cévennes mountains in the southeast. Flowing north, it cuts through the high plateau region of the Massif Central before turning west and widening into a broad valley—France's agricultural heartland. The Loire widens into an estuary at Nantes before flowing into the Atlantic at the northern part of the Bay of Biscay.

If you want to savor wine in its homeland, this is a fascinating region to visit. The cool climate produces light-bodied, refreshing white wines. Now let's look at the districts of the Loire region.

The Loire River nurtures the world's longest viticultural region.

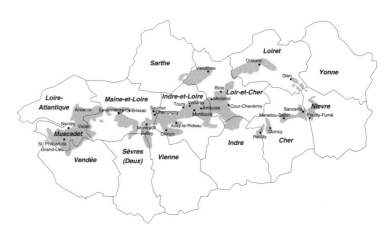

Muscadet

Let's begin at the river's mouth, near the city of Nantes where the Loire forms a large estuary. Here vineyards produce the Muscadet, or Melon grape. Muscadet wines are light-bodied, pleasant, slightly fruity wines.

170

Muscadet wines are refreshing, and their prices are too. You can find a good Muscadet for $5 to $8 a bottle. Buy it while it's still young—at its best. It retains a zesty effervescence and piquant vinous character for about one year from its vintage date.

The best Muscadet wines will bear the name of the Sèvre-et-Maine region on the label. Also look for the term "sur lie" (from the lees). These are bottled right from the cask with no racking. This procedure gives the wine freshness, and sometimes a lively little prickle of carbon dioxide on the tongue. The most refreshing and flavorful Muscadet is bottled sur lie, best drunk as early as possible.

Tasting Tip

The best Muscadets are crisp and bone dry. Muscadet is an excellent companion to oysters, clams, and delicate fish. It's also a great summer drink.

Pouilly-Fumé

Pouilly-Fumé is a Sauvignon Blanc wine made in the vicinity of the town of Pouilly-sur-Loire. It is somewhat fuller than Sancerre and can have aromas of gun flint and spicy flavors.

Pouilly-Fumés range from slightly thin and ordinary wines to more aromatic, slightly complex premium wines. Pouilly-Fumé can be quite a fine wine when made by a good producer like Ladoucette. Richer than Sancerre, Pouilly-Fumé complements poached salmon, veal, and chicken.

Pouilly-Fumé wines range in price from $10 to $25 per bottle. It is best enjoyed young, within three or four years of the vintage.

Sancerre

In the eastern end of the region, about 80 miles south of Paris, are the towns of Sancerre and Pouilly-sur-Loire, on opposite banks of the river. Here thrives the Sauvignon Blanc grape, which makes lively, dry wines. These offer spicy, green-grass flavors that can range from ordinary to outstanding and can be very distinctive.

Compared with Pouilly-Fumé, Sancerre is somewhat lighter in body and more refreshing. It's a good match with shellfish or delicate fish like rainbow trout, and it's an enjoyable summer beverage. Sancerre wines fall into the same price range as Pouilly-Fumés ($10 to $25 per bottle). Also, they are best drunk within three or four years of their vintage.

Vouvray

The central part of the Loire Valley region, near Tours, features both Vouvray wines and several palatial châteaux. Most Vouvray wines are white, made from the Chenin Blanc grape, which does well in this terrain, once trod by royalty.

171

Heard It Through the Grapevine

The wines of Vouvray are produced in three distinct styles—dry, medium–dry, or sweet (called moelleux). These last are luscious and, at their best, super-premium. These sweet wines can be made only in vintages of unusual ripeness, which occur infrequently. That makes these both rare and costly. Vouvray also produces sparkling wines that are pleasant and inexpensive.

The best Vouvray wines are agers. These require several years to develop. With their high acidity, they can last years without risk of becoming salad dressing. These begin in the $12 to $17 range.

The Sommelier Says

The Rhône Valley wine region is split into northern and southern divisions. Strangely, the part of the Rhône Valley that lies in between does not afford growing conditions suitable for wine production.

Rosés of the Loire

The Loire Valley produces rosé wines in huge quantities. Most come from an area around Anjou. These popular Anjou rosés are a lovely pink-orange color. They are low in acidity, appealingly fruity, and sometimes slightly spritzy. They range from slightly to very sweet in finish.

The Rhône River Valley

In southeastern France, south of Beaujolais and between the city of Lyon and the area of Provence, is the warm, sunny, and wine-rich Rhône Valley. The region is divided into northern and southern parts.

These regional reds are full, robust, and hearty with good color and a ripe, fruity character. There's not much complexity here, but there's nothing wrong with simple, straightforward red wine. The whites age well and are light- to medium-bodied, rich, and earthy.

Northern and southern Rhône divisions produce distinctively different wines. The greatest distinction, however, may be in the amount of wine produced: About 95 percent comes from the southern Rhône. The prime varietal in southern Rhône is the Grenache, which produces wines high in alcohol content. Most Rhône wines are simple, inexpensive, and enjoyable—great for an informal evening at home. The section that follows describes the different districts of the Rhône.

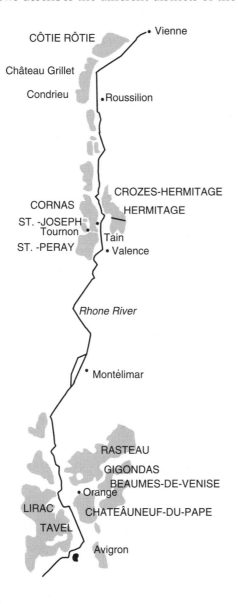

The Rhône River Valley produces some superb wines.

Côtes du Rhône

The Côtes du Rhône and Côte du Rhône-Villages appellations offer a number of highly drinkable red and white wines. Reds are more available in the U.S., ranging from $5 to $12 per bottle. Wines from the higher appellation—the 17 villages that make up Côtes du Rhône-Villages—are fuller and occupy the higher end of the price spectrum.

Heard It Through the Grapevine

France's Rhône River, its second-longest, originates high in the Swiss Alps. In Switzerland, it's punctuated by the Lake of Geneva (near where the famous watches are made). The Rhône enters France east of Lyon where it turns southward. Then it flows through its eponymous wine region and into the Mediterranean at Marseilles, where the French wines had their origin.

The reds generally are fruity and light-bodied, similar to inexpensive Beaujolais. Uncomplicated by nature, they can withstand a slight chilling to bring out their fruity vinosity, low acidity, and light tannins. The result is thoroughly pleasant drinking. The less common white Côtes du Rhône bottlings are mildly fruity, somewhat coarse and rough—earthy wine at its best!

Hermitage

Hermitage reds are mid- to super-premium wines, rich and full-bodied, with great aging potential. They are made from the noble Syrah grape. They are not quite up to Côte-Rotie wines in finesse, but are high in tannins and alcohol and develop complexity and vigor when fully aged.

The best vintages will mature in-bottle for 30 years or more (1988, 1989, 1990, 1991, and 1995 were stellar years for the northern Rhône; 1989 was the finest for Hermitage). The three best producers of Hermitage are Chapoutier, Jean-Louis Chave, and Paul Jaboulet Aîné. The best Hermitages range from $35 to $60, but you can find Hermitages from lesser producers for as little as $15 to $25 a bottle.

Hermitage also produces a small quantity of white wine, made from the Marsanne and Rousanne grape varieties. White Hermitage is a full, rich, earthy wine that needs six to 10 years to really develop.

Condrieu

Condrieu is made 100 percent from the Viognier grape variety, and it's another excellent white wine from the northern Rhône. This is one of the most fragrant and floral wines you can find. It has flavors that are delicate yet lush, with fragrant fresh apricot and peach nuances. Drink it young. Condrieu sells for $18 to $25 a bottle.

Côte-Rôtie

Côte-Rôtie wines are almost uniformly high in quality, with many reaching super-premium status. They are more subtle than Hermitage wines. Firm and long-lasting, they develop a berry and truffle flavor with aging, and their smooth texture gives them finesse as they mature.

Peak vintages of Côte-Rôtie possess aging potential of 20 years or more (1991 was a great year). The most celebrated producer of Côte-Rôtie is Guigal. La Mouline, La Landonne, and La Turque, Guigal's single-vineyard wines, are superb (although quite expensive). You can find most Côte-Rôties for $20 to $45 a bottle.

Gigondas and Vacqueyras

Gigondas and Vacqueyras are two former members of Côtes du Rhône-Village that now merit their own appellations. Gigondas, especially, is robust, rich, and a good ager. A superior vintage can thrive for 10 years or more in the bottle. At $10 to $15 a bottle, it's an excellent buy.

Chateâuneuf-du-Pape

Chateâuneuf-du-Pape is the pride of the southern Rhône Valley. Its intriguing name evokes the fourteenth century, when the popes resided in nearby Avignon. The vineyards with this venerable appellation extend over 8,000 acres, producing more than a million cases of wine.

Chateâuneuf-du-Pape is a robust red wine made from a blend of up to 13 grape varieties. The primary grapes are Grenache, Mourvedre, and Syrah. Quality ranges from mid-premium to an occasional super-premium. At the upper levels are slow-maturing, hard, sturdy, and tannic wines. The best have a full body and are rich, complex, and high in alcohol. Some more accessible wines are fruitier, less complex, and rounder.

Tasting Tip

The best Chateâuneuf-du-Pape vintages age well in-bottle for 15 to 20 years. One of the very finest, Château Râyas, differs from type by being 100 percent Grenache, made from very old vines. Château Beaucastel is a notable wine that can mature for 20 years or longer.

Tavel and Lirac

A close neighbor of Chateâuneuf-du-Pape, Tavel excels in producing the world's best—and most expensive—rosés. Less celebrated than Tavel, Lirac produces both reds and rosés, though the latter do not equal the quality of their Tavel cousins. However, they offer tasty, refreshing wines, reasonably priced. The wines from both areas are made primarily from Grenache and Cinsault grapes.

Alsace—the German Wines of France

Located in Northeast France and bordering Germany, Alsace is separated from the rest of France by the Vosges Mountains. Wines from Alsace differ in several ways from those from all other French regions. First, they differ in character and style, bearing a closer kinship with the wines of Germany. Next, most Alsatian wines carry a grape variety name and bear the appellation "Alsace." Finally, Alsatian wines come in a tall, thin, tapered bottle, unlike any other French wine bottles.

The Alsatian vineyards are situated on the lower slopes of the Vosges Mountains, west of the Rhine River. These are among the most beautiful in the world, dotted with picturesque villages and impressive cathedrals. Despite the northern latitude of the Alsatian region, the climate is temperate, sunny and dry—the kind of climate grapes (and grape growers) love.

Heard It Through the Grapevine

Until the close of World War II, the territory and people of Alsace have been variously French or German. Originally part of the Holy Roman Empire, Alsace lands were acquired by France over a span of several hundred years. The entire Alsace-Lorraine region was annexed by the German Empire in 1871, after the Franco-Prussian War. The territories reverted to France after the First World War, only to be taken over by Germany during the Second. Periods of German rule and affiliation have left a mark on the style of Alsatian wines. These fine wines are far closer in character to German wines than to their French counterparts. As in Germany, most Alsatian production is white wine.

Alsatian vineyards largely are planted in German varieties—Riesling, Sylvaner, and Gewürtztraminer, along with some Pinot Blanc, Pinot Gris, Pinot Noir, and Muscat varieties. The small quantity of light-bodied Pinot Noir is vastly outnumbered by the 93 percent of Alsatian wines that are white. The climate and vinification endow the Alsatian whites with a fuller body, stronger alcohol content, and greater austerity and dryness than their German counterparts. The Alsatian whites, Gewürtztraminer especially, have a spicy character unique to the region.

Riesling

In Alsace, the Riesling is king of wines (as it is in Germany). Here, however, it is produced in a relatively dry style. Alsace Rieslings have a flowery bouquet, but with a firmness that belies its flavors.

Most Alsatian Rieslings are made to be consumed young. But certain wines from outstanding vintages are made in the late-harvest style and can be aged for a decade or more. Rieslings show up here in the $10 to $20 a bottle price range, with late-harvest bottlings going for upward of $50 a bottle or more.

Gewürtztraminer

For dry, spicy Gewürtztraminers, Alsace has no equal. The Gewürtztraminer grape has a personality all its own—pungent and intense, with a unique spicy flavor. Either you like it, or you don't!

High in alcohol and low in acidity, its impression is rich and mellow. Gewürtztraminer goes well with strong cheeses, spicy Asian cuisine, and your favorite fruit. Also, it's fine all by itself, before or after a meal. It sells in the same price range as Alsatian Riesling, but it doesn't age well.

Pinot Blanc

Alsace Pinot Blanc is the lightest of the Alsatian wines, with a mellow, fruity character. While it generally is dry, some producers make it medium-dry to appeal to wine drinkers who do not like an austere style. You cannot tell from the label which style is which, so you should ask your wine merchant. In either style, these wines are best young. Alsatian Pinot Blancs range from $5 to $15 a bottle.

Other Varieties

The Sylvaner grapes make slightly fruity, highly acidic table wines. Only a small quantity is sold in the U.S. Similarly, Muscat d'Alsace, a slightly bitter, usually dry white wine, is found here only in small quantities. Tokay d'Alsace, made from Pinot Gris, is a full-bodied, rich, and spicy wine with a lot to offer. Like Gewürtztraminer, it is low in acidity and high in alcohol. It sells in the $8 to $15 category and makes a good complement for spicy meat dishes.

Les Autres

Les Autres means simply "the others." The two areas in this section—Côtes de Provence and Pays D'Oc—produce simple, affordable wines.

Côtes de Provence—Land of Sunshine

Côtes de Provence is located in the south of France, bordering the French Riviera, in the hilly region between Marseilles and Nice. It produces vast quantities of refreshing and simple red, white, and rosé wines, along with tiny amounts of sparkling wine.

The white wines are labeled primarily "Côtes de Provence," "Cassis," or "Bandol." When well-made, these relatively dry wines are fruity and pleasingly refreshing, with some amount of distinction. White wines from the Appellation Controlée Cassis tend to be more austere and richer in flavor. The numerous rosés from this region are uncomplicated and dry to slightly off-dry. The red wine from Bandol, made primarily from the Mourvedre varietal, is tasty and pleasant. (But it tends to be overpriced.)

Vin de Pays D'Oc—Simple Wines for Everyday

This is a large district in south-central France, stretching along the Mediterranean coast from Provence to the Spanish border, that formerly was known only for very cheap vins ordinaires. However, thanks to innovation and technology (and maybe some strong motivation on the part of the region's winemakers), these wines have improved in quality.

These are straightforward, simple wines, reasonably priced and fine for everyday drinking. They range in price from $4 to $10 a bottle and frequently offer fine value. Some examples of the better wines available from this region are Faugeres, St. Chinian, Fitou, Corbieres, Minervois, Côtes du Roussillon, Côteaux du Languedoc, Pic-Saint-Loup, Vin de Pays de L'Herault, and Urn de Pays D'Oc.

The Least You Need to Know

➤ There are many fine wine regions in France.

➤ The wines of the Loire are mostly white, young, and refreshing.

➤ Côtes de Rhône wines are simple, delightful, and fine for everyday drinking.

➤ The wines of Alsace are more in the German style than French.

Ah! l'Italia!

Italy is the largest wine producer in the world, beating out France, Spain, and the U.S. Practically all of this mountainous country supports wine growing, from the Alpine soil in the north to the sunny shores of the Mediterranean to the south.

Wine is an essential part of any Italian dinner. So perhaps you won't be surprised to learn that people have made wine on the Italian peninsula for three millennia. But guess how long Italy has had a formal system of wine classification? For little more than three decades! And even today, Italy still lacks anything like the French "cru" system of vineyard classification.

Italian grapes are not only provincial, they're patriotic! Even the finicky Pinot Noir has conceded grudgingly to perform outside of France. In contrast, the Italian grape varieties—such as Sangiovese, Nebbiolo, and Barbera—are outstanding performers only on their native soils.

But the Italian growing environments are unique as well as varied. Some vineyards thrive high in the mountains. The altitude seems to protect the vines from the withering heat of the lowlands. In fact, the only wines in the world made on the slopes of an active volcano are the white wines of Mount Etna.

Italy has 20 wine regions, corresponding to its political jurisdictions. The wine regions here are called zones (as in Twilight) to avoid any particular political connotation. For generations, Italians kept the best premium wines for their own consumption. But today it's possible to find great Italian wines. It takes just a little homework.

The best wine districts of Italy.

The Basic Three

For the purposes of this book, I'm going to rank Italian wines into three categories:

1. Inexpensive red and white wines often sold in magnums, for everyday drinking.

2. The better wines, which range from simple to mid-premium quality.

3. A select number of wines that are of super-premium or noble quality.

In the first category we find one of the best-known Italian wines for casual drinking. I mean Lambrusco, that effervescent, slightly sweet red wine that rose to popularity in the U.S. in the 1970s. It continues to please drinkers who want a pleasant, undemanding wine.

In the second category are most of the wines I'll describe in this chapter, plus many others space doesn't allow me to discuss.

The third category includes wines the Italians have created to emulate the finest wines of Bordeaux and California as well as the very best homegrown wines—Barolo, Barbesco, Gattinara, and Brunello.

What's Up, Doc?

For years, when we heard the term "Italian wine" we pictured a cheap and largely undrinkable product in a straw-covered flask, with "Chianti" on the label. (Some of these wines actually were from Chianti, but many were not.)

Tasting Tip

If you've avoided Italian wines—in favor of those from France or California—because you think they are inherently inferior, think again! Italian vintners have been turning out many new products that have enjoyed worldwide acclaim.

As you might imagine, a number of Italian winemakers who took pride in their creations felt they were unfairly stigmatized. So they set about to correct things, to provide a viable structure for their national wine industry. And they got the government to help them.

So Italy enacted a body of laws called the *Denominazione di Origine Controllata* (DOC). Introduced in 1963, the DOC went into effect in 1967.

DOC laws control the quality of Italian wines through legal definitions of viticultural districts, regulation of yields-per-acre, specification of grape varieties, specifications for alcohol content, and minimum requirements for cask aging. The terms "Superiore," "Riserva," and "Classico," which appear on wine labels, took on legal significance.

The lowest category of Italian wines, rarely exported, is simple table wine, which does not fall under DOC regulations. The second, most of what we see in the U.S., is DOC (*Denominazione di Origine Controllata*) wine. This runs from simple, everyday wines to super-premium. Look for the phrase *Denominazione di Origine Controllata* on the label.

Vino Vocab

In Italy, **DOC** stands for **Denominazione di Origine Controllata**, the exact Italian equivalent of the French *Appellation d'Origine Contrôlée*, which means, simply, "controlled place name."

Heard It Through the Grapevine

Currently there are 250 DOC-designated districts in Italy. An appellation of a Classico region, with more stringent standards than the broader DOC, provides a second tier at this level. (Chianti Classico is an example.)

Only 13 Italian wines have earned the respected *Denominazione di Origine Controllata e Garantita* (DOCG) designation. DOCG wines that fail to pass the tasting test are declassified as ordinary table wine rather than DOC wine. This motivates winemakers to produce a superior product.

At the very top *is Denominazione di Origine Controllata e Garantita* (DOCG). This elite category, mostly in the super-premium quality category, must meet additional standards for winemaking and taste testing.

All Roads Lead to Wine

Italy has hundreds of wine districts, too many to cover in this book. Instead, we'll look at those that produce wines readily available in the United States.

Italy's Main Wine Regions

Red Wine	White Wine	Grape Variety
Piedmont		
Barbaresco		Nebbiolo
Barbera d'Alba and similar DOCs		Barbera
Gavi		Cortese di Cortese Gavi
Roero Arneis		Arneis
Barolo		Nebbiolo
Gattinara		Nebbiolo, Bonarda[1]
Tuscany		
Brunello di Montalcino		Sangiovese Grosso
Chianti, Chianti Classico		Sangiovese, Canaiolo, and others

Red Wine	White Wine	Grape Variety
Tuscany		
Vernaccia di San		Vernaccia Gimignano
Vino Nobile di Montepulciano		Sangiovese, Canaiolo, and others[1]
Carmignano		Sangiovese, Cabernet Sauvignon[1]
Super-Tuscans[2]		Carbernet Sauvignon, Sangiovese
Veneto		
Amarone della Valpolicella		Corvina, Rondinella, Molinara[1]; semi-dried
Bardolino		Corvina, Rondinella, Molinara[1]
	Bianco di Custoza	Trebbiano, Garganega, Tocai[1]
	Lugana	Trebbiano,
Soave		Garganega,Trebbiano, and others[1]
Valpolicella		Corvina, Rondinella, Molinara[1]
Trentino-Alto Adige		
	Chardonnay	Chardonnay (various DOCs)
	Pinot Grigio	Pinot Gris (various DOCs)
	Pinot Bianco	Pinot Blanc (various DOCs)
	Sauvignon	Sauvignon Blanc (various DOCs)
Fruili-Venezia Giulia		
	Chardonnay	Chardonnay (various DOCs)
	Pinot Blanco	Pinot Blanc (various DOCs)
	Pinot Grigio	Pinot Gris (various DOCs)
	Sauvignon	Sauvignon Blanc (various DOCs)
	Tocai Friulano ·	Tocai Friulano (various DOCs)
Umbria		
	Orvieto	Trebbiano

1 *Blended wines, made from two or more grapes*
2 *Nontraditional wines produced mainly in the Chianti district (see Tuscany)*

Tuscany—Where It All Began

Tuscan winemaking began 3,000 years ago with the Etruscans who inhabited this northern piece of Italy. Now that's what I call tradition!

The name of the region's most famous wine, Chianti, appears in records from 1260 B.C.E.[sc] (only then it referred to a white wine). In an interesting twist of fate, white wine from Tuscany may not legally be called Chianti today.

The best wines of Tuscany come from near Florence, a city known for its Renaissance art. The vineyards of Chianti, the largest DOC zone, are situated among olive groves, stone farmhouses, and an occasional castle. It's only a short hop from bucolic, picturesque vineyards to some of the world's most impressive art and architecture.

Chianti is divided into seven subdistricts: Classico, Colli Fiorentini, Montalbano, Rufina, Colli Aretini, Colli Senesi, and Colli Pisani. All of them turn out good wine (in fact, all hold DOCG status), but Chianti Classico is the undisputed *numero uno*. Second in quality is Chianti Rufina.

Heard It Through the Grapevine

Chianti wines carry the name of the district (or simply "Chianti"). "Chianti" by itself may mean the wine was blended from grapes from two districts. The cépage (blending of grape varieties) in Chianti is carried out at the producer's discretion. In Chiantis, only certain grape varieties are permitted; certain ones are required by DOC law.

Sangiovese is the dominant grape—a required 50 to 80 percent—with the other red grape, Canaiolo, at 10 to 30 percent. The blend requires 10 to 30 percent from the white grapes Trebbiano or Malvasia. Many producers make their Chiantis almost entirely from the Sangiovese grape. Although not consistent with the DOC regulations, I think it makes for a better wine.

Chianti wines vary according to subdistrict and, to a lesser degree, grape blending. They also vary in style and quality. Ordinary Chianti, at the lower end of the price range, is a prickly, fruity wine and is made to be drunk young. The middle range embraces simple to mid-premium wines, Classico or otherwise. These age well in the bottle for several years, but you can enjoy them when you buy them.

The highest quality is the Riserva, the product of a special selection of vines or harvest, greater care in winemaking, and longer aging before release (at least three years). Riservas frequently are aged in French oak for a minimum of 10 years. Many will age well for 20 or 30 years.

Chianti is a very dry red wine that goes well with food. It is a vinous wine that frequently has an aroma of cherries and sometimes hints of violets. Its taste sometimes is similar to that of tart cherries, but for the most part, Chianti is best described as, well, tasting like Chianti. The best Chiantis are high in acidity and do not reach their peak until four to eight years after the vintage. Some of the better Chiantis, particularly the single-vineyard examples, can age for 10 years or more in great vintages.

Chianti is not the only red wine of Italy. (It just seems that way!) One important Tuscan red wine currently taking bows hails from the town of Montalcino, south of Florence in the Sienna hills. This relative newcomer emerged from a clone or variant of the Sangiovese, known as the Brunello or large Sangiovese. The resulting wine, Brunello di Montalcino, brings the highest prices of any Italian wine.

Brunello di Montalcino is one of those overnight successes that's been around for ages, literally. In 1970, the Biondi-Santi family (the leading producer in Montalcino) decided its wines could use some publicity. So they invited some leading wine writers to a tasting of rare vintages. Needless to say, these 1888 and 1891 vintages were a smash! Brunello immediately became one of the most sought-after wines in Italy. Twelve years after its harvest, the 1971 reserve bottling retailed in the U.S. for $130 a bottle. Even by the extravagant standards of the 1980s, that was pretty pricey for a young wine in no way ready to drink.

The publicity for this DOCG wine has been mixed. Not all bottlings deserved the prices they demanded. Now that the rage has died down, however, there is general agreement that Brunello di Montalcino has the potential to be one of the world's most superb and long-lived red wines. Prices begin at $25 to $40 a bottle and scale upward.

The Sommelier Says

The Brunello variant on Chianti is a huge, full-bodied, and intense wine, with concentration and astringent tannins. But to enjoy its qualities, you may need to age it up to 20 years. Now some producers in Montalcino are making a more accessible version of Brunello, one that is ready to drink in about five years.

From vineyards surrounding the hilly town of Montepulciano comes another red wine: Vino Nobile di Montepulciano. Vino Nobile is close to a Chianti Classico, but responds better to aging. Its minimum age is two years; a Riserva must have three years, and with four it can be designated Riserva Speciale. Just as there is a younger and lighter version of Brunello Rosso di Montalcino, there's a younger Vino Nobile as well: Rosso di Montepulciano.

The Carmignano district west of Florence produces a red wine that owes a good part of its high quality to the incongruous (but welcome) presence of Cabernet Sauvignon. Essentially a Chianti with a French flair, Carmignano can be made with up to 10 percent of the noble Bordeaux grape.

Possibly descended from the white wine of the ancient Etruscans, Vernaccia di San Gimignano bears the name of a medieval walled village west of the Chianti Classico zone. Vernaccia is vinified to be drunk young. It is a refreshing white wine with a slightly viscous texture with hints of almonds and nuts. Most Vernaccias sell in the $6 to $8 price range.

Super Tuscans—Triumph of Technology

During the 1970s, certain visionary winemakers decided to transcend the limits of traditional winemaking and experiment with unorthodox blendings in a quest to make wine of Bordeaux classified-growth stature. Producers like Piero Antinori gained worldwide attention by creating new wines (for example, Tignanello and Solaia) that became known collectively as super-Tuscans. Like Carmignano, these blends were usually Sangiovese and Cabernet Sauvignon.

Today there's considerable variability in the blends of the super-Tuscans. Some producers use Cabernet Sauvignon; others use Merlot or Syrah, while others stick to native Tuscan varieties. There's a considerable range in price, too: from $30 up to $100 per bottle.

Tasting Tip

The super-Tuscans are not cheap! But you can be sure of one thing: They all are of superb quality—super-premium or better. The most famous super-Tuscan wines, Sassicaia and Solaia, are much sought after by wine aficionados, costing upward of $200 in great vintages.

Piedmont—Alba and Asti

Situated in the extreme northwest at the base of the Swiss Alps, bordering France and Switzerland in an area that combines agriculture, industry, and mountaineering, Piedmont is the site of two very important wine zones. Alba (which means "white") is known for its red wines. Asti is famous for its sparkling wines (see Chapter 21, "A Bit of Bubbly").

Piedmont produces some of the greatest Italian red wines. Some wine lovers call it the noble wine region of Italy, a reputation it owes to the distinguished Nebbiolo varietal. This sensitive grape is the pride of the Piedmont. Nowhere else does it really express itself.

Barolo and Barbaresco both come from the central part of the Piedmont region. Made entirely from Nebbiolo grapes, they hail from the Langhe hills near Alba. Both Barbaresco and Barolo are full-bodied, robust wines—high in tannin, acidity, and alcohol. Their aromas evoke hints of tar, violets, strawberries, and black truffles. Barbaresco tends to be less austere than Barolo and slightly lower in alcohol content. It is softer and more delicate and can be consumed earlier.

Heard It Through the Grapevine

The red Nebbiolo grape lies at the heart of three of Italy's best DOCG wines: Barolo, Barbaresco, and Gattinara. (In Gattinara, Nebbiolo is known by its local name, Spanna.) A decade ago, Barolo was the undisputed king of the mountain, followed by Gattinara. These days, Barbaresco seems to have gained in popularity, but Gattinara remains a superb (if underrated) wine.

Traditionally made, Barolo and Barbaresco are agers—some (Barolo especially) need 10 years of aging or more before they are ready to drink. And you should open these a few hours before drinking to give them adequate breathing. Some producers make these wines in the Bordeaux style, so you can enjoy them sooner. The vintners use French oak barrels for aging to give the wine an oaked character.

Barolo, Barbaresco, and Gattinara all are excellent complements to a meal. Fine Barolos and Barbarescos are a bit pricey: $25 to $45 a bottle. But from a good producer and a good vintage, they are worth the ticket. You might want to start with Gattinara. It offers Nebbiolo style and verve at a more manageable price: $12 to $18 a bottle.

Tasting Tip

Roughly half of Piedmont's wine production comes from the Barbera grape. This is the everyday table wine of the Piedmont region. Drink Barbera while it's young, though you might age a good vintage. This is a rich, fruity wine with high acidity but little tannin. You'll find Barbera d'Alba is somewhat more rich than the more austere Barbera d'Asti.

Dolcetto is another Piedmont district favorite everyday red wine. If you know some Italian and you think "Dolcetto" means this is a sweet wine, you're wrong. Actually, it's the grape that's sweet. The wine is quite dry. It's vinous in quality, low in acidity, and rich in soft tannins. I find it easy to drink, even with its slight bitter undertone.

Heard It Through the Grapevine

Recently, Barbera has soared in popularity in the U.S. That means it's widely available and in a reasonable price range. You will find two types of Barbera.

The traditional style is aged in large oak casks, but they impart only a minimum of oak flavor. These wines retail in the $8 to $15 range. The newer method is aging in *barriques* (French oak barrels). These smaller containers offer more wood–wine contact, in proportion to volume, than those giant casks. This endows the wine with more of an oaky flavor, but at a higher price: $20 to $40 per bottle. Oaky is in, but don't be afraid to go for tradition. Both you and your wallet may prefer the old style.

Nebbiolo d'Alba is another Piedmont red you might try. Lighter in body than Barolo or Barbaresco, it often has a sort of fruity, sweet undertone. It retails at $10 to $15.

The Red Queen in Lewis Carroll's *Through the Looking-Glass* would love Piedmont, no doubt about it! Here reds dominate. However, there are two whites you might try.

Gavi is a very dry, refreshing wine with high acidity, named for a town in southern Piedmont. Most Gavis sell for $10 to $15 a bottle; however, some of the best examples go for as much as $35 a bottle and are worth the price.

The second white wine is Arneis, from the Roero zone near Alba. It is named for its grape variety, Arneis. Arneis is a medium-dry to dry wine with a rich flavor and texture. It reveals its best qualities when consumed within a year of the vintage. It sells for $12 to $18 a bottle.

Friuli—Putting Whites on the Map

The Friuli-Venezia Giulia district is nestled up against Austria and Slovenia in the northeast. This prolific zone has notified the world that Italy's wines come in two colors. In this zone, white bottles outnumber red 4 to 1. Over the past 25 years, white wines from Friuli-Venezia Giulia (better known in the U.S. simply as Friuli) have made their way to New World shores and stores.

The districts of Collio and Colli Orientali del Friuli are the top winemaking districts in Friuli. The cool climate produces wines that are crisp and clean. The grapes of Friuli include Riesling (both Rhein and Italico), Müller-Thurgau, Chardonnay, Sauvignon Blanc, Pinot Bianco, and Pinot Grigio. Add to this impressive collection of white varietals two local winners, Tocai Friulano and Ribolla Gialla.

Tasting Tip

And now for something really different: One Friuli wine that falls into no category is Picolit, an unusual (and expensive) white dessert wine. It makes a good conversation piece when wine lovers gather.

Umbria—Volcanic Vineyards

Umbria lies to the south of Tuscany, almost in the center of Italy. According to legend, its best-known wine, the white Orvieto, has been planted since Etruscan times.

The vineyards grow on volcanic rock, which gives the wine a distinctive, earthy character. Made from the Trebbiano grape, Orvieto also has a Classico zone and is produced as both a dry and a semidry wine. You can find a good Orvieto for less than $10.

Sicily and Sardinia

Although Sardinian wines have achieved some popularity in the U.S., most are no more than ordinary. However, Sicily produces some interesting wines, notably from Regaleali's vineyards (intriguingly situated on the slopes of Mount Etna). The white DOC wines of Etna have a, and I don't have another word for this, *volcanic* character that makes them particularly interesting.

Regaleali produces red, white, and rosé wines; these range from mediocre to extraordinary, with reds that are among Italy's finest. As one producer of note in Sicily, Count Regaleali's best red wine is called Rosso del Conte. He makes a Chardonnay that rivals those of the Côte d'Or. Regaleali also makes a dry rosato (rosé) that sells for about $8.

Sicily sends us some good sparkling wines, ranging from the brut to the sweet, muscat-flavored spumantes from the Island of Pantellaria (see Chapter 20 "From the Lands Down Under"). This Mediterranean island also produces a fortified wine known as Marsala, which ranges in style from dry to very sweet, and in quality from average to very refined. Marsala is used both as an apéritif and for cooking (see Chapter 22, "Fortified Wines," for more on Marsala).

Three Gentle Wines of Verona

Veneto lies just to the west of Friuli in the north. The best wines from this zone come from vineyards surrounding the beautiful city of Verona. Verona's three leading wines are among the most well-known and are widely available here. These are two reds,

Valpolicella and Bardolino, and a white, Soave. (It's too bad the Montagues and the Capulets didn't raise a glass of one of these to settle their differences!)

Valpolicella and Bardolino both are made primarily from the Corvina grape. The Valpolicella district resides on a series of hills, some of which overlook Verona. Bardolino is named for the charming village situated on Lake Garda. It also has a Classico zone where the better wines are made. Bardolino is a light, fruity wine, pleasant when young. It's closer in style to Beaujolais than to its Corvina cousin, Valpolicella. Try a chilled Bardolino on a hot summer evening (and imagine you're on the beautiful lake in the Italian countryside).

Heard It Through the Grapevine

Valpolicella is fuller in body than Bardolino, with more color, alcohol, durability, depth, and complexity. Those labeled "Classico" come from the best growing area. An exception is Valpantena, made from a valley to the east. It doesn't have the Classico label, but its quality is as good as Classico, sometimes better. If you see *Superiore* on the label, it means a minimum of one year's aging. Some Valpolicellas improve in the bottle for several years.

Another classification of Valpolicella is Recioto. It's made from grapes grown high up on the hillside and dried on straw mats in lofts or attics to concentrate their sugars and fruits before vinification. Recioto contains 14 to 16 percent alcohol, and it's made in three different styles.

Vino Vocab

When fermentation ceases before all the sugar is converted, it's said to be **stuck**. One reason for this is development of high alcohol, which kills the yeasts.

The first is a sparkling wine, rarely seen in the U.S. The second, labeled simply "Recioto," is sweet because fermentation stopped (referred to as *stuck*) before all the sugar fermented. Finally, there is Amarone Recioto (or Amarone della Valpolicella, or just Amarone), which has fermented completely. Amarone is one of those special wines of Italy that deserves super-premium classification. Amarone is velvety, round, soft, well-balanced, and full of character. You can age the best of these 10 to 15 years, though most are delightful after five years.

Soave is an easy-to-drink white wine that's grown near Valpolicella. Made predominantly from the Garganega grape, along with some Trebbiano, Soave is available as both Classico and non-Classico wine. Most of the better Soaves come from the Classico zone, an area to the northeast of the picturesque town of Soave itself.

We Americans love the flavors of Valpolicella, Bardolino, and Soave. And we like their prices as well. Most retail in the $5 to $8 range. Two other white wines of the region, Bianco di Custoza and Lugana, fall into the same range.

The Top of the Boot

Trentino-Alto Adige, located at the most northerly "top of the boot," actually comprises two very distinct zones. To the south, we have the Italian-speaking Trentino; to the north, the German-speaking Alto Adige (or South Tyrol). These interesting wines differ no less than the languages of their vintners.

Most of the red wines from this border region go to Austria. The white wines rival those of Friuli. Pinot Grigio, Chardonnay, and Pinot Bianco from Alto Adige retail in the $6 to $15 range.

Lombardy—Master Wine Craftsmen

Once famed for its expert craftsmen, Lombardy is less renowned for its wine. To be sure, the region offers some delightful red and white wines.

The best white is Lugana, produced from the slopes bordering Lake Garda. Four mid-premium reds come from the Valltellina region, high up in the pre-Alps, just below the Swiss border. The predominant grape is Nebbiolo, known here as Chiavennasca. The four light-bodied red wines are Sassella, Inferno, Grumello, and Valgella. All are highly drinkable and affordable, too: usually less than $10. Drink them while they're young.

Latium—Near the Coliseum

Latium (or Lazio) occupies the west-central part of Italy, around Rome. Its best-known wine is Frascati, made from the Trebbiano grape and produced on the volcanic slopes of the Colli Romani southwest of Rome. Named for the town Frascati, this wine should be light, fresh, charming, and fragrant.

Most of these wines are dry (labeled "asciutto" or "secco"), but there also are sweeter versions (cannellino, dolci, or amabile). Enjoy these while they're young. Vast quantities of Frascati are produced, and quality can vary.

The Sommelier Says

Latium turns out prodigious quantities of Frascati, both red and white. Quality varies greatly. If you find one not to your liking, it's worth your while to try another.

191

Emilia-Romagna

Emilia-Romagna lies in the northeast, along the Adriatic, south of Veneto. It's best known for the city of Bologna and the ocean of soft, effervescent Lambrusco wine it produces each year.

Abruzzo

Abruzzo lies along the Adriatic, just south of Emilia-Romagna. In the U.S. we know this region for its red Montepulciano d'Abruzzo. This inexpensive wine frequently is sold in magnums for only $4 to $6. It's easy to drink, with low tannins and low acidity.

Marche (The Marches)

Moving further south along the Adriatic, we come to Marche. This region lies outside most tourist routes, offering few historical attractions. But it's very much on our wine map!

Heard It Through the Grapevine

What's in a name? *Marche*, in English, means "the Marches." The what? Well, this old term refers to the borderlands of a country or empire, what we call "buffer states." In the third century B.C.E., long before Rome had encircled the Mediterranean with its empire, the ancient city had annexed the land to the east, still called Marche.

The region's white wine, Verdicchio, gives Marche some distinction. The most famous zone here is the large Verdicchio dei Castelli di Jesi. The grapes used here are the Verdicchio, with up to 20 percent of Trebbiano Toscano and Malvasio Toscano permitted. This is a dry, simple wine to be enjoyed young, within two years at most.

On the Slopes of Mt. Vesuvius

Campania lies to the southwest, just south of Latium, the land of Naples and Mount Vesuvius. Just northeast of Naples we find some outstanding wines, ranging from mid-premium to (sometimes) noble quality. These are the work of Antonio Mastroberardino. It's worth your while to negotiate the six syllables of this name to sample some of his superb product!

Greco du Tufo and Fiano di Avellino are Mastroberardino's unique whites. Greco is viscous and quite strong in bouquet and flavor. Sometimes it can be a bit strong in alcohol, but it's always well balanced. Its flavors have a bitter almond edge that increases with bottle age. It retails in the $12 to $18 range. Fiano has greater elegance of body and texture and a sort of toasty bouquet.

Apart from the excellence of these two whites, Mastroberardino's masterpiece is his rich, full-bodied, and tannic Taurasi. This DOCG wine is made from the Aglianico grape, grown at 1,000 feet or higher. The great vintages of Taurasi age well for 10 or 20 years and can attain near noble status. The single-vineyard Taurasi, named Radici, is especially recommended.

A Sea of Wine

Apulia and Basilicata, along with Calabria, lie at the extreme south of "the boot" (the shoe part) of Italy. These dry, sunny regions produce a veritable sea of wine.

Apulia, the heel of the boot, essentially is one gigantic vineyard. But only over the past two decades have vintners there invested in the modern winemaking technology necessary to make good wines. In the past, these wines had been heavy in alcohol and often sunbaked. Today, the wines of Apulia are fruitier, fresher, and lighter. The Aleatico di Puglia grape is used for a red DOC dessert wine.

Basilicata, the toe of the boot, has achieved its distinction through Aglianico del Vulture, a superb DOC red wine that improves with age. This is a mid-premium wine, quite smooth, with a caramel background and lots of fruit.

The Least You Need to Know

➤ DOC (Denominazione di Origine Controllata) and DOCG (Denominazione di Origine Controllata e Garantita) are indicators of Italian wine quality.

➤ Every region of Italy produces wine. Each is distinct in character and reputation.

➤ Italy produces some super-premium and noble wines that rival the best from France.

➤ Italian wines provide excellent values.

Wines with a Spanish Spirit

Spain ranks third, behind Italy and France, in wine production. The table wines of Portugal, Chile, and Argentina are similar in taste, flavors, and styles to those of Spain. Similar, but with a few surprising differences. Wines from all these countries, though, offer excellent values for what you get in the bottle. You should consider these wines for your everyday drinking.

In this chapter we'll survey the traditional wines of Spain and Portugal. Some examples are the Riojas from Spain and the Daos from Portugal. Then we'll visit the eclectic wines of Chile and Argentina. This New World viticulture, introduced by Spanish colonists, has undergone centuries of change, as successive generations of immigrants have played their parts. All the countries covered in this chapter produce substantial quantities of agreeable wine of good value. I think they all deserve greater worldwide visibility.

Olé! Red Wines; Good Value

Spain evokes images of bright sunlight on distant mountains, Flamenco dancers, festive toreadors, guitars, and (if you're up on your architecture) that strange-looking Antonio Gaudi hotel in Barcelona. Wine? Red, of course, with quality ranging from ordinary to superb.

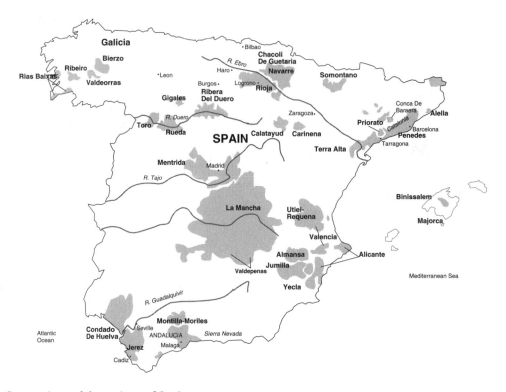

The finest wines of the regions of Spain.

Tasting Tip

Despite the fact that Spain is among the world's wine giants, few Americans are familiar with that country's wines, beyond their fortified Sherry or the red Rioja. In today's market, Spain offers a wide variety of wine styles. With careful selection, you'll find an impressive number of wines at bargain values.

One reason the world hasn't acknowledged Spanish wine may be the lack of a uniform classification system, coupled with laxity of enforcement where laws do exist. In recent years, this has changed considerably. Spain's wine laws, like Italy's, have a dual-level classification: *Denominaciones de Origen* (DO), which means "place name," and the higher classification, *Denominaciones de Origen Calificada* (DOCa).

The higher tier was added only in 1991, and so far, its sole occupant is Rioja, the popular red wine from the Rioja region. Wines with no DO classification fall into the category of table wines, Vino de la Tierra, which are comparable to the French Vins de Pays.

Rioja—Fame and Fashion

Located in north-central Spain, Rioja is the one region you're most likely to have heard of. Rioja is divided into three districts: Rioja Alavesa and Rioja Alta, which have a cool climate; and Rioja Baja, which has the warm climate more typical of Spain.

In the Riojas, the predominant grape is Tempranillo, though Rioja wine typically is a blend. The fruity Grenache (known in Spain as Garnacha) is one of the better-known varieties used in blending. The best Riojas usually are made of grapes from the two cooler districts, or they may contain grapes from all three.

In earlier years, Rioja reds had been aged in small oak barrels (from America). Nowadays, stainless steel and bottle-aging have replaced cask-aging, resulting in fresher, crisper, fruitier wines. While American oak remains traditional, there is some movement toward French oak, which imparts more character to the wine.

Before modernization and DOCa classification, *Reserva* on a red wine label meant only that the wine was aged. No hint of quality was to be implied. Today, "Reserva", used exclusively for red wines, denotes a minimum quality as well as aging.

The Sommelier Says

In the Rioja district, the traditional winemaking methods too often resulted in wines that turned out mediocre and flat, suffering the combined effects of overaging and poor winemaking. In recent years, however, Rioja has progressed from traditional to modern winemaking, with impressive results.

There are several types of red Riojas. Some Riojas are young wines with no oak-aging. Others, labeled *crianza*, are aged in oak and then in bottles for two years; reservas are aged for three years (and now, quality is demanded). The finest Riojas are aged five years or longer and bestowed with the status gran reserva.

Heard It Through the Grapevine

A sizable portion of Spain's sparkling wine bubbles up from the Penedes. In the town of San Sadurni do Noya, located in the El Penedes Central, are the leading producers, including Codorniu, the world's largest producer of sparkling wines by the *Méthode Champenoise* (Champagne method), and Freixenet, which is growing in production and popularity.

Red wines make up 75 percent of Rioja's total output, with rosé wines accounting for 15 percent. (These full-bodied rosés are made from the Garnacha grape.) Prices, generally, are reasonable: Crianza reds begin at about $6 to $7 per bottle. Gran reservas may run up to $25 on average, with some renowned labels selling for upward of $100. The top recent vintages from Rioja are (in order of quality) 1982, 1989, 1981, 1990, and 1994.

Penedes—Outstanding and Inexpensive

The Penedes region in Catalonia, south of Barcelona, is less famous than Rioja, but this is where you go for table wines. Its two leading producers, Torres and Jean Leon, are known for their outstanding red wines, which start in the $6 to $8 range, with the better wines going for up to $30 a bottle. These wines are made in both varietal renditions as well as blends.

Ribera del Duero: Up-and-Comer

Ribera del Duero, north of Madrid, is Spain's up-and-coming wine region. Several new vintners are bringing new wines to market from there, and you might want to look for these.

Until recently, the legendary Vega Sicilia winery dominated this region. It produces Spain's most renowned wine, Unico (which means "unique"). Made from Tempranillo, with a little Cabernet Sauvignon, Unico is an intense, tannic, and concentrated red wine that requires long aging after its 10 years in the cask and several more years in-bottle at the winery. It sells for more than $100 a bottle.

Rueda—Slightly Sweet

Located west of Ribera del Duero, the Rueda region is known for one of Spain's best white wines. Made from the Verdejo grape, slightly sweet and round on the palate, the wine is stylish with a fruity character. The price is attractive, from $6 to $8 a bottle.

Albarino Means White

Galicia, on the Atlantic in northwestern Spain, has one specific district, Rias Baixas, that boasts an exhilarating new wine. This is a white, Albarino, that displays an intense acidity, flowery scents, and delicate flavors reminiscent of a Condrieu. (See the section "The Rhône River Valley" in Chapter 14, "The Tour de France.") Albarinos range in price from about $8 to $17 a bottle.

Sherry Central

Jerez is a large wine region in southern Spain best known as the home of *Sherry*. The wines from Jerez are subject to the country's highest regulatory standards. The predominant grape here is the Palomino, a delicious variety that undergoes a unique process to produce the fortified Sherry.

Sherry is proof of the importance of soil and climate to wine production. As a viticultural area, Jerez is divided into three sections, all based on soil type. The most prized (but least productive) regions have soils characterized by *albariza*, a soil that is mostly chalk, with lots of limestone and magnesium. The topsoils (which actually are white) bear the best Sherry grapes. By law, at least 40 percent of the grapes used in Sherry must come from these famed albariza soils.

Barro, another soil division (literally "clay"), is more productive. Finally, *àrena*, the third region (it means "sand"), bears vines that are immensely productive but weak in character.

Sherry is made in large volume by modern, efficient methods of crushing and vinification. But Sherry is a fortified wine, so I'll have much more to say about it in Chapter 22, "Fortified Wine."

Vino Vocab

Why are the fortified wines from Jerez called **Sherry**? Because that's how English-speakers heard the Spanish name Jerez (formerly Xerez), mistaking it for the plural form of the name of this wine.

Deciphering the Spanish Wine Label

These are the most important terms you will find on a Spanish wine label:

Term	Meaning
Crianza	For red wines, the wine has been aged for at least two years, including a period of oak aging; for white and rosé wines, Crianza means that the wines are a minimum of one year old.
Reserva	Red reservas must be aged in oak and bottle for a minimum of three years; white and rosé reservas must be aged for a minimum of two years, including six months in oak. Reservas are produced only in good vintages.
Gran Reserva	Red wines must be aged in oak and bottle for a minimum of five years; white and rosé gran reservas must be aged a minimum of four years, with a minimum of six months in oak. Gran Reservas are made only in exceptional vintages.
Cosecha or Vendimia	The vintage year.
Bodega	Winery.
Tinto	Red.

continues

continued

Term	Meaning
Blanco	White.
Viejo	Old.
Viña	Vineyard.

Portugal—More Than Mateus

If you came of age in the 1970s, there's a good chance your first wine either was Mateus (which nobody seems to pronounce correctly—maTOOS) or Lancer's. These two medium-dry, somewhat effervescent rosés in their distinctive bottles are Portugal's most familiar wines. But the country's most famous wine is the dark dessert wine, Port. (Many more Americans have heard of port than have experienced an authentic one.)

You might be surprised to learn that most Portuguese drink table wines, red and white. These are less well known outside of their own country. However, the current trend of modernization and stronger quality control should ensure Portugal higher status and visibility in the expanding world wine market.

Within the Portuguese classification system, the highest tier is the *Denominação de Origem Controlada* (DOC). Only 11 wine regions have received this distinction.

The next tier, the *Indicação de Proveniencia Regulamentad* (IPR), has been awarded to 32 regions, many of which aspire to elevation to DOC status. IPR corresponds roughly to the VDQS status of France.

Heard It Through the Grapevine

Port has its own system of classification, implemented and enforced by the rigid Instituto do Vinho do Porto. The appellation system for Port is called the *Denominação de Origem* and follows stringent standards.

The designation Vinho de Mesa Regional ("regional table wines"), corresponds to the Spanish Vino de la Tierra and the French Vins de Pays. All remaining wines are known simply as Vinho de Mesa.

Wines of Portugal.

Green Wine!

Vinho Verde means "green wine." The color refers to the grapes, not the wine! This DOC region, between the Minko and Douro Rivers, is the country's largest wine-producing region.

The most widely available Vinho Verdes are the brands Aveleda and Casal Garcia, which sell for $6 to $7 a bottle. These are medium-dry wines meant to be served chilled. Rarely are they any better than ordinary. More expensive Vinho Verdes are made from the Alvarhino grape from the subregion of Monção (as in the Spanish Albarino). These retail for $12 to $20 a bottle. The higher quality Vinho Verdes are more complex, with some potential for aging. They may be hard to find but are worth the effort.

Dao—The Best Table Wine

Dao is the country's finest table-wine region. The best Dao wines are the reds, although there are some good whites as well.

Most of these wines are blends from within the region, and some are vintage-dated. Those that are aged in wood casks are entitled to Reserva status. This cask-aging makes them soft and mellow. Dao reds typically are smooth and full-bodied, while the whites are light and simple. Few stand out as distinctive, but they offer pleasant drinking at equally pleasant prices.

Douro—Porto

Located in northeastern Portugal, the Douro River region produces Portugal's most renowned wine, *Port*, officially known in Portugal as "Porto." The steep and hilly terrain, with hot summers moderated by cool evenings, is ideal for growing the deep-colored, full-flavored grape varieties needed for Port. (See the section on Port in Chapter 21 for more details.)

The region produces some interesting table wines from the same grapes used to make Port. These wines are intense and robust, requiring years of aging.

Sweet, Strong, and Misunderstood!

The excellent fortified sweet wines of Moscatel de Setúbal still suffer from an erroneous and unfortunate

Tasting Tip

Vinho Verde wines are made for early consumption as fresh, fruity wines. Their tart, bracing, refreshing character is enhanced by a distinct degree of effervescence. As the name suggests, the wines are acidic and have a pleasantly under-ripe character. White Vino Verde wines can add a unique flair to your favorite seafood dish. Yes, there are red Vinho Verdes, but the description "acidic" is an understatement—definitely an acquired taste.

Vino Vocab

Contrary to what you might have heard, the term **Port** is not short for "Portugal." Rather, it comes from "Oporto", the city at the mouth of the Douro River, which has had a wine trade for more than 300 years. Authentic Port from Portugal is called **Porto** as opposed to Ports made in other countries.

association with the inferior, American-made Muscatel. To be sure, the two are forti-fied wines. But the resemblance ends there!

Setúbal wines are deeply colored with a strong, complex Muscat character, and they improve with long aging. I find it interesting that the producers sell both six-year-old and 25-year-old bottlings. You will find these in fine wine stores, often at an attrac-tive price for a wine of such high quality.

Unlocking the Language

These are the important terms you will need to know to be comfortable with Portuguese wines:

Term	Meaning
Reserva	A vintage wine of superior quality.
Garrafeira	A reserva that has been aged a minimum of two years in cask and one year in bottle for a red wine; six months in cask and six months in bottle for a white wine.
Quinta	Estate or vineyard.
Colheita	Vintage year.
Seco	Dry.
Adega	Winery.
Tinto	Red.
Vinho	Wine.

Chile—Old World and New

Chilean winemaking displays a cosmopolitan tradition. The first vineyards were planted in Chile by Spanish colonists in the mid-sixteenth century. Then, in the nineteenth century, a wave of immigrants, mostly Italian, brought with them their own winemaking legacies.

To this we add Chile's unique soils and climate, that sometimes favor grapes we asso-ciate with France or Germany. Many Chilean vineyards are planted in Bordeaux grape varieties, like Cabernet Sauvignon, Chardonnay, and Merlot. A few regions seem per-fect for the Riesling, yielding wines that are delightfully fresh, dry, and austere—similar in style to the German Steinwein. (See Chapter 17, "From the Rhine to the Aegean," for more on the German Steinwein.)

It's surprising to see such European variety in a country that's geographically isolated—on that long, narrow strip between the formidable Andes and the broad Pacific. But high coastal ranges protect much of the growing land from excess humid-ity, and the soothing Pacific protects it from excess heat.

Heard It Through the Grapevine

The Central Valley, located between the coastal mountains and the Andes, is the main grape-growing area. Here, vineyards are categorized according to latitude. The best wine-making grapes are grown in the middle region, which spans an area from roughly 50 miles north of Santiago to 150 miles south of this major city.

In the northern part of the Central Valley, it's warmer. (Remember, this is the Southern Hemisphere!) Here vintners grow table grapes, along with the grapes used in Pisco, the Chilean brandy. The southern part is the home of Pais and Moscatel—popular grapes for the domestic wine market, though little of this is exported.

From south to north within the Central Valley, the wine regions are

➤ **Maule**   This is where the Curico district is located. It is cooler and less dry than Rapel; parts of this region grow the Pais.

➤ **Rapel**   This is where the Colchagua district is located. It is a cooler region than Maipo.

➤ **Maipo**   This is where many of the major wineries are located. It is a relatively small region.

➤ **Aconcagua**   This region is north of Santiago and is the warmest area for quality grapes.

➤ **Bio Bio**   This region is planted mainly with Pais and Moscatel.

➤ **Casablanca**   Casablanca is near Santiago to the north and is known for its new plantings of white grapes.

The Sommelier Says

About 25 years ago, Chilean Merlot and Cabernet Sauvignon got some international acclaim, but export efforts were minor and inconsistent. Only since the mid 1980s has winemaking for export become a serious industry.

Chile is a relative newcomer to the export market. If you tell your friends you're buying a Chilean wine, you may get a blank stare. The Pais grape, which locals have enjoyed for centuries, is hardly a household word outside of its native land.

Chilean producers of Cabernet Sauvignon, Merlot, and Chardonnay wines are modernizing to help them capture a share of international markets. Today, the number of vines bearing these varietals has multiplied, and so has the number of bottlings designated for export.

Foreign investment has had a great influence. The Miguel Torres winery in Curico has a Spanish owner. Even a California winemaker, Augustin Huneeus of Franciscan Vineyards, has become a developer of the new Casablanca wine region.

Finally, it was inevitable that Chile's reputation for French-style reds would inspire the interest of Bordeaux's best. Château Lafite-Rothschild now owns the Los Vascos winery. Also, the Vina Aquitania is a collaboration of the noted Bordeaux châteaux, Château Cos d'Estournel, and Château Margaux. In Chile, !Si! !Si! is turning into Oui! Oui!

Chilean reds are not yet contenders in making world-class wines. However, Chile has the potential, exemplified by the outstanding Don Melchor made from Cabernet Sauvignon by Concha y Toro, a winery known for its excellent, inexpensive varietal wines. The Chilean wine industry is moving toward producing better varietal wines, and in a decade or so, it should be a significant world player.

Tasting Tip

Like California wines, Chilean wines carry varietal names, usually in conjunction with the region and sometimes the district. Many of Chile's white wines resemble inexpensive magnum wines from California. The reds are better, offering excellent value, ranging in price from $4 to $12 a bottle.

Argentina—Smoothing the Rough Edges

Argentina produces about the same amount of wine as the U.S. It is the fifth largest wine-producing country in the world, with a per capita annual consumption of more than 22 gallons—one of the world's highest. (Maybe this explains why so little is exported!)

In Argentina, the historical pattern of grape-growing and vinification is similar to Chile's. Spaniards planted the first vineyards in the sixteenth century. In the nineteenth century, immigrants, mostly Italian, influenced and expanded this industry. Today, Argentinean winemaking is under strict government control.

Most of Argentina's vineyards are concentrated in the hot, arid Mendoza region in the west, shielded from the ocean by the Andes. The next largest wine producing area is San Juan, in the hotter and drier lands north of Mendoza. La Rioja lies further north, still.

Most grapes grow in the flatlands, though the better vineyards are situated at higher elevations where the climate is more temperate. Daytime temperatures during maturation can exceed 110 degrees Fahrenheit, which encourages high sugar content but can give the wines a peculiar sunbaked flavor.

Heard It Through the Grapevine

Historically, the Malbec had been Argentina's predominant red grape. This contributes body and substance to many French wines. Recently, this grape seems to have been displaced by the Italian Bonarda. Other red varietals that manage to thrive in the *caliente* environment include Tempranillo, Barbera, Syrah, Lambrusco, Cabernet Sauvignon, and amazingly, Pinot Noir.

Among the whites grown here are the Pedro Jiminez, Moscatel, Torrontes, Chardonnay, Riesling, Chenin Blanc, and Semillion. The red varietals remain better than the whites.

With the exception of a few superior reds, Argentinean wines seem rough on the palate and ordinary in quality, ranging from powerful and hot to powerful and volatile (that is, bordering on vinegar). With the trend toward modernization, this should soon be in the past. Heading this modernization movement is the vast Penaflor winery—one of the world's largest. In the meantime, you can shop Argentina for many good-value reds between $4 and $7 a bottle.

The Least You Need to Know

➤ Spain, Portugal, Chile, and Argentina all offer excellent values in simple, inexpensive table wines.

➤ The best reds of Spain come from Rioja.

Chapter 17

From the Rhine to the Aegean

In This Chapter

➤ A look at the wine regions of Germany

➤ Appreciating Austrian wines

➤ Hunting for wines from Switzerland

➤ Greece offers more than retsina

➤ Finding wine from Hungary

Germany offers some of the most varied and enjoyable experiences the world of wine has to offer. Some of the driest and some of the sweetest wines come from this country. (Even wines made from grapes that have become frozen raisins!)

German wine labels, with their strange, long words may seem intimidating. However, German wine laws are logical (you expected otherwise?), and these labels can tell us quite a lot. That is, once we recognize a few terms. That's one reason for this chapter.

Later, we'll discover that German-speaking Austrians have some very original (and delicious) ideas about wine. And the German-Italian-French-speaking Swiss have several notions of their own.

Then we'll visit a bit of the ancient world of Greece where we can sample some unusual beverages made in a very, very old-fashioned way.

We'll finish with some wines that made the Hapsburgs happy, the distinguished products of Hungary.

The finest wine regions of Germany.

The Sommelier Says

For a wine-producing country, Germany is pretty far north. There's little of that bright golden sunshine needed for red grapes to flourish. As a result, at least 85 percent of German wine produced *is* white.

Germany—Süss und Trocken

Have you ever tasted a German red? Chances are you were within a few kilometers of the Rhine. Few German red wines are ever exported. All the German wines you'll see in your favorite wine shop are white.

Regardless what you've heard, not all German wines are sweet. Some even carry the word "Trocken" on the label, which means "dry." In general, though, German whites run medium-dry to sweet. They are floral, fragrant, and refreshing—and never oaked.

Microclimates and More

Germany's wine districts differ from those of other countries in one regard. Instead of having one generalized climate, each German wine district may comprise several microclimates. These vary with every turn of the winding rivers (principally the Rhine and the Mosel) on which they locate their choicest vineyards. The flowing rivers temper the harsh extremes of weather and help protect the vulnerable grapes.

The best vineyard slopes face south. Every element of topography can affect the wine: the steepness of the slope; the amount of sun reflected from the adjoining rivers; the nearness of a wind-sheltering forest or mountain peak; altitude; and, as in other winegrowing areas, the soil constituents. German wine conditions not only vary from place to place, but (more than in other lands) year to year. With German wines, vintages do matter!

Where Riesling Reigns

Germany is the first home of the noble Riesling, which unlike most vinifera, is no sun worshipper. It is, however, something of a snob. Only in Germany's best vineyards does it ripen consistently. As a result, it represents only 21 percent of all viticultural plantings.

The most prolific German grape is the Müller-Thurgau. Some say this varietal is a cross between Riesling and Sylvaner. Other say it's the marriage of two Riesling clones. It ripens earlier than Riesling, yielding a soft, round, fragrant wine. However, it's not in Riesling's exalted class.

Müller-Thurgau loves the cool German climate, just as German winegrowers love it. Germany cultivates other white varietals. These include Sylvaner, Kerner, Scheurebe, and Ruländer (Pinot Gris). The red varietal Spätburgunder (Pinot Noir) is grown in the warmer parts of the country.

German Wine Laws: Simplifying Complexity

One very striking thing about the German language is the length of some of its words. This occurs through compounding, the cementing of several words to form a new one. German wine label designations are somewhat the same, building from separate elements until some become quite long. (At least there are spaces between these words.)

Let's begin with the place of origin, the town. Bernkastel is a good choice. (To this name Germans add the suffix -er, for reasons of German grammar.) Next comes the name of the vineyard, say, Badstube. Then comes the name of the grape. How about Riesling? So now we have *Bernkasteler Badstube Riesling*. Isn't that easy?

Now we come to something that's unique to German wines, at least to the finer wines: a measure of ripeness dictated by when the grape was harvested. This is a real quality assessment. It's called *Prädikat* (the same word Germans use for report-card grades). But before we continue, let's look at the broadest quality designations under the 1971 German wine laws.

At the bottom, we have *Tafelwein* (table wine), or *Landwein* (table wines with some regional designation). These are everyday stuff, not good enough to export. Then comes *Qualitätswein*, short for *Qualitätswein bestimmter Anbaugebiet* (QbA), which means "wines of quality from a specified region."

Heard It Through the Grapevine

The Qualitätswein designation describes most of the lower-priced German wines that are exported. Some popular and colorful generic names you might see are *Liebfraumilch* (Milk of the Virgin), *Naktarsch* (bare bottom), *Schwatze Katz* (black cat), and *Black Tower*.

Now we return to *Qualitätswein mit Prädikat* (QmP), "wines of quality with special ranking," the highest level.

This system of assigning rank to ripeness isn't so strange, actually, when we consider the cool German climate in which ripeness is the desired, but sometimes elusive, goal. There are five Prädikat levels, the higher usually indicating a higher (riper) quality. From the lowest to the highest, these are

➤ Kabinett

➤ Spätlese (late harvest)

➤ Auslese (select harvest)

➤ Beerenauslese (selected grape-by-grape)

➤ Trockenbeerenauslese (selected grape-by-grape, with the grapes on their way to becoming raisins)

Vino Vocab

There is a category within Beerenauslese called **Eiswein** (ice wine). It's very rare. The grapes, when harvested individually, are dried out and frozen on the vine.

Now there's no need to be intimidated by such a descriptor as "Bernkasteler Badstube Riesling Trockenbeerenauslese." In the case of German wines, word count is a reliable indicator of quality.

The finest wines at each level are made from the Riesling grape, although the quality of wines made from other grape varieties improves as riper grapes are used. Kabinett wines generally

210

are somewhat dry and fruity, though well-balanced. Wines graded from Spätlese upward indicate some degree of selection. Spätlese wines are made from grapes ranging from fairly ripe to greatly mature, and can come to us from fairly dry to slightly sweet.

The 1971 German wine laws also define viticultural areas as follows:

➤ **Bereich** is an enormous region, which may be subdivided into one or more Grosslagen.

➤ **Grosslage** means "large locale." It's essentially a large vineyard that contains smaller vineyards (Einzellagen), sometimes several hundred acres with thousands of vineyards, all of which produce wines of similar quality and character. A wine from a Grosslage is identified on the label with a generic name that looks just like a vineyard name. To tell the difference, you need to know the Grosslagen names.

➤ **Einzellage**, literally "single-cell locale," is the smallest defined region, an individual vineyard that is at least 12 acres. The Einzellage is indicated on the label after the village name.

Tasting Tip

Prädikat is assigned according to the *Oechsle* scale, a measure of sugar in the grape juice prior to fermentation. Not all finished products will be sweet, though. At the two lower Prädikat levels, the grape juice may be fully fermented to dryness. Above these levels, the amount of sugar in the ripe grapes guarantees us a sweet wine.

Milk of the Virgin

Liebfraumilch, which means "milk of the Virgin," is a delightful, refreshing, enjoyable wine. (Who can dislike a wine with a name like that?) Actually, the name originates from an old vineyard that had surrounded the Liebfraustift (institution dedicated to Our Lady) at Worms in the Rheinhessen region. Liebfraumilch may be the best-known German wine in the U.S. and, for many people, their first taste of Vitis vinifera.

Yellow in color, with a slight greenish hue, Liebfraumilch is a blend of several grape varieties, primarily Müller-Thurgau with Riesling, Silvaner, and/or Kerner. It's produced generally in the Rheinhessen or the Pfalz region, with lesser quantities produced in the Nahe and the Rheingau. Liebfraumilch is ranked Qualitätswein (or QbA). Typically low in alcohol, it is medium-dry with a refreshing acidity and a pleasant fruity flavor. It is definitely meant to be enjoyed young. Liebfraumilch sells for $5 to $7 a bottle.

Heard It Through the Grapevine

Liebfraumilch and many other inexpensive German wines are produced using a method called süss Reserve (sweet reserve), which helps maintain a desired level of sweetness. The wine is fully fermented to create a dry wine of low alcohol and high acidity. But here's the trick: Before fermentation, a small quantity of grape juice is withheld to be blended later with the fermented wine.

The unfermented grape juice, or süss Reserve, adds its natural, sweet, fruity flavor to the finished wine. Wines produced in this style are termed "lieblich," which means "lovely" or "gentle." They are fruity, light-bodied wines with a pleasing sweetness, perfect to drink on their own.

Yes, There Are Dry German Wines

Outside of Germany, most people are familiar only with lieblich-style wines. But there are other styles, less sweet, that have become trendy in their homeland. The driest category is *trocken* (dry). Trocken wines have virtually no residual sugar and range in taste from austere to tart. *Halbtrocken* (half-dry) wines are midway between trocken and lieblich. More mellow than trocken wines, they have a certain amount of residual sugar and a fairly dry taste. They are somewhat higher in alcohol than Kabinett or Spätlese wines.

Tasting Tip

Auslese (and higher) wines are made from overripe grapes that endow the wine with a fuller body and a higher concentration of flavor. Their sweetness usually is balanced by sufficient acidity.

Overripened, Rotted, and Expensive

Wines from the Auslese category on up are made from grapes that may be overripened, rot-infected, or even frozen. Remarkably, these are among the world's finest wines—and unique in their aromas and flavors.

Beerenauslese (grape-selected) wines are made from grapes that have overripened and generally display the noble rot, *Botrytis*. This gives them a honeyed and luscious opulence. Winemakers choosing to make a Beerenauslese are gamblers. They risk losing their entire crop to frost as the grapes are left on the vine to ripen. As a result, only small numbers of Beerenauslese are produced each year. Yes, it can be expensive.

Trockenbeerenauslese (dried on the vine) wines are at the very top of the hierarchy. These berries are harvested individually and usually show signs of *Botrytis* (although it's not a legal requirement). These wines possess a concentrated lusciousness like nectar. (This, I understand, is Wotan's favorite beverage in Valhalla.)

The intense lusciousness is the combined effect of the grape's essence, the flavor of noble rot, and the high level of residual sugar (which may approach 20 percent). This wine is a killer to make. It's not only risky, it's a difficult wine to vinify and requires superior skill and loving dedication throughout the process. Prices easily can run into the three-figure range.

Maybe it is the cool climate—or maybe it's the same spirit that gave us Zeppelins, dachshunds, and lederhosen—but the German winemaking industry has some truly strange offerings. Perhaps the strangest is *Eiswein* (ice wine), made from grapes left on the vine to freeze. (Talk about turning a liability into an asset!)

Once harvested, the grapes are crushed gently to retain the sweet, concentrated grape juice, minus the ice. The juice left to undergo fermentation is richly concentrated in sugar, flavor, and acidity. Depending on the skill of the winemaker, this opulent wine can better the late-harvest German wines. You'll find these rare wines in half-bottles, sometimes at obscene prices.

Vino Vocab

Four of Germany's wine regions bear the name of the renowned river: **Rheingau**, **Rheinhessen**, **Pfalz** (formerly called **Rheinpfalz**), and **Mittelrhein**.

Das Rheingold

In *Das Rheingold*, the first of Wagner's four-opera *Ring Cycle*, a gold hoard, fashioned into a ring, grants its owner ultimate power. (The remaining 13 hours of the plot are too hard to explain here.) Some of the *Rhine* River's most golden treasures come in tall, amber-colored bottles. And you don't have to blackmail the goods to obtain them. (Admittedly, they're not as easy to find in wine shops as their French or Italian counterparts.)

Rheingau

The Rheingau is a tiny wine region (only one-quarter the size of the Mosel, which we'll get to in a moment), but along with the Mosel-Saar-Ruwer, it is the most important in Germany. It's divided into 10 Grosslagen and 120 einzellagen (individual vineyards) among 28 communities that jut quaintly along the river's banks. Riesling grapes account for more than 80 percent of the vineyard plantings, producing the finest wines of the region. The Rieslings tend to be round, soft, and deep in color.

The following are the leading Grosslagen:

➤ **Hochheim** produces full-bodied and fruity wines, often with a trace of earthiness. The best vineyards include Domdechaney, Hölle, and Sommerheil, whose wines fall within the mid-premium quality range and are comparable in quality to wines from Johannisberg (see the last item in this list). The finest estate is Schloss Eltz, followed by the vineyards of Taubenberg and Sonnenberg.

➤ **Erbach** is noted for its sturdy wines, with full-bodied flavors and long life. Erbach gained its stature primarily on the reputation of the wines produced by the Marcobrunn estate; in the best vintages, these noble wines rank with the world's best.

➤ In **Hattenheim**, the Steinberg estate produces superlative wines. The wines of other Hattenheim vineyards are somewhat more delicate and less firm than the noble class Steinbergers.

➤ In **Winkel**, the Schloss Vollrads vineyard eclipses all others. Its wines are characterized by ripeness and great fruit—unquestionably noble, quality material. Their Kabinett and Spätlese rank in the mid- to super-premium range.

➤ Wines from **Rauenthal** are characterized by a distinctive sense of fruit and an almost spicy flair. Most of the wines fall into the mid-premium range, but some of the better Lagen—Baiken, Wülfen, Langenstrück, and Nonnenburg—are capable of producing wines of noble stature.

➤ **Eltville** produces wines that are pleasing, fine, soft, and have good bouquet. Although less distinguished than the wines of the Rauenthal, they are highly drinkable, simple to mid-premium quality wines.

➤ **Johannisberg**, the village, is the most famous name of the Rheingau. The wines made here range from simple to super-premium in quality, with the Schloss (castle) Johannisberg standing out for its noble wines from the great vintages. Johannisberger wines are distinguished for their finesse and fine bouquet. Schloss Johannisberg wines have an extra dimension of breed, placing them among the world's great wines.

Rheinhessen

The large *Rheinhessen* region produces a greater variety of wines—ranging from small table wines to *spritzenwein* (wine you mix with soda)—than any other German wine district. Its most famous export is Liebfraumilch, which is made by nearly all of the region's 167 villages. The Rheinhessen accounts for 50 percent of all German wine exports.

Heard It Through the Grapevine

Rheinhessen wines tend to be soft, with a pronounced character that makes them the easiest to identify of all German wines. But because of a temperate climate, the wines lack the character they might have had if they had to fight for their lives.

The popularity of the Rheinhessen wines probably is based on their intense bouquet and straightforward sweetness. Most Rheinhessen wines are made from the Müller-Thurgau grape, which produces juicy, soft, fruity wines. The next most widely used vine is the Sylvaner, which produces full, round wines.

The Rheinhessen comprises three *Bereichs*: Bingen, Nierstein, and Wonnegau. The highest-quality wines come from Nierstein (and its towns, Oppenheim and Nierstein). Its long-lived Rieslings are unquestionably the best Rheinhessen wines. They are soft, full-bodied, and elegant, with a unique, easily identified, marvelous bouquet.

In the Bereich of Bingen, the village of Bingen itself produces wines similar to those of the Nahe, which are fuller, heavier, and more concentrated than the average Rhine wine. The wines here profit from warmer microclimates that give them a special fullness and ripeness. With time, Riesling wines develop elegance and style, and Sylvaner wines gain in distinction.

Tasting Tip

On the whole, wines from the town of Nierstein have more elegance than those from Oppenheim, although in some vintages (particularly hot, dry years), Oppenheim wines reign superior. Remember, in Germany, vintages count.

Wines from the finest vineyards of Nachenheim have great bouquet and are remarkable for their elegance, finesse, and class. The best wines combine depth, fire, spiciness, and delicacy in marvelous and noble harmony.

Wonnegau is where the city of Worms is located. Alzey, the center of the inland area, and its surrounding towns produce good, clean-tasting lieblich wines.

Die Pfalz

The Pfalz region is close in size to the Rheinhessen. Situated along the Rhenish wine road (the Weinstrasse), its enchanting and scenic vineyards grow on a high plateau above the river's western bank.

In the finer vineyards, the soil contains large amounts of *Schist* (slate), which retains the day's heat during the cool evening hours. A long, warm fall fosters grape maturity, which enables the area to produce intense, sweet wines ranging from Spätlese to Trockenbeerenauslese. Some of these high-ranked Prädikats achieve super-premium or noble status.

As in other areas, the finest wines come from the noble Riesling, though this grape accounts for only 14 percent of all vineyard plantings. Pfalz Rieslings offer an attractive and remarkable balance. They're fuller than those of the Mosel, less mild and soft than those of the Rheinhessen, and less overwhelming in bouquet than those of the Rheingau. This region produces some of the world's finest Auslese and Beerenauslese wines.

The predominant grape here is the Müller-Thurgau, which yields pale, fresh wines. The Sylvaner accounts for 20 percent of vineyard production, ranging in quality from simple premium to mid-premium. A small amount of spicy wine is produced from the Gewürztraminer. Recently, Kerner, Scheurebe, and Blauburgunder (Pinot Noir) have gained in importance.

Mittelrhein

Mittelrhein, along the banks of the northern Rhine, is one of Germany's smallest wine regions. It is noted mainly for its Rieslings.

Vino Vocab

Sometimes you will see and hear the River **Mosel** (MOH–zl) as **Moselle** (moh–ZELL). The river rises in France, so either is correct.

The Mosel (Moselle)

The Mosel region comprises the vineyards dotting the slopes of the serpentine *Mosel* and its tributaries, the Saar and Ruwer. Officially, it's known as the *Mosel-Saar-Ruwer* (or MSR). Divided in two, the area includes the Mittelmosel (Central Mosel), which produces the greatest wines of the region, and the Saar-Ruwer, which produces good, if not necessarily distinctive, wines.

More than half (55 percent) of the plantings are Riesling. Mosel Rieslings are light in body, delicate, and refined. They often are described as floral wines, evoking images of flowers in spring meadows. They have a lively and refreshing taste, low in alcohol, often exhibiting a slight effervescence. These are wines that you must drink while they're young.

Bereich Bernkastel is the best-known region in the Mittelmosel, and premium and noble wines are produced by four of its six Grosslagen: Michelsberg, Kurfürstlay, Münzlay, and Schwarzlay. The two others, Probstberg and St. Michael, produce simple-premium wines.

➤ The villages of the Grosslage Michelsberg produce some of the most distinctive wines in the Mosel. There are the fresh, light wines of Trittenheim and the more intense wines of Neumagen. The best and most famous village in this Grosslage is Piesport.

➤ In the Grosslage Kurfürstlay, the two best wine-producing villages are Brauneberg and Bernkastel. Brauneberg wines are very full-bodied, rich in flavor, and long-lived. When from the best vineyards, such as Juffer, they can reach super-premium class.

➤ In the Grosslage of Münzlay, the three villages of Graach, Wehlen, and Zeltingen yield wines capable of achieving super-premium or noble status. These wines are well-balanced and fragrant, although the style can vary from vineyard to vineyard and range from fine, fragrant, and delicate to full-bodied and big. Wehlen is the home of some of the finest Mosel wines, many of which come from the renowned Prums estate. The fuller-bodied wines of Zeltingen range from ordinary quality wines to super-premiums, ranking alongside Graach and Wehlen.

➤ The Grosslage of Scharzberg is where we find the Saar of Mosel-Saar-Ruwer (MSR). The quality of wine from here varies greatly, depending on the whims of Mother Nature. Scharzhofberger is the noble estate and wine of the Saar.

➤ The tiny Ruwer valley gives us the lightest and most delicate of the MSR wines. The top-quality names are Maximin Grünhaus and Eitelsbach.

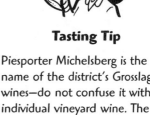

Tasting Tip

Piesporter Michelsberg is the name of the district's Grosslage wines—do not confuse it with an individual vineyard wine. The Kabinett wines usually are of mid-premium quality, with typical Mosel delicacy. Those of Auslese and above, from the better vineyards, can achieve super-premium quality—richly sweet, complex, and flavorful.

Leaving the Main Road

The Nahe River region, west of the Rheinhessen, produces agreeable, pleasant wines that are somewhat fuller, heavier, and more intense than most German wines.

Baden, the southernmost and, consequently, the warmest region, produces fairly full-bodied, pleasant, straightforward wines. The wines of Franconia are unlike other German wines. They are fuller in body, higher in alcohol, and have an earthy and steely character that replaces the typical flowery, fruity wine profile.

Wines from the Land of Waltzes

The Austrian people enjoy their native wines! Annual per-capita consumption is roughly 10 gallons. Strangely, no Austrian wines come from near its borders with its wine-producing neighbors, Germany, Italy, or Switzerland. The best wines of Austria come from Langenlois, Krems, and Wachau, all in its eastern provinces. Baden, near Vienna, produces light, fruity-style wines.

Most of Austria's red wine is produced in Burgenland, one of the country's warmer regions bordering Hungary. The red wines are medium- to full-bodied, with a fruity character and moderate tannins.

Austrian wine laws follow the German model. Better wines are divided into Qualitätswein and Prädikatswein classifications. The only difference from the German laws is that in Austria Prädikat begins with Spätlese. The minimum ripeness required for each level is higher in Austria than in Germany, and Austrian wines typically are higher in alcohol.

The German system of labeling also applies to Austrian wines, including linking the varietal name with the place name. There are some exceptions. For example, in Burgenland, the wines generally carry varietal names followed by the region.

Heard It Through the Grapevine

Eighty percent of Austria's wines are white, full-bodied, and refreshing, with herbal and, occasionally, vegetable flavors. The most popular are made from the indigenous white Grüner Veltliner. Austrian growers plant Müller-Thurgau, along with Welschriesling, a grape frequently used to make ordinary table wines in Eastern Europe. These wines excel in quality in Austria and are light, soft, and aromatic.

Sylvaner, the noble Riesling, and Ruländer (Pinot Gris) also are planted. Wines made from these grapes are similar to German wines. Though they rarely reach the same flavor heights, Austria's sweet, late-picked, berry–selected, and dessert–style wines have received international acclaim. Austria's crisp, dry whites, ranging from light- to full-bodied, are beginning to gain recognition.

Switzerland—Interesting, but Rarely Exported

Like the Austrians, the Swiss enjoy their wines. Annual per-capita consumption is close to 12 gallons. Unfortunately for the rest of the wine world, the Swiss enjoy their wines so much that they keep most of them at home.

The canton of Vaud is the largest winegrowing region. To the south is the Valais. As with Germany, roughly two-thirds of Switzerland's wines are white. Swiss wines tend to be expensive for their quality and not a good value. They do, however, offer a certain unique character.

> **Tasting Tip**
>
> Switzerland is well situated for winemaking, nestled along with Germany, France, and Italy. Vineyards dot all regions, German-speaking, French-speaking, and Italian-speaking.

Vaud

Most of the vineyards here are located on slopes surrounding beautiful Lake Geneva. The two major subregions are Lavaux and La Côte. (Guess which language they speak here!)

With its southern exposure, Lavaux enjoys the tempering effect of Lake Geneva. The predominant grape variety is the Chasselas, which yields a grapey, if neutral, white wine. Chasselas wines tend to be fairly full-bodied, with dry and straightforward earthy flavors. La Côte, on the northern shore, produces similar wines to Laveaux.

Valais

The Valais has a few warmer growing sites, particularly on the slopes near the Rhône River. Chasselas is known here by its local name, Fendant. In the temperate (for Switzerland) Valais, it develops full body and offers good balance. Dôle is the local name for red wine, made from either Gamay or Pinot Noir. Petit-Dôle is another name for Pinot Noir.

> ### Heard It Through the Grapevine
>
> Rèze has some historical—or mythical—importance: It was once (according to the story) used to produce a wine, *vin de glacier*, made by mountain peasants and reputed to remain fresh for decades when kept at high elevation.

In Valais, wines from the Müller-Thurgau grape are called "Johannisberg." Malvoisie is a soft, sweet, dessert-style wine made from the Pinot Gris grape. The area still cultivates several local wines such as Arvine, Amirgne, Humagne, and Rèze.

Neuchâtel

The region around Lake Neuchâtel in the northwest corner is adept at producing good quality in both red and white table wines—something a bit unusual this far north. Remarkably, the fussy Pinot Noir yields a delicate, fruity style of wine. The village of Cortaillod offers some of the better light Pinot Noirs.

Ticino

Ticino is located in the southern corner, known as Italian Switzerland. Most of the vineyards here are planted in red varieties. Nostrano is the name for a light, blended red. Viti is the name for fuller-bodied reds made from the Merlot variety.

Greece—Dionysus Country

Greece is one of the oldest winegrowing regions in the world. In fact, ancient Greeks honored their own wine god, Dionysus.

The Greek wine palate is rather different from ours, stemming perhaps from the traditional red-and-black clay vessels from ancient times. In those ancient days, the Greeks kept their wine from spoiling by adding preservatives such as herbs and spices—even goat cheese! A few vestiges of this practice remain. (I don't know of any wines today with goat cheese!) Resin flavorings still are added to the white Retsina and the rosé Kokkineli.

Retsina is quite popular in Greece. If you're planning some travel in Greece, you may want to sample this in its home territory. A word of caution: Many similarly inclined wine lovers have been so unnerved by their first taste of Retsina, they have forgotten their desire to sample other native Greek wines, some of which are very good.

There are some pleasant and fruity wines produced in Greece. Most are not distinguished, but they don't taste like Retsina. (Incidentally, Retsina is flavored with resin, a plant substance used in the manufacture of varnish.) But hey! Greek olives are an acquired taste, too!

Attica, the home of the Parthenon, is a leading wine-producing area in Greece—and where most of the Retsina is made. The Peloponnese, an area of Sparta, is the largest wine district, producing mostly sweet wines. Wine is made also on many of the Greek islands, including Crete, Samos, Santorini, Rhodes, and Corfu. Little of it is exported to the U.S., but if you're planning a trip to Greece, there's plenty of it waiting.

Fortified dessert wines are the second most important Greek wine type. First in prestige is the dark red Mavrodaphne, similar to California Port, although lower in alcohol.

Hungary— Blood of the Bull

Hungary continues to uphold a centuries-old tradition of turning out many good to fine wines. Many of its grape varieties are indigenous. Others, like the Sylvaner and the Walschriesling, have been adapted successfully to the area.

Hungarian wines are quite distinct in style, made to suit the tastes of the local populace. But unlike that of the Greeks, Hungarian taste is not so different from ours. The result is a variety of good wines, many of them reasonably priced and a good bargain. However, they may not be easy to find.

Tasting Tip

Some pleasant fruity Greek table wines, red and white, are exported to the U.S. They're very drinkable and relatively inexpensive. The largest producers are Achaia-Clauss and Andrew Cambas. Boutari is a name linked with quality.

The most important Hungarian wines are the whites. Some pleasant white wines come from the region of Transdanubia (across the Danube), near Lake Balaton. They're usually labeled "Badacsonyi," followed by a grape name, such as the widely planted Furmint.

Heard It Through the Grapevine

For the wines of Tokay, you'll see the word *aszu* (AH-soo) as the descriptor for "sweet." Tokay varies from slightly sweet to the richly concentrated celestial wine, Tokay Eszencia (Tokay essence), which is made from *Botrytis*-infected grapes in a manner similar to the German Trockenbeerenauslese. Rare and always expensive, Eszencia can be close to 50 percent sugar! Alcohol levels, though, often are very low. Over the centuries, it has been the preferred beverage of the European nobility and was once considered to have curative, therapeutic powers.

On a Tokay Eszencia wine label, you'll see the term *puttonyos*, which refers to the measure of sweetness as determined by the quantity of *Botrytis*-infected, overripe grapes that were added to the wine. Wines labeled "3 puttonyos" are moderately sweet; those labeled "5 puttonyos" are very sweet and concentrated.

The most distinguished wines are made from *Botrytis*-infected Furmint. These are the legendary whites from Tokay, in the Northern Massif region. Unsweet versions of Tokay, otherwise known as dry- to off-dry wines, are labeled "Tokay Szamorodni." They have a slightly nutty, slightly oxidized character.

Probably the best-known of Hungarian wines is the red Egri Bikaver, which literally means "Bull's Blood of Eger." The name comes from its deep color, so don't expect it to have some hemoglobular property. It's a dependable, full-bodied red wine with some potential for aging. Eger also makes a sweet-style Merlot, with the local name Médoc Noir, but it's seldom seen outside of the country.

In recent years, foreign wine companies have made major acquisitions in Hungary, introducing traditional European varieties. You can find Cabernet Sauvignon, Merlot, and Chardonnay wines from a number of fine producers.

The Least You Need to Know

➤ German wines range in quality from simple wines to some of the best in the world.

➤ German wine labels can tell you much, if you know what to look for.

➤ Good wines are made in Switzerland, but they are expensive.

➤ Good, inexpensive wines come from Austria, Greece, and Hungary.

Go West!

America doesn't share Europe's long tradition for wine. Wine, older than history, is relatively new in the Western Hemisphere. You could say the American wine industry dates from the nineteenth century, when European immigrants transplanted vines into the U.S., Chile, and Argentina. However, it wasn't until the 1970s, thanks to California, that the U.S. had a large enough commercial output to sit among the world's great wine producers.

Those pioneer wine growers arrived in the New World with their native grapes, their skills, and their respect for wine, but they left behind the rigid Old World laws that had regulated their craft.

Vintage Laissez-Faire

American vintners face fewer rules than those of other wine-producing countries. To be sure, the U.S. does have a system to let us know where the wine was grown. These are the *AVAs*, standard names (appellations) designating the American winegrowing regions. However, there are no rules regarding which varieties may be planted where and no limits on yields per acre.

Vino Vocab

AVA stands for **American Viticultural Area.** This is like the French word **appellation,** which means, simply, "name."

Tasting Tip

If the bottle says "California," you can be 100 percent sure that the grapes were California-grown. (Other states require only 75-percent content.)

The Sommelier Says

"Estate bottled" and "Grown, produced, and bottled by" sound pretty impressive. However, these terms can be applied to some of the least distinguished and interesting wines. So these terms are no assurance of quality.

American wines displaying a varietal name must be made at least 75 percent from the juice of that grape. But some of these varieties offer quantity for the producer rather than quality for us consumers.

An AVA on the label means at least 85 percent of the grapes came from the specified place. That doesn't tell us much, because some AVAs may include areas that produce only mediocre grapes along with some that yield the very finest.

Some other words on the label have standard meanings. The terms "Grown, produced, and bottled by" and "Estate bottled" mean the producer owned or controlled all the grapes that went into that wine. If you see "Produced and bottled by," that means the vintner actually made and bottled at least 75 percent. Now watch out! The phrase "Made and bottled by" means the winery may have produced as little as 10 percent of that wine. (Pretty tricky, huh?)

Vintage date, when listed on the label, is pretty reliable. At least 95 percent of that wine must have been grown and fermented that year. But watch out! There are no rules whatsoever for the use of such nice-sounding embellishments as "reserve," "special reserve," or "vintner's reserve." Producers often add such promising descriptions to their mediocre, large-volume production as a marketing gimmick, while their superior wines are shipped with no extra words on their labels. Other wine-producing countries are quite strict about the meaning of every word, but as you can see, such regulation in the U.S. is quite spare.

For us wine consumers, I suppose, that's both good news and bad. On the plus side, we buyers of American wines face an amazing selection from among thousands of producers. On the minus, the label can't tell us much about the quality of what's inside.

Sure, there's a varietal name on the label, and the bottle has a cork instead of a screw top. But that's no real help. Both a region's very best wines and its very worst actually may show the same information on their labels. So when you buy American, you simply have to know your producer!

A California Odyssey

In France, each winegrowing region specializes in wines made from only one or two grape varieties. But in California, most AVAs produce wines from most grapes. In the following California appellations, you will learn which varieties to seek in which AVAs.

California, Here I Come!

This is one giant category! The grapes may have been grown anywhere at all in the Golden State. (You can be sure the contents are 100 percent California grown, though.) Wines falling under this broad appellation range from ordinary everyday to simple-premium in quality.

Tasting Tip

Just as you would expect, some varietals excel in certain areas but flop in others. Many of the failures represent some grower's unsuccessful experiment. You shouldn't have to pay for these! Learn to associate AVAs with those grapes that do best in them.

Appellation North Coast

You can be sure the wines designated "North Coast" are from one of the better winegrowing regions of the state. These range in quality from everyday to mid-premium. This popular AVA includes wines from

> ➤ Napa Valley
> ➤ Sonoma Valley
> ➤ Mendocino County
> ➤ Lake County

Operator, Get Me Central!

Welcome to Central Valley, jug-wine country! This hot, fertile, sunny valley, about 100 miles long, features those so-so but high-yielding grapes that feed California's bulk-wine pipeline. But don't reject the Central Valley out of hand! Some producers, Robert Mondavi, for instance, now grow some better varietals in the Lodi area to sell in magnums at low prices.

California's Best

Now let's zoom in closer and explore those particular California AVAs that give us the best (or most interesting) wines.

The best-known wine regions of California.

Growers Don't Nap in Napa

Ask anybody to name a California winegrowing region, and chances are good the response will be "Napa Valley." But for all its fame, this modest region accounts for not quite 5 percent of California's production. Some say this is California's "Bordeaux Region." Maybe not. Some pretty mediocre wines have been bottled here, along with some of the finest.

The Napa Valley lies just northeast of cosmopolitan San Francisco. In this small growing region, more than 200 wineries compete for precious acreage. Its picturesque character makes this region a popular tourist destination.

The small Napa region contains eight AVAs, plus the Carneros AVA, which is shared by Napa and Sonoma:

➤ Spring Mountain and Mount Veeder, in the western mountains

➤ Howell Mountain, Stags Leap District, Atlas Peak (which are all hilly or mountainous); and Wild Horse Valley—all in the eastern portion of Napa

➤ Rutherford and Oakville—on the Valley floor

Heard It Through the Grapevine

Higher is better—elevation, that is. Napa wines from Montain vineyards—on the slopes of the Mayacamas Mountains to the west or the Howell Mountains to the east—generally are superior to those from the Valley floor.

Let's begin with the white wines and the varietal most closely associated with Napa, the Chardonnay. The very finest of these have a ripe aroma and flavor, frequently spicy, offering a mélange of apricot, pineapple, and citrus. The texture is rich and the alcohol high—13 percent or more—giving these fine wines a certain headiness when young.

Some of these may be fermented in oaken barrels, in the true Burgundian fashion, or even in small, French oak casks. This endows these vintages with a slight oaky bitterness and a vanilla character that goes well with its varietal personality. Mid-premium Chardonnays may be made from less-ripe grapes or have spent less time aging. They are fruity, appley, but less complex.

The Sauvignon Blanc (also called Fume Blanc) is Napa's second most famous varietal. The very best of these resemble their French namesakes, but rarely can they rival the finest from the Graves or the Médoc. (Then again, Sauvignon Blancs from other French regions can't, either.)

The Sommelier Says

A "Napa Valley" appellation alone cannot guarantee greatness. Napa Valley wines range from mediocre to sublime. So there's no substitute for doing your homework. You need to know your growers and what they produce.

These distinguished Sauvignons range from subtle, light, and moderately oaked to powerful, warm, and heavily oaked. It all depends on the winery. In general, the Napa style lies in the direction of full ripeness, counterbalanced by assertive oak flavors. Don't worry about age. Though capable of good bottle-aging, they're fine when they're young.

The Napa Valley is not well known for its Rieslings (usually labeled "Johannisberg Reisling"). Few of Napa's drier Rieslings can match the charm of the authentic Rhines and Mosels from Germany. But they easily equal those from elsewhere.

When we come to the late-harvests, Napa's Rieslings can stand up against Germany's very best. These Napa grapes, along with some from Sonoma and Monterey Counties, can develop the "noble rot" (refer to Chapter 17, "From the Rhine to Aegean") that allows the production of late-harvest wines in the true German tradition.

Heard It Through the Grapevine

There are no direct U.S. equivalents to the German mit Prädikat designations, so just look for the term "Late Harvest" on the label. These rare wines can achieve super-premium or even noble status. With them, you enjoy the characteristic Riesling floral together with the **Botrytis** complexity—honeyed aroma, hint of almonds, with acid balance to the innate sweetness.

Now let's sample Napa's red wines, beginning with that region's Cabernet Sauvignon. When Napa producers go for it, this wine can rank among California's very best. Well-made Napa Cabernets present a berryish, herbal aroma. They are full of body, with ample tannins and some warmth. The super-premiums have a riper character that's reminiscent of cassis, dried sage, and black currants. These wines often develop a cedary "cigar-box" characteristic with bottle-aging. The very best of these can be set aside a decade or more.

You must have noticed how Merlot has become very popular. It's easy to see why. Its tannins are less harsh, less astringent than Cabernet's, and Napa is on top when it comes to excellent Merlots! The best are very ripe and herbaceous in aroma and flavor. In character, they are round, soft, and voluptuous. With some, you may notice a finish that's slightly sweet.

The Zinfandel grape thrives in Napa Valley when grown on hillside sites and allowed to develop high sugar levels. It does less well on the valley floor. Superpremium Zinfandels come from hillsides or from very old vineyards. Zinfandel reigns in the Calistoga region, the area's warmest subregion.

Tasting Tip

Napa Valley Cabernet Sauvignons made from grapes grown north of Yountville generally fall in the mid- to super-premium range. A select few from vineyards in Rutherford, Oakville, or the Stags Leap District can achieve noble status.

Most Napa Valley Zinfandels are berry-like and medium-bodied, with moderate tannins and a tart finish. That's red Zinfandel we're talking about! The blush wine, called White Zinfandel, recently has soared in popularity. But it's quite different—a light, sweet, and fruity wine good for summer and more leisurely drinking.

Heard It Through the Grapevine

Bordeaux-style blended wines are showing up now in greater numbers. The reds usually are made from the red Bordeaux varieties (Cabernet Sauvignon, Cabernet Franc, Merlot, and sometimes Malbec and Petit Verdot). The whites usually are made from the white Bordeaux grapes (Sauvignon Blanc and Semillon). Some of these blends are known by the name Meritage, although rarely does this name appear on the label.

Some Place, Sonoma!

The Sonoma winegrowing region is not the picturesque tourist trap Napa is, but it's home to some of California's most successful wineries. This region is much larger than Napa. Its climate is similar, except along the cooler coast. The grape varieties grown here are mostly the same as in Napa, but the style and character of the finished product often are quite distinct.

These are the designated AVAs of Sonoma:

➤ Sonoma Valley

➤ Sonoma Mountain

➤ Dry Creek Valley

➤ Alexander Valley

➤ Russian River Valley

➤ Sonoma-Green Valley—contained within Russian River Valley

➤ Chalk Hill—contained within Russian River Valley

➤ Knights Valley

To make things just a bit confusing, Sonoma County contains parts of two other AVAs: Northern Sonoma, encompassing Russian River Valley, Alexander Valley, Dry Creek Valley, and Knight's Valley; and Sonoma Coast, which includes land situated along the coast in western Sonoma.

Tasting Tip

Sonoma Chardonnays tend to be fruitier and leaner than Napa's, and long bottle aging improves them.

Sonoma offers mid- and super-premium Chardonnays. The Dry Creek and Alexander Valley districts feature a fruity varietal aroma with a lemony flavor; they have a medium-bodied, slightly viscous texture. Only the Dry Creek district is noted for its Sauvignon Blancs.

Sonoma is the home of many mid-premium Cabernet Sauvignons. Most are vinous and straightforward, medium-bodied, moderately tannic, and early maturing with a slightly weedy, peppery character. These traits are especially evident in wines from Dry Creek, Alexander Valley, and the Sonoma Valley.

Super-premium Zinfandels come from a number of hillside vineyards in Dry Creek and Alexander Valley. Alexander Valley Zinfandels range from mid- to super-premium and offer a distinct, ripe cherry, blackberry character, along with richness and depth.

Heard It Through the Grapevine

Not many California wineries can manage the finicky Pinot Noir grape as well as some do in Sonoma, particularly in the Russian River Valley. In these wines, you will discover the characteristic Pinot Noir fruitiness; a slightly cherry, smoky character; medium body; and slight tannins. Successful California Pinot Noirs are the result of continuing experimentation.

Wines Flow at Dry Creek

The Sonoma appellation "Dry Creek Valley" gets its own listing. Dry Creek is celebrated for its Chardonnays, Sauvignon Blancs, Cabernet Sauvignons, and Zinfandels. In fact, Dry Creek Valley is Zinfandel heaven! These grapes are noted for richness and depth. The best of the Dry Creek red Zinfandels have an earthy, peppery character that distinguishes them from others.

Carry on, Carneros!

Carneros is the single most important winegrowing district in California. It runs from the southern part of Napa Valley into Sonoma County. Temperatures there are moderated by cooling breezes from the Pacific and the mists that roll in from San Pablo Bay. So look here for cool-climate grapes, such as Chardonnay, Pinot Noir, and several white varieties that make high-quality sparkling wines.

As in Sonoma, many winemakers in Carneros have tamed the Pinot Noir grape, creating a few mid- to super-premium wines. The Pinots typically are deep-colored, with herbal, cherryish, and slightly roasted aromas and flavors with a velvety texture, some depth, and a long finish.

Leaping Cabernet!

Two words sum up the Stags Leap District in Napa: Cabernet Sauvignons! This is where you will find the most exceptional examples of this renowned grape.

Goin' to Monterey

This scenic coastal area is a haven for writers and artists in Carmel, the little town at the end of the Monterey Peninsula. And it's home to many superb vineyards and wineries. Monterey has two centers: the Salinas Valley near Soledad and King City in the southern portion. The northern half is dry, cool, and windy—ideal for growing white grapes.

Monterey is a microcosm of contemporary California viticulture: modern science in service to winegrowing. Through careful experimentation, growers and winemakers here have eliminated many faults that beset their product in the 1970s. For instance, Monterey Cabernet Sauvignon has managed to shed its vegetable-garden image as innovative winemakers have learned to cope with their unusual regional trait, and even use it to their advantage. Today these Cabernets have an herbal, spicy flavor; a moderate, peppery overtone; and good varietal character.

Monterey is a great place for Sauvignon Blanc. At mid-premium quality status, it yields a characteristic grassy, weedy, or black pepper flavor.

The Sommelier Says

If you had sampled some of Monterey's Cabernet Sauvignon in the 1970s, you might have complained it tasted like uncooked asparagus and smelled like bell peppers. (And it did!) But no longer, as Monterey growers have learned how to create great wines.

Heard It Through the Grapevine

Monterey vintners have applied the techniques of Burgundy winemaking to coax their Chardonnays to their full potential. These Chardonnays tend to have more varietal character in aroma and flavor than those from further north, with an accent on fresh, varietal fruitiness. Many display a unique, green, or grassy character; a medium body; and a sharp, crisp finish.

Tasting Tip

Gewürztraminer is an important varietal in Monterey. These wines are characteristically spicy in fragrance and fruity in flavor. Some retain a slight degree of Muscat character, which adds complexity. The best are well structured for bottle aging.

Monterey offers some dry-styled or slightly sweet Rieslings. Flowery yet firm, they're similar to the German Kabinett harvest. These "soft Rieslings" can be opulently fruity and flowery; they're low in alcohol and meant for simple sipping.

Mendocino Vino

The name "Mendocino" has a lyrical ring, evocative of the quaint, picturesque town itself. This AVA lies due north of Sonoma and has two main subdivisions. Ukiah is a large area with a prolific growth of vineyards; Anderson Valley, the smaller of the two, has a cool climate and the highest level of rainfall of all California's winegrowing regions.

All the popular varietals thrive here. Initially best known for Zinfandel and Cabernet Sauvignon, they've been joined by Chardonnay, Riesling, Sauvignon Blanc, Gewürztraminer, Pinot Noir, and grapes for sparkling wines. Parducci was the first winery to operate in the area; today it shares its renown with Fetzer.

The Anderson Valley recently has made a name for itself in the sparkling-wine industry, featuring such operations as Roederer Champagne, Scharffenberger, and Handley.

Mendocino Chardonnays usually are lemony and crisp, characterized by a firm, lean style. They don't pretend to be anything more than enjoyable beverages, and their quality is consistent. Mendocino-style Sauvignon Blanc is early-maturing; soft and light-bodied, its grassy, black pepper varietal flavor is somewhat muted. The Rieslings are slightly sweet, like the German Kabinett, with low acidity.

There's a lot of Zinfandel grown here, and the range is extensive. They are berry-like, medium-bodied, with moderate tannins and a tart finish. The regional Pinot Noirs offer varietal fruitiness; a slightly cherry, smoky character; medium body; and slight tannins.

Heard It Through the Grapevine

Mendocino-grown Zinfandels vary from simple and berry-like to riper and excessively tannic, depending on climate. They often have an appealing ripe fruit aroma, redolent of berries and herbs, but more astringent and tannic. In the mid-premium category and above, they have a fresh violet and plum-like character, with moderate (less than 13 percent) alcohol content.

Another Great Lake

Lake County, to the north of Napa, recently has gained in popularity. It's primarily planted in the red wine grapes of Cabernet Sauvignon and Zinfandel. The regional versions of these varietals tend to be light-bodied but with straightforward flavor. A few strongly varietal Sauvignon Blancs are made from Lake County grapes.

Meet Me in San Luis!

San Luis Obispo is another area that continues to gain in importance. Its main subdistricts are the warm and hilly Paso Robles (featuring Zinfandel, Cabernet Sauvignon, and Pinot Noir) and the cool and breezy Arroyo Grande and Edna Valley (planted in Chardonnay and Pinot Noir). Its Cabernets and Chardonnays are similar in style to those from Santa Barbara (see Magnificent Santa Barbara later in this chapter).

Adorable Amador County

Amador is located in the Sierra foothills where weary prospectors once panned for gold. Few of them found any, but the winegrowers who discovered the native Zinfandel did much better. Zinfandel grapes reach full ripeness in this region. They're generally warm, fruity, and very tannic.

The foothills are located southwest of Sacramento, where Amador shares some of its winemaking fame with El Dorado County. The most prominent grape-growing areas are Shenandoah Valley and Fiddletown in Amador. Vineyards in hot, dry El Dorado are planted at high altitude to counteract the summer heat.

Tasting Tip

Amador County grows and bottles small amounts of Cabernet Sauvignon, Sauvignon Blanc, and Riesling, but its Zinfandel is tops.

Cruisin' in Santa Cruz

Santa Cruz is a beautiful, mountainous area that runs from San Francisco south to the town of Santa Cruz. A decade ago there were only a dozen small wineries here, but the numbers have grown, some now the very best in California. This is a cool growing region, with sea breezes on both sides of this partial peninsula. Pinot Noir grows happily on the Pacific side, while Cabernet Sauvignon prefers the San Francisco Bay area on the other side of the Santa Cruz mountains. Chardonnay likes them both.

The appellation "Santa Cruz" appears on many big-styled ripe Chardonnays and Pinot Noirs.

Magnificent Santa Barbara

Some of California's very first vineyards were planted by Spanish missionaries in Santa Barbara County. This area of beautiful rolling hills earned its place on our map in 1975, when pioneering Firestone Vineyards began producing its famous Pinot Noirs, Rieslings, and Chardonnays.

Initially, most of the region's wines used the "Santa Ynez Valley" appellation, but the Santa Maria and Los Alamos Valleys are now gaining notice.

Heard It Through the Grapevine

Santa Barbara Chardonnays mature early, and they are similar in style to their cousins from San Luis Obispo. They have a unique grassiness and, depending on sugar development, they range from very firm and hard in style to rounder and softer (although few have the rich texture that earmarks Napa Chardonnays). They have excellent acidity and a slight silky texture.

Some Sauvignon Blanc is produced in Santa Ynez. Though it tends to have an aggressive, pronounced aroma of grassiness, black pepper, and fruit that needs to be tamed and rounded by cask aging, bottle aging, or blending with a small percentage of Semillon. (Remember that in California, wines are often blended with grapes from other regions.)

Santa Barbara Cabernets also share some traits with the San Luis Obispo version. Both have moderate, Bordeaux-like alcohol levels (less than 13 percent) and a rich, herbal, berrylike aroma and flavor made complex by a weedy overtone. In some cases, we notice an oakiness from long aging in small casks. These tend to have a short finish compared to the regal, lingering aftertaste found in the Cabernets of Napa and the middle Médoc of Bordeaux.

A good part of Santa Barbara's growing wine reputation is founded on the affinity of the Pinot Noir grape for its soil and ocean air. The Pinots often are deep-colored, with herbal, cherryish, and slightly roasted aromas and flavors; a velvety texture; some depth; and a long finish.

California's Best Wine Deals

It's easy to shop smart among California wines. The very best values lie in that state's everyday and simple- to mid-premium wines. California vintners turn these out in great quantities, and you benefit from the savings. On the other hand, California's best are not priced competitively with their counterparts from Bordeaux, Burgundy, Italy, and elsewhere.

The Sommelier Says

Collectors find value beyond what's intrinsic to that which they collect. Wine collectors know that some small-production bottlings, in a few years' time, will bring ridiculous prices at wine auctions. If you're a collector, go for it! But if you buy fine wines only for their drinking pleasure, better look elsewhere.

Heard It Through the Grapevine

Don't be in a hurry to remove that cork! While many California wines are meant to be consumed when bottled, the super-premium and noble-quality wines benefit from bottle aging. Chardonnays benefit from two to four years' bottle-aging. Red varieties, like Cabernet Sauvignon, Merlot and the better Zinfandels, can benefit from five to ten years' aging. (Sometimes even more.)

Don't Forget the Pacific Northwest!

Guess what! California isn't the only source of fine wines from the West Coast! Just to the north in Oregon and Washington, there's a thriving wine industry. The Cascade Mountains cut through both states and give rise to their distinctive climates.

Washington Never Slept Here

Growers in Washington State began growing vinifera varieties in the 1960s, although few commercial wineries existed until two decades later. Most of these are situated in the East, where the climate is agreeably dry.

The winegrowing regions of Washington follow:

➤ The **Yakima Valley** in the Southeast has cool summer weather and a long growing season. It's not the biggest region, but it has more wineries (22) than the larger Columbia Valley.

➤ **Columbia Valley** has the most sizable grape-growing terrain, supporting 11 wineries. Puget Sound wineries often use grapes from this region.

➤ The **Walla Walla Valley** accounts for less than 1 percent of the state's viticultural output, from only six wineries.

Choice Washington State Offerings

Gewürztraminer and Johannisberg Riesling do well here, with excellent varietal character and with a less-sweet style than their California cousins. Riesling grapes thrive in the few vineyards located west of the Cascades, in the Puget Sound area.

Washington State Sauvignon Blancs are noted for their powerful character. The ubiquitous Chardonnay is widely grown, although its quality can be inconsistent. Chenin Blanc, Cabernet Sauvignon, and Merlot round out Washington's more common varietals. Washington's Columbia Crest Merlot currently is the biggest selling Merlot in the U.S.

Busy in the Beaver State

Oregon's main winegrowing region is the Willamette Valley, followed by the Umpqua Valley and the Rogue River Valley.

Are We in Willamette Yet?

The Willamette AVA is a sizable area south of the city of Portland. Its summers are quite cool, with plentiful rainfall during the harvest. Pinot Noir favors a cool climate, and Oregon winemakers have made their name on this most finicky of grapes.

In Willamette's winery-rich Yamhill County, all of the wineries produce Pinot Noir. Oregon Pinot Noirs first received acclaim in the early 1980s, and their reputation has soared since. Recently, Pinot Noir has been joined in Oregon by that other Pinot, Pinot Gris.

What We Saw in (Umpqua)

The Umqua Valley is warmer than Willamette, though still rather cool. This AVA is the home of Oregon's pioneering winery, Hillcrest Vineyards. Pinot Noir thrives in Umpqua, along with Riesling, Chardonnay, and Cabernet Sauvignon.

Remember the Rogue River Valley

The Rogue River Valley is a relative newcomer. It's the warmest of the Oregon growing regions, ideal for Cabernet Sauvignon and Merlot and, of course, Chardonnay, which really took well the advice of "Go West!" The Pinot Gris now is finding a happy home there, too.

Tasting Tip

Historically, Rieslings have been Oregon's second most important varietal after the Pinot Noir. Hillcrest, which began Oregon's wine industry in 1962, is noted for its fine Rieslings.

The Empire State's Wine Empire

To most people, New York State is the home of the Yankees, the Adirondacks, and Niagara Falls (the American side, at least). But not many people outside the Empire State realize that New York is second only to California in wine production.

The western states are relative newcomers to the wine industry, but they dug right in with Vitis vinifera, experimenting and cloning, and figuring out how to overcome their regional peculiarities. By contrast, New York's wine staple has always been Vitis lambrusca, which is great for jams, jellies, and unfermented beverages, but not so great for fine wines.

It wasn't until the 1950s that the first vinifera grapes were cultivated in New York, in the Finger Lakes region, by the Russian Dr. Konstantin Frank. In 1961, the first of these wines emerged from his winery, called (guess what?) Dr. Frank's Vinifera Wine Cellars. So in 1961, New York was already ahead of California, but it couldn't have held that lead.

The reason? Climate. Harsher growing conditions mean more labor, and more labor means higher costs. There are no warm Pacific zephyrs blowing across New York! So, except for some low-priced champagnes, Empire State wines cannot compete successfully with those from the Golden State.

Heard It Through the Grapevine

America's oldest winery, the Brotherhood Winery in New York's Hudson Valley, was founded in 1839. And the second oldest? That would be the Canandaigua Wine Company in the Finger Lakes region of New York, which also is the country's second largest.

Linger at the Finger Lakes

The cold climate of the Finger Lakes district in western New York is tempered somewhat by these four large bodies of water. About 85 percent of the state's wines come from this district, although not all are vinifera. Riesling and Chardonnay are the two most successful varietals. During the 1980s, wineries like Glenora and Hermann J. Weimer began paving the way toward high-quality vinifera wines.

Not Just the Hamptons!

The Northern Fork AVA, near the end of Long Island, shows great promise with several vinifera grapes, notably Riesling, Pinot Noir, and Cabernet Sauvignon. Recently, Merlot and Sauvignon Blanc have thrived there. Long Island's second AVA consists of the Hamptons on the Southern Fork. But that area is far more celebrated for its luxurious summer homes than for its wines. Wines from these regions tend to be purchased by the Smart Set who summer in the Hamptons.

Rip Van Winkle Did Sleep Here

The Hudson River Valley, a mere 40 miles north of Manhattan, is home to Benmarl, Clinton, and several other wineries, including the historic Brotherhood, which caters to the region's many tourists. They have shown good progress with the better French hybrids, and they succeed occasionally with these vinifera grapes. This region also grows lambrusca varieties, which may be sold to wineries in the Finger Lakes district.

The Least You Need to Know

➤ The U.S. has few regulations governing what's on the label. It helps to know your American winegrowing regions.

➤ California produces many varietal wines from many areas. You need to know the producers to know which are good and which are not.

➤ California's very best wines are not that state's very best buys.

➤ Oregon and Washington produce some very fine wines.

➤ New York State has a large wine industry and some very good wines, but the best may be hard to find outside their locality.

O Canada!

Canadian wine? Why not! North of the U.S. border, summer days are longer (though at the expense of longer winter nights). And in a few special regions, soil and climate conspire to produce wines of the highest quality, some unique in the world.

Canada has had commercial vineyards for more than a hundred years, but the Canadian wine industry we're going to explore has existed for little more than 10 years. The 1980s were a big decade for Canadians. In 1982, there was the Canada Act, under which Canada obtained complete national sovereignty. And in 1988, there was the U.S.-Canada Free Trade Act, which stimulated the rebirth of Canadian wine. In this chapter we'll look at that remarkable renaissance, and we'll visit Canada's wine regions, both east and west.

Canadian Wine? Yes!

Historically, Canadian wineries used native American grapes, *Vitis lambrusca*, rather than the European *Vitis vinifera*. The lambrusca varieties make wonderful jams and jellies—grape juices, too, but fine wine grapes these are not!

Heard It Through the Grapevine

In 1853, horticulturist Ephraim Bull exhibited a new variety of the native American grape species, *Vitis lambrusca,* at the Massachusetts Horticulture Society. This was the first Concord grape. Within 10 years, this grape was planted throughout eastern North America.

In 1869, a dentist in Vineland, New Jersey, Thomas Welch, began manufacturing a pasteurized grape juice from the Concord grape he grew in his back yard as a substitute for the alcoholic wines used in his church's communion service.

(Canada is recovering only now from the stigma of the commercially successful Concord and other lambrusca varieties.)

Yes, the 1980s were a time a change. The world became more aware of fine wines, but these did not include wines from Canada. The Canadian wine industry was quite aware of this situation. And these growers, vintners, and shippers decided to do something about it.

VQA You Can Trust

Canada's biggest handicap to entry into the market of fine wines was that it had cultivated the wrong grape species, *Vitis lambrusca,* instead of the traditional European *Vitis vinifera.* But would they be willing to uproot (in some cases) 100 years' worth of growing tradition and start over? Yes. But with a little help from Ottawa.

In 1988, Canada signed a Free Trade Agreement with the U.S. That meant no more price protection for wines from the inferior lambrusca grape. Now they would have to face competition from wines of higher quality, fairly priced.

The Canadian government began a five-year program to subsidize those lambrusca growers who decided to plant something else. In Ontario, this meant other grapes, the best-known vinifera. In British Columbia, it meant, mostly, replacing lambrusca with other crops. However, in that province, about a third of the original vineyard acreage was kept in grapes but switched to the better European varietals.

New grapes meant new winemaking technologies—and heavy capital investment. Canadian vintners proved their dedication to the new opportunities the new grapes provided. These savvy business folk had planned their rebirth very carefully. In 1989, the Ontario growers organized the *Vintners Quality Alliance* (VQA), under which they would show the world they could make fine wines.

The VQA provided regulations to cover everything from the grape to the glass. The regulations went into effect nationwide in 1990. In 1998, the VQA introduced a new labeling system, one that the world has quickly come to recognize.

The VQA name and symbol on a Canadian wine label is your assurance that

➤ The wine is made from 100-percent Canadian-grown grapes.

➤ The wine has been made to VQA standards set by the provinces of Ontario or British Columbia.

➤ The wine has been sampled by a provincial panel of tasters. (But, as elsewhere, the tasting panel might have had flawed palates or just a bad day.)

Vino Vocab

When you see the words **Vintners Quality Alliance** (or the letters **VQA**), think of the French AOC or the German QmP. This is Canada's strict code for wine production and a reliable mark of quality.

The new Canadian wine labels are very easy to read. As Joe Friday, the police detective in the 1950s TV show *Dragnet* used to say, "Just the facts, ma'am."

In addition to bottle size, alcohol content, and vintage (where applicable), the new Canadian labels show

➤ The producer's name (though sometimes in code).

➤ The producing region.

➤ Where the wine was bottled.

➤ Quality level.

Tasting Tip

In the world of wine, the VQA is the newest national wine-rating system. It's also one of the simplest and most reliable.

I'll discuss that last, quality level, as we look at Canada's two wine-producing provinces.

Big Province, Big Wine!

Ontario is a very large province of about 400,000 square miles. However, its three *Designated Viticultural Areas* (DVAs) are found on that tiny bit of the south that nestles along Lakes Erie and Ontario. These lie at the same latitude as the southern wine districts of France, the northern winegrowing regions of Italy and Spain, and the West Coast region of the U.S. between the Mendocino Valley of California and the winegrowing regions of Washington State.

Compared with France's wine regions, Ontario wine country experiences hotter summers and colder winters. This allows Ontario (and also British Columbia) to produce ice wines (see the section on German wine laws in Chapter 17, "From the Rhine to the Aegean") on a consistent basis. Soils in this glacier-scraped region range from sandy loams to gravel to sand and clay.

Heard It Through the Grapevine

More than 200 years ago, in the German duchy of Franconia, ice wine (Eiswein) was discovered quite by accident when winemakers tried to rescue their crop by pressing grapes that had frozen on the vine. Germany has produced it ever since, but only in small batches, because conditions that allow it are rare.

Not so in Canada's winegrowing provinces! Long days of hot summer sunshine allow grapes to develop high sugar and complexity. But the days shorten drastically in the fall, and temperatures fall readily into the 8 to 21 degree Fahrenheit range required for a good ice wine harvest. Ontario and British Columbia now lead the world in the production of this rare and wonderful dessert wine.

Ontario accounts for 80 percent of Canada's wine production, with 38 wineries producing to VQA standards. Many vintners of this cosmopolitan province were trained in France, Italy, Germany, Austria, and the United States. Growers plant most of the leading European varietals, including Chardonnay, Pinot Blanc, Riesling, Gewürztraminer, Pinot Noir, Gamay, Cabernet Sauvignon, and Merlot.

In Ontario, the VQA recognizes two levels of quality. (Both are superior.) The first is the *Provincial Designation*. To use the term *Ontario* on the label, the wines must meet four requirements:

➤ Wines must be made from approved grapes—classic European varietals and hybrids.

➤ If labeled as a varietal, the wine must be made from no less than 85 percent of that grape.

➤ Whether varietal or blend, all grapes must have been grown in Ontario.

➤ All varieties must meet stipulated minimum sugar levels.

The higher VQA level is the Geographic Designation. Ontario has three *Designated Viticultural Areas* (DVAs), which we will discuss later in some detail.

In addition to the standards for the Provincial Designation, these wines meet certain additional requirements:

➤ Only classic European varieties are allowed.

➤ If the vintner wishes to designate a vineyard, it must be in a DVA, and all the grapes must come from that vineyard.

➤ Wines labeled "estate bottled" must be made entirely from grapes from one DVA that are owned or controlled by the winery.

➤ Minimum sugar levels are set for vineyard-designated wines, estate-bottled wines, dessert wines, and ice wines.

Tasting Tip

The Ontario *Vintners Quality Alliance* (VQA) sets standards and checks all VQA candidates for compliance with these standards for production and labeling. Additionally, the VQA issues vintage reports for each *Designated Viticultural Area* (DVA). Wine consumers benefit greatly from this information.

All VQA wines are evaluated and sampled by a panel of wine experts before they may display the VQA symbol. But the panel may not always be up to par or may look the other way. The quality of these wines varies from superb to not so good. As with other wine regions, you must get to know the producers or rely on wine critics to avoid mediocre wines.

Now let's take a look at Ontario's three DVAs.

The Niagara Peninsula

This Designated Viticultural Area lies between the southwestern shore of Lake Ontario and the Niagara Escarpment. The latter is the amazing geological feature responsible for Niagara Falls. It's a wall of granite, 100 to 150 feet high, that runs west-to-east between Lake Erie and Lake Ontario.

The most interesting aspect of the Niagara Peninsula is the microclimate interplay between Lake Ontario and the Escarpment. In the fall, the lake still holds summer heat. Warm air rises from the lake and moves inland, but when it hits the Escarpment, it falls and returns to the lake for further warming. This unique circulation allows an extended season for the development of sugars in these grapes.

Heard It Through the Grapevine

When the Ice Age glacier receded, it left behind minerals and trace elements from many rocky strata, which have become part of the soil. These contribute to the development of complexity in the flavors of the area's wines.

Lake Erie North Shore

This area lies along Lake Erie's northwestern shore. The vineyard slope cultivation enjoys a southern exposure and the moderating effect of the lake on temperatures. Lake Erie is the shallowest of the Great Lakes, so its surface temperature tends to be the warmest.

Pelee Island

Pelee Island, situated in Lake Erie about 15 miles south of the mainland, is Canada's southernmost point. Because of both latitude and the warming effect of the lake, this DVA enjoys a growing season 30 days longer than on the mainland.

Tasting Tip

Ontario's Lake Erie North Shore climate is very similar to that of France's Bordeaux region. So it's not surprising that some of Ontario's finest wines come from this DVA.

Heard It Through the Grapevine

Pelee Island is the site of Canada's first commercial winery, the Vin Villa, which opened in 1866. Of course, through most its history, this winery had used the native lambrusca grapes. But in 1980, all of Pelee Island was replanted in the European vinifera.

The soil here is similar to that of the mainland—glacial deposits of sand, loam, and clay over limestone bedrock.

North America's Other West Coast

The mountainous far-west province of British Columbia (B.C.) has its own Vintners Quality Alliance. This was established through a law of 1990. Under this law, the British Columbia Wine Institute establishes regulatory controls for growing, production, and naming. Following are some highlights:

➤ The designation "Product of British Columbia" means all the grapes were grown in that province.

➤ Wines bearing a viticultural name contain a minimum of 85 percent grapes grown in that area.

➤ Wines designating a grape variety must be made at least 85 percent from the juice of that grape.

➤ A vintage date on the label guarantees no less than 85 percent of the wine came from that harvest.

➤ Wines labeled "estate bottled" must be produced entirely from grapes grown in a vineyard owned by the winery, with all steps—from crushing to bottling—done at that winery.

There are 53 VQA wineries in B.C. The very first vineyards were planted in the 1860s at a mission located in the Okanagan Valley. The first commercial winery dates from 1932, in the same locale.

Most of B.C.'s wine industry lies in lowland areas guarded by coastal mountains to the west and the Rockies to the east. This makes for summers that are surprisingly sunny, hot, and dry. Such conditions allow good development of sugar and flavors.

The leading varieties cultivated by B.C.'s best wineries are Chardonnay, Pinot Blanc, Pinot Noir, Merlot, Riesling, and Gewürztraminer.

British Columbia has four Designated Viticultural Areas: Okanagan Valley, Similkameen Valley, Fraser Valley, and Vancouver Island.

The Sommelier Says

Many thought the Free Trade Act of 1988 would put an end to British Columbia's wine industry. In that year, acreage in wine-grape production crashed—from 2,500 to only 800. Now, with vineyard renewal in vinifera and superior quality control through the VQA, B.C. has increased its wine cultivation to where it's planting more acres than ever before.

Okanagan Can!

The Okanagan Valley is B.C.'s oldest wine-producing region. This area features more than 30 wineries that produce from premium grape varieties.

The south end of the valley has an annual rainfall of less than 6 inches, making it the only part of Canada classified as desert. Growers must use some irrigation as they plant this part of the valley in classic red viniferas.

Heard It Through the Grapevine

Colona Wines has operated in British Columbia continuously since 1932, western Canada's oldest commercial winery. It is situated in the northern part of the Okanagan Valley, near the town of Kelowna.

The northern end of this long north-south valley offers a cooler and wetter climate. This favors the French and German white varietals that are planted here.

Assimilating Similkameen

Through the mountains, just west of the southern part of the Okanagan Valley, lies the high-desert cattle range that's the Similkameen Valley winegrowing area. The small plots are planted along the banks of the Similkameen River, with some irrigation.

Here the summer days are long and the rainfall sparse. The microclimate of the area and its soils, mostly gravel and clay, provide superb conditions to grow both red and white grapes—Merlot, Pinot Noir, Chardonnay, and Vidal.

Fraser's Praises

In the southwestern corner of British Columbia, a short drive up the Fraser River from Vancouver, you will find a few small vineyards that enjoy a climate somewhat different from that of the interior.

Here along the coast, hot, dry summers are followed by warm, rainy winters. Growers here need to irrigate their plots of award-winning Chardonnay, Pinot Blanc, Riesling, and other white varietals.

Vancouver Island

Lying just off the southwestern coast of B.C., Vancouver Island is the province's newest winegrowing region. Most of these few acres of grapes are located near the town of Duncan.

Here you will find Pinot Gris, Pinot Noir, Muscat, and Müller-Thurgau. Look for some of their late-harvest *Botrytis*-infected bottlings.

Awards? Yes!

It's reasonable to say that the Canadian wine industry began only in 1989 (Ontario) and 1990 (British Columbia), as wines from these provinces came under the VQA insignia of quality.

Canadian vintners have entered their wines in international competition—in Europe, Asia, and the Americas. And in less than a decade, they have scored hundreds of medals, including many golds. Canadian wines occupy a secure position among the fine wines from France, Italy, Germany, and the U.S.

Let's Visit Canadian Wineries

Though its wine industry is new, Canada's appeal to tourism is quite old, particularly in the country's two wine provinces, Ontario and British Columbia.

If you plan a trip to Niagara Falls or to Toronto, you're quite close to Ontario's viticultural areas. All you need to do is get a list of VQA wineries. Then call a few up! Most will be delighted to meet you and let you sample their finest.

You can get a list of Ontario VQA wineries from

> Wine Council of Ontario
> 110 Hannover Drive, Suite B205
> St. Catherine, Ontario
> Canada L2W 1A4

The winegrowing regions of British Columbia are worth a visit, even without the wine. They offer some of North America's most spectacular and memorable scenery.

But do visit the wineries! Most of them offer tours. And if you are driving up the Okanagan Valley, be sure to visit the Wine Museum at Kelowna.

You can get a list of B.C.'s VQA wineries from

> British Columbia Wine Institute
> Suite 5
> 1864 Spall Road
> Kelowna, B.C.
> Canada V1Y 4R1

249

The Least You Need to Know

➤ The Canadian wine industry began anew in the late 1980s, with plantings of vinifera varieties.

➤ The Vintners Quality Alliance assures reliable quality and labeling of wines from Ontario and British Columbia.

➤ Canada is the world's leading producer of ice wines.

➤ Canadian wines have won many international awards.

From the Lands Down Under

G'day! Yes, I know, mate. The term "down under" refers to Australia and New Zealand. But I'd like to extend it (just here) to include another English-speaking wine producer from beneath the Southern Cross, South Africa. Y'got a problem with that, mate?

Australia already has a secure position in our wine shops' shelves. But now New Zealand and South Africa are up-and-coming players, and you can use material from this chapter to seek out their wines (and to enjoy them).

Our Aussie cousins hate to admit it, but they are becoming positively refined! (Okay— I mean their wines are.) Those rough-and-tumble wines from an earlier day are now being replaced by respectable, good-quality whites and reds that can grace any table.

Australian wines offer good value. And what the heck: An Aussie wine bottle is a great conversation starter! Australia's southeastern neighbor, New Zealand, also is working to create a new wine industry, one better in tune with current export markets.

Then there's South Africa. With its new (1993) government and no more international boycott, it is looking hungrily at a significant export market. And believe me, they have some wines worth exporting! They're not too easy to find yet, but they're worth looking for.

Wine from the Outback

Over the past two decades, a wine renaissance has taken place in Australia. Not too long ago, all we could find were cheap, fortified wines. Today we see a brand new Australian wine industry—one that's earned itself an honorable standing in the world wine market.

This turnaround is not unlike California's. In California, we used to have screw-capped jug wines. In Australia, it was *bag-in-the-box*. You can find both in both places today, but you also will find an embracing of technology that results in world-class medal-winning wines.

There's one difference between Australia and California: California is Zinfandel's first home. Australia has no wine it can exclusively call its own.

Vinifera vines first made their appearance in Australia in the late eighteenth and early nineteenth centuries from Europe by way of the Cape of Good Hope. Fortified wines were a common thing in warm climates, especially in the days when spoilage was a serious problem. So it's not surprising that rich, sweet wines dominated Australian production. (Even today, Australia makes some of the best Sherry outside of Spain.)

Vino Vocab

Bag-in-the-box refers to a new kind of wine container that looks like a large milk container. Inside the box is a plastic bag that collapses as the wine is consumed to prevent the wine from being oxidized. Very popular in Australia, this type of container is making inroads with American producers of jug-quality wines.

Blends: Australian for Wine

The predominant grape used in Australia's better wines is Syrah, known there as *Shiraz*. Shiraz is the name you'll see on the label, which, California-style, bears the varietal name. The named grape must make up at least 85 percent of the bottle's contents.

Australian vintners commonly blend two vinifera and use both varietal names. The dominant grape comes first. Examples: Shiraz/Cabernet Sauvignon and Cabernet Sauvignon/Shiraz. You may find these blends a bit unusual. Most winemakers follow the classic French prototypes, such as Cabernet Sauvignon with Merlot and Cabernet Blanc or Semillon with Sauvignon Blanc. But with no special tradition, Australia has created two original styles of wine: Shiraz with Cabernet Sauvignon and Semillon with Chardonnay, both of which are quite good and provide an interesting wine.

Tasting Tip

Those raunchy reds and hot-tasting whites that made up Australia's first varietal efforts are now tamed, tuned, and styled into wines of refinement, balance, and charm.

Heard It Through the Grapevine

Untamed, sprawling Australia is a long way from historic France in style, no less than geography. The majority of Australian wines carry the appellation "South Eastern Australia." This means the grapes could have been grown in any one of the three states in this immense territory. You will find others that reveal wines from several appellations, with the percentage of each frequently listed. If you're looking for distinctive, stylistic, regional nuances, you must look for wines from a single, more narrow appellation.

The other important Australian varietal is Semillon. Some are aged in oak, similar to Chardonnay, with tastes of vanilla and oak with complexity. Others are unoaked, which produces simple white wines when young. These same wines become complex and honeyed with bottle aging.

For all their idiosyncrasies, Australian wine labels are very informative and easy to read. Most blended wines list their grape varieties on the label, and the percentages of each grape are usually included. There is one catch, though: There's no restriction on where the grapes used in blended wines are grown, so there are many transregional blends.

The Sommelier Says

Australian wine labels don't always speak your language. If you're in the market for an Australian Riesling, look for the name "Rhine Riesling." If the label reads simply "Riesling," chances are it's Semillon.

Southern Hemisphere Napa-Sonoma

Australia's main viticultural regions are geographically and climatically similar to California's Napa and Sonoma Valleys: dry, not too humid, and ranging in temperature from moderate to fairly warm in some parts.

The most important wine-producing state is South Australia, which accounts for approximately 60 percent of Australia's wine. It has two distinctly different faces. The Riverlands region produces the inexpensive jug-style wine that is the staple of the bag-in-the-box industry. Closer to the state capital, Adelaide, are the vineyard regions, which are gaining renown for their fine wines. These include the following:

Tasting Tip

The ever-popular Shirazes are made in several styles, from very light, quaffable, simple-premium wines to serious, complex wines that require bottle-aging. They deserve your attention.

➤ **Barossa Valley** Lying north of Adelaide, this is one of the coolest vineyard regions and one of the first to be associated with fine wines. It's also the largest area, highly influenced by Germanic wine styles. Both its Rhine Riesling and Riesling are light and delightful. The Shiraz and Cabernet Sauvignon are solid, consistent, and continually improving.

➤ **Coonawarra** The climate is cool, and the region is esteemed for its classic reds, Cabernet Sauvignon, and Shiraz. There can be wide vintage variations, but in fine years, the Cabernets have been standouts!

➤ **Clare Valley** The climate is diverse, and the winemaking is eclectic. This yields a good variety of wines, from crisp Rieslings to full-bodied reds.

➤ **McLaren Vale** Located south of Adelaide and cooled by the ocean, this is white wine territory. It's known primarily for Chardonnay and Sauvignon Blanc.

➤ **Padthaway** Another white-wine area situated north of Coonawarra.

New South Wales was Australia's first viticultural state. Today it accounts for approximately 30 percent of the country's wine. Its main wine region is the Hunter Valley. During the 1980s, Hunter Valley attracted wealthy investors and lifestyle seekers, making it sort of a Napa-Down-Under. The Hunter Valley consists of two distinct locales:

➤ **Lower Hunter Valley** Close to Sydney, it is warm and humid, with heavy, rich soils.

➤ **Upper Hunter Valley** Drier and further inland, Shiraz and Semillon are the classic varietals, with Chardonnay recently gaining in stature. Riesling and Pinot Noir have also yielded some impressive efforts.

Here are some other important wine-producing regions of South Australia:

➤ **Mudgee** Situated inland near the mountains due west of Hunter Valley, this lesser-known wine region offers Chardonnay, Merlot, and Cabernet Sauvignon.

➤ **Victoria** In eastern Australia, Victoria is the site of many small wineries. It offers quantities of everyday white, red, and sparkling wines and remains a center for fortified wines. The wines produced here range from stylish Pinot Noirs to rich, fortified dessert wines. Among the key winegrowing regions in the state of Victoria are ....

➤ **Rutherglen, Glenrowan, and Milawa**   Situated in the northeast, the warm climate of these regions lends itself to the making of fortified wines, including fortified Muscats and Tokays.

➤ **Goulburn Valley**   This central area is known for its Shiraz and Marsanne.

➤ **Great Western**   This is the mainstay of Australia's sparkling wine industry.

➤ **Yarra Valley**   This cool region, located close to Melbourne, yields some fine Pinot Noir, Cabernet Sauvignon, and Chardonnay.

Australia's Best Values

Australian bag-in-the-box wines are Australia's best values: inexpensive, and they provide good value. You can find them in some stores, but they're not yet popular in the U.S.

Australian Chardonnay, Shiraz, and Cabernet Sauvignon, priced around $6 to $8 (U.S.), provide good value in well-made wines. The more expensive Australian wines, $20 or more, compare with their counterparts from other parts of the world. However, these are not the bargains their lower-priced mates are.

Wine Under the Ocean Spray

Think of Australia, and the next country that comes to mind usually is New Zealand. Somewhat behind its larger neighbor, New Zealand is emerging in the world wine market. It still has a way to go.

New Zealand lies a little farther south than Australia, where it's cooler. Actually, New Zealand is two large islands, both of which are subject to the effects of the ocean spray.

The warmer North Island is known for its red wines, particularly Cabernet Sauvignons, which come from the area around Auckland and Hawkes Bay. These are produced along with less-costly Müller-Thurgau-based wines. The South Island contains Marlborough, New Zealand's largest wine region, which is gaining acclaim for its white wines—notably, Sauvignon Blanc and Chardonnay.

New Zealand's whites generally are unoaked, with rich flavors and sharp acidity. Its reds are similar to those of Australia. The wines of New Zealand tend to be priced higher than comparable wines from Australia and elsewhere, but they do provide an interesting wine experience.

The Sommelier Says

Compared with Australia, New Zealand has quite a bit of catching up to do. But who knows? In a few years, New Zealand wines may be the latest rage. (Then you can claim you have discovered them first.)

255

New Beginnings in South Africa

Since Dutch settlers introduced the first European vines 300 years ago, South Africa has produced a good variety of wines. Later the Dutch were joined by French Huguenots, who contributed their Gaelic winemaking knowledge and techniques.

Tasting Tip

South Africa's rich, dessert-style Muscat wine, Constantia, became legendary during the early history of South Africa. It was considered a delicacy in the royal courts of Europe.

Aside from a continental regard for South Africa's Constantia dessert wine, few countries other than Great Britain displayed any interest in this country's wines. Up until 1918, quality regulation was poor to nonexistent, and overproduction resulted in inferior wines. To combat this effect, the government adopted a regulating body, the KWV (a cartel-like winegrower's association), to control an anarchic industry.

The strict quota system of the KWV has come under a lot of criticism, especially in recent years. In 1992, the KWV finally loosened controls, permitting independent wineries greater production. In 1972, the government implemented a type of appellation system, granting an official "Wine of Origin" seal to certain wines and certain estates to ensure accuracy of label information.

With the death of apartheid, the writing of a new constitution, and the election of Nelson Mandela to the presidency, South Africa has gained new recognition in the world. More important, it was able to reenter markets that had been closed through an international boycott of the apartheid system.

Few of the country's 5,000 grape growers are wine producers. They deliver their grapes to one of the 70 cooperatives run by the KWV. Approximately half the crop is turned into distilled alcohol or grape concentrate. Most of the remaining grapes are used for Sherry or Port. However, more and more of this production is being used to make dry, unfortified wines. New independent wineries are cropping up, and South Africa is gaining a reputation for higher-quality, estate-grown wines.

Although South Africa ranks eighth in worldwide wine production, only 20 percent is exported. The U.K. remains its biggest customer.

Wine of Origin

The implementation of the *Wine of Origin* (WO) appellation system resulted in the creation of 10 wine districts (and their subdistricts). Most of South Africa's viticultural land is located in Cape Province near the southeastern coast (in the vicinity of Cape Town). The vineyards are known collectively as the Coastal District vineyards. The two most prominent districts are Paarl and Stellenbosch, but several others are emerging (including one subdistrict). Currently the five key wine districts are

➤ **Stellenbosch**   This region is the largest in area and production and is renowned for its high-quality wines, particularly reds. It's situated east of Cape Town.

➤ **Paarl**   Located north of Stellenbosch, it's the site of the KWV and the impressive Nederburg Estate. Paarl is recognized for its high-quality white wines.

➤ **Franschloek Valley**   This subdistrict of Paarl is a center for experimentation and innovation in winemaking.

➤ **Constantia**   Located south of Cape Town, this historic region created the luscious dessert wine that wowed the nobility of Europe.

➤ **Durbanville**   Located north of Cape Town, this region is noted for its rolling hills with well-drained soil.

Heard It Through the Grapevine

Despite changes, both in winemaking and in government policy, the giant KWV cartel still runs the show. The growing table-wine industry is dominated by the **Stellenbosch Farmers' Winery (SFW)** Group. The Nederburg Estate, regarded as one of South Africa's most esteemed winegrowing properties, is part of the SFW. Another important table wine producer is the Bergkelder Group. Eighteen wine estates, including some of South Africa's best, are affiliated with this firm.

South Africa's WO legislation is modeled after the French Appellation Contrôlée system. That is, it includes strict regulation of vineyard sites, grape varieties, vintage-dating, and so on. Under South African law, varietal wines must contain at least 75 percent of the designated grape. (Those produced for export to the European Union, however, must have at least 85 percent of the named grape.) Roughly 10 percent of South Africa's wines now earn the WO seal.

Steen Rules

Chenin Blanc, called *Steen* in South Africa, is the reigning grape variety. And no wonder: It's one versatile vinifera! Though used mainly to make medium-dry to semisweet wines, it also makes dry wines, late-harvest *Botrytis* wines, rosés, and sparkling wines. Sauvignon Blanc and Chardonnay also are gaining in popularity.

257

The predominant red grape traditionally has been Cinsault, the same as the Rhône variety (formerly called the *Hermitage* in South Africa). The Cinsault grape produces an ever-popular wine by the same name. It's been getting a few rivals lately, notably Cabernet and Merlot, and to a lesser degree Pinot Noir and Shiraz.

The table wines of South Africa have always included a few crossbreeds. The best known is the distinctive Pinotage, a hybrid of Cinsault and Pinot Noir. Pinotage combines the berry fruitiness of Pinot Noir with the earthy qualities of a Rhône wine, producing an easy-to-drink, light- to medium-bodied, simple-premium wine.

The Least You Need to Know

➤ Australia produces some interesting white and red varietal wines that provide good value, and some excellent selections of everyday wines.

➤ The wines from New Zealand are improving, but they provide less value than their counterparts from Australia and elsewhere.

➤ The wines from South Africa are gaining a renewed popularity, and some are worth seeking out.

Chapter 21

A Bit of Bubbly

In This Chapter

➤ Styles of sparkling wine

➤ How sparkling wine is made

➤ Recognizing true Champagne

➤ Sparkling wines of the world

His first name wasn't really "Dom." That's a title attached to the names of Benedictine monks. His name was Pierre—Pierre Pérignon. He was blind.

In 1688, Dom Pérignon was put in charge of the wine cellars at the Abby of Hautvillers, near Reims in France's Champagne province. It was he who first decided to quit worrying about those annoying bubbles that developed in the bottles of the abby's wines and to start perfecting this strange, "mad" wine. The world of celebration and mirth hasn't been the same since!

From those old Fred Astaire and Ginger Rogers movies to the latest James Bond, we know what sophisticates do, don't we? They sip Champagne! And so does everyone else, it seems—at weddings, birthday celebrations, and of course, New Year's Eve bashes.

Most of us have experienced Champagne (or imagine we have). But no one has described this lively beverage better than the blind monk himself. They say he held his glass and exclaimed, "I am drinking stars!"

In this chapter we'll explore the science and the art that allow vintners to create those stars.

Champagne Is a Province

If bubbles alone were the key to Champagne's opulent image, we could celebrate our triumphs and delights with soft drinks. But Champagne is much, much more than bubbles.

In Champagne, the French province east of Paris, vintners apply the most exacting standards and costly procedures to create that sumptuous beverage we find just right for special occasions. With its precisely delimited growing region, authentic French Champagne is limited in production, and rising prices reinforce its image as a luxury wine.

Yet there are many other sparkling wines we may endow with at least some of Champagne's mystique and pleasant associations. Of course, we shouldn't call these "Champagnes." Except in the U.S., only wines from the Champagne region may bear that label. We call the others *sparkling wine* or *vin mousseux*.

The Sommelier Says

When designer Yves Saint Laurent created a perfume he named "Champagne," the Interprofessionnel du Vin Champagne—the trade organization for Champagne wines—took him to court to force him to change the name of the perfume, and they won. The vintners of Champagne guard their distinguished name very carefully!

Heard It Through the Grapevine

Under French legislation, Champagne is a sparkling wine produced only within the defined geographic boundaries of that district and made under the strict regulations of the Appellation Côntrolée.

To make Champagne, only certain grape varieties may be used, and only one procedure—the Méthode Champenoise. Sparkling wines from elsewhere in France are called vin mousseux, never Champagne, even if the same grapes and methods are used.

You can get sparkling wines of good quality at reasonable prices, comparable to those for good table wines. So it's easy to enjoy some effervescence before dinner. Or with dinner. Or to celebrate some special occasion (like finishing that report or giving the dog a bath).

It's no harder to select a sparkling wine than any other type of wine. A little knowledge, some label reading, and maybe a few phone calls, and that's it! Remember, you're the one drinking the stuff, not some wine snob who wants to tell you what you ought to buy. If you enjoy it, it's the right selection.

Vino Vocab

The word "brut" is not very precise. **Brut** can range from 0 to 2 percent residual sweetness.

Extra Dry; Slightly Sweet: Huh?

The hardest part of selecting a Champagne is figuring out the label. Why, you might ask, is *Extra Dry* sweeter than *Brut* (which means "heavy")? When we discuss *still* (not sparkling) wines, drier means less sweet!

Then there's *Demi-Sec* (half-sweet), which suggests half as sweet. But in the case of Champagne, it means twice as sweet!

Confused yet? Well, before I confuse myself, let me lay them all out for you, from driest to sweetest:

Term	Meaning
Extra Brut, Brut Nature, or Brut Sauvage	Bone dry
Brut	Dry
Extra Dry	Medium dry
Sec	Slightly sweet
Demi-Sec	Fairly sweet
Doux	Very sweet

Whether your palette judges it dry or semi-sweet is a matter of personal judgment. And preference. But there are some things you can look for to assess the quality of a sparkling wine or Champagne:

Tasting Tip

Sweetness in Champagnes can easily mask defects—either a weak *cuvée* (blend) or a winemaking flaw. The drier a Champagne is, the more perfectly it has to be rendered. Its flaws and weaknesses can't be concealed. The most delicate Champagnes, particularly those called *Grand Marks* or *Tête de Cuvée* by the producer to signify the best, must be flawless.

➤ Look at the bubbles (known as the bead). They should be tiny, bursting somewhat above the surface of the wine. (Think of those cartoon depictions where the bubbles float skyward from the glass.) The bead should endure in your glass for 10 minutes, at least.

➤ Check the mouthfeel. The finer the wine, the tinier the bubbles. These will be less aggressive on your palate.

➤ Assess the balance between sweetness and acidity. This marks the difference between a good-tasting sparkling wine and one that is unpleasant.

➤ Sparkling wine made by the Méthode Champenoise (I'll explain shortly) will have a slightly creamy mouthfeel, the result of its extended aging on the lees.

➤ Now the finish: It should be crisp, refreshing, and clean. Bitterness on the finish of a sparkling wine is a sign of poorly made wine.

Authentic Champagne has a recognizable subtle and refined yeasty flavor and unique character that rarely is equaled in other regions producing sparkling wine.

The Night They Invented Champagne

What Dom Pérignon described as stars actually was no more than carbon dioxide retained in the bottle following a second fermentation of residual sugar by live yeast that had remained from the original fermentation. In the case of that abbey near Reims, it was unintended. Short growing seasons meant late harvests. Early cold weather stopped the fermentation before it was complete. This resumed in the warming spring, after winter bottling.

Heard It Through the Grapevine

How many bubbles are in that bottle of bubbly? Yes! This is a serious question! American scientist Bill Lembeck wanted to know. So he found out. First Lembeck established that the average gas pressure in a bottle of Champagne is about 5.5 atmospheres (typical inflation pressure for the tires of a large truck). Then he measured the sizes of bubbles in the glass using an optical comparator. (They run about a fiftieth of an inch.) Finally, subtracting the gas that lies above the liquid, he divided the remainder by the volume of these tiny bubbles. The answer? Forty-nine million bubbles!

Dom Pérignon didn't discover Champagne, he exploited its virtues and eliminated its imperfections. In doing so, he turned what had been considered a failure into his region's greatest success. Pérignon was a fastidious monk who devoted years to experimentation with grape blends and to developing superior methods of clarifying his wines. Champagne, like the Germans' first *Eiswein*, is an example of defeat converted into triumph.

The fermentation gases added sparkle to wine, and high pressures. Many of Pérignon's bottles exploded. So the Dom substituted stronger glass bottles, developed by the English. And he experimented with improvements on the wooden or oil-soaked hemp bottle stoppers in use at the time.

About a hundred years later, in 1805, Barbe-Nicole Cliquot Ponsardin took over her husband's small winery after his death. Madame Cliquot was a remarkable woman, totally dedicated to perfecting what Dom Pérignon had begun. It was she who developed the mushroom-shaped champagne cork we know today. She also invented riddling, which is essential to the production of authentic Champagne. Madame Cliquot's house still turns out excellent Champagnes under the name "Veuve (widow) Cliquot. "

France's Champagne province wasn't the only part of the winegrowing world that experienced incomplete fermentation in its wines. Many sparkling wines come from cool areas where vines are slow to ripen. A still wine from such a region might be excessively acidic, harsh, and thin—in a word, awful. But through the intricate processes of refermentation, this potential salad dressing becomes a winning touchdown.

In the U.S., sparkling wine and champagne (note the lowercase c) get their sparkle during a second fermentation in a sealed container. The choice of grape varieties is up to the producer, with no restrictions on growing conditions or bubble-producing techniques. The only legal limitation is that these bubbles must be produced naturally and not added by artificial carbonation.

The terms "champagne" and "sparkling wine" are used interchangeably. I prefer to use the term "Champagne" the way Madame Cliquot and the Appellation Controlée intended it. So I will refer to all effervescent wines from outside the Champagne district as "sparkling wine."

French Champagne derives its quality from a series of time-proven, exacting methods. Permissible grape varieties are the noble Chardonnay and Pinot Noir, with minor blending grapes that, even in Champagne's cool climate, develop character when picked at low sugar levels ranging between 15 and 19 degrees Brix. (The norm for table wine is 20 to 23 degrees.)

Tasting Tip

For U.S. wines, believe it or not, the term "sparkling wine" on the label is a better indicator of quality than the word "champagne." Sparkling wine is a perfectly respectable appellation. Beware of cheap imitation champagnes from California and New York that sell for less than $7 and have the nerve to describe their contents as "champagne."

These grapes ferment conventionally into wine. Then the Champagne maker assembles them into a base wine, or blend, known as the *vin de cuvée*. The blend may be entirely from one vintage, but usually it consists of wines from two or more years, acquired to suit different markets. For example, the blend may be drier for export to the U.K. or sweeter for U.S. tastes. Despite this variability, the vin de cuvée usually is made within an established house style.

The *Méthode Champenoise* is the original, and most involved, technique. Other, lesser methods are the transfer method and the bulk, or Charmat, process. So let's divide our hypothetical cuvée into three batches and begin with the Méthode Champenoise.

Méthode Champenoise: It's in the Bottle

The most important thing to remember about the Méthode Champenoise is that the second fermentation of your wine took place in the actual bottle you got from your wine shop. The cuvée that was the basis for your Champagne was fermented and bottled. Then the vintner added a bit of sugar and yeast before the bottles were sealed, with either a temporary cork or metal crown cap. Then these bottles were placed on their sides for the second fermentation of three or four months. That's just the beginning.

By law, the wine must remain in contact with the dead yeast cells for at least one year. Some remain as many as five years. Time "on the yeast" adds flavor complexity through a process of yeast *autolysis* (breakdown), which contributes richness and a desired yeasty character. Virtually all the top-line French Champagnes spend several years on the yeast.

Once the bubbles are created and the flavors are developed, the vintner must remove the yeast sediment from each bottle. This technique is called *dégorgement* (disgorgement). This is what distinguishes the Méthode Champenoise from the less-costly transfer-process shortcut. Prior to dégorgement, the Champagne undergoes a laborious and time-consuming process called *remuage*, or riddling.

The Sommelier Says

The labels of all U.S. sparkling wines must indicate how they were made. If they were produced by the French Champagne method, you will see "Méthode Champenoise" or "Fermented in *this* bottle." But be careful! Wines labeled "Fermented in *the* bottle" are from the cheaper transfer process. What a difference one word makes!

For remuage, the bottles are placed neck-down in special A-frame racks. Each day, cellar workers riddle (slightly shake and rotate) each bottle, causing the sediment to creep gradually from the side of the bottle to the neck area. After about six weeks, the sediment is lodged in the neck, up against the closure. At this stage, the bottles are carefully removed—neck down— and taken to the dégorgement room.

Dégorgement can be done either by hand or machine. The principle remains the same. The neck of the bottle is immersed in a below-freezing brine solution, which traps the sediment in a plug of ice. The bottle is opened, the plug expelled by the pressure, and voilà!—No more sediment!

Some liquid always is lost in the process, and it's replaced according to house style—either with Champagne or a solution of Cognac and a sugar syrup. This tiny squirt actually determines the sweetness of the finished Champagne. Known as the *dosage*, it usually contains some sugar.

Following dégorgement, a special multilayered cork is inserted, the protective wire hood attached, and the Champagne set aside for further bottle-aging to allow dosage and wine to marry.

Transfer Method: Fake?

Tasting Tip

French Champagne is ready to drink at the time you buy it, no matter how long the vintner has seen fit to age it. (A good thing, too! Who wants to wait?)

If you follow the steps of the Méthode Champenoise, it's not difficult to see why fine French Champagne is *très cher* (very expensive). A less costly method for making sparkling wine (note the distinction) is the transfer method, a time- and labor-saving shortcut to bottle-fermented wine. It differs from the Méthode Champenoise in two ways.

First, though the wine undergoes its second fermentation in *a* bottle, it's not the *same* bottle you'll find on the shelf. Second, there's no riddling or disgorging. Both steps are replaced by filtration.

During the transfer process, the wine is transferred into a large, pressurized tank via a special machine designed to prevent loss of pressure. Once in the tank, it's filtered to remove the yeast cells and all other sediment. Then it's bottled. The process ensures that the sparkling product is free from sediment, and it's far less costly than the Méthode Champenoise. The catch is that some of the character developed during fermentation may be filtered out along with the yeast.

Actually, the distinction can be quite subtle. If the cuvées are similar, the distinguishing factors are the length of time the wine spends on the yeast and the degree of filtration used. Both are an influence on the flavor. But unless you have comparable bottles in front of you, it can be difficult to distinguish between a fine sparkling wine made by the transfer method and one made by the Méthode Champenoise. (Even for wine experts, regardless of what they may have you believe.)

The transfer method still can give us sparkling beverages with the sought-after tiny beads and persistent effervescence that are the hallmarks of a fine sparkling wine.

Charmat Process: Bubbles in Bulk

With our third batch of cuvée, we come to the Charmat, or bulk process (named for Eugene Charmat, the Frenchman who invented it). After its initial fermentation, the cuvée is poured directly into a closed tank, with an added solution of yeast and sugar.

The size of the tank varies, but it's usually several thousand gallons (bigger than any bottle). The second fermentation takes three to four weeks, at which point the wine is filtered and bottled.

What about those oversized Champagne bottles you might see at your local wine shop? You probably know that the two-bottle size is called a *magnum*. But what about those bigger ones? Here's a list:

Name	Volume	Number of Bottles
Jeroboam	3 liters	4
Rehoboam	4.5 liters	6
Methusalah	6 liters	8
Salmanazar	9 liters	12
Balthazar	12 liters	16
Nebuchadnezzar	15 liters	20

The bulk process makes sparkling wine, but it's unlikely Madame Cliquot would have approved. (Nor, perhaps, will you.) Bulk-process sparkling wines generally form larger bubbles that dissipate quickly. They also lack the traditional yeasty character, because they spend little time, if any, in contact with the yeast.

Basically this merely is wine made bubbly—not always pleasantly so. Charmat lends itself to large volume and an efficient use of time, labor, and equipment. It's used to make inexpensive sparkling wine, often from neutral- or even poor-quality grapes.

The True Champagne

Champagne's opulent aura may be a bit overdone, but just as in Hollywood, there is such a thing as star quality. And just as a great director brings out the best in a star, a great Champagne maker gets Academy Award nominations for all the grapes!

Champagne as a Fine Art

Making Champagne really is more of an art than a science. The wine artisan must create the cuvée carefully—by tasting and retasting potential components (which may be up to 200 different wines). Then there's monitoring the time on the yeast. Then riddling the bottles, with just the right touch. Finally there's disgorging the sediment. This is not mere manufacturing! It's medieval craftsmanship.

The Sommelier Says

Sparkling wines made elsewhere than Champagne use the same descriptors for sweetness. Though these terms have legal definitions in Champagne, they may be inconsistent in other places.

But the final product, with its small, delicate bead, persistent effervescence, subtle yeastiness, and intricate balance, justifies the extraordinary time and care demanded by the Méthode Champenoise.

Champagne is the northernmost winegrowing region in France. Its cool climate makes grape-growing, especially red grapes, for table wines a real gamble. But it's ideal for achieving those sparkles. And its chalky limestone soil is perfect for the Pinot Noir that adds fullness and body to the cuvée.

Most of the major Champagne houses reside in two cities within the district. The first is historic Rheims, where Joan of Arc led the Dauphin Charles to be crowned King of France. The second is the smaller Epernay, located south of Rheims. Surrounding these historic towns are the vineyard sites where the three Champagne grape varieties— Pinot Noir, Chardonnay, and Pinot Meunier—are cultivated.

➤ **The Montagne de Reims** (south of Rheims) is where the best Pinot Noir grapes grow.

➤ **The Côte des Blancs** (south of Epernay) is where we find the best Chardonnay.

➤ **The Vallée de la Marne** (west of Epernay) favors the Pinot Meunier (a black grape). However, all three varieties are grown here.

French Champagne makers are perfectionists. (Under strict French law, they have to be!) Both grape varieties and their yields are closely regulated, with quality uppermost in mind. Pinot Noir contributes fullness, body, structure, and longevity. Chardonnay offers finesse, backbone, delicacy, freshness, and elegance. And Pinot Meunier provides floral scents and fruitiness. In the end, though, the proportions depend on the Champagne maker's style and vision.

Heard It Through the Grapevine

The highest-quality product comes from free-run juice, the juice that runs off the grapes from their own weight before pressing. Pressing is an art in Champagne because it's essential to avoid tainting the juice of the dark-skinned grapes with anything more than the slightest hint of color or bitterness of flavor. The Champagne district has about 300 crus (vineyards) that are graded for quality. The highest-ranked vineyards are sought after by the prestigious houses especially for their top-of-the-line Grand Mark.

Certain vineyards are esteemed for Pinot Noir, while others are cherished for Chardonnay. Except for the Blancs de Blancs, which are made entirely from white grapes, the usual ratio is two-thirds black grapes to one-third Chardonnay. Of the two black grapes, it's Pinot Noir that dominates; only a small amount of Pinot Meunier is used. There's also a Blanc de Noir, made entirely from black grapes.

Non-Vintage Champagnes—House Style

Contrary to legend, most Champagne (85 percent of all produced) is non-vintage (NV). That is, you'll find no vintage year on the label. It's all in the blending. In addition to the myriad wines in the cuvée, NV Champagnes are allowed to contain wine from three or more harvests.

Non-vintage Champagnes are created according to the favored house style. One house may seek elegance and finesse, while another will strive for fruitiness, and a third might consider body and full flavor as paramount. Every Champagne house has its own style, and it's rarely tampered with. After all, Champagne drinkers don't differ from other consumers. Most remain loyal to their preferred style of Champagne.

As noted in our earlier discussion of the Méthode Champenoise, most Champagne producers age their product long beyond the one-year minimum. The usual time for NV Champagne is two-and-a-half to three years. This additional aging provides greater marrying time for the blend and enhances the wine's flavor and complexity as it absorbs the lees in the bottle.

Vintage Champagne—Crème de la Crème

It occurs only a few times each decade—a year when the weather in Champagne is so friendly that a good cuvèe can be made exclusively from the vines of that year, without blending from reserve wines from previous harvests. When this happens, we have a vintage Champagne.

There are two categories of vintage Champagnes:

➤ Regular vintage lies within the $25 to $50 a bottle price range. The label will carry the name of the house, plus the vintage date.

➤ Premium vintage (tête de cuvée or prestige cuvée). Some examples are Taittinger's Comtes de Champagne, Roederer's Cristal, and Veuve Clicquot's La Grande Dame. These run from $50 to $200 per bottle.

No doubt you'd like me to give you some reasons for spending a substantial sum for a vintage year on the label. Okay. Here's why I feel vintage Champagne is unquestionably superior:

➤ The cuvée is made from the finest grapes from the finest vineyards (without exception for tête de cuvée).

➤ Vintage Champagne is usually made from the two noble varieties only: Pinot Noir and Chardonnay.

➤ Vintage Champagnes are usually aged two or more years longer than non-vintage Champagnes, giving them greater complexity and finesse.

➤ The grapes all come from a superior, if not superlative, vintage.

Vintage Champagne is richer in flavor than non-vintage Champagne. Also, it may be more full-bodied and more complex, with a longer finish. Whether a vintage Champagne is worth its extra cost is something you'll have to decide for yourself after trying one.

Blanc de Noirs

This rare and exotic Champagne specimen (the name means "white from blacks") is made exclusively from black grapes—sometimes 100 percent Pinot Noir. It's at the upper end of the tête de cuvée price range. Bollinger's Blanc de Noirs Vielles Vignes ("old vines") is the crème de la crème of these rare creations.

Blanc de Blancs

Blanc de Blancs literally translates as "white from whites." (If you're feeling artistic, think of it as white-on-white.)

Blanc de blancs is made 100 percent from noble Chardonnay grapes. It can be either vintage or non-vintage, and it's usually priced a bit higher than other Champagnes in the same class. Blanc de blancs are lighter and more delicate than other Champagnes.

Rosé Champagne

Commonly (maybe too commonly) known as pink Champagne, rosé Champagnes actually are a cut above average. Unfortunately, being pink and sparkling makes people take them less seriously. They're usually made from Pinot Noir and Chardonnay only. Like blanc de blancs, they can be either vintage or non-vintage, and they cost a bit more than regular Champagnes in the same category.

The Sommelier Says

Don't pop that cork! While it might be fun to launch that cork like a mortar shell, it's very wasteful of those expensive bubbles. There's a much better (and classier) way: With a firm grip on the cork, turn the bottle, allowing the cork to emerge slowly. When it's nearly out, let the gas escape slowly. Then pour.

The Premier Producers

As I explained earlier in this section, all of the best Champagne houses develop their own signature style. Here's my list of premier producers categorized according to style:

Light and Elegant

➤ Billecart-Salmon

➤ Charles de Cazanove

➤ de Castellane

➤ Jacquesson

➤ Laurent-Perrier

➤ Perrier-Jouet

➤ Philipponnat

➤ Ruinart

➤ Taittinger

Medium-Bodied

➤ Charles Heidsieck

➤ Deutz

➤ Hiedsieck Monopole

➤ Möet & Chandon

➤ Mumm

➤ Pol Roger

➤ Pommery

Full-Bodied

➤ Bollinger

➤ Gosset

➤ Henriot

➤ Krug

➤ Louis Roederer

➤ Salon

➤ Veuve Clicquot

If you're in the market for tête de cuvée, here's a guide to some of the best, so you'll know you're getting superior quality for your investment:

➤ Billecart-Salmon: Blanc de Blancs (1986, 1985)

➤ Bollinger: Blancs de Noirs Vielles Vignes (1985)

➤ Cattier: Clos du Moulin (the only non-vintage on the list)

➤ Charbaut: Certificate Blanc de Blancs (1985)

➤ Charles de Cazanove: Stradivarius (1989)

➤ Charles Heidsieck: Blanc des Millenaires (1983)

➤ Gosset: Grand Millesime and Rosé (1985)

➤ Hiedsieck Monopole: Diamant Bleu and Rosé (1985, 1982)

➤ Jacquesson: Signature (1985)

➤ Laurent-Perrier: Grand Siecle (1988, 1985)

➤ Louis Roederer: Cristal (1988, 1986, 1985)

➤ Möet & Chandon: Dom Pérignon (1988, 1985, 1982)

➤ Mumm: Rene Lalou (1985, 1982)

➤ Philipponnat: Clos de Goisses (1986, 1985, 1982)

➤ Pol Roger: cuvée Sir Winston Churchill (1986, 1985)

➤ Pommery: cuvée Louise Pommery (1988, 1987, 1985)

➤ Ruinart: Dom Ruinart Blanc de Blancs (1988, 1985)

➤ Salon: Le Mesnil (1983, 1982, 1979)

➤ Taittinger: Compte de Champagne (1988, 1985)

➤ Veuve Clicquot: La Grande Dame (1988, 1985, 1983)

Vin Mousseux—Not Quite Champagne

As I've mentioned, most sparkling wines made in France outside of the Champagne region are called *vin mousseux*. The most popular of these wines come from the Loire Valley, with a few appearing from the Rhône and Midi regions.

The Loire sparklers can be quite good and relatively inexpensive. The difference is they are made from different grape varieties than Champagne and spend less time on the yeast. Saumur is the Loire Valley's biggest appellation for vin mousseux, which may or may not be made by the Méthode Champenoise. A word of caution: It tends toward oversweet, and quality varies.

When made by the Méthode Champenoise, the wine may be labeled "Crémant." Grape varieties do not have to be the ones used for true Champagne and usually will be those typical of the region. Most sell in the $8 to $15 range.

Good Taste Without the Designer Label

You've probably imbibed California sparkling wine, and chances are you've had some Italian sparklers from the famous Asti wine zone. Or maybe you've tried some of the Spanish sparkling wine that's become increasingly popular in recent years. These may not be Champagne, but they're worthy beverages in their own right.

Tasting Tip

Cava made by the Méthode Champenoise can be well-balanced with a fine, steady bead. The distinction is in the grapes. Most Cavas use local Spanish varieties, although the finer cuvées contain Chardonnay. Cava production is dominated by two huge wineries, and both have produced catchy commercials, making them well-known to U.S. consumers: Freixenet and Codorniu.

The Cavas of Spain

Spain is the up-and-comer in the sparkling wine market, and most of its bubbly is available for less than $8. Sparkling wine is called *Cava* in Spain, and the best of it comes from the Penedes region near Barcelona.

Sekt from Germany

Theoretically, the cool German climate makes it the perfect place for sparkling wines. Unfortunately, this theory does not translate into practice. Germany produces some of the finest white wines of the entire wine world, but Sekt just isn't one of them.

Sekt is produced by the Charmat method, which can make it coarsely bubbly. The better brands can be fruity and fresh, but only a handful of brands make a decent Sekt. The best are made from Riesling grapes, which can provide an interesting taste experience.

Spumante from Italy

Italy is one of the leading volume producers of sparkling wines, formerly known as *spumante* ("sparkling").

Unfortunately, the term *spumante* came to be associated with a fruity, oversweet beverage resembling a soft drink. So sparkling wines now bear the regional name without any mention of spumante. The Italians do prefer their sparkling wines sweet, so even those labeled "Brut" tend to be on the sweet side. But it's not impossible to find good Italian sparkling wines that are bone dry.

The major production center is the Piedmont, which gives us Asti. This well-known Italian sparkler is made from the Muscat grape, which has a musk-like or pine-like aroma that's attractive but not overpowering in a well-balanced wine. A good Asti is delicious and fruity, with flavors reminiscent of pine. Made by the Charmat method, Asti is non-vintage and is meant to be consumed soon after purchase.

Heard It Through the Grapevine

Before Dom Pérignon and Madame Cliquot tamed that bottle-fermented product that became Champagne, the French had some interesting names for it. One was *saute bouchon* ("cork-popper"), because of the numbers of accidental openings (before the corks were tied in place). Another was *vin diable* (devil wine), after the tendency of many of the bottles to explode in their cellars.

Some very good-quality sparkling wine is produced by the Méthode Champenoise in the Oltrepo-Pavese and Franciacorta wine zones of Lombardy. Until recently, only small quantities were exported, but now they're not difficult to find. This is where you'll find the bone-dry bubbly; the dry sparkling wines are made with little to no dosage.

Domestic Bubbles

Most of the domestic sparklers you'll find in your wine shop come from California or New York. Happily, both producers have outlived a reputation for making inferior, mass-produced, grapey imitations of the real thing. Made by the Méthode Champenoise, the bubbles have gotten smaller and more persistent, and the quality has improved vastly.

Some of the best California sparkling wines come from French Champagne houses that have set up shop on the West Coast. Led by Möet & Chandon, which began California production in 1973, Roederer, Taittinger, and others have heard the siren call of the Golden State.

Remember, for the best quality, look for the words "sparkling wine" on the label, not "champagne." The only bottle-fermented bubbly I know that uses the name "champagne" is Korbel, which sells for about $9. Two fine sparkling wine producers in New York State are Château Frank and Glenora. Their wines retail in the $12 to $14 price range, and both are made by the Méthode Champenoise.

Tasting Tip

The California bubbly made by the French Champagne houses is definitely a different wine than the Champagne they make in Champagne. The California versions are fruitier and more direct.

> **The Least You Need to Know**

➤ All sparkling wine is not Champagne.

➤ True Champagne can come from only the Champagne district of France.

➤ Sparkling wines from regions other than Champagne can be quite good.

➤ American wines labeled as "champagne" (with a lowercase c) usually are inferior and go flat quickly.

Chapter 22

Fortified Wines

In This Chapter

➤ Learn about real Porto wines from Portugal

➤ A tour of Ports of the world

➤ Sherry—sunshine from Spain

➤ Madeira—from the island

Historically, people added alcohol to wines to give them stability. No bottle fermentation (or bubbles) wanted! The higher alcohol stopped fermentation. This *fortification* ensured the survival of wines that were transported over long distances.

By definition, a fortified wine is any wine with alcohol content boosted through the addition of brandy or neutral spirits. Fortified wines usually range from 17 to 21 percent alcohol (by volume), somewhat higher than the 14 percent limit for table wines.

Portugal and Spain insist that the fortifying agents come from within their borders, often within a delineated region, and that they are made from specified grape varieties. (This has nothing to do with quality control. It's just a protectionist measure.)

In this chapter you will learn all about the fortified wines of Spain and Portugal (both mainland and the offshore island, Madeira). Fortified wines differ from table wines in style and alcohol content.

Body Building for Wine

Fortified wines are made in two ways. In the first, the vintner selects grapes for their ability to develop a high sugar content, with the potential to ferment to high alcohol levels. The *must* (juice) from these select grapes is inoculated with special, powerful yeasts, capable of thriving at high alcohol concentrations. The alcohol level will reach 17 or 18 percent before fermentation finally stops. Sweetness can be adjusted later.

In the second (and more traditional) method, the vintner adds a fortifying agent to increase the level of alcohol and, where necessary, to halt fermentation. Most Ports, Sherries, Marsalas, and Madeiras start with grapes high in natural sugars. They may be fermented to dryness or fortified to stop fermentation while there is still some sweetness. The selection of the brandy or neutral spirits used as the fortifying agent is important to the quality of the product. Some fortified wines are aged in wood for smoothness, while others are left raw and rough.

Porto—The Real Thing

A decade or two ago, the Portuguese changed the name of their Port to "Porto" to avoid confusion in a marketplace filled with "Ports" from many other countries. Only Port from Portugal may be called Porto. But in this chapter, I'll refer to Porto as Port, because here we're looking (nearly) only at authentic Port, from Portugal.

Heard It Through the Grapevine

The foremost authority on Port was H. Warner Allen, a noted wine writer from the early part of the century. He wrote, "Vintage Port has a lushness, unctuousness, delicacy, and refinement that make Port unparalleled by any wine of its type in the world."

Port has long been a favorite of the English gentry, and some swear it's a British invention. When faced with a shortage of French wine in the late seventeenth century, the resourceful (and thirsty) British imported wine from Portugal. To ensure its stability on the journey to England, they added a touch of brandy to the finished wine.

In 1670, the first English Port house, Warre, opened its doors in the seaport city of Oporto, Portugal. Oporto is still the home of true Port. As Port became an important commodity, the process for making it became more refined. Instead of adding the brandy as an afterthought the (mainly British) producers began to add the brandy during the fermentation process.

Today, a Port producer can make as many as six different styles of Port, depending on the taste preferences of the intended market. True Port has gotten sweeter by design to meet market demands, but the basic process remains the same.

Port is made from a blend of grapes grown on the steep slopes of Portugal's Douro region, where the soils are a gravelly schist (slate) and the climate is warm to hot. As many as 15 different local grape varieties may go into the making of Port. These grapes truly are unsung heroes. Even the most important of them are relative unknowns: Touriga, Sousão, Bastardo, and the Tinta (red) versions—Tinta Cão, Tinta Madeira, and Tinta Francisca.

These local grapes are chosen for their ability to develop high sugars, good color, and when used in concert, character and finesse. After they're gathered from the terraced hillsides, the grapes are fermented and brought to Oporto for prolonged aging, blending, and bottling. The quality of Port is derived from the vintage, the aging, and the blending. Variations in these elements account for nuances in style.

Vintage Port

Vintage Port is the top-of-the-line among Ports. It's produced only in exceptional vintage years, capable of producing wines of great depth and complexity. Individual producers set the standards, but a vintage year generally is declared by consensus. It's unusual to find a lone producer declaring a vintage year (although it's not impossible).

Usually made from selected lots, vintage Port is capable of aging and developing complexity for many, many years. Once it's been fermented, fortified, and adjusted for sweetness, vintage Port must be aged for two years in wood before bottling.

Before aging, vintage Port is concentrated and rich, to the point of being undrinkable. In bottle aging, the spirits and flavors marry, and the wine throws a heavy deposit or sediment. Ten years in the bottle represents mere infancy. It takes 20 or 30 years before vintage Port comes into its own. Some of the best vintage Ports are 70 years old (sometimes much older).

Most good vintage Ports sell in the $30 to $50 range when they are young (and years away from being ready to drink). You can expect to pay $50 or more for a Port with a decade or more of aging. A fully mature Port can cost from $80 to $200 a bottle in a great vintage.

The Sommelier Says

Bottle-aging leaves a crusty sediment on the bottom and along the sides of the bottles of vintage Port. You really need to exercise care when you handle and open these fine wines. You also should decant them before serving to ensure that you don't ruin your experience with the bitter deposits.

Late-Bottled Vintage

Late-bottled vintage Port comes from one vintage that is cask-aged for at least four years before bottling. Most of the sediment will settle during cask-aging, making late-bottled vintage Port a compromise between vintage and non-vintage varieties. It is less expensive, less complex, and sometimes made from young vines or less traditional grape varieties. It sells for about $15 to $20.

Ruby Port

Ruby Port is a blend of vintages, usually lacking the intense purple colors and flavors of a better-quality Port to begin with. It's cask-aged for roughly three years. Ruby Ports are blended for consistent color and style. Usually these are the least expensive Ports (around $8 or $10). They're the youngest of the Port family and are rougher and less harmonious than their Tawny cousins, described next.

Tawny Port

Some *tawny* Ports are deep garnet or brownish in color, but they need no more aging than a ruby. The best lie in cask for many years, until the color becomes light or tawny through oxidation. Some well-aged tawny Ports can be marvelous and subtle. Expect to pay about $15 for a longer-aged tawny; the lesser-quality tawnies can be found for as low as $6 or $8.

Tasting Tip

Occasionally, a tawny Port will be so outstanding that it is not blended with Ports of other vintages but aged individually. This single-vintage tawny will be labeled either "Port of the Vintage" (as opposed to "Vintage Port") or "Colheita Port." An exceptional Colheita can be a fine example of an aged Port, but it is distinctively different from vintage Port.

The very best tawnies state their average age (the average of the ages of wines from which they were blended) on the label—10, 20, 30, or 40 years. Ten-year-old tawnies cost about $15 to $25, and 20-year-olds sell for $35.

White Port

White Port rarely is seen outside Portugal or France. Made from white-grape varieties, it has a golden color, and it's usually finished dry, bottled young, and drunk as an apéritif. The sweet-finished version usually is inferior in quality. (You can find much better apéritifs.)

Vintage Character Port

Vintage character Port is a blend of premium ruby Ports from several vintages, cask-aged for about five years. They are full-bodied, rich, ready to drink when bottled, and sell for about $12 to $15. Vintage character Ports are sold under a proprietary name like Boardroom (made by Dow).

Port at Home

Like other fine red wines, vintage Ports should be stored on their sides in a cool environment. Other Ports may be stored upright like liquor, because they're already fully developed. With the exception of ruby and white, all Ports will keep several weeks after opening.

You should serve your Port at cool room temperature, 66 to 68 degrees Fahrenheit. Ports go well with nuts and strong cheeses. Try walnuts with Stilton cheese.

Ports of the World

The name "Port" refers, properly, to the city of Oporto. But the term has been borrowed and used generically, like (sorry, Kimberly-Clark!) "Kleenex."

California and South Africa have an unfortunate history of producing dull and ordinary Ports, tainted by baked qualities and coming from grapes inappropriate to a hot climate. Today, these regions have set their sights on producing high-quality Port. Now, vintners in both places plant local grape varieties as they search for finer fortifying spirits.

In California, winemakers have developed several very interesting Ports made either from blended grapes or from blends in which Zinfandel predominates. Among the Port revivalists, Amador County and parts of Sonoma County have gained attention as respected Port wine regions. South Africa, a country traditionally noted for making fortified wines, has awakened our notice with its finer Port wines. Some South African versions are nearly indistinguishable from the Oporto products.

The Sommelier Says

Non-Oporto ports simply are dessert wines made in many countries. Some are good; some are adequate; and some are cheap, baked-tasting, sweet wines bearing little resemblance to the real thing. Perhaps the best Ports to be seen outside of Portugal come from Australia. Look for Yalumba, Chateau Reynella, and Lindemans.

From Jerez to Sherry?

Originating in the Jerez (Andalucia) region of southern Spain, "Sherry" is the Anglicized pronunciation of "Jerez." This ancient Moorish town is the site of many Sherry *bodegas* (wineries), but it is just one part of the Sherry-producing region.

The coastal village of Puerto de Santa Maria, located southwest of Jerez, also boasts several bodegas. The sea air is believed to be an important element in the making of dry *fino* (a type of sherry). Ten miles northwest of Jerez, another coastal village, Sanlucar de Barrameda, is so renowned for its sea breezes that the lightest and driest of sherries, *Manzanilla*, legally can be made only there. (It does not appear possible to make wine of this quality elsewhere.)

The predominant grape variety used in Sherry is the *Palomino*, a prolific vine with delicious, edible fruit, but which normally yields thin, neutral, and sometimes harsh table wines. Once again, inventive winemakers have turned a liability into a plus.

This wine oxidizes easily during aging, yielding the characteristic and desirable nutty aroma and flavor that are the hallmarks of a fine Sherry. *Pedro Ximenez* is a secondary grape for Sherry, yielding a very sweet wine that is often used as a blending or sweetening agent. *Moscatel* (Muscat) sometimes is used for dessert Sherries.

On the Flor

Sherry is a fortified wine made in large volume. Most producers use modern, efficient methods of crushing and vinification. The Sherry-to-be begins as a wine that is fermented in stainless steel tanks.

The first-year wine is then aged at the bodega in *butts* (U.S.-made oak barrels with a capacity of 158 gallons) filled to about one-third capacity. What evolves over the next year or two is a drama of self-fulfillment. Some butts will reveal a propensity toward developing the unique, thick, white film yeast called *flor* in Jerez. Others won't.

The wine's progress in each butt is chronicled, and based on the intrinsic character and development of the flor, the wine is channeled into one of three directions:

➤ Wines without any flor character and with weak flavors either will be distilled into spirits or made into vinegar.

➤ Wines that develop only a small degree of flor, but have good body and flavors, are marked as "Olorosos" and introduced into a solera. (You'll learn about soleras soon!)

➤ Wines that are light in color with a thick layer of flor are marked as "Finos" and sent to another solera.

Within the bodegas, butts marked "Fino" will be made into three different styles of Sherry: Fino, Manzanilla, and Amontillado. The Olorosos will be made into Oloroso, cream Sherry, or brown Sherry. The crucial factor in achieving quality in a Sherry lies in the aging process. Most sherries are non-vintage wines, and almost all are the product of the *solera* system of blending and aging in butts.

The *solera* itself is a configuration (usually triangular) of barrels containing Sherry of various ages. It's usually composed of three tiers or rows, with each successive tier representing a younger wine. There is a method behind this.

The system is based on the premise that newer wines "refresh" the older ones, and the union releases a host of flavors. This procedure, called fractional blending, marries old wine with newer wine from different tiers of the solera.

The oldest Sherry resides in the bottom tier. Above it are the *criada*, sort of a nursery in which the Sherries mature. In an established solera, the butts remain. The wine moves first laterally, and then down from one tier to the next. (Think of it as one of those mechanical puzzles with the sliding wooden squares.)

When the wine is bottled, the bodega master drains off part (no more than one third) from each butt on the bottom tier and replaces it with wine from the tier above. As Sherry moves throughout the solera, it's continually in the process of fractional blending. (Mathematically, each bottle will have at least a little of the very first wine that was present when the solera was established.)

Vino Vocab

The word **solera** is derived from **suelo**, the word for "bottom" or "ground," referring to the bottom tier of the solera.

Fino

Fino, the finest Sherry, is always produced and aged within Jerez or in Puerto de Santa Maria. It has a pale color, a yeasty, slightly nutty aroma, delicate flavors, and is usually dry, sometimes slightly bitter. Its scent is often reminiscent of almonds. The alcohol content ranges from 15.5 to 17 percent.

Manzanilla

Manzanilla is Fino produced in Sanlucar de Barrameda. It is pale, straw-colored, delicate, and light-bodied. Some say the wine's slightly bitter, tangy, and pungent character is due to the salty flavors picked up from the sea air.

Wines made in Sanlucar but sent to Jerez for aging in solera do not develop the typical character of Manzanilla. So maybe there is something to this sea spray idea. More likely, the temperate sea climate causes the flor to grow more thickly. Manzanilla is the driest and most intense of all the Sherries. Serve it well chilled.

Amontillado

Amontillado is an amber-colored, aged Fino that's spent a longer time in the solera. It's medium-bodied with a more pronounced, nutty flavor. Amontillado is dry and pungent. True amontillado is seen often, and it's expensive. Some lesser Sherries are labeled "Amontillado." If you find an Amontillado selling for $6 or less, it is not worth buying. Serve Amontillado slightly chilled.

Tasting Tip

Amontillado has been esteemed by Americans for a very long time, as you can infer from Edgar Allen Poe's classic tale of horror, *The Cask of Amontillado.*

Oloroso

Oloroso is deep in color and boasts a rich, full-bodied style with a scent of walnuts. Because of its prolonged aging, it lacks the yeasty flor pungency. Olorosos are customarily dry wines, sometimes sweetened to suit market demands. They usually contain between 18 and 20 percent alcohol. Serve at room temperature or very slightly chilled.

Palo Cortado

This rare breed of Sherry is the best of the non-flor Sherries. It begins life as a fino with a flor, but develops as an Amontillado after losing its flor. Later, it resembles the richer, more fragrant Oloroso style, while retaining the elegance of an Amontillado. Palo Cortado is similar to an Oloroso in color, but its aroma is like Amontillado. (Got that?) Serve at room temperature or slightly chilled.

Medium Sherry

Medium Sherry is an Amontillado or light Oloroso that has been slightly sweetened.

Pale Cream

Pale cream Sherry is a slightly sweetened blend of fino and light Amontillado Sherries.

Cream Sherry

Cream Sherry is made from Oloroso wine, often of poor quality. Once sweetened, the sweetness will mask the defects.

The wine is sweetened and the color darkened by the addition of wines from Pedro Ximenez grapes, which are left to sun-dry for seven to 10 days for extra sugar development. Pedro Ximenez is a thick, concentrated, very sweet wine; so not much is required to make a cream Sherry. However, its character is a key factor in the quality of the finished product. Cream Sherries are very popular.

The Sommelier Says

Many fortified wines labeled "Sherry" are out-and-out impostors! Few made outside Spain go through the solera process. Even the best solera sherries don't measure up in flavor and interest to the real product from its Spanish homeland.

Brown Sherry

Brown Sherry is a blend of Oloroso, Pedro Ximenez, and an added sweetening agent. It's very dark, very syrupy, and very, very sweet. The style is far more common in the U.K. than the U.S. *East India* is a type of brown Sherry that is even sweeter and darker in color.

Pedro Ximenez and Moscatel

Pedro Ximenez and Moscatel are extremely sweet, dark brown, syrupy dessert wines that can be used as a sauce on desserts. They are made from raisined grapes of these two varieties and are low in alcohol.

Montilla

Montilla is located northeast of the Jerez region. The wines made here are similar to the Fino, Amontillado, and Oloroso styles of Sherry. Unlike Sherry, they are not fortified to higher alcohol levels, but derive their strength naturally during fermentation. The main grape variety is the Pedro Ximenez. The leading brand for Montilla is Alvear, usually priced at $8 to $9. Once seldom seen in the U.S., it's now widely distributed.

Ready to Serve

Always buy Fino and Manzanilla when you're ready to serve them. They're at peak flavor and complexity when first opened, but an open bottle can keep in the refrigerator up to a month. (After such storage, it won't taste quite like the intricate blend the bodega master intended, but it's still drinkable and delightful.)

Appendix A, "Recommended Wines," lists recommended Sherry producers.

Legendary Madeira

Once famous as the beverage of choice in colonial America, *Madeira* is named for the Portugal-owned island off the Atlantic coast of Morocco. The grapes for this legendary fortified wine are grown on very steep hillsides that ring the perimeter of the island. The wines of Madeira often are identified by their predominant grape variety. These include, principally, Verdelho, Sercial, Bual (or Boal), and Malvasia.

To say that Madeira is hardy is an understatement! It's not just its robust character, but also its ability to age. If a wine can be called a survivor, Madeira is it. The prime Madeiras are vintage-dated from 1920 all the way back to 1795, when the colonists were still around to enjoy their favorite drink. Even the rarest, most noble Château Lafite is a mere infant by comparison.

The styles of Madeira range from sweet to moderately dry. As the juice of the grapes (or *mosto*) is fermented in large vats, the wines destined for a dry style will complete fermentation. The sweeter versions will have fermentation arrested through the addition of brandy.

Madeira employs one unusual production technique that accounts for its unique character. It's baked. The process is called *estufagem* (from *estufas*, or ovens). But the wine isn't put into baking dishes and placed into bread ovens or anything like that. Traditionally, it was placed into large casks that were left out under the hot sun.

Today, the slightly roasted or smoky tang is achieved by aging in heat-controlled vats. In the estufas, the temperature increases gradually until it reaches about 110 degrees Fahrenheit, where it remains for several months. The sugars in the wine become caramelized, and some of the wine components oxidize, a process called *maderization*. After estufagem, the Madeira is allowed to cool and recover for the same period of time. Finally, it is fortified and aged in wood casks before being bottled.

Heard It Through the Grapevine

The *estufagem* technique was discovered quite by accident. This was back in the days when Madeira was shipped in the holds of sailing vessels. En route to the East Indies, ships passed through the tropical heat. In the overheated hold, the wine changed character. The resulting heady flavor was a hit.

Okay, I admit it! Madeira is an acquired taste. Technically, this is a white wine, though even the most robust Chardonnay literally pales beside it. Madeira's characteristic color is a dark, rich amber. It has a rich, nutty aroma, a sharp tang to its flavors, and a finish as long as its age.

Most Madeira is sold under proprietary names. Authentic vintage Madeira usually comes from a single cask. Many Madeiras are aged in solera, and with those that are labeled as solera, the dates refer to *when the solera was established,* not to the entire contents of the bottle. (Though the bottle actually does contain a little wine that really is that old.)

Twenty years is the designated cask-aging time for a vintage Madeira, although the wines were once aged even longer. Special Reserve Madeiras are a blend of wines about 10 years old and are less expensive. Reserve Madeira is about five years old.

The styles of Madeira are differentiated both by the grape and the level of sweetness. These names reflect either the grape variety or style:

➤ **Sercial**   The finest dry Madeira, Sercial has a lightness and delicacy that lends itself well to enjoyment as an apéritif. The grape is grown at the highest altitude, so it's one of the latest to ripen. It offers the most distinctive aroma and a dry, tangy taste on the palate.

The Sommelier Says

With most wines, particularly whites or rosés, maderization is bad news. Both the color and the taste are destroyed, generally through age or bad storage. In the case of Madeira, though, it's the touch that brings out its best character.

➤ **Verdelho**   Slightly sweeter and rounder on the palate than Sercial, it has a more typical Madeira aroma that can best be described as a toasted, nutty character.

➤ **Bual (also Boal)**   Sweeter than Sercial or Verdelho, much fuller in body, and darker in color with flavors of raisins and almonds, it makes for a nice wine to serve with dessert.

➤ **Malmsey**   Made from the Malvasia grape, Malmsey is the sweetest of all—dark amber in color, with a smooth, luxurious texture and a very long finish.

➤ **Rainwater**   Well-known in the U.S. (not surprising, from its name, which was once the proprietary name given it by a shipper in Savannah, Georgia), it can be variable in sweetness. But, as its name implies, it will be rather pale in color.

➤ **Terrantez**   Between Verdelho and Bual in style, it is a powerful, medium-sweet, fragrant Madeira with a lot of acidity. It is rarely seen these days.

Tasting Tip

Are you interested in antiques? How about nineteenth-century vintage Madeiras? Yes, you can find them, and for about $100 to $200 a bottle. Not bad for such a distinguished bit of wine history. And don't worry—it won't be spoiled. Just remember the Madeira motto, "Nothing can keep a good wine down."

Setúbal

Setúbal is a Portuguese dessert wine from the town of Azeitao, south of Lisbon. Made from the Muscat grape, it is somewhat similar to Port, with grape spirit added to halt fermentation. It's a rich wine with longevity.

Marsala

Italy's most famous fortified wine, *Marsala*, takes its name from its prime production center, the town of Marsala in western Sicily. In vogue as a chic beverage in the late eighteenth century, it has since been reduced to the status of a cooking ingredient—a common dessert wine at best.

Despite its tarnished reputation, Marsala does bear some resemblance to Madeira, and devotees (and producers) are bent on a Marsala revival. It is dark in color, with amber, red, or gold versions.

Marsala has a caramel aroma, tending to be very sweet, but there are dry and semidry versions. The sugar comes from allowing the grapes to dry in the sun prior to fermentation or, more commonly, from the addition of grape concentrate after fermentation. Dry Marsala often is blended in a solera system. Dates on Marsala bottles refer to the founding of the solera, not to a particular vintage.

The best Marsalas are labeled "Superiore" or "Vergine." Marsala Vergine is unsweetened, uncolored, and aged longer than other styles.

Vermouth

Vermouth, a flavored, fortified wine, derives its name from the German word *Wermut* ("wormwood," the plant that yields a bitter extract). It's made in many wine regions throughout the world. It boasts an intriguing list of flavoring agents: herbs, juniper, coriander, and, of course, *wormwood*, to name but a few.

Vino Vocab

Actually, there are neither worms nor wood in **wormwood**, the bracing bitter flavor in **Vermouth**. The word is a corruption of the German word *Wermut*, which means "man-strength."

Vermouth normally begins as inexpensive, bland white wine. The herb infusion, which has been steeped in alcohol, is then added, and the whole is quickly blended to marry. The herb formula varies from brand to brand, and Vermouths vary from fairly dry to quite sweet. Vermouth is inexpensive, ubiquitous, and used as an apéritif or mixer. (Without Vermouth, a martini would be nothing but gin and an olive.)

The Least You Need to Know

➤ Fortified wine is made by adding alcohol to wine to raise its alcoholic content.

➤ Port is produced throughout the world, but authentic Port is produced only in Portugal and is officially called Porto.

➤ Sherry is produced throughout the world, but authentic Sherry is made in the Jerez region of Spain.

➤ Madeira is produced only on the island of Madeira off the coast of North Africa.

Organic Wine

Today, 1 percent of the U.S. food supply is grown using organic methods. That seems like only a little, but it's about $4 billion! (And growing rapidly, as you must have noticed the last time you passed your supermarket's produce counter.) Organic foods have left the specialty stores and small cooperatives, and they have entered the merchandising mainstream.

Many restaurant chefs now use organic produce, because they perceive superior quality and taste. Organic food has gained acceptance worldwide, with Japan and Germany becoming important international markets for organic foods.

Organic wines are mainstream now, with significant production in the U.S., France, Germany, and Canada. You'll see them at your local wine store. This chapter explores some reasons why you might choose organic. And we'll try to peek a little inside the bottle.

Why Pick Organic?

For many shoppers, the word "organic" is a valuable assurance that what they consume is not tainted with man-made fertilizers, antibiotics, herbicides, hormones, or pesticides. Increasingly, this consciousness has extended to wine. The reasons are various. You may agree, or disagree, with any of these. But as a wise consumer, you'll want to understand your options.

In certain wine regions, organic farming results in a more full-flavored and complex wine as the vine roots have to grow deeper to seek the nourishment they would otherwise receive from chemical fertilizers. Not all organically farmed wines adhere to the abstinence of sulfites or other chemicals. We must distinguish those that do from those that don't.

To Your Health

Does soil management make a difference in the taste and quality of food? Some people believe it does. Research demonstrates that for higher-quality wines, organic farming can lead to superior grape quality.

What about pesticides and herbicides used in wine growing? Do some residues linger in the wine we drink? Unquestionably. But harmful? Those who set limits and standards say no. But many others say yes. Or at least that there's a cumulative effect of strange chemicals from hundreds of sources entering our bodies through food, drink, and air.

One thing we can say for sure: Organic products don't add anything harmful to our diets. In fact, the term "organic" used to be defined more in terms of what it lacked than for what it offered.

Sulfite Sensitivity

To a large number of American wine drinkers (estimated at 1 in 250), "organic" on the wine label means one thing: lower *sulfite* levels (or even no sulfites at all). These are the people who are very sensitive to sulfites, who may experience unpleasant side-effects, from mild to severe. In actuality, U.S. government regulations for organic products permit a level of sulfites higher than many nonorganic wines contain and may be too high for persons with sulfite sensitivity.

Vino Vocab

What are **sulfites**? These are chemical compounds that contain an SO_3 arrangement. They are a by-product of treating wine with sulfur dioxide gas (SO_2). The SO_2 gas reacts with the water in wine to form a very weak sulfurous acid solution, H_2SO_3. Much of this will consume the small amount of oxygen trapped in the wine to prevent harmful oxidation in the bottle. But a little may react with some of the natural compounds in wine to form sulfites.

Once wine is bottled for final consumption, any remaining microbes—including yeast or bacteria—could spoil that wine. Also, you might remember that many of wine's delicate flavor compounds can be ruined through oxidation. A small amount of SO_2 gas, added to the wine at various stages of production, kills "wild yeasts" and bacteria. It also consumes dissolved oxygen, as sulfites become sulfates. In the U.S., sulfites are limited to 350 parts per million (ppm) or less, with all forms of sulfur counted, although wines usually contain considerably less. European and Australian limits are similar. Organic certification typically allows sulfites of up to 90 ppm for red wines and 100 ppm for whites. However, most organic growers come in at less than 40 ppm.

Sulfites occur naturally in grapes, and they are a by-product of fermentation. In some cases, sulfites could reach as much as 40 ppm with no added SO_2 gas! Somehow, a very few organic vintners have managed to make a product so low in sulfites that they are undetectable.

Under Bureau of Alcohol, Tobacco, and Firearms (BATF) labeling requirements, anything with more than 10 ppm of sulfites must have the words "contains sulfites." Wines with less need not display that warning, but neither may they claim "sulfite-free" (except in those rare cases in which sulfite levels are undetectable). This is not based on the "honor system." Such vintners must include a sulfite analysis from an approved testing laboratory when they apply to the BATF for approval of their wine labels.

There is an important bit of leeway in BATF-approved labeling, though. Organic vintners may (where applicable) use the words "no added sulfites" or "naturally occurring sulfites only." The minority who make no use of sulfur dioxide in their wine production want you to know they went to this special trouble. (Also, you need to know this when it comes to storage and keeping properties.)

Sulfur dioxide gas has been used for centuries as a fruit preservative. The amount appearing in wines has fallen throughout the world as countries impose stricter limits. These limits vary with the type of wine being treated. If you are sulfite-sensitive, or if you can taste these compounds in your wines (some people can), organic wines might be your best choice.

Lifestyle Choice

Organic agriculture is more than the sum of its parts. It's a philosophy, one that considers the ecological context of all human activity, that val-

> **Tasting Tip**
>
> Most organic vintners do use sulfur dioxide gas. Without any, most wines would soon spoil—particularly white wines, which lack the tannins of reds. But they use it in great moderation, yielding a product lower in sulfite than most other wines. Organic wines without any added sulfites are a rarity, as such wines are susceptible to oxidation.

ues diversity and natural biological processes of competition, growth, death, and regeneration.

Many conscientious consumers try to reward environmental "good behavior" by selecting products produced by growers and manufacturers who share their concerns. This shows up in the strong growth we have seen in the (still small) market share garnered by organic vintners.

What Makes Organic Organic?

Many decades ago, the term "organic" was pretty clear. It meant, simply, growing crops without manufactured fertilizers. Organic gardening and farming used manure and compost instead of manufactured phosphates and nitrates.

Later, "organic" began to embrace other aspects of growing: pesticides, soil management, biodiversity, animal husbandry and food processing. Several states and many countries implemented standards for labeling products "organic." But there was no U.S. national standard.

In 1990, Congress passed the Organic Food Production Act, which directed the U.S. Department of Agriculture (USDA) to develop national standards for foods labeled "organic." The federal Natural Organic Standards Board (NOSB) has set to work developing standards for food and wine.

The Sommelier Says

How can it take 10 years to develop national standards for organic foods and beverages? Part of the answer lies in the utter complexity of the whole problem. Another answer lies in politics. Different producers have different interests. From the grower's standpoint, the best rule would be one that embraces all of that particular grower's practices—but no others.

These standards will cover all organic crops and processed foods, including produce, grain, meat, dairy, eggs, and fiber. (To learn more about the proposed rule, visit the National Organic Program's Web site at www.ams.usda.gov/nop/)

The Organic Grapes into Wine Alliance (OGWA), a producers' association, has been diligent in presenting model standards to both BATF and USDA. But as this is written, the USDA still has not decided which rules belong and which do not.

When it comes to wine, regulatory authority is distributed over many agencies. The BATF regulates wine labeling. The Federal Trade Commission (FTC) governs organic food advertising. The Food and Drug Administration (FDA) decides which foods may be labeled "organic." And the USDA figures out what ingredients belong in organic foods.

"Certified organic" on the label means products that have been grown and processed according to strict uniform standards, verified annually by independent state or private organizations. Certification includes inspection of farm fields and processing facilities. The label "certified organic grapes" means only that the grapes have been grown organically.

Farm field inspections look at long-term soil management, buffering between organic farms and neighboring conventional farms, and record keeping. Processing inspections include reviews of the facility's cleaning and pest control methods, ingredient transportation and storage, and record keeping.

Organic wine is more than wine made from organically grown grapes. The concept extends to the winemaking itself. In this section, we'll discuss both.

Organically Grown

Organic farming systems avoid both pesticides and manufactured fertilizers. That doesn't mean organic growers are indifferent to soil fertility or to pest damage. Far from it!

Organic farming is not a throwback to primitive agriculture. Instead, it's very scientific, within whatever constraints organic certifying bodies or the growers themselves place on it. Organic growing requires a deep understanding of the ecology of soils and the plants that grow in them.

Soil is much more than bits of rock and other minerals. Healthy soils are teeming universes of microbial life and microscopic bits of plant debris. There are dozens of active processes—not unlike fermentation—that render dead plant material into available nutrition for living plants.

In natural settings, growth and decay are in balance. Agriculture upsets that balance as crops are harvested and removed. Crop rotation helps delay nutrient depletion, but most modern farmers have had to turn to manufactured fertilizers to obtain good (and profitable) yields.

Tasting Tip

Individual states have their own organic certification and certifying boards. This makes it tough for organic wineries that, naturally, want to market their goods nationally. So far, the only label designations approved by BATF are "Certified Organic Grown" and "Certified Organic Viticulture."

Tasting Tip

When we hear of organic farming, we think of California, where social and cultural trends seem to begin. But in the case of organic wine, California was a real laggard. France was the first to get into organic wine in a big way, followed by Germany. California (along with Canada and Australia) is a relative newcomer. But a very quick learner!

Heard It Through the Grapevine

The healthiest soils are those that are in constant use, with nothing removed. As nutrients are released by dead matter, they are taken up by roots of living matter before they can be washed away. Organic winegrowers grow cover crops along with their grapes. These are plowed under each season. Cover crops also help with pest control and erosion from both wind and water.

Organic grape growing returns much of the crop (everything but the grape *must*) to the soil. It plants other crops (cover crops) to fix nitrogen and to control pests. These crops will be plowed back into the soil each season. As needed, organic growers augment their soils with natural fertilizers, such as composted manure.

Vino Vocab

Bordeaux mixture is lime, copper sulfate, and water. It leaves no residue in the wine you buy. The mixture's use against plant disease was discovered a hundred years ago in the Bordeaux wine region of France. Though Bordeaux mixture doesn't occur in nature, certifying bodies allow its use in organic growing, possibly because it's old and uses no petrochemicals.

The organic grower's first line of defense against pests is prevention. With planting diversity, there is pest diversity. This means no particular pest develops a dense population. And overall biodiversity—in soil organisms, insects, and birds—ensures that no one pest population will grow large enough to damage the wine crop.

When pests do become a problem, there are other ways than poisons to deal with them. These include introduction of insect predators, mating disruption (through the use of synthetic pheromones!), traps, and barriers. As a last resort, organic farmers will apply natural, plant-derived pesticides, only as much as needed.

Bacteria and fungi can be as devastating to a crop as insects. Organic growing certification bodies allow the application of Bordeaux mixture—lime, copper sulfate, and water—to crops and soils. It's effective and leaves no toxic residue in the must or wine. However, overuse of this mixture can add excess copper, which in acidic soils can reduce grape yields.

The most effective preventive factor in plant disease is climate. Hot, dry conditions mean little disease. In fact, some winegrowers who don't seek organic certification have adopted chemical-free agriculture. In cooler or moister climates, organic winegrowing can be very difficult.

Weed control depends on increased cultivation, along with cover crops, mulches, and flame weeding. (Burned plant material maintains all its mineral nutrients.)

Organic growers spend nothing on manufactured fertilizers and pesticides. But they must apply considerably more labor to meet their production goals, and crop yields are somewhat smaller. Yes, it costs more. But many consumers are willing to pay the organic premium.

Vino Vocab

Would you like to sample French organic wine in its country of origin? Well, don't ask for **organic wine**. In France, it's called **vin bio** (short for *vin biologique*).

Organically Produced

Just as organic growing is not primitive agriculture, neither is organic winemaking a throwback to some preindustrial period. We could argue, in fact, that organic viticulture is the most modern of all, because organic producers are only now developing and learning methods that ensure good quality and keeping properties.

Some who sampled organic wines, say, 10 years ago might have been disappointed in a product that was off-color, sometimes with little bits of material visible in the liquid. Today's organic wines are clear, clean, and fresh.

Organic winemakers pay close attention to three things: yeast, fining (clarification), and sulfur dioxide.

Many organic vintners use only the yeasts that settle and grow naturally on the grape skins (as do many nonorganic producers). Crop sprays used in conventional viticulture sometimes kill these yeasts. In any event, many conventional winemakers prefer the predictability of cultured yeasts.

Wild yeasts do add an element of variability to organic winemaking, but I've not known this to interfere with the fermentation of any crop. On the other hand, we may see greater year-to-year variability than with more controlled uses of cultured yeasts.

Organic vintners clarify their wine with minimal physical handling. Such handling can introduce oxygen, which increases the need for sulfur dioxide gas for preservation. For some reason, organic certification does not permit the use of the centrifuge.

Tasting Tip

Fining (clarification) processes may add trace amounts of foreign matter to the final product. For example, beaten egg white is a common and very effective fining agent. But it does leave a very small quantity of protein in the wine. Some organic vintners sell into markets that seek foods and beverages with no animal products, so egg whites are not suitable in their operations.

(See Chapter 8, "Hot Off the Vine.") So far, no one has given me a good reason for this rule.

Filtering is not uncommon in organic wine production, often making use of sterilized cellulose material. Another effective filtering agent—and a natural, nonanimal one—is diatomaceous earth, microscopic siliceous remains of certain species of algae.

Finally, as we discussed earlier, some organic winemakers minimize their use of sulfur dioxide gas in the growing and production of their product. In fact, some organic growers have proved it's possible to produce good wines without any added sulfites whatsoever. Of course, these wines have poorer storage and keeping properties.

Serving Organic Wines

Even if you're not someone who seeks out organic foods and wines, don't turn your back on organic wines. Organically grown can mean fuller flavor and more complex wine from the better wine-producing regions of the world. Organic winegrowers are a dedicated breed—wild-eyed, even, some of them. That means loving care and attention throughout the process, from cultivation to bottling. And think of the adventure: that your beverage was fermented from (gasp!) wild yeasts!

Heard It Through the Grapevine

The words "certified organic" on the label mean only that the methods of growing or production were certified by one of several certifying organizations throughout the world. All the world's organic agriculture groups belong to the International Federation of Organic Agriculture Movements, or IFOAM. (What a great name that would have been for a brewer's organization!)

Many organic wines are quite good, and you can serve them with confidence. You must, however, serve them with a little extra care if the sulfite level is not high enough to prevent oxidation. With minimal processing and preservatives (sulfur dioxide), these wines can be very fragile.

Don't Spoil a Good Thing

Did you ever cut an apple into slices and watch them turn brown before your eyes? This is oxidation—a cosmetic problem for apples, a disaster for wines. Here's the reason: The parts of your wine that oxidize are generally those that give it its flavor.

The Sommelier Says

Molds present on the grape at the time of crushing hasten the chemical reactions that cause changes in color or taste. So without the use of sulfur dioxide gas to inhibit oxidation, organic growing requires extreme care.

Actually, oxidation becomes a problem the instant the grape is crushed. As soon as the juice is exposed to air, oxidation begins. Oxidation can destroy the appearance of any white wine. And conversion of certain acids can cause a wine to taste herbaceous, like leaves.

Once wine is bottled, the only oxidation you need to worry about is from the little bit of air trapped in the bottle (or dissolved in the wine). But when you open your low-sulfite or no-sulfite wine, mischief begins immediately.

Of course, there's rarely any need to open your organic wine early to let it breath. (See Chapter 2, "Savvy Serving.") It's best to open it just before you serve it. And, if reasonable, try to finish the whole bottle. (If it's dinner for one, that would be a bit too much. But read the next section ....)

Saving for a Rainy Day

Sometimes you have to store your organic wines. Before opening, that's not too hard. If sulfites have been added, even below the lower limits imposed on organic vintners, your bottled organic wine should keep for months, even years. That assumes you are quite careful. The same rules apply as with most other wines: Keep it away from heat, bright light, vibration, and avoid rapid temperature changes.

Once your wine is opened, though, you do have to take special care. Refrigeration slows the processes of oxidation or spoilage, but it cannot stop them altogether. Try to drink the remainder of your low-sulfite wine shortly after opening. Or you can put your organic leftovers into your refrigerator for a day or two (see Chapter 2) and keep it a little longer.

The Least You Need to Know

➤ Organic wines can be lower in sulfites than other wines, but this is not always the case.

➤ Organic certification requires special techniques for growing and vinification.

➤ France, Germany, U.S., Australia, and Canada are leading producers of organic wines.

➤ Low-sulfite wines degrade quickly after exposure to air.

Chapter 24

Kosher Wine

In This Chapter

➤ The why and how of kosher wine

➤ Why you should consider kosher wine

➤ Who makes it and where

Jewish or not, you have kosher foods in your house. Check the packages or the labels. See that little letter *U* inside the circle? Or that little letter *K*? These are registered symbols of two organizations that certify foods as kosher. You might see one (or both) of these symbols on a bottle of wine, too.

No, kosher is not another grape varietal. And from the standpoint of grape, winemaking style, or country of origin, kosher is inapplicable. Kosher wines come in many varieties and styles and from many lands. Many of these are superior wines in every regard. And a few are, well, unusual—resembling certain wines that were popular in the U.S. 50 years ago.

Kosher? Whazzat?

"Kosher wine? Oh, yeah! It's that purple pancake syrup in the fat bottle." Want another guess? "Okay. It's wine that's blessed by some rabbi." Uh, not quite. Actually, the concept of kosher wine is quite simple.

Heard It Through the Grapevine

If kosher wines are just like other wines in varietal, style, and origin, how can you tell what's kosher and what isn't? The easy answer is to check the label for the symbols of either of two organizations that certify food and beverages as kosher.

One is the Orthodox Union, a 75-year-old international body. Its symbol is the letter *U* inside the letter *O*. The other is Kosher Overseers Associates of America, which uses a stylized letter *K*. Producers of food and drink may submit their products to one (or both) of these organizations for kosher certification, for which they pay a small fee.

This is smart marketing, because many observant Jewish families purchase only dietary products that are certified kosher.

Kosher wine, like any kosher food, is wine prepared according to *kashrut*, the body of Jewish law and tradition that's concerned with dietary practices. Any wine made in accordance with kashrut is kosher.

The strictest Jewish dietary observance doesn't permit consumption of meat and dairy products in the same meal, or even the use of the same dishes and utensils for both. If even the smallest amount of meat or dairy product is present in the production of food or drink, this will be noted with the kosher symbol, sometimes with just an *M* for *meat* or a *D* for *dairy*.

Kosher foods that are neither meat nor dairy are labeled *pareve*, which is Yiddish for "neutral." (The word *pareve* may or may not appear on the label.)

There is only one other important restriction: During the eight days of Passover, certain leavened grains and legumes may not be eaten. Foods that do not contain these products may be labeled "Kosher for Passover" or with the letter *P*.

Vino Vocab

Kosher is from the Hebrew word that means "fitting" or "suitable." **Kashrut** (kash-ROOT) is the Jewish law and tradition of kosher diet. **Pareve** (PAH-reh-veh) is Yiddish for "neutral," neither meat nor dairy.

What Makes Wine Kosher?

Wine is a special case in Jewish law and tradition. Wine is an integral part of rituals in synagogues or households, such as the Kiddush, a sanctification spoken over wine on the eve of the Sabbath or of a holiday (such as Passover).

For this reason, the *kashrut* for wine is somewhat stricter than that for other foods and beverages. Wine consumed for sacramental purposes must meet certain very strict requirements.

Special Handling

Kosher certification requires attention to all parts of the wine production process. Certifying bodies inspect wineries to ensure continued compliance of the following:

➤ All equipment used in growing, fermentation, aging, and bottling must be used exclusively in the production of kosher products.

➤ The grapes and wine may be handled only by Sabbath-observing Jews. If the wine is *mevushal*, i.e., pasteurized, this requirement is waived.

➤ Only kosher-certified products may be used in the winemaking process. These include yeasts and filtering agents.

Tasting Tip

About a third of the food and drink we consume is certified as kosher. That is, it's prepared from ingredients that are themselves kosher using equipment that only comes into contact with ingredients that are kosher.

Mevushal Does the Trick

Jewish commentators believe the Torah (the books of the Bible attributed to Moses) excludes non-Jews from the winemaking process as a means of preventing intermarriage. After all, wine, in all its aspects, is a great socializer.

Mevushal (pasteurization) is a different issue. Observant Jews may not drink any wine that could be used in pagan worship. Tradition dictates that wine that has been boiled is unfit for such use, making it okay for Jewish use.

Wines that are pasteurized need not be handled only by observant Jews. However, all other requirements of kosher certification must be met.

The Sommelier Says

The temperatures of pasteurization destroy bacteria but also can destroy the flavor components in the wine. Fortunately, technology has come to the rescue. It's called flash pasteurization. Now it's possible to run wine through special apparatus that heats it and returns it to its original temperature in a fraction of a second—enough time to kill microbes, but not enough to destroy the flavor.

Not Just for Sacramental Purposes

Fifty years ago many Americans, regardless of religion, could name only two brands of wine: Mogen David and Manischewitz, both kosher wines. Today, many wineries from several countries offer certified kosher wines, in great variety, often of very high quality.

Heard It Through the Grapevine

Most kosher wines are flash pasteurized, or mevushal. Under kashrut, these wines need not be handled exclusively by observant Jews. This is a practical consideration, since a bottle of wine might pass through many hands on its way to your table at home or in a restaurant.

So the best reason to drink a kosher wine is the best reason to drink any wine: because you like it. Remember, you already buy dozens if not hundreds of certified kosher foods through your everyday shopping. The kosher certification has nothing to do with quality or value.

Another reason you might consider kosher wines, particularly if you have a cellar and do much entertaining, is to have some on hand to serve guests who are kashrut-observant. They'll appreciate your consideration no less than you'll appreciate their joining you in wine toasts.

Finding Kosher Wines in Your Hometown

Kosher wines are made in most major wine-producing countries. They range in quality from the most ordinary to the genuinely extraordinary. But you may have trouble finding any in that little wine shop in Smallville.

The nice thing about finding one kosher wine is that you likely will find several in that same wine store. Some importers specialize in locating kosher wines from all over. One with a worldwide reputation is the Royal Wine Corporation in New York City.

Kosher wines are produced in the U.S., France, Italy, Israel, Chile, Canada, and Australia. Not all make it into export markets.

New York

New York state is the original home of the American kosher wine industry. Grapes for these wines come from both the Finger Lakes district and the Hudson Valley. In both regions the superior vinifera grape is harvested, as well as the more traditional lambrusca species.

Heard It Through the Grapevine

Owned and operated by members of the Herzog family, the Royal Wine Corporation has made kosher wines since 1848. After the upheavals of war in their native Czechoslovakia and the communist takeover in 1948, the family relocated to the U.S., where they produce, import, and distribute the finest kosher wines from around the world.

The Royal Wine Corporation operates vineyards and a winery at Milton in the Hudson Valley, where it produces some excellent vinifera-based wines as well as the older-style sweetened wines. The Shapiro Wine Company of New York City is America's oldest kosher winery, with its vineyards located in the Finger Lakes region.

California

The Royal Wine Corporation is a major presence among the kosher wine producers of California, under the Baron Herzog brand. In the Golden State, this house makes wines ranging from good to superb. Its Alexander Valley Special Reserve Cabernet Sauvignon of 1995 is very highly regarded.

Other major players in California's kosher wine trade are Hagafen Cellars and Weinstock Cellars. Also, there are many small but dedicated vintners supplying demand for kosher wines.

Celebrating? Look for the kosher symbol on some bottles of non-vintage Korbel Brut sparkling wine.

France

When you think of France, you think of Bordeaux. And Bordeaux evokes the name Rothschild. Yes, that distinguished name has been on a kosher label since 1986 (after an absence of 100 years), thanks to the efforts of U.S.-based Royal Wine. This is under the label "Barons Edmond et Benjamin de Rothschild."

Royal Wine also is responsible for Château de la Grave Herzog Selection Dry Red, a Bordeaux. There are many other kosher Bordeaux, some quite good, such as Château Giscours (Margaux) and Château Yon-Figeac (St.-Emilion). Also, you will find some excellent kosher wines from Alsace, including the Arbarbanel Gewürztraminer.

Italy

In the Tuscan hills, there is a very old Jewish community at Pitigliano. Near the village is a kosher winery that markets a red and a white under the name La Piccola Gerusalemme, which means "Little Jerusalem," Pitigliano's nickname.

From Asti, we find the kosher Bartenura Asti and Bartenura Moscato d'Asti. There are several smaller Italian producers of kosher wines, but many of these are never exported.

Israel

Let's not forget: Israel is a Mediterranean country, and its semiarid climate and harsh soils make for some pretty good wines.

Tasting Tip

You don't even need to look on the label. All Israeli wines imported into the U.S. are kosher for the Passover.

Tiny Israel has five official wine growing regions: Galilee, Golan Heights, Samaria, Samson, and Negev. These regions grow popular European varietals, according to the regional conditions of soil, drainage, rainfall, and temperature.

A major producer in the Sansom region is Carmel, a brand that has been exported for many decades. Many years ago these wines closely resembled those oversweet kosher wines of the U.S., and many in their line still do. (They know their market well!) However, Carmel's varietal wines are similar to those inexpensive ones from California. They even market a White Zinfandel. Or you might try their Cabernet Sauvignon.

The Yarden Gamla winery of the Galilee region sells a Sauvignon Blanc that's quite good.

Your Grandfather's Kosher Wine

To many people, the term "kosher wine" means wine that's excessively sweet. Indeed, Americans of a certain age remember when wine meant bottles of Manischewitz or Mogen David, both nationally advertised brands.

The association of kosher with sweetened wines made from the unsuitable lambrusca grape species is one of history and geography, unrelated to Jewish dietary laws.

Heard It Through the Grapevine

The Shapiro Wine Company of New York is America's oldest kosher winery—more than 100 years old. Yes, they still make syrupy-sweet fermented Concord grape products in fat bottles. But now they also make lighter and drier wines (also in fat bottles) for more modern tastes.

To visit the Shapiro Wine Company, at 126 Rivington Street, New York City, is to step out of a time machine. Some of their oak and cedar casks are as old as the winery itself.

Around the turn of the century, America took in large numbers of Jews who had fled pogroms in Russia and central Europe. A large portion settled near their port of entry, in and around New York City. And what kinds of grapes were grown then in the American Northeast? That acidic and ubiquitous Concord grape!

Today even the oldest kosher wineries produce a variety of fine wines from the superior European vinifera grapes, wines no one would be embarrassed to serve. And yet, the old sweet stuff in the fat bottles remains in these wineries' catalogs. Why? Tradition! Many old-timers (not necessarily Jewish) will drink nothing else.

The Least You Need to Know

➤ Kosher means that a product has been produced in strict accordance with Jewish dietary laws.

➤ Large numbers of food and beverage products are certified kosher, including wine.

➤ Kosher wines offer greater quality and more variety than ever before.

➤ Kosher wines are produced in many countries around the world.

Part 4

Let's Go Wine Shopping!

This is the Information Age, right? Aren't you just bursting with information from the first three sections of this book? Or maybe you're bursting with curiosity, wondering where to buy these wines you've read about. How to shop wisely. How to get even more information. Well, it's all here in this part!

We'll start with the wine bottle itself, so you can read that label as well as the greatest wine expert. Then we'll move on to wine merchants, as you learn to select the one that's best for you. Then we'll enter the Wine Information Highway, with well-marked exits to books, periodicals, newsletters, and Web sites. After that brisk drive, we'll visit a restaurant. There, we'll apply what we've learned to that intimidating wine list (and to dealing with that intimidating wine steward).

Then back home, where we can enjoy our wine experience every day with, well, everyday wines. And finally, we'll explore the world of winetastings: pleasant, educational and cost-effective ways to develop and refine our wine palates.

Chapter 25

Decoding the Wine Bottle

In This Chapter

➤ Recognizing basic wine bottle shapes

➤ How to read a label

➤ Bottling terms that describe origin, style, and quality

At one time, the shape of a wine bottle told us exactly what was inside. Each part of the world and each style of wine had its own distinctive bottle. But bottles have become somewhat standardized, and the information they communicate has become rather fuzzy.

I find it interesting that the most unusual bottles point to wines that fall on opposite ends of the quality spectrum. The most expensive Champagnes, for instance, typically are bottled in special shapes that are unique to the brand. But then, some of the cheapest plonk attempts to disguise its lack of character with an attention-getting container.

This chapter introduces you to the things you need to know about wine bottles. Then we'll deal with the labels. I hope all this will help make you a savvy wine-shopper.

Shape Matters

Wine bottles come in several general shapes, each with its own variations. Here are the most common:

Vino Vocab

The terms **Claret** and **Hock** once referred, respectively, to the reds of Bordeaux and the whites of the Rhine. They both seem a bit quaint today. Neither term on a label has any legal standing.

The Sommelier Says

This rule of brown for Rhine wine and green for Mosel no longer is 100-percent true. Some Rhine wines arrive now in blue bottles, but at least you won't see Mosel in brown or Rhine in green. The Hock shape is used throughout the world, but be warned: It is not a sure indicator of the kind or quality of wine within.

➤ **Claret**   The Claret bottle (also called Red Bordeaux) has straight sides with sharp shoulders. This shape is used for wines made in the Bordeaux style, as well as wines grown and bottled on Bordeaux soil. Red Bordeaux, Sauternes, and Graves wines all are packaged in this squared-off bottle. California varietals such as Cabernet Sauvignon, Merlot, Sauvignon Blanc, Semillon (all Bordeaux vinifera), and Zinfandel also are considered Bordeaux styles.

➤ **Burgundy**   Wines fuller in body or richer in perfume than Claret-styled wines generally are bottled in the rounder, slump-shouldered Burgundy bottle. California Chardonnay and Pinot Noir—Burgundy varietals—are sold in the Burgundy bottle. Fuller-bodied Spanish wines and the sturdier Italian wines (such as Barolo and Barbaresco) find their way into variants of this shape.

➤ **Hock (Rhenish white wine)**   The German Hock bottle is tall, slender, tapering, and brown in color. Its variant is the similar but green-colored Mosel. (The traditional rule in Germany is Rhine wine in brown bottles, Mosel in green.)

Most wines from Alsace are bottled in a shape similar to the hock. So are many California Rieslings, Gewürztraminers, and Sylvaner varietals.

➤ **Bubbly bottles**   The Champagne bottle is a variant of the Burgundy bottle—sort of a fatter and sturdier cousin. It usually has an indentation, or punt, at the bottom and thick walls to withstand the pressure of the carbonation.

As mentioned at the beginning of this chapter, the most expensive Champagnes usually are bottled in signature shapes. The flaring Champagne cork—the legacy of Madame Cliquot, along with the sparkling wine bearing her name—is a laminated seven-piece closure constructed to guarantee a tight seal with plenty of strength once it is in the bottle neck.

The reason for the deep green or brown color of most wine bottles is more than aesthetic: The color protects the wine from sunlight. (You wear sunglasses, why shouldn't your wine?)

Brown glass may give better protection than green, and often it's used for low-alcohol, sweet-finished white wines. But technology is supplanting tradition. With advances in winemaking and better methods of stabilizing wines for bottle aging, clear glass has become more popular. Even traditional winemakers are giving honor to the phrase "What you see is what you get."

Tasting Tip

If you're the proud owner of a brand-new pleasure vessel or vehicle you'd like to christen with a magnum of bubbly, sparkling wine vintners make special christening bottles for that purpose. You would need an awful lot of muscle to smash the solid, reinforced glass of a real Champagne bottle.

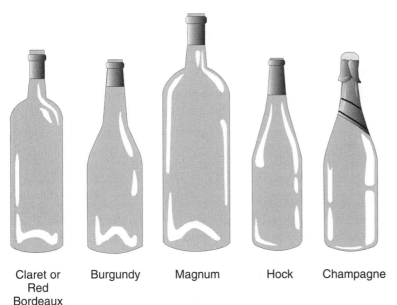

The varied shapes of wine bottles.

Claret or Red Bordeaux   Burgundy   Magnum   Hock   Champagne

Magnums and More

In addition to different shapes, wine bottles come in varying sizes. The standard size (worldwide now) is 750 ml, which is approximately four-fifths of a quart (a fifth of a gallon). The other more common sizes are 375 ml, which is a half bottle, and the magnum (two bottles, or 1.5 liters). A double magnum (3 liters) contains four standard bottles. A wine bottle containing six standard bottles is a Jéroboam, and a bottle containing eight standard bottles is an Impériale.

In Champagne, bottle nomenclature is somewhat different (see Chapter 21, "A Bit of Bubbly"). A magnum is still a magnum, but a bottle containing four standard bottles is called a Jéroboam. A Rehoboam contains six standard bottles; a Methuselah contains eight standard bottles; a Salmanazar contains 12 standard bottles; a Balthazar contains 16 standard bottles; and a Nebuchadnezzar contains 20 standard bottles (perfect for Babylonian orgies or other big celebrations).

A Vintage—Not Just a Year

The date on the bottle is the wine's vintage. It tells you the year the grapes were harvested and nothing more. The fact that there is a date on a bottle is not an indication of quality by itself. However, most wines with a vintage are better wines.

Some everyday wines for which the vintage is of no importance might carry a vintage date to make them appear better than they are. To determine whether the region's vintage is good, great, or poor, you need to consult a vintage chart such as the one on the tear-out card in the front of this book. Or look in wine magazines or newsletters, which provide the scoop on the latest vintages.

Earlier chapters discussed the requisites for a great vintage: the right amount of rainfall at the right times, ideal day and night temperature profiles, and sunshine. A great vintage is Mother Nature's nurturing smile on the tender succulents, allowing them to bathe, nap, and gradually reawaken, refreshed and energetic, with just the right balance of acid, sugar, and flavors.

There have been some great vintages! Every flavor nuance is ready and waiting to incite your nose and taste buds into a peak sensory experience. The balance is secure, the breed is bred, and the wine has a body and concentration that other wines can only envy.

How do you know what vintages have been so favored? As I said earlier, you need to consult your vintage chart. Investing in a fine wine should not be a matter of trial and error. Sometimes it's just a good idea to let someone else do some of the work.

Heard It Through the Grapevine

Avoid poor vintages. The wines will be feeble, insipid, vapid—not exactly what you want to start your wine collection with! There are exceptions, though. Every poor vintage has at least some properties that can make a good wine. You can find out which wines are good by reading reviews in wine magazines or newsletters, or by surfing the on-line services or the Internet.

Wine drinkers tend to malign average vintages, but doing so really is unfair. True, average vintages lack the complexity and finesse of great vintages, but they're quite capable of providing a savvy consumer with some perfectly delightful wine drinking, and usually at reasonable prices.

Don't Ignore the Back Label

The back label is the one that doesn't have the picturesque scene of the vineyard or the name like "Château d'Yquem" with its royal crown. This label hardly seems important enough to read. However, it may contain information that is useful to you, or at least interesting. It's certainly worth a peek.

Laws control the exact content on the front label, but they say nothing about the back. That's left to the vintner's (or exporter's) imagination.

The back label is where bottlers may tell you what foods are a good match for the wine or what temperature brings out its peak flavor. Or the label may offer an engaging story about the wine or the winery. Or maybe a map of the winegrowing region. Or a history of the grape. Or maybe some technical gobbledygook about pH or Brix. But you won't know if you don't look.

Where's It From?

We've examined wine labels throughout this book. So now you're up to speed on your AO, QmP, DOG, and VDQS, right? Or do you imagine the wine label is some kind of legal document or a geeky home page on the Web? Actually, it is a legal document, the purpose of which is to let you know what is in the bottle you just might take home with you.

Tasting Tip

All imported wines must conform to both the mandatory label requirement of the U.S. and to the regulations of the country of origin. (Individual states may impose their own regulations, but these may not conflict with federal standards.)

Labels on wines sold in the U.S. are approved by the Bureau of Alcohol, Tobacco, and Firearms (BATF), part of the Treasury Department. In addition to collecting alcohol taxes, BATF must ensure that the information on a wine bottle is truthful, accurate, and complete.

American labels are simple. This has its good and bad points. On the plus side, more concise labeling is less likely to be misleading. On the negative side, American wine labels tell us very little about the contents of the bottle. (By law, at least. Many producers choose to provide excellent information.)

Of course, the European Union (EU) countries have strict standards for labeling, which make labels relatively easy to read—as long as you know what to look for.

Terms of Origin

The origin descriptor tells us where the wine comes from. The descriptor starts with the country of origin. Some examples are *Product of France* and *Product of Spain*. All imported wines have these.

Next, we run through region, state, vineyard, château—whatever level of description is allowed for the particular type or quality of the wine. Not all vintners will use all the descriptors they're entitled to. Some renowned French estates, such as Château d'Yquem, list only the vineyard and the name of its producer. (Hey! What more is needed?) On the other hand, an origin descriptor on the label of a superior German wine may set a world record for syllable count.

Terms of Quality

Under EU regulations, a label with the vineyard name indicates better quality than one that lists only a region.

AOC, DO, DOG, and QmP are quality indicators at their most basic. In France, there are the *crus*: *Cru Classé* (classified growth), *Premier Cru*, and *Grand Cru*. These indicate both origin and quality. In Italy there is *Classico*—referring to a special, smaller wine zone—and *Riserva*, which indicates extra aging. Spain has *Reserva* and *Gran Reserva*. In Portugal these words are *Reserva* and *Garrafeira* (although requirements differ somewhat). And in Germany we have *Prädikat*, which means the wine has something special to report of its quality and style.

U.S. wines carry quality descriptors like *Late Harvest* or *Botrytis*, and sparkling wines are required to state whether they are produced by the *Méthode Champenoise* (fermented in *this* bottle) or the transfer method (fermented in *the* bottle). (Only true Champagne may use the French term *Méthode Champenoise* on the label.) Other than these quality descriptors, you're on your own.

What's the Style Mean?

Style descriptors are required legally only on German wines and on Champagne. These descriptors indicate the wine's sweetness or dryness (percentage of residual sugar). Some non-German wine labels do include style descriptors, but these are at the whim of the individual producer. (In the absence of a style descriptor, you have yet another reason for knowing your wines.)

The Sommelier Says

I'm a little amused when I see a label on a bottle of U.S. wine with the words *Classic* or *Reserve*. In terms of legal standards, they mean nothing, nothing at all!

General Terms: Something for Every Wine

The most basic terms are white, red, and rosé (in the language of the wine's native land). A few variations exist. For example, Italian wines may be labeled "Nero" (black), which means very dark red. But really, you need to judge color gradations for yourself. (In your glass—not in the green bottle!)

These general terms include most of those things that don't fall into the other categories. There's the term *Table Wine*, for instance, that's required on imports but optional on U.S. wines. And there are instructions that are entirely optional, such as to serve at room temperature or to serve chilled. The vintage can also fall into the category of general information. (If you know your vintages, it is a quality descriptor as well.)

Mandatory Information

Along with the country of origin, alcoholic content and bottle volume are imperative on all labels. Volumes of imported wines are listed in standard metric units—milliliters (ml) or centiliters (cl)—and the bottles conform to approved sizes. The name and address of the importer, producer, and/or négociant are required on all labels. For California wines, the name and address of the bottler and the Bonded Winery (B.W.) license number are required.

Quality labeling of wines from EU countries is required, conforming to EU, national, and local regulations. These are not required for U.S. wines. (On the other hand, varietal names are mandatory only on American wines.)

Heard It Through the Grapevine

American labels provide the consumer with a lot of data concerning who owned the grapes and who selected, bottled, produced, and cellared the bottle's contents. But if you're looking for a quality assessment, you may feel as though you're reading a weather report for every city but your own.

Translating the French Wine Label

The French wine label provides a lot of information that gives you clues to the quality of the wine. The label provides exacting information through its system of Appellation Controlée regulations, which are linked to carefully defined geography.

By law, the smaller the piece of property named, the more stringent the regulations are for methods of cultivation and production. Other than names of properties and estates, the names of the négociant (if any) and importer must appear on the label, so knowing the reputations of these companies is useful. Frequently, the name of the négociant or shipper is a clue to the quality of a wine from an unknown property.

The Sommelier Says

Be careful! *Mis dans nos caves, Mis par le propriétaire,* and *Mis en bouteille a la propriete* all may sound as though they describe estate-bottled wine. But they don't! Some sellers put these terms on the bottle to deceive the consumer into believing that the wine is estate-bottled when it isn't. Such terms have no legal definition.

French Origin Descriptors

The abbreviation *AO* or *A* on a label stands for *Appellation d'Origin Controlée. VDQS* stands for *Vins Délimités de qualite Supérieure,* the second rank below AO of delimited wine areas. *Vin de pays* is the next rank below AO.

Cave is the French word for "cellar" (easy to remember). *Château-bottled, Mis au Château, Mis en bouteilles au Château, Mis au* (or *du*) *Domaine,* and *Mis en bouteilles au* (or *du*) *Domaine* all mean estate-bottled, and they have legal significance.

A *Négociant* is a businessperson who purchases wine from growers and bottles it under a proprietary brand (or under the individual château name). An *Eleveur* is a négociant who buys young wine from the grower and matures it in his own cellars. *Propriétaire-récoltant* means owner and manager of a property.

A Bordeaux wine label.

Wine name — CHÂTEAU LA MISSION HAUT-BRION

District — PESSAC-LÉOGNAN

Appellation Contrôlée designation — APPELLATION PESSAC-LÉOGNAN CONTRÔLÉE

Classification — Cru classé des Graves

Vintage year — 1992

Name of producer — DOMAINE CLARENCE DILLON S. A.

Estate-bottled designation — MIS EN BOUTEILLES AU CHATEAU

Alcoholic content

Importer

A Burgundy wine label.

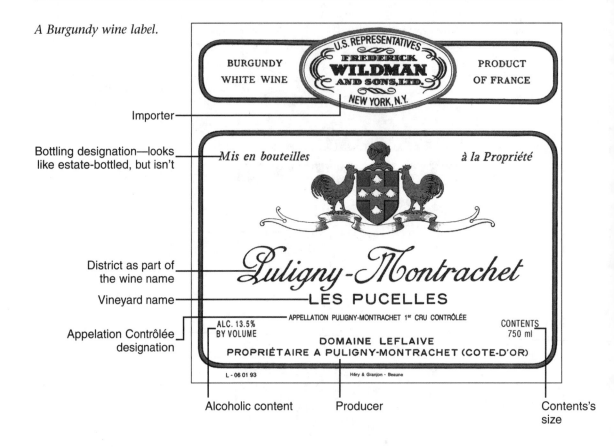

Importer —

Bottling designation—looks like estate-bottled, but isn't —

District as part of the wine name —

Vineyard name —

Appelation Contrôlée designation —

Alcoholic content   Producer   Contents's size

French Quality Descriptors

Appellation Controlée is both an origin descriptor and a quality descriptor, as French geographical designations are linked to quality regulations. *Cru Bourgeois* in Bordeaux refers to the many good vineyards just below the classified growths in quality.

Cru Classé is a classified growth of Bordeaux, the most famous of which is the 1855 classification of the wines of the Médoc. (See Chapter 11, "The Noble Wines of Bordeaux.") This is preceded by the level of the cru, such as *Premier Cru Classé. Cru Exceptionnel* is a Bordeaux classification between cru Bourgeois and Cru Classé. *Grand Cru* means "great growth"—in Burgundy the highest level of classified vineyards, in Bordeaux the highest of the five levels of classified growths.

Grand Vin means "great wine," but it has no legal definition. Anyone can use this term! *Premier Cru* means "first growth"—in Burgundy the second level of classified growth; in Bordeaux, the top level of classified growth. *Méthode Champenoise* (fermented in this bottle) is the legally defined term for the Champagne method of sparkling wine production. *Supérieure* indicates that the wine is at least one degree of alcohol above the minimum required for a particular AOC. (Note: The term does not mean that the wine is better or superior.) *VDQS* and *Vin de pays* relate to the quality of a non-AOC wine.

French Style Descriptors

Vin Blanc means "white wine," *Vin Rouge* means "red wine," and *Vin Rosé* means "rosé wine." *Sur lie* refers to wines bottled off the lees, without racking or filtering. *Pétillant* means "slightly sparkling" or "crackling." *Mousseux* refers to sparkling wine other than Champagne. *Blanc de Blancs* refers to a white wine made entirely from white grapes. (You usually see the term on Champagne bottles.) With Champagne and Mousseux, *Brut* means "almost dry," but *Extra Dry* means slightly sweeter than Brut. *Brut Sauvage* or *Sauvage* means "completely dry." *Demi Sec* means "semi-sweet," which is quite sweet. Finally, *Doux* means even sweeter than quite sweet.

French General Terms

Année means "year." *Recolte* means "crop" or "harvest," and *vendange* means "grape harvest," (used synonymously with année). A *chai* is an aboveground building where wine is stored in casks. *Chambré* is the French word for bringing a red wine from cellar temperature to room temperature (as in *Servir Chambre*). *Servir frais* means to serve chilled. *Château* in Bordeaux refers to a single estate—elsewhere it may be part of a brand name. *Domaine* means wine estate. *Clos* means walled vineyard. *Côte* refers to a slope with vineyards, as opposed to *graves* or flatter land. *Cru* means "growth" and refers to a legally defined vineyard. *Cuvée* is a vat or batch of wine.

Tasting Tip

Do you like your Champagne extra dry? Then don't get *Extra Dry*, which is sweeter than *Brut*. You want even drier? Look for the word *Sauvage*.

Deciphering the German Wine Label

The German wine label is exceedingly precise as to quality. Its descriptions are linked closely to growing regions—large down to tiny; to a designation of quality; and also to the degree of ripeness achieved by the grapes that went into the wine.

These labels appear more complicated than they are. They are less intimidating once you learn the system. The region in which the wine is produced and the ripeness of the grapes are the two main elements, and both items play important roles on the label.

The German Grosslage wine label.

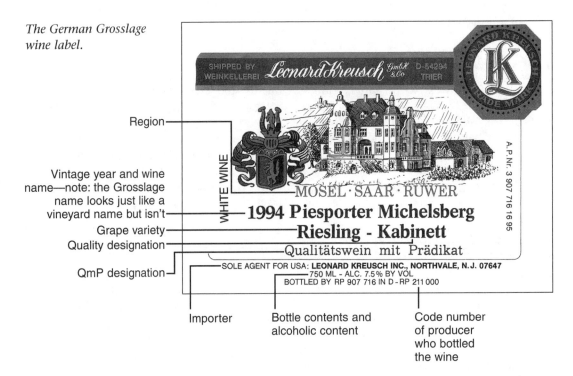

Region

Vintage year and wine name—note: the Grosslage name looks just like a vineyard name but isn't

Grape variety

Quality designation

QmP designation

Importer

Bottle contents and alcoholic content

Code number of producer who bottled the wine

The German Einzellage wine label.

Vintage year and wine name—this is an authentic vineyard name.

German Origin Descriptors

A *Gebiet* is one of Germany's 13 major wine regions. A *Bereich* is a large subregion of a Gebiet. A *Grosslage* is a subdivision of a Bereich consisting of numerous adjoining vineyards that may span the boundaries of many villages.

Grosslage names sound like individual vineyard names. So you need to memorize Grosslage names to avoid buying a village wine when you want higher-quality wine (see Appendix A, "Recommended Wines"). An *Einzellage* is an individual vineyard site with a minimum size of approximately 12 acres. Vineyards smaller than 12 acres are given the name of a nearby Einzellage and are of similar quality and style.

Stillwein is the German word for still wine, and sparkling wine is called *sekt*.

An *Abfüller* is a bottler, and *Abfüllung* means a bottling, as from the producer's own estate. *Aus Eigenem Lesegut* and *Erzeuger Abfüllung* mean estate-bottled. *Eigene Abfüllung* means bottled by the producer. A *Keller* is a cellar, and a *Weinkellerei* is a place where wine is made but not grown. (Isn't this logical?)

A *Weingut* is a wine estate. And a *Weinhändler* can be a wine shipper, wine merchant, or vintner. *Winzergenossenschaft* and *Winzerverein* both mean winegrower's cooperative. (*Amtliche Prüfungsunummer*) (AP)is the official testing number found on all better German wines. This encodes the place of origin, the producer's individual number, the individual lot number, and the year (not necessarily the vintage) that the lot was submitted for testing.

Vino Vocab

The German word for "still wine" is pretty easy to figure out. It's **Stillwein**. The term for "sparking wine" is not so obvious. It's **Sekt**. (But sometimes, Sekt means only "dry wine.")

German Quality Descriptors

Tafelwein is wine, the lowest level of quality. Tafelwein may not bear a vineyard site name. *QbA* (*Qualitätswein bestimmter Anbaugebiete* or just *Qualitätswein*) refers to a wine from a specific origin and is the middle level of German wine quality. *QmP* (*Qualitätswein mit Prädikat*) refers to wine with special attributes, the top level of wine quality consisting of six degrees of ripeness. No chaptalization ever is permitted for these wines!

German Style Descriptors

Kabinett is the basic grade for QmP wine that must be made from grapes with sufficient natural sugar to produce a wine with a minimum of $9^{1}/_{2}$ percent alcohol. *Spätlese* means "late-picked" and refers to a wine made from fully ripened grapes. *Auslese* is a term describing very ripe, late-picked grapes that render a fairly sweet and luscious dessert wine. These are hand-selected bunch by bunch.

Beerenauslese is a very sweet wine made from even later-picked, overripe grapes, selected grape by grape. Some of these may have been shriveled by *Botrytis* (noble rot). Trockenbeerenauslese is wine made entirely from grapes shriveled by Botrytis. During the harvest, the pickers keep these grapes separate from the others. Eiswein is a sweet, concentrated wine made from frozen grapes that may or may not be affected by *Botrytis*.

German General Terms

There are some general sweetness descriptors in use. *Trocken* refers to a wine that's completely dry. *Halbtrocken* is half-dry or off-dry wine. Some other general terms are *Perlwein*, a mildly sparkling wine, and *Sekt*, a sparkling wine.

Moselblümchen is a generic wine from the Mosel that is in the Tafelwein class. Liebfraumilch is a generic wine from the Rhine region that is in the QbA class. A *Fass* is a cask, and a *Fuder* is a very large cask. *Rotwein* means "red wine," and *Weisswein* (written in the German alphabet as *Weißwein*) means "white wine." A *Schloss* is a castle, in this case, a wine estate. *Staatswein* refers to wine from government-owned vineyards.

Tasting Tip

German sweetness rankings are quality indicators, though not in the sense of one being better than another. Which one you choose will depend on how you'll serve it and on your preferences. A cool, crisp Kabinett makes a wonderful apéritif. A rich, fruity Auslese goes well with many dinner entrées. And what better dessert wine than a perfumy, syrupy (and expensive) Trockenbeerenauslese!

Interpreting the Italian Wine Label

Italian wine labels provide a fair amount of meaningful information regarding what is in the bottle. Nomenclature for certain wines is regulated under laws enacted in 1967, modeled after the French, but without the refinement of official classifications. The Italian wine-regulating system, the *Denominazione di Origine Controllata* (DOC) is government approved and defines growing regions.

If a grape name is not accompanied with a place (*Nebbiolo d'Alba*, for example), chances are the wine lacks distinction. *Denominazione di Origine Controllata e Garantita* (DOCG) is the highest grade of Italian wine and is granted only to regions making the highest-quality wine.

Heard It Through the Grapevine

For several types of wine, the DOC guarantees certain minimum standards of production. Good-quality Italian wines indicate the place, either as the name of the wine itself (*Chianti*, for example) or linked to a grape variety, such as *Barbera D'Asti*, or through a DOC designation. Not all places have earned DO status, but most better Italian wines sold within the United States are DOC wines.

The Italian wine label.

NOZZOLE —————— Wine name

CHIANTI CLASSICO ————— Wine district
DENOMINAZIONE DI ORIGINE CONTROLLATA E GARANTITA ————— DOCG quality designation

RISERVA 1993 ————— Riserva quality designation with vintage date

ESTATE BOTTLED BY ————— Estate-bottled designation
TENIMENTI AGRICOLI VALDIGREVE S.A.S. ————— Producer
GREVE - ITALIA
RED WINE   750 ML ————— Bottle contents
PRODUCT OF ITALY   13% ALC. BY VOL.
————— Alcohol content

Italian Origin Descriptors

Classico refers to a wine made in a legally defined inner section of a wine district. It's supposed to denote a higher quality. *DOC* refers to a wine from a delimited wine district, produced in accordance with DOC wine laws. *DOCG* is wine made from a delimited district that has earned this highest-quality designation.

Cantina means "winery" or "cellars." *Cantina Sociale* is a wine-growers cooperative. *Casa Vinicolá* means "wine company." A *Consorzio* is a local winegrowers association with legal recognition. *Infiascato alla fattoria, Imbottigliato nel'origine, Imbottigliato del produttore*, and *Messo in bottiglia nel'origine* all mean "estate-bottled." *Imbottigliato nello stabilimento della ditta* means "bottled on the premises of the company, but not estate-bottled." A *Tenuta* is a farm or agricultural holding.

Italian Quality Descriptors

As you know, DOC and DOCG are quality descriptors. *Riserva* means aged in wood for a time specified by law. *Riserva Speciale* means aged one year longer than Riserva. *Stravecchio* means very old, but you'll see that rarely.

Vino Vocab

You've heard of **Spumante**, sparkling wine from Italy. But what do Italians call semi-sparkling wine? **Frizzante**!

Italian Style Descriptors

Secco means "dry," while *amaro* means "very dry" (bitter). *Abboccato* and *amabile* (literally, "lovely") mean "off-dry" or "semisweet," with amabile being sweeter than abboccato. *Dolce* means "sweet." *Cotto* refers to a concentrated wine. *Passito* refers to wine made from semidried grapes. *Vin santo* is wine made from grapes dried indoors.

Italian General Terms

Vino da Tavola means "table wine." *Bianco* means "white wine"; *rosso* means "red wine," and *rosato* means "rosé wine." *Nero* is very dark red. Oh, and those funny little bottles with the woven straw? They are *fiasci* (plural of *fiasco*).

The Sommelier Says

Yes, it's true: Some U.S. wine districts are reputed to be better than others. However, a well-made wine from a lesser district can be far superior to a large-yield wine from a more respected district.

Reading the United States Wine Label

In terms of legally defined nomenclature, very little on an American wine label helps us to tell a high-quality wine from an ordinary wine. Terms such as *Reserve, Special Reserve, Vintner's Reserve*, and so on, have no legal regulation, and they are used routinely on mediocre or poor wines.

American wine districts are limited solely to defining geography, with no concomitant regulations as to grape varieties that may be grown, to yield, or to production methods, such as those used by the French, Italians, and Germans. To tell the difference between two wines from a particular wine district (Napa Valley, for example), you must have a real knowledge of the individual producers.

With American wine, *caveat emptor* is the rule. The U.S. government seems to have no interest in giving us quality clues.

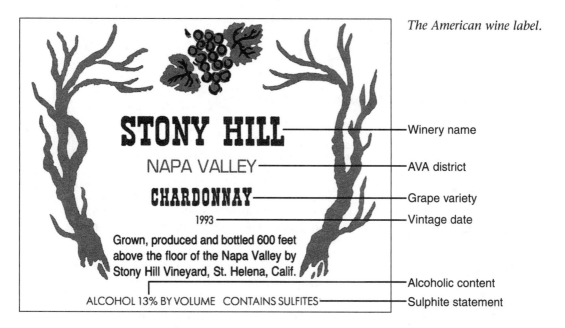

The American wine label.

STONY HILL ———— Winery name

NAPA VALLEY ———— AVA district

CHARDONNAY ———— Grape variety

1993 ———— Vintage date

Grown, produced and bottled 600 feet above the floor of the Napa Valley by Stony Hill Vineyard, St. Helena, Calif.

———— Alcoholic content

ALCOHOL 13% BY VOLUME   CONTAINS SULFITES ———— Sulphite statement

American Origin Descriptors

The single word *American* means American wines; the wine can be a blend of wines from different states. A state name means that 75 percent of the wine must be from the named state—unless it's California, where regulations require it to be 100 percent Californian.

A county name means that 75 percent of the wine must be from the named county. All valley, district, and regional designations on the label must be BATF *approved viticultural areas* (AVAs), and at least 75 percent of the wine must come from the named area. The rule-of-thumb is that the smaller the geographical area specified, the better the quality. Just remember, such a descriptor provides no quality guarantee.

Something that looks like *B.W. No. 0000* is the bonded winery's license number. *Grown by* means the grapes were grown by the named winery. *Selected by* means that the wine was purchased by the named winery. *Made and Bottled by* means that the named winery fermented at least 10 percent of the wine and bottled all the wine. *Cellared and Bottled by* means that the named party blended and/or aged or otherwise treated and bottled all the wine.

Produced and Bottled by, *Proprietor* (or *Vintner*) *Grown*, and *Bottled by* mean that the named party fermented at least 75 percent of the wine and bottled all the wine. *Estate Bottled* means that the named party fermented all the wine from grapes 100 percent from the named AVA; that the grapes came entirely from the party's own vineyards or vineyards in which the party controls the viticultural practices; and that the wine was bottled on the same premises where it was made.

American Quality Descriptors

Reserve, Vintner's Reserve, and *Special Reserve* are mere label puffery with no legal definition. In some cases, these terms may appear on the best of the producer's wine. But in other cases, the wine is of the same, or maybe of lesser, quality as the producer's regular line. *Rare* and *Classic,* usually seen on the least expensive wines, have no legal definition. Such wine rarely is either rare or classic!

Nouveau refers to wines that are quickly fermented by carbonic maceration and bottled immediately after fermentation. *Late Harvest* means the wine was made from overripe grapes that may or may not have been affected by *Botrytis.*

Brix is a measure of potential alcohol based on the sugar content of the grape when it was harvested. *Residual sugar* refers to the amount of remaining natural sugar in the wine after fermentation is completed. (More than 1 percent tastes sweet.) *Off-dry* refers to wine that has a little residual sugar but not enough to be sweet. *Botrytis* means the grapes were affected with *Botrytis* (noble rot). And remember, *Fermented in* the *bottle* refers to sparkling wine made by the transfer method, while *Fermented in* this *bottle* refers to sparkling wine made by the Méthode Champenoise.

American General Terms

In the U.S., the term *table wine* refers to wine that is less than 14.5 percent alcohol and made without additional alcohol. *Dessert wine* is more than 14.5 percent alcohol, usually a sweet wine fortified with additional alcohol. *White* is, well, white wine. And *red* is, uh, red wine. (You knew that, already. But did you know rosé wine can be called either *rosé* or *blush*?)

The Least You Need to Know

➤ Wine bottle shapes are a clue to what is in the bottle.

➤ A magnum contains two standard wine bottles. Standard bottles hold 750 ml.

➤ Wine labels must contain certain information as a matter of law, such as the country of origin and the alcoholic content.

➤ Back labels frequently provide some very useful and interesting information, such as the history of the winery or wine region or a description of the taste of the wine.

➤ Labels on U.S. wines say little or nothing about quality.

Chapter 26

Swimming in the Wine Market

> **In This Chapter**
>
> ➤ Finding a good wine merchant
>
> ➤ Money-saving techniques for buying wine
>
> ➤ All about wine auctions
>
> ➤ Secrets of the wine trade

Think of wine-buying as a challenge. If you're buying a car, a TV, or some other big-ticket item, what do you do to make sure that salespeople really know their stuff? You ask questions! Unfortunately, most purchasers of wine are intimidated by the process.

There's no need to be. In this chapter you will learn how to locate the best wine store. You'll learn, also, how to identify and use other sources of wine.

Finding a Good Wine Merchant

The best wine merchant is the one who understands wines and can advise you on selections that meet your budget and complement your palate. You should spend a little time finding that wine seller.

Be careful: Wine merchants aren't registered stockbrokers who go to jail if they give you bad information or if they manipulate your account too much. They're just shop owners, who come in as many varieties as the wines they sell.

Did someone here say "varieties?" More than 30,000 different wines sell in the United States alone! Even the real pros can't possibly know them all. Sometimes, visiting a wine store is like visiting a foreign country. Everything looks familiar until you read the names. Then they're all different. I've had that experience more than once in wine stores that feature private brands and obscure producers.

So you ask questions, just a few strategic questions that will tell you if a merchant is knowledgeable, honest, and accessible.

Here are a few questions I use to separate the knowledgeable from those who merely push cash-register buttons:

➤ What's the difference between a Bordeaux and a Burgundy?

➤ Why is a bottle of French Burgundy more expensive than a comparable bottle of French Bordeaux?

➤ What do you recommend in a bottle of dry white wine for less than $10? A domestic sparkling wine for less than $16 to go with roast chicken?

By using this tactic, you are not just testing the merchant, you also are showing yourself as a savvy wine consumer. And if all goes well, this could be the start of a beautiful friendship.

Good wine knowledge is only one criterion. You need also to consider price, service, selection, and storage.

If the Price Is Right

Price is an excellent reason for shopping around (and for knowing your wines). Prices are set by the retailer, not the producer or importer. (Yes, sometimes they are set by state governments.) Generally, you won't see a big difference from one shop to another, except in the case of those shops known for rock-bottom prices. But a couple dollars here and there can add up—especially if you're just beginning to build a wine cellar.

Heard It Through the Grapevine

If you know in advance what you want, check out one of those wine "supermarkets" or giant wine and spirits emporiums. The owners or sales help in these giants are not always knowledgeable about their wares, but the prices can be the best around. With a bit of homework, you can find substantial savings.

On the other hand, if you do need advice to help with your selection, it's worth paying more for the right bottle than paying less for the wrong one. In choosing wines, as in most other items, you need to strike a balance between store loyalty and self-interest. No one retailer will satisfy all of your needs.

Service, Service, Service

When you visit a large wine shop, you may feel as though you've walked into a hotel ballroom full of strangers. Perhaps you'd like someone to greet you and introduce you around a bit. Willingness to assist is important. As customers, we have a right to cordiality from the wine shop's personnel.

So be critical: Do the merchant's suggestions parallel your desires and requirements? Does the seller share information about new arrivals or good bargains? Ultimately, your judgment will be some combination of savvy and pure gut. By all means, enjoy the rapport you feel with a merchant who seems informed, friendly, and willing to show you around. Just be sure you're sold on more than charm.

Never be afraid to apply your own knowledge. Building your confidence is as important as building your wine cellar, and it can keep you from overspending, too.

The Sommelier Says

Watch out for the helpful merchant who may be too helpful. You don't need pressure. You do need to know the person who's helping you choose the right Bordeaux for the boss's party or the California white for the barbecue is someone you can trust. A willingness to give advice is great, but only if you can rely on it.

What's Your Wine Budget?

I strongly recommend framing your questions within a particular price range to indicate you are a value hunter, not a candidate for a quick, high-profit sale. If the merchant responds with a haughty look or with an attempt to steer you to a higher price range, you'll know you're in the wrong place.

Speaking Up

Asking the right questions is not the only way to test the merchant's expertise and customer attitude. But I do think it's the only way to get what you need. Some people who have no problem asking for help when shopping for clothing or furnishings wilt at the thought of having to explain their wine preferences.

It's all part of the wine mystique. You may think, "What if they think my taste is gauche? Or worse yet, cheap? What if I use the wrong language? Or what if they think I'm just plain ignorant?" Forget that voice. Instead, listen to the voice that says, "I know what I want, and I'm going to find it!"

When you shop, you rely on the expertise of someone who is there for two reasons— to help you and to help the store sell its goods. One way to assure yourself that you'll be explaining your needs correctly—and directly—is to make a checklist of all the points you need to cover to get the right wine:

➤ Informal, formal, or momentous?

➤ What foods (if any)?

➤ Personal preferences and those of guests?

➤ More than one wine to be served?

➤ Expect to have leftover bottles?

➤ Budget for the occasion?

Don't be afraid to use words like *fruity*, *oaky*, *truffles*, *vanilla*, or any of the things you've learned. A knowledgeable merchant won't judge your taste. (And if the merchant does not understand these terms, you are definitely not in the right place.)

If the suggested wine seems a bit pricey, the merchant's intent may not be to make more money, but to imply tactfully that a better wine may be more appropriate for your occasion. Buying wine is an interactive experience. Establish a dialogue with the retailer. Explain your needs, listen to answers, and don't be afraid to question advice. A good wine merchant will be as happy as you are to see you go home with the right wine.

The Importance of Selection

The type, range, and assortment of wines are important considerations in choosing your retailer. You may want to avoid the big emporiums when you're in the market for something special. If you're after a vintage Madeira or the right Trockenbeerenauslese to complement your Bavarian pastries, you simply won't find it in some establishments.

A good wine store will have a selection of wines to meet the needs of discerning customers. Most large wine stores stock a number of fine wines—at lower prices than you may find in a smaller shop. Many stores stock expensive and rare wines that are not on display, so make sure to inquire. (I remember that time I found a $125 Château Haut-Brion Blanc for $25 less at a discounter who kept it hidden in the basement!)

Shops with a limited selection may neglect certain important wines. These shops may have a large selection of several popular wines—Chardonnay, Beaujolais, and Pouilly-Fuissé—and quick-selling California jug wines. You may find, also, a few expensive Champagnes and big names (usually off-vintages) from Bordeaux. But beware. This merchant may not have taken the time or effort to learn about wine.

Another example is the merchant who stocks mainly well-advertised brands. Then there are the stores that feature unknown brands from producers or importers who specialize in bargain versions of well-known wine types. These wines may offer good drinking and value, but typically, they're not up to snuff.

Heard It Through the Grapevine

A good selection of wines is one that offers a variety of tastes, styles, occasions, and budgets. The shop should be both well-stocked and well-organized. Look for shops that group wines by country and wine type, and frequently by price. And look for rack or aisle markers that can help guide you to your selection.

Some fine shops arrange wines by similar characteristics: Red Bordeaux with California Cabernet Sauvignon, German Rieslings with California Johannisberg Rieslings, Chardonnays and White Burgundies, and so on. This method makes comparison shopping easier. It also encourages comparative tastings by type, nationality, and by smaller regions and subregions.

Wine Storage at the Store

Wine bottles may look good shelved upright in rows like liquor bottles, but stocking better wine this way is deplorable! Especially if the inventory doesn't turn over rapidly. Shops should store wines just as you store them at home. The bottles should be protected from direct sunlight, and bottles with corks (anything better than jug quality) should be lying on their sides.

Window dressing is a key part of selling, but no wines belong in sun-drenched windows. Better shops display only empty or sample bottles in their windows. No good merchant ever sells a bottle from a window display!

Inside the shop is another matter. Most of us like to touch and handle bottles while shopping. (How else do you read the back label?) The better shops keep a bottle of each available wine in a large rack or stacked in such a way that you can reach for it without risking an avalanche. The rest of the stock should be kept in perfect, temperature-controlled storage spaces.

Temperature control for wine is always important. In the main area, you should find temperature that's constant and cool. If the entire stock is not within sight, I may check to see where the cases are stored. Sometimes, the back rooms of a shop or central warehouse area are far from ideal in climate and general storage conditions. You want to know where the wine has lingered. Storage is especially important if you are buying wines by the case or purchasing old and rare wines.

Most wine shops offer a chilled-wine section featuring whites, rosés, and Champagnes. This section is offered as a convenience to customers buying wines for immediate drinking. These wines may tempt you, but you don't know how long those wines have been chilled. You're better off buying at store temperature and chilling at home.

Tasting Tip

If a wine has been in a cooler for weeks, chances are it's lost some of its freshness or liveliness. Some shops have a chilling machine that can chill your wine in three or four minutes without harming it. If not, buying a bottle and chilling it yourself for about half an hour is far better than taking a chance with prechilled wine.

What About Wine Ratings?

Have you ever gone to a movie that received unanimous raves, four stars in the newspaper review, only to be disappointed, dismayed, or just plain disgusted? Fortunately, rating wines is not as subjective as rating movies. Critics evaluate wines using standard criteria developed to assess acidity, tannins, sweetness, and so on.

In recent years, a 100-point system has been adopted by most wine publications and wine critics. But watch out! No one can evaluate wine on such a system with any degree of accuracy (more on this subject in

Chapter 27, "The Wine Information Highway"). When reading wine reviews, look for complete and comprehensive tasting notes to guide you to the wines you like. Trouble is that many wine critics do not fully describe a wine in their published tasting notes. But their critique is better than nothing.

You need to look beyond the numbers. A wine may have a superlative rating, but when you go through the adjectives, you may realize the wine is not going to titillate your taste for tannins or awaken your oaky aesthetic. A judicial assessment of words and numbers can help you combine your own knowledge and preferences with the critic's. Studying ratings also helps you become a better rater yourself. (For a list of wine publications, see Chapter 27.)

The Sommelier Says

Because magazines survive on advertising, they may not be your best source for wine ratings. Newsletters and updated consumer guides are more impartial and generally more thorough.

How to Save Money at the Wine Store

Nowadays, very few wine shops sell wine at a full markup. Some sell at better prices than others. (Not true, of course, in state-run stores.) Here are some ways to save money when you buy wine.

Discount Stores

A discount or mass merchandiser is a good source for bargains. If you're in the market for an everyday wine, don't be afraid to try unknown or private-label brands. And if you decide you like them, don't be afraid to say so! Forget the wine snobs. You may live in a state where wines are sold in supermarkets, convenience stores, or even drug stores. These places usually are good sources for everyday wines. The prices are reasonable, and you can match the wine with the food right at the source.

Private Labels

Large wine shops, or those that are part of a chain or franchise, often carry private-label wines bearing the name of the outlet or some trademark the retailer owns. Some of these can represent good values. The merchant buys a certain percentage of wines in bulk and has them bottled under the store label. Without the prestigious name of the winery, the wines can be sold for much less.

This concept is the vinous equivalent of designer fashions without the designer prices. Or more closely, supermarket "generic" products that are made by the same brand-name folks. Yes, quality can vary from batch to batch, but chances are that the merchant who seeks to build a reputation on the store name or exclusive trademark will choose wisely. You may come home with a great bargain.

Second Labels

When a winery selects its wines to make its brand-name wine, it frequently has some lesser-quality (but still good) wine left over. These wines may be from younger vines or vineyard sites that did not ripen to optimum maturity. Often these products are sold under another name, such as Les Forts de Latour (Château Latour's second label), or an unrelated name.

Second-label wines can provide excellent drinking. Some wineries also want to increase the amount of wine they sell, making optimum use of their marketing personnel, but they lack sufficient wine to meet the standards for their primary label. The winery may create a second label to market wines of a lesser quality.

Tasting Tip

You can find excellent bargains among better winemakers' "second labels." Keep in mind the expertise from making prime-label wines also goes into making second-label wines. Frequently these are quite good.

Returning a Bottle of Wine

Stores' return policies fall under the heading of customer service. You've paid for your wine, taken it home, cooked the perfect meal, used your best corkscrew technique, and voilá! The odor of rancid corn chips hits you! Okay. It's rarely that obvious, but you are entitled to a product without flaws. You would return a defective CD or a spoiled container of milk, right? You also should return wine that is not up to your standards.

The wine merchant is in business to please consumers, not to alienate them. If the wine seems flawed or the bottle damaged, generally you'll have no problem returning it. If you are returning an unopened bottle (you've changed the menu or found out your guest hates Cabernet Sauvignon), use the same principle that guides the return of most retail items: Return it within a few days of purchase. After a week or two, the merchant is justified in refusing the bottle. (After all, how does the retailer know how you may have stored the bottle?)

Buying Old Wines

Many wine enthusiasts feel the lure sooner or later. It's like the people who start with a few nostalgic knickknacks and suddenly find themselves drawn to the finest antique shops. Someday you may survey your wine collection and think it could do with a few vintage Ports or Madeiras. Or you may look to old and rare wines as an interesting financial investment. Or you may host a dinner that calls for a mature bottle from a great vintage. I assure you, those Grand Crus Bordeaux from an excellent vintage can provide for some very exciting wine experiences!

Yes, these wines may be quite expensive. But when you consider the value added from careful long-term storage, the price for some of these wines may really be quite reasonable. With older wines, storage and handling is of the utmost importance. You need to ask how the wine was stored and where it came from. Inquire about getting a refund if the bottle is not what it should be, because older bottles can have considerable bottle variation.

The Sommelier Says

Some wines from a single case of expensive old wine can be superb, while others are defective. Just remember, when you buy, buy with caution.

Investment or Expensive Hobby?

Only the tiniest number of wines are good financial investments. Fortunately, you can spot them, because they share certain qualities:

➤ Excellent potential for longevity.

➤ Both press and the industry have given them unanimous commendations.

➤ Superlative vintages.

➤ A track record of appreciation.

➤ Rarity, such that demand drives up the price at a higher rate than with other wines. (Romanée Conti and Château Pétrus are prime examples of wines that command astronomical prices after a decade or so.)

Insider's Look at Auctions

Regulation of the purchase or sale of wine at auction is determined by each state. Auctioning wine is totally legal in Illinois and California (of course), and allowed in New York several years ago. The lifting of restrictions in New York has made it a haven for wine-lovers, eager to bid on those beckoning bottles or to sell from their own collections. Many other states permit charity wine auctions, but some states prohibit wine auctions altogether. Check with your local wine merchant to find out the story where you live.

Heard It Through the Grapevine

Even careful attention to the guidelines in this section does not ensure that you are making a good investment. No matter how careful your selections, you always face a major risk. More investment wines depreciate than appreciate in value when you factor in the cost of storage. If you are seriously thinking of becoming an investor, do the same thing you would if you were investing in stocks or commodities: Seek the help of a qualified expert. Some large retail firms can offer advice on investment wines.

Regardless of how modest or expansive your desires, you want assurance that you are dealing with a reputable auction house. In New York, call these places:

➤ Morrell & Company: 212-688-9370

➤ Sherry-Lehmann/Sotheby's Auction House: 212-606-7207

➤ Acker, Merrall & Condit: 212-787-1700

In the Midwest, call

➤ Chicago Wine Company: 847-647-8789

➤ Davis & Company Wine Auctioneers: 312-587-9500

In California, call

➤ Butterfield & Butterfield Auction House: 415-861-7500

If you want to sell your wine, bear in mind a few facts about most auction houses and retail stores:

➤ They deal mainly with valuable, prestigious, or rare wine.

➤ They want to know where the wine comes from. Be ready to prove that the wine has had optimum storage.

➤ They charge a commission for their services, ranging from 10 percent to 25 percent of the sale price, depending on the deal you make. (The customary rate is 25 percent.) Some auction houses collect a 10- or 15-percent premium from the buyer.

➤ Some retailers pay you only after they sell your wine; others pay you when they receive the wine. Look for the best deal.

Buying wines at auction has one great advantage: You can find wines you won't find in most wine shops. In most instances, you can purchase old and rare wines only at auction or from a wine company specializing in buying wine collections for resale.

The disadvantage of buying wine at auction is that frequently you don't know the provenance (storage history and ownership) of the wine. If the wine comes from a well-known collector or an establishment known for impeccable storage and care, the auction catalog says so, and such wines usually command a premium price.

Tasting Tip

Auctions are no place to seek younger wines or mature wines that still are in the sales pipeline. With few exceptions, you'll find these wines at better prices elsewhere. (Auction fever frequently results in paying higher than market price.) And remember, at some wine auctions, you may be assessed a buyer's premium, typically 10 or 15 percent.

Mail-Order Wine

Many large wine shops sell wine by mail or telephone order. They ship to any state that subscribes to a reciprocity agreement with their state. And some may ship the wine even if your state doesn't permit it, so check out your local regulations. Here's a list of mail-order shops you may look at:

➤ Ambrosia, Napa, CA: 1-800-435-2225

➤ Bel-Air Wine Merchant, West Los Angeles, CA: 310-474-9518

➤ Big Y Liquor Super Market, Northampton, MA: 413-584-7775

➤ Brookline Liquor Mart, Allston, MA: 617-734-7700

➤ Calvert Woodley, Washington, DC: 202-966-4400

➤ Central Liquors, Washington, DC: 1-800-835-7928

➤ Chicago Wine Co., Niles, IL: 847-647-8789

➤ Crossroads, New York, NY: 212-633-2863

➤ Duke Of Bourbon, Canoga Park, CA: 1-800-434-6394

➤ Garnet Wines & Liquors, New York, NY: 1-800-872-8466

➤ Geerlings and Wade, Sommers, CT: 1-800-782-9463

➤ Golden West International, San Francisco, CA: 1-800-722-7020

➤ Horseneck Wines and Liquors, Greenwich, CT: 1-800-667-6529

➤ John Hart Fine Wine, Chicago, IL: 312-944-5385

➤ MacArthur Liquors, Washington, DC: 202-388-1433

➤ Marin Wine Cellar, San Rafael, CA: 415-459-3823

➤ Morell & Company, New York, NY: 212-688-9370

➤ New York Wine Warehouse, New York, NY: 212-956-2250

➤ North Berkeley Wine, Berkeley, CA: 1-800-266-6585

➤ Northridge Hills Liquor & Wine, Northridge, CA: 1-800-678-9463

➤ Pop's Wines & Spirits, Island Park, NY: 516-431-0025

➤ Red Carpet Wine & Spirits, Glendale, CA: 1-800-339-0609

➤ Rosenthal Wine Merchant, New York, NY: 212-249-6650

➤ Royal Wine Merchants, New York, NY: 212-689-4855

➤ Sam's Wine Warehouse, Chicago, IL: 1-800-777-9137

➤ Schneider's of Capitol Hill, Washington, DC: 1-800-377-1461

➤ Sherry-Lehmann, New York, NY: 212-838-7500

➤ Silver Spirits, Saint James, NY: 1-800-998-4411

➤ Stafford's Wine Warehouse, Irvine, CA: 1-800-723-9463

➤ The Wine Connection, Westchester, NY: 914-764-9463

➤ The Wine Stop, Burlingame, CA: 1-800-283-9463

➤ Tinamou Wine Company, Sonoma, CA: 1-800-388-6390

➤ Wine Cask, Santa Barbara, CA: 1-800-436-9463

➤ William Sokolin & Co., Southampton, NY: 1-800-946-3947

➤ Wine Country, Signal Hill, CA: 1-800-505-5564

➤ Wine Exchange, Orange, CA: 1-800-769-4639

➤ Wine Spectrum, Santa Rosa, CA: 1-800-933-8466

Another recent innovation is that of the wine-of-the-month clubs, which ship a selection of two to six different wines each month. (If you like the wine, you usually can buy more.) Here are some worth exploring:

➤ Ahlgren Vineyard Wine Club: 408-338-6071

➤ Ambrosia Wine Club: 1-800-435-2225

➤ California Wine Club: 1-800-777-4443

➤ California Winemaker's Guild: 1-800-858-9463

➤ Gold Medal Wine Club: 1-800-266-8888

➤ Oregon Pinot Noir Club: 1-800-847-4474

➤ Passport Wine Club: 1-800-867-9463

Wine Trade Secrets

A knowledge of the inner workings of the wine trade not only is useful in understanding how wines get to your store and how they are priced, but it's fascinating in its own right.

Importers

Although each state has its own regulations, the imported wine trade in the U.S. basically is a three-tiered system: Wine importers and producers sell to distributors or wholesalers; distributors and wholesalers sell to a retail merchant or restaurant; and shops and restaurants sell to you. (Of course, the price increases each step of the way.)

Needless to say, the wine industry loves this type of system. It provides the industry players with limited competition, guaranteed profits, and the luxury of legally legislated debt collection. This system especially benefits retailers in states where minimum profits are maintained by law. Can you blame a merchant who is protected from supermarket competition for fighting to keep the status quo? Unfortunately, consumers pay millions of dollars a year for this legally sanctioned protectionism.

There was a time following the repeal of Prohibition that liquor companies concentrated on high-profit distilled spirits and left imported wines to smaller specialists. (Remember, back then there was no domestic wine industry as we know it today.) During this period, names such as Frank Schoonmaker and Alexis Lichine became famous for their high-quality imported French or German wines.

The renowned Lichine literally barnstormed the country, city to city, persuading restaurants to serve French wines. He also convinced the French to package their wines to appeal to American consumers. Other wine promoters soon joined in courting American buyers.

With a few exceptions, the great old-time wine importers became mere trade names submerged in an industry devoid of any real wine savvy. Today, many wine importers offer a mixed bag of goods—some bad, some good, and some superb. Ironically, the names of several of the most prestigious importers of bygone years are now associated with what one should avoid rather than what one should buy.

But don't get cynical! You can still count on a number of importers to maintain their tradition of quality by selling only dependable merchandise. These firms are few in number, but they specialize in selecting fine wines and particular vintages on a personal level. From these importers you can buy any wine with the confidence that you are buying a superb bottle (some importers distribute domestic wines as well):

Heard It Through the Grapevine

During the mid 1960s and early 1970s, giant conglomerates took a serious interest in the wine business and bought several of the fabled wine companies, once renowned for excellent wines. The result was that a number of liquor executives, ignorant both of wine and the wine trade, were unable to exercise control over their suppliers or choose new ones with any expertise. Today it's a different story, with prestigious vineyards being bought up by conglomerates that want to improve the quality and reputation of the property.

➤ Admiral Wines

➤ Austin Nichols

➤ Banfi Vintners

➤ Clicquot, Inc.

➤ Dreyfus, Ashby & Co.

➤ European Cellars (Eric Solomon)

➤ Frederick Wildman & Co.

➤ Jeffrey Davies/Signature Selections

➤ Kobrand Corp.

➤ Kysela, Père et Fils

➤ Louis/Dresner Selections

➤ Marc de Grazia

➤ Neil Empson Selections

➤ Parliament Imports

➤ Peter Vezan Selections

➤ Robert Chadderdon Selections

➤ Robert Kacher Selections

➤ Seagrams Château & Estate Wine Co.

➤ Select Vineyards

➤ Steve Metzler/Classical Wines from Spain

➤ Terry Theise Selections

➤ Vineyard Brands

➤ W.J. Deutsch & Sons

➤ Weygandt-Metzler Importing

➤ William Grant & Sons

➤ Winebow

➤ Wines of France/Alain Junguenet Selections

Distributors

The distributor is the wholesaler who sells the wine to the retailers and restaurants. Sometimes distributors import wine for distribution limited to their market area.

Direct Import

Some wine merchants have discovered clever loopholes in the regulations that give them an edge over their competition, provide better value for customers, and earn them generous profits. The most significant example is direct import.

Here's how it works: The merchant buys wines abroad (wines that are unavailable in the U.S.) and arranges for an importer/wholesaler to bring them into the country. Although many states rule that the wines must be "posted" at a legal resale price to everyone, these wines belong to the merchant, who is free to set the price. For doing the paperwork, the importer receives a stipend per case, sometimes as low as $1 or $2 and sometimes as much as $20, depending on importing and warehousing costs.

The importer tells other retailers that these wines are out of stock—which they are, because the entire shipment went to only one merchant. The merchant can sell these wines for roughly 30 percent below the price of comparable wines from a national importer. Frequently these wines are even better.

Similar arrangements exist for domestic wines. This situation can complicate your comparison shopping, because a higher-priced wine can be notably lower in quality than a little-known bargain brand. If you play your cards right, however, you can emerge the winner. The two keys to

Tasting Tip

Direct import can mean value for you. Any wine merchant who goes to all the trouble of direct import generally has a good palate—and an eye for a good deal.

343

bargain-finding success are an experienced palate and good book knowledge. If you have a novice palate, don't despair. Just do a little more homework (especially sipping).

Master of Wine

Master of Wine (MW) is a title bestowed by the Institute of Masters of Wine in London. To qualify, candidates must have considerable knowledge of wine and the wine trade. They need to be well-versed in the wines of the world and in each country's wine regulations and requirements. The prestigious MW is awarded only after passing a rigorous written and tasting examination. The title ensures a high level of competence. (Of course, not all MWs are created equal.)

Once the sole province of the United Kingdom, preparatory programs for the MW are currently offered in the U.S., Australia, and continental Europe. Only a small number of Americans so far have qualified for the title. Most of the 195 Masters of Wine are in the U.K.

For information on how to study for and take the test, write to the Institute of Masters of Wine, Five Kings House, 1 Queen Street Place, London EC4R 1QS, England.

Boutique Wineries

California and other states have many small wineries, called boutique wineries, which specialize in finer-quality wines. Many of these wineries were established in the late 1970s and 1980s.

The Sommelier Says

American wines remain one of the few domestically produced products to face severe restraints in interstate trade. With few barriers to sales of wine in the various states, we consumers would have larger choices at lower prices.

For years, many of California's finest wines rarely left the state. No, it wasn't some conspiracy by Californians to keep the good stuff from going east. Instead, the lack of national attention reflected a prejudice against domestic wines by the rest of the country. The chain of distribution was weak or nonexistent. But as the number of California wineries grew, the local market could not absorb all the wine produced, and the wineries were not equipped to market their wines nationally.

Marketing organizations quickly cropped up to fill the void. Today many boutique wineries are promoted by these marketing firms or by national wine importers who have shrewdly recognized these small wineries as a good source of profit. Spotty distribution still remains a problem with many small California, Washington, Oregon, and New York state producers.

Some wineries just do not produce enough wine to spread around. Others don't care to be involved with the regulations—which vary from state to state—imposed on the sale and movement of wine. Still others simply can't afford to pay the prohibitive fees imposed by states for registering a brand for sale within its borders.

A number of these wineries sell directly to the consumer—in their tasting room or by mail or telephone order. Some producers offer their wines through mail-order organizations that feature wines in attractive and informative catalogs.

Tasting Tip

Gallo has enjoyed great success in achieving a more upscale image. (Remember when Gallo meant "cheap jug wine"?) The firm now produces some superb mid- and super-premium wines in its Sonoma County line.

The Giants

When it comes to winemaking, domestic production is dominated by a handful of large and powerful producers in California and New York state. Some of these producers are owned by importing firms or have their own national distribution network, usually through wholesalers.

You can find wines from these producers in virtually every wine store throughout the U.S. (Pretty good marketing, huh?) Gallo commands the largest share of the market. Along with a few other biggies, this group takes the lion's share of space in American wine stores. Most of these wines are ordinary jug or simple-premium quality.

The Least You Need to Know

➤ Shopping around for a good wine merchant is an important step in your involvement with wine.

➤ You can return a bad bottle if you don't wait too long.

➤ Private labels and direct imports can provide some bargains.

➤ You can buy wine by mail or telephone, if permitted in your state.

The Wine Information Highway

In This Chapter

➤ Understanding scoring systems for wine

➤ Selecting wine magazines and newsletters

➤ Finding wine online

➤ Choosing books for further reading

You think it's hard selecting from among tens of thousands of wines? What about tens of thousands of books, magazines, articles, brochures, news columns, videotapes, and Web sites about wine? Actually, tens of thousands is an understatement. A recent look around the Internet turned up 65,000 references to red wine, 55,000 to white wine, and 7,500 to Champagne, alone. In fact, the Internet search engine I use found nearly three million references to wine of some kind or another!

But going online isn't the only way to get up-to-date wine information. Old-fashioned hard-copy information sources are proliferating as well. But how can we go through this mountain of printed information? How can we get information that's both useful and reliable? That's what I'll try to cover in this chapter.

A Word on Scoring Systems

How many times have you heard, "On a scale of 1 to 10 ..." Everybody does it: Everybody rates things—from school report cards to consumer magazine tests of automobiles, home-theater systems, and computer printers.

With cars and other machines, raters measure things and convert measurements into scores. When perfect scores are added up, you get an even hundred. To read any number of wine magazines and newsletters, you'd think their 100-point rating systems were no less quantitative. But no. We're not rating Champagne bottles for their resistance to breakage under pressure. Instead, we have writers working under pressure to tell us how much they enjoyed a particular Champagne.

It's all subjective. In a blind-tasting, it's unlikely any two wine experts will give identical ratings to, say, a half dozen wines. It's unlikely a single expert will give the same product the same rating six times! That doesn't mean wine ratings are useless. Experts do reach a general consensus on the good, the bad, and the downright ugly.

Heard It Through the Grapevine

The 100-point wine rating system was conceived by Robert Parker, a former government lawyer who published his ratings in a newsletter, *The Wine Advocate.* Parker must have been aware that his system was not laboratory accurate, but he bet that the system's appeal would sell newsletters. He was right. Parker's newsletter is one of the foremost in the field.

Today, however, many experts consider the newsletter's numerical ratings unreliable and often controversial. But that hasn't stopped many others from emulating Parker's success. Most wine periodicals do the 100-point thing, regardless of its shortcomings.

The problem with wine rating stems from the fact that humans aren't calibrated laboratory instruments. As we wine critics taste wines, we become fatigued from the stress and effort of concentration. And (spitting aside) alcohol still gets into our systems. So wines sampled later in the tasting are at a serious disadvantage, as the palate no longer can perceive those wine's attributes fully.

Even an extraordinary wine tasted late in a tasting of a large number of wines may be considered mediocre. As publisher of *Vintage Magazine*, I had the opportunity to test the palates of some of the A-list tasters who write for magazines and newsletters. Unknown to the participants, I put the same wine in the tasting several times. The expert critics scored the same wine vastly differently each time. In a 100-point system, some scores varied as much as 30 points!

Other experiments have shown that tasters cannot match their tasting notes or numerical ratings with any wine when it is presented a second time. The scores are all over the place.

But don't discard the scoring system entirely. Instead, think of the scores as helpful clues to what will be in that bottle. Concentrate on the qualitative descriptions in wine publications and see how closely your tastes match those of the writers.

I advocate a letter system: A, B, C, D, F, just like school. This is a concise way for getting the point across. (A five-star system works just as well.) *The Connoisseur's Guide to California Wine* newsletter uses this type of system with stars. The wines are evaluated in a manner similar to movie or restaurant ratings. You're given a point rating with enough information to assist you in making a decision. No pretension, no fuss. Just clear and concise information. (That is, unless you would feel comfortable rating movies or restaurants on a 100-point scale.)

Tasting Tip

For the most part, the scores you see in magazines like *Wine Spectator*, *The Wine Advocate*, and *Wine Enthusiast* are guesstimates. Although the tasters are knowledgeable and experienced, there is no reliable system of palate calibration.

Wine Magazines

Wine magazines are a good source of information about wines that are new on the market. Also, you get articles and commentary on topics of interest to wine enthusiasts. Some magazines specialize in providing lots of up-to-the-minute information. Others offer a more leisurely read. You also can find ads about wine tours, wine education programs, and wine-related equipment and products. These magazines are among the most popular:

➤ **Vintage** This magazine is edited specifically for you, the reader of this guide. It is written for the beginning or novice wine drinker and contains elementary articles on wine and spirits. Gourmet cuisine is covered as well. It is available for free in many wine stores throughout the country. Ask for it.

➤ **Decanter** Published in London, *Decanter* is of interest primarily in the British market. The magazine audaciously proclaims on its stationery that it is the "best" wine magazine. *Decanter* does succeed in being the most authoritative magazine, as many writers are professionals in the trade or full-time wine writers. Monthly, $80 a year. Telephone (USA): 1-800-875-2997.

➤ **Wine Spectator** This publication is arguably the best wine magazine in terms of production values and graphics, with more pages, features, and wine recommendations than the others. However, it often publishes inaccurate vintage assessments and bizarre wine reviews.

The magazine rates its wines on a 100-point system that rarely is useful. Its tasting notes are useful although sometimes incomplete. Many of the wines reviewed are of such limited production that they cannot easily be found. The magazine presents the insider's view of the wine world, and everyone in the wine trade reads it.

Decanter is more authoritative, but the slick, full-color design of *Wine Spectator* makes that magazine more attractive. Large format, 18 issues, $40 a year. Telephone: 1-800-752-7799.

➤ **Wine Enthusiast**   This publication is a *Wine Spectator* wannabe. The main business of this magazine's publisher is wine accessories. The features frequently are written by freelancers who have wine as an avocation and are employed full time in other professions. *Wine Enthusiast*'s paper quality and ratings on the untenable 100-point system do not make it a worthy competitor for *Wine Spectator*. Large format, 14 issues, $24.95 a year. Telephone: 914-345-8463.

➤ **The Wine News**   This attractive magazine covers the world's major wine regions and includes tasting notes. In production details, it is not on a level with *Wine Spectator,* but it's worth reading. I recommend it. Large format, bimonthly, $24 a year. Telephone: 305-444-7250.

➤ **Wine & Spirits**   This publication covers spirits as well as wine. Its writers are mainly freelancers who are employed full time in other professions. Wine reviewers use the 100-point system. Eight issues a year, $22 a year. 212-695-4660.

Reading a wine magazine will keep you abreast of the world of wine as well as steer you toward some good wines. If you intend to become serious about wine, a wine magazine is essential reading.

Tasting Tip

One or many tasters? Some wine newsletters base all their judgments on the palate of a single taster (who also is writer, editor, and often, publisher). Others compile the experiences and judgments of others. If you find your tastes coincide with those of a single taster, that's the one you want to heed.

Newsletters

Newsletters are concise, up-to-date, and informative. Many newsletters reflect the opinion of one expert (with whom you may or may not agree). Others present the views of several writers. You won't find picturesque accounts of a holiday in Bordeaux or a weekend in sunny Sonoma, but you will find extensive tasting notes and buying guides. You might consider these newsletters:

➤ **The Vine**   England's Clive Cotes MW is a Master of Wine, and his expertise is apparent in this excellent publication. Cotes is an authority on Bordeaux and Burgundy and one of the world's best wine tasters and wry writers. I highly recommend this newsletter for the avid wine enthusiast. Monthly, $120 per year (www.clive-coates.co.uk).

➤ **The Wine Advocate**   This newsletter is probably the most influential publication in the wine world but is not the most authoritative. It achieved this status by instituting a 100-point system to score wines. Retailers quickly jumped on the bandwagon, quoting Parker's ratings in their advertisements. Despite Parker's use of the 100-point system, he does provide solid, useful information and tasting notes that are usually on the mark. Bimonthly, $45 a year. Telephone: 410-329-6477.

➤ **Stephen Tanzer's International Wine Cellar**   This is the most influential newsletter after Parker's and, in my opinion, a better read. In addition to wine reviews, Tanzer publishes interviews with important members of the winemaking community, more background information on the vintages, and guest experts' writings on various subjects. This publication is a must-have if you are serious about wine. Bimonthly, $48 a year. Telephone: 1-800-946-3505.

➤ **Connoisseur's Guide to California Wine**   As its name implies, this publication specializes in California wine. Its writers tend to have a California palate (they prefer big, chewy wines). Wines are evaluated by a panel and are rated on a three-star system. Monthly, $50 a year. Telephone: 510-865-3150.

Free Winery Newsletters

A number of wineries, large and small, publish their own newsletters. These handy sheets contain announcements of new releases, news of happenings at the winery, and opportunities to buy wine directly from the winery. These newsletters are too numerous to list here, but if you want, send me your name and address, and I will forward it to the wineries on your behalf. Put your name and address on a postcard, and send it to Winery Newsletters, 201 E. 87th Street, Suite 5E, New York, NY 10128.

Wine Online

America Online and CompuServe online services have wine forums where wine hobbyists meet to post their tasting notes, read news of the wine world, chat, and exchange ideas. All forums are similar, with minor variations. My favorite is CompuServe because its forum leader is the most knowledgeable and adept.

Heard It Through the Grapevine

The World Wide Web (WWW) is a wonderful resource, with more information on more topics than you'll ever need (or even find). Tens of thousands of new Web sites are born daily, some even on the subject of wine! But easy come, easy go, they say. Most Web sites are maintained at the pleasure of a single individual. That superb wine site you found last week may not be around next week.

(The Web sites mentioned in this book have exhibited some permanence.)

More and more wineries, wine shops, and wine entrepreneurs are creating pages on the Internet or joining a larger Web site with a wine focus. Many thousands are devoted entirely to wine. Several of these pages have links to hundreds of other sites.

These sites and the ones listed in Appendix E, "Wine Accessories," are worth visiting:

The Wine Reporter newsletter (www.winereporter-usa.com)

Fujiwine (www.netins.net/showcase/fujiwine)

Pascal's Wine Page (www.speakeasy.org/~winepage)

Burgundy Cellar (www.burgcellar.com)

Mark Squires' E-Zine (marksquires.com)

Wine Bargain Page (www.iglou.com/why/wine.html)

Virtual Vineyards (www.virtualvin.com)

One easy way to surf the wine Web is to visit vine2wine.com. This site has nearly 2,000 links to other wine sites, with descriptions of the sites.

Wine Accessory Catalogs

The Wine Enthusiast (1-800-356-8466) and International Wine Accessories (1-800-527-4072) mail-order companies both produce slick, full-color catalogs with a wide variety of corkscrews, wine racks, wine storage units, glassware, and other accessories. Both sell the same merchandise, pricey with high markups. A new entry to this field is Wine & All That Jazz (1-800-610-7731), which has a great-looking catalog with good values. I highly recommend it.

Wine Courses

Wine courses can range from informal tastings conducted by a wine expert to professional-level courses. The latter are not restricted to members of the wine trade, but some level of proficiency is a requisite. Wine courses of various lengths and levels are conducted at numerous locations throughout the country. For information on the courses offered in your area, write to the Society of Wine Educators, 8600 Foundry Street, Savage, MD 20763, 301-776-8569.

Wine Clubs

A wine club is an rganization where wine lovers get together at wine tastings and gourmet dinners to enjoy the fruit of the vine. A large national wine club by the name of Les Amis du Vin used to exist. The club had more than 30,000 members, but it went bankrupt. The individual chapters across the nation either disbanded or went their own ways.

A wine club may exist in your locality. The best way to find out is to contact the wine and food editor of your local newspaper or your local wine retailer. If no wine club is in your area, you may want to start one yourself. Wine clubs provide an excellent way to exchange information about wine, make new friends, and pursue your interest in wine as a hobby.

The Sommelier Says

Both Wine Enthusiast and International Wine Accessories promote the Vacu-Vin wine-keeping device, which scientific studies have shown to be completely ineffective.

Tasting Tip

If you decide to start your own wine club, use your local newspaper to publish notices of your meetings so your organization can grow. You may find a local wine retailer who wants to get involved by providing wine for free or at a discount.

Books for Advanced Reading

In addition to encyclopedias, pocket guides, and general reading, you can find a wealth of books offering in-depth information on specific topics related to wine. Books are available on Burgundy, Bordeaux, Cabernet Sauvignon, and Chardonnay. You can find books on old wines, like Port and Madeira, and books hailing the pleasures of wine from obscure wine regions. Here is a brief list of some books that might enhance your enjoyment and appreciation of wine (for a comprehensive list, see Appendix C, "Recommended Books for Further Reading"):

➤ *Bordeaux* (Third Edition), by Robert M. Parker, Jr., 1998. This book reviews thousands of wines and vintages and provides comprehensive information about the region. (Unfortunately, this book uses the 100-point system to rate the wines.)

➤ *Bordeaux* (Second Edition), by David Peppercorn, 1991. This book offers sketches of whatever the author deems important—good vintages, history, general characteristics of the wine, and information on several hundred wineries of the region.

➤ *Burgundy* (Second Edition), by Anthony Hanson, 1995. Hanson is deeply immersed in the Burgundy wine trade and shares his immense knowledge of the subject. It includes considerable detail on the practices and growers of the region.

➤ *Burgundy* (Second Edition), by Robert M. Parker, Jr., 1996. Parker rates the growers and reviews their wines. He provides an in-depth evaluation, as well as comprehensive details on the region.

➤ *Hugh Johnson's Modern Encyclopedia of Wine*, by Hugh Johnson, 1991. A complete explanation of wines, including grape growing and winemaking, of all wine-producing areas of the world.

➤ *Hugh Johnson's Pocket Encyclopedia of Wine*, by Hugh Johnson, 1999. This annually updated book provides country-by-country ratings of many vintages of over 5,000 wines. The book has maps, label guides, vintage charts, and more.

➤ *Parker's Wine Buyer's Guide* (Fourth Edition), by Robert M. Parker, Jr., 1995. This comprehensive guide rates more than 7,500 wines. Parker rates the producers of every winegrowing region on a five-star system but reviews specific wines using his 100-point system. Read the reviews, but don't take the precision of the ratings too seriously.

➤ *Port* (Fourth Edition), by George Robertson, 1992. A very readable account of the entire Port winemaking and maturation process by the chairman of Croft & Co.

➤ *Sherry* (Fourth Edition), by Julian Jeffs, 1992. Includes the history of Sherry, from Chaucer's time to present, and the entire grape growing and winemaking process.

➤ *The New Connoisseur's Handbook of California Wines* (Third Edition), by Norman S. Roby and Charles E. Olken. Comprehensive and authoritative coverage of more than 800 wineries with critical ratings of thousands of individual wines and vintages. The book uses a viable three-star system to rate wines.

➤ *The Oxford Companion to Wine*, edited by Jancis Robinson, 1994. This 1,086-page tome includes just about every detail you would want to know about wine. The book is written by experts in each field.

➤ *The Wine Atlas of California*, by James Halliday, 1993. An excellent book on California wine, as well as a comprehensive and detailed compendium of maps of the region.

➤ *The Wines of Italy*, by David Gleave, 1989. An in-depth coverage of the wines of Italy providing details of all the important regions.

➤ *Vintage Talk: Conversations with California's New Winemakers*, by Dennis Schaefer, 1994. Conversations with winemakers from 20 wineries, such as Simi, Sterling, Acacia, and Au Bon Climat. Excellent insight into the role of the winemaker.

➤ *Wine Price File*. This is a data book of wine auction and retail store prices with 70,000 listings of more than 15,000 fine and rare wines.

➤ *World Atlas of Wine* (Fourth Edition), by Hugh Johnson, 1994. This book provides detailed maps of the major wine regions of the world, along with informative commentary.

Heard It Through the Grapevine

There are hundreds of wine books out there. An excellent place to find them is Kellergrin's Specialty Book Company, a mail-order firm.

The Least You Need to Know

➤ You can advance your wine education by reading wine magazines, newsletters, and books—and by participating in online forums.

➤ The 100-point system used by most wine publications isn't as useful as it seems, primarily because it's based on small differences in the changeable taste perceptions of humans.

➤ Look for a wine course or wine club in your locality. These are an enjoyable, social way to increase your wine knowledge.

The Wine List, Monsieur!

Life offers no finer experience than a superb meal with a noble wine. The experience is particularly rich in the opulence of a three-star restaurant, such as Le Régence in New York City, with dining companions who share your appreciation of wine and cuisine.

Sadly, unless you have money to throw away, your aspirations quickly will dissipate as you discover that a $400 bottle of Le Montrachet is $1,200, a $30 bottle of Volnay is $95, a $26 bottle of Champagne $65, and a mere $8 Beaujolais Village is $20. A three- to five-times retail markup is not unusual at better restaurants.

I will not pay such prices, and I recommend you don't either. Actually, I've discovered that the full body, silky mouthfeel, and complex aromas of the expensive coffee blends these restaurants serve are an acceptable substitute for the wine experience. You may want to do what I do, which is to order a cup of coffee during the meal and enjoy two or three refills for a dollar or two.

But that's just me. Most wine-lovers feel that no fine dining experience is truly complete without wine. But trying to complement a restaurant menu can be a frustrating and sometimes futile experience. Three things can go wrong here:

1. Exorbitant prices from outrageous markups.

2. A small wine list that's limited to a choice of undistinguished wines, varied only in their degrees of mediocrity.

3. The appearance of a key-jangling *sommelier* (wine steward), overtly condescending and, pretensions to the contrary, not necessarily familiar with the wines, their vintages, and availability.

Put these three all together, and we can make a great case for ordering a cold beer or a cup of coffee.

Okay, let's be fair: Some restaurants do offer a good selection of wines, meticulously matched to the cuisine. A few even afford an opportunity to try wines unobtainable elsewhere. When the wines are fairly priced (some restaurants have realized that affordable wines may encourage people to enjoy more than one bottle), dining with wine can live up to your greatest expectations. Or even surpass them.

Wine By the Glass

Ordering wine by the glass seems like a good idea. For one thing, it's easy. Your choices are red or white (sometimes rosé). Ordering wine is as trouble-free as choosing between tea or coffee, cola or ginger ale. The problem is, after you taste the house wine, you may wish you had chosen the cola!

Depending on the restaurant, your single glass of mediocre wine can cost anywhere from $3 to $7.50. As the next section explains, you can order wine by the glass without being disappointed (or ripped off).

Tasting Tip

What if you are the only person at your table who wants wine? Or the red wine chosen by your meat-eating companions would easily overpower your delicate filet of fish? Wine by the glass might be your best choice, even though the selection will be poorer.

House Wine

House wines are sold by the glass or carafe. Rarely do you find a house wine that is a superb choice. Well, you may (possibly) if you are dining in wine country—Napa or Sonoma—but for most of us, that's a long way off. Even then, you still need to be very sure of your restaurant.

House wines generally are your ordinary California or Italian generic wines, purchased in large containers and then marked up—frequently to 10 times over cost. Think of it: You're paying more money per glass for your nondescript wine than the restaurateur paid for the whole bottle! The word for most house wines is *avoid*.

Better Pours

Some restaurants include a selection of premium wines by the glass. Yes, this does mean a higher price, but it also means better quality. Premium wines by the glass usually range from $5 to $10 (sometimes more) per glass for wines that retail for $5 or $6 a bottle.

What if premium wines are not available by the glass? One trick is to be a little enterprising. If you see no premium listing—or if only one or two wines are listed and they are not to your taste— don't be afraid to ask about other selections. Specify what type of wine you want. The worst your server can say is that something is not available, and a helpful and knowledgeable server may suggest something comparable.

The Sommelier Says

Many wine-by-the-glass menus list only one premium white and one premium red as well as their cheaper wines. A few may include several of each, but other restaurants list no premium wine by the glass.

Pricing Bottles of Wine

Determining a "fair" restaurant price for a bottle of wine is difficult. Here's one guide-line I offer: For wines that require neither aging nor special handling, twice the retail price is probably more than fair. And for the more expensive wines, full retail price plus $10 is what you can expect.

Generally, restaurants mark up wine to three times the retail, which is four to five times their cost. In other words, you can expect to pay $20 for a bottle of wine retail-ing for about $7 at your local wine shop. Some restaurateurs go six or seven times above cost!

For prestigious or scarce bottles, the markup can be even higher, with an expensive wine carrying a markup of several hundred dollars or more. All this for no greater effort than buying the wine by phone and pulling the cork at the table!

In my opinion, no wine, no matter how rare or expensive, should be marked up more than $50 over retail. After all, the restaurant only needs to store the wine, but the retailer must store the wine and provide costly display space. If the retailer can make a profit selling the wine at retail, the restaurant can too.

For a restaurant, profits from wine sales (and other beverages) go directly to the bot-tom line. Overhead, advertising, and staff expenses are calculated in setting the food prices. When a restaurant charges from $12 to $20 for $2 worth of chicken, it should not gouge the customer who wants to enjoy a bottle of fine wine with his dinner. I refuse to pay these prices and instead seek out restaurants that permit customers to bring their own wines, either for free or for a modest corkage charge ranging from $5 to $10 a bottle.

Heard It Through the Grapevine

To the unwary consumer, older wines can present a real risk. Cashing in on the vintage mystique, many restaurants assume any older wine is better and worthy of exorbitant prices. Old is not necessarily better. Nor is it always good.

I have seen poor or past-their-prime vintages of prestigious labels, like Château Lafite-Rothschild or La Romanée-Conti, offered at astronomical prices. Once, I found a 1965 Lafite-Rothschild—one of the worst vintages in many years that retailed for $4 a bottle when released—listed at $70. At this particular resort hotel, the wine was selling quite briskly, though it was nothing short of dead!

Rating the Wine List

There is an old joke among wine-lovers. There's a restaurant that has a wine list that looks like this:

1. Chablis
2. Burgundy
3. Rosé

Please Order Wine by Number

That joke is not so funny when you're trying to select a wine that will complement your meal and enhance your dining experience. Variations on this theme are all too common. My motto for ordering wine in a restaurant is the Scouts' motto: "Be prepared!"

I feel fair treatment on the wine price list contributes to a restaurant's mood, no less than a well-matched wine to enhance the dining experience. The first step, of course, is the wine selection. If the list offers nothing worthy of the meal you order, you're stuck.

Whenever I decide to order no wine, I make my objections clear to the owner, manager, or maitre d'. I feel he or she ought to know my reasons. Then again, many restaurants with a poor wine policy attract me frequently anyway. The ambiance is excellent, the cuisine superior, or both.

The Short List

The list of one white, one red, and one rosé may be a joke, but in all humor, there is truth. Abbreviated wine lists with maybe two wines per color, one or two wines from an "exotic" location (anything other than France, Italy, or California), and perhaps some sparkling variety are still too common. A restaurant with this type of list is one that goes through the motions of serving wine without any sensitivity to its customers or desire to attract wine-lovers.

The Familiar List

Does that wine list give you a feeling of *déjà vu*? Hmmm. That red leatherette cover is strikingly familiar! You know what wines are there even before you open it. And you don't check for vintages because you know, somehow, they aren't there at all.

That wine list was not compiled by the restaurant at all, but by a wholesaler or distributor whose primary motive was self-interest. I mean, why not supply the binder and printing for a list stocked with the distributor's most profitable wines!

You may see such a list in an Italian restaurant one weekend, in a small French restaurant the next. The restaurateur using this list opts for economy, convenience, and minimal personal effort. (I wonder how much attention the food gets!)

The Brand List

This is a variation on the familiar list. Suspect any wine list with a preponderance of major, nationally distributed brands: B&G, Mouton Cadet, Bolla, Paul Masson, for example. These wines are not necessarily bad, but a list dominated by one or two popular brands is much too restrictive.

> **The Sommelier Says**
>
> Prices outrageous? Try to bargain by ordering two bottles at a lower price. A small profit on each of two bottles is better than none at all, and the restaurateur may get a loyal customer out of it. It's worth a try. Just call in advance to negotiate a deal to avoid an embarrassing confrontation in front of your guests.

Offering wines that are commonly available and all too familiar suggests the restaurateur prefers to allow a sales representative to prepare the wine list, making no effort to match the wine with the cuisine. The wine cellar has neither imagination nor creativity. (Chances are that both are missing in the kitchen as well.) Check to see if most California wines come from one producer or if most imported wines are from one shipper/importer. If so, you have a brand-dictated list.

The Fat Wine List

Although an extensive wine list is always nice, one that reads like a doctoral thesis or a Henry James novel can bog you down when you're trying to make a simple selection to go with dinner. The best-managed restaurants provide an extended list for patrons willing to lose themselves in wineland and an abridged version for those who simply are trying to match their meal.

The Good Wine List

I love wine lists that offer variety and global appeal—that is, a wide selection of wines from the major wine regions of the world. Of course, I also like an indication that the owner exercised a modicum of care in the wine selection. Here are examples of a good wine selection:

➤ Bordeaux from different châteaux

➤ Different vintages of the same wine

➤ Wines spanning a wide price range

➤ Wines from a local producer

➤ Wines chosen to complement the restaurant's menu

These wines are the beginning of a good wine list. This type of list shows that the owner or beverage manager is quite knowledgeable about wines. Generally, this person will be enthusiastic in suggesting wines within your price range.

The Reserve Wine List

No, a reserve wine list does not mean that all the wines on the list are "reserve" wines. A few upscale restaurants offer a special list of rare wines in addition to the regular wine list. If the occasion is really special, and cost is no object .... Well, why not? On the other hand, if you have any doubts, stick with the regular list. Should you choose the reserve list, ask for assistance from the sommelier. You do not want to be stuck with a very expensive mistake.

Bringing Your Own Bottle

We all know about BYOB (bringing your own bottle) where the restaurant has no liquor license. Small ethnic restaurants often fall into this category, along with restaurants that have just opened and for which the license is still pending.

What most people don't realize is that BYOB is also a time-honored tradition at restaurants with a weak wine list, or even a restaurant with an adequate list, when you want to enjoy a special wine of your own. First check your local regulations to be sure you're allowed to bring a bottle of wine to a licensed restaurant. Some places say no; others, yes. Second, be sure you follow a sensible protocol and are prepared to pay a corkage fee. You are not out to alienate the proprietor. BYOB is appropriate under the following conditions:

➤ The wine you want to bring is something special, not on the list.

➤ You consider ordering another bottle from the list to maintain goodwill.

➤ You call ahead to ask for approval and to find out the corkage fee.

➤ You are a fairly regular client.

➤ You include a reasonable value for the wine when you are calculating your tip.

Bringing your own bottle of special wine will add to the dining experience while permitting you to save money. A reasonable corkage fee is anywhere from $5 to $10. Some restaurants try to discourage the practice by charging an exorbitant fee. If this is the case, visit a restaurant that realizes that a reasonable corkage fee makes for a loyal customer.

Go Ahead! Send It Back!

The question is a big concern for many restaurant patrons: Under what conditions can you refuse and return a bottle of wine? (This option seems to be exercised quite often by an elite few and not at all by the vast majority.)

Don't break out in hives. The decision simply comes down to this: Don't accept defective or flawed wines. The confusion for some people lies in deciding whether a wine's taste and smell are defective or just unfamiliar and unusual. (But isn't this one supposed to smell like skunk?)

The Sommelier Says

If a white wine is dark yellow or brown in color and smells like Sherry, it is over-the-hill and likely maderized. (See Chapter 22, "Fortified Wine," to understand the Madeira reference!) Red wines past their prime are somewhat brown in color, often orange around the rim. A dull flavor—like the smell of dead leaves—and a sharp, short finish are sure indicators of when to send the wine back.

Tasting Tip

A good sommelier is supposed to taste the wine to determine its quality before serving it to you. (You could check by asking a few of the questions you used to evaluate your wine shop.) When a sommelier is present, the practice of tasting wine at your table is an acceptable ritual and not a charade.

Of course, if you see, smell, or taste any of the defects mentioned in this book, do not hesitate. Send it back. (See Chapter 8, "Hot off the Vine," to review how to spot a bad wine.) However, experience is the best teacher for helping you detect the most common off-aromas.

When in doubt, ask your server to sample the wine. If the server is confused about its merits and acceptability, then you are off the hook and another bottle should be forthcoming. But never return a wine you ordered out of curiosity but then did not like!

In my experience, a well-run restaurant will not quibble or get into a battle of wills with its customers. Customer service is the hallmark of the hospitality trade. "The customer is always right" has always been the policy in the food industry and is used more often these days with wine. Just remember: Don't abuse the restaurant's good will.

Rating Your Sommelier

In many higher-priced restaurants, the wine list and your order are handled by a sommelier. A sommelier, or wine steward, should be knowledgeable and familiar with the wines listed. Better yet, the sommelier may have bought, stored, and cared for the beloved wines and even trained the rest of the staff in wine protocol. France, Italy, and a few other countries have professional schools to train sommeliers. A few comparable programs exist in the U.S., but it has yet to catch up with the Old World.

Therefore, you must learn to distinguish between the well-informed, full-fledged sommeliers and the impostors who strut around with pomp, ceremony, and haughtiness (and whose sole purpose is to intimidate and ultimately coerce people into buying wines with high markups or wines purchased in some big-quantity deal). Worst of all, these characters survive because customers, unsure in their own knowledge, are afraid to speak up.

Taking Home the Rest of the Bottle

You have half a bottle of wine left, and you're sure that one more glass will be imprudent. Wine is an awfully expensive commodity to leave sitting on the table! How do you ask for a doggie bag for your wine?

Wine etiquette has no protocol that forbids requesting to take your unfinished bottle home with you. In some states, however, the practice is restricted by law, so your request for the bottle may be turned down. Don't blame the owner or manager for being difficult or haughty. Of course, you might ask the restaurateur to keep the corked bottle refrigerated until your next visit.

The Sommelier Says

If your white wine arrives at your table iced like a beer bottle, beware. Wines kept too cold for too long lose their verve. You don't want an overpriced flat wine. (You are better off to have white wine delivered to your table at room temperature than placed in an ice bucket for 15 minutes.)

Getting Good Service

As a paying customer—especially at the price restaurateurs charge for wine—you are entitled to fair service. These few suggestions can help you get a fair deal:

➤ Make sure you see the bottle you order. Check producer, type, vintage, etc.

➤ See that the wine arrives with cork and foil capsule intact. The possibility exists that a bottle may have been refilled with inferior wine or returned by another diner.

➤ Take some time away from your friends and guests to study the bottle. Slow the sommelier or server down to your pace—it's your money.

➤ Hold the bottle and check its temperature. A red wine, unless it is Beaujolais Nouveau, should be at room temperature. A bottle that's too warm can indicate poor storage. White wines should be chilled, not frigid.

➤ Do not let the sommelier open the wine bottle until you have given your official approval. Do not let the sommelier pour the wine into other glasses until you have tasted and accepted it. Most important rule: Don't rush.

Tasting Tip

Smell the empty glass. I know. This sounds silly. But the slightest smell of soap or detergent ruins Champagne and impairs most table wines. If you detect a detergent smell, ask the waiter to scrub the glasses carefully. When he returns, don't be afraid to recheck. A once-over light rinse won't always do the trick.

➤ Check the wine glasses for size and type. If you are not satisfied, ask for others. Champagnes and sparkling wines are best served in glasses without hollow stems. Flutes are preferred, but an all-purpose wine glass may be your only alternative.

➤ Make certain the capsule is cut neatly and the cork is removed cleanly. The cork should be offered to you, and it certainly should not crumble under your touch. Of course, Champagnes and sparkling wines should be uncorked with a minimal pop, if any. That movieland pop will land half your expensive bubbles on the carpet.

The wine should not just smell clean and free of defects, its bouquet should be consistent with its type. These characteristics assume some knowledge on your part, which you are developing if you've read this far. (Of course, if you select an unfamiliar wine at random and discover it's not to your taste, that's your problem. Live and learn.)

If you followed the sommelier or server's recommendation and description, but the wine does not resemble what was described, the problem is the restaurant's. You can refuse the wine. Be persistent.

Heard It Through the Grapevine

A word about timing. Far too often, about the time your food arrives, you are informed that the wine you ordered is not available. Because some of us plan the meal around the wine selected, this is bad news! You can avoid this dilemma by requesting that the wine or wines be presented and brought to the table well ahead of the food.

Vintage wines deserve special mention. If you intend to bring an old vintage with you or contemplate ordering a really old wine from the list, check ahead for several reasons. Old wines mean old bottles, and they are subject to enormous variations in storage. Find out if the management stands by the quality of the vintage bottles in its cellar. If you're bringing your own dowager wine, inquire if the restaurant has the necessary decanter, glasses, and a person experienced in decanting old wines.

An old wine is like a special entrée: It should be ordered ahead of time, allowing the staff to make proper preparations that include standing the bottle upright for several hours or more, preferably the day before. The wines should be ready to decant when you arrive.

The Least You Need to Know

➤ You may get better wines by the glass in restaurants if you ask about premium pours.

➤ A fair price for a $6 retail bottle of wine is $12 in a restaurant. A fair price for a wine selling for $25 or more in a wine store is full retail price plus $10. Few restaurants practice such a pricing policy.

➤ A mediocre wine list or one prepared by the wholesaler is an indication of a dining establishment not fully conversant with its craft.

➤ You may be able to bring your own wine into a restaurant by paying a corkage charge of about $10 or so.

➤ In many states, you can take home a partially filled bottle if you have not finished it during your meal.

Chapter 29

Wines for Everyday

In This Chapter

➤ Everyday wine quality

➤ Savings in packaging

➤ How everyday wines differ

Throughout this book, we've looked at the very finest wines you can buy anywhere in the world. And we've looked at some of the most expensive (not necessarily the same wines). I've noted excellent wines from many countries that I think are pretty good values—and some pretty good wines that are excellent values. So why should we even bother with the sorts of everyday wines that anybody can buy at any time or any place (and without any special wine knowledge, either)?

Because everyday wine has its place. Sometimes it's perfect in a punch bowl recipe or as an ingredient in a summer "cooler." Ordinary wine may be good any time you might feel like enjoying a sip.

Everyday wines lack the flavors, the authority, and the complexity of better wines. (We'll not mention breeding and finesse!) But still these wines are the product of fermentation of grapes, a process that yields unique flavors, found nowhere else in nature. If your everyday wine hasn't been doctored with nonwine ingredients, it can still offer you at least a few of wine's many pleasures—and for surprisingly little money.

Cheap Doesn't Mean Bad

Do you remember how much personal computers used to cost? And color TVs? (And how much less capability you got for your money, too!) Many everyday things have become much cheaper over the years, not even counting inflation. (Movie popcorn is another matter.)

The reason is technology: new tools, new materials, new manufacturing methods, and new distribution systems. They all work together to deliver more value at less cost.

To some degree, this has worked in wine production, too, but mostly at the cheap end of the price spectrum. When it comes to superior and noble wines, there's no substitute for the intensive skilled and semiskilled labor that goes into their making. Technology—say, temperature-controlled stainless steel fermentation tanks—may help make quality more reliable, but it does little to reduce labor costs.

As we move down a few price and quality grades, though, there are more opportunities for automation, replacing expensive labor with machinery. And at the very lowest level, winemaking has more in common with mass-production manufacturing than with any art or craft.

Heard It Through the Grapevine

Comparing wine prices over time is a little tricky. You have to correct for consumer price inflation. When I noticed that it was possible to buy some California white wines for only $1.35 a bottle (equivalent), I was curious. So I checked: In terms of consumer price inflation, that $1.35 is equivalent to 22 cents a bottle in 1960, 30 cents in 1970, 66 cents in 1980, and a dollar in 1990. We never before saw wine at those prices!

This isn't a bad thing, actually. Good wines are still good—and still expensive. What we call jug wines, however, have become better because of the quality control that automation allows. And they have become cheaper. I've seen some wines in 5-liter packages sell for the equivalent of $1.35 a bottle!

For Less Than Five Bucks

There's a lot that goes into the price tag on that bottle of imported wine from France, Australia, or Argentina. There's shipping (the glass bottle as well as its contents). There are import duties. And profits for winery, broker, importer, and retailer. Oh, and federal, state, and local taxes. Still, we can buy a bottle of imported wine for less than $5.

Some of the larger wine outlets—the ones with the big price display signs in their windows—offer a surprising selection of inexpensive wines from France, Italy, Spain, and Argentina. And let's not forget California, though such bargains can be a little scarce when we're buying these by the single bottle.

For this little money, you can afford to experiment now and then. I mean, select a bottle—a red Bordeaux or something white from Italy. Take it home and serve it. You might like it. Or bring one home and save it for your next brown-bag wine-tasting. See how it scores. (You might risk embarrassing a few friends, though.)

Tasting Tip

Here's where you can forget all about that knowledgeable wine seller at your favorite store—the one who stocks fine wines and great vintages. Such a store cannot afford to give space to these cheapest wines. If you're looking for a bottle of wine for less than $5, you're best off in one of those large chain discount stores (if they allow them in your state).

Before I continue, let me remind you what you're giving up when you choose something for less than $5:

➤ **Body**   Some alcohol, but little else.

➤ **Finish**   Once it's swallowed, it's gone.

➤ **Texture**   Little more than from tap water.

➤ **Complexity**   About as complex as a tiddlywink.

The experience isn't without value. You'll still get the grapey winery flavors. You'll sense the alcohol. But mostly, you'll enjoy the economy.

Miserly Magnums

A magnum is two bottles. Once upon a time, this was the giant economy size for wines. One bottle, one label, and one cork (or screw cap) all mean a better price. Also, a magnum takes less room in your refrigerator than two bottles, if it's something you need to chill for a party.

I have seen magnums of lesser French wines, honest vin du pays, selling for $7 to $10, Italian wines for $8 to $12, and unpretentious wines from California for $6 to $10, including some at the lower end from Gallo, in interesting pinch-waist bottles.

Affordable Jugs

There was a time when the least-expensive wines came in glass jugs, generally a gallon. In fact, the term "jug wine" became another way of saying "cheap wine."

Wine in jugs is even cheaper than wine in magnums, but not because it's inferior. The lower price reflects the lower packaging cost. A gallon jug holds five standard bottles (plus a few drops more).

Most jug wines you'll see (assuming you look) will be from California. How much money? About $10. That gets us down to only $2 a bottle.

Bargains in a Bag

Wine in a bag. Bag-in-the-box. This is a triumph of packaging technology. Wine in a rectangular box, inside a polyethylene bag, solves three problems: cost, space efficiency, and storage.

First, these bag-in-the-box setups hold 6.67 standard bottles! And the cardboard and plastic components cost less than a single glass bottle. It costs less per bottle to warehouse and ship, too.

Next, as the folks at UPS will tell you, a box is more efficient than a cylinder. Large, rectangular bottles are hard to make, and they're more fragile than their rounded cousins. (Can you imagine a chicken laying rectangular eggs?) But a plastic bag inside a cardboard box makes for a rectangular package that's both cheap and strong.

These boxes fit easily on a deep shelf in your refrigerator, taking less than four inches of horizontal space.

Imagine, if you will, three of these boxes, side by side. Now imagine the 20 standard wine bottles they replace. Space efficiency? No contest!

The Sommelier Says

If you want to serve everyday wines, but are embarrassed to remove a screw cap, look to imports. Most inexpensive magnums from Italy, Spain, France, and Argentina come with corks. Many from the U.S. come with screw caps. I find the screw caps more reliable when it comes to preventing oxidation, but corks do have their charm.

Tasting Tip

There's some sort of counterculture cachet to jug wines. The kind that actually comes in jugs, that is. These heavy glass containers, with their finger loop near the neck, evoke the life of a starving artist—or of a carefree vagabond.

Finally, the bag-in-the-box can protect your wine from its worst enemy: oxygen. At no time is the wine exposed to air, even when the bag-in-the-box is nearly empty.

Heard It Through the Grapevine

Some people call the package "wine in a box." But of course, you don't pour wine directly into cardboard boxes. The wine's in a polyethylene bag, which is equipped with its own spigot. The bag protects the wine. And the box gives it its shape. The bag-in-the-box concept has been used for fruit juices and other liquid foods, but it's wine that seems to have taken most strongly to this packaging.

You've seen packaged plastic bags, perfectly flattened. That's how the polyethylene bags look before they are filled with wine. When the wine is pumped into them, there's no air to pump out. In other words, there's no ullage (the air space between the wine and the top of the bottle or jug).

And when you fill your glass from the built-in spigot, you'll hear no glug-glug sound, which would have been air entering to replace the liquid that's lost. The bag simply collapses as it's emptied. No air gets in at all.

When you're storing five liters of inexpensive wine or *plonk*, you may be keeping it in your refrigerator for weeks, if not months. Forget about its losing flavor. The simple flavors of this inexpensive wine aren't the sort that time can destroy. What's important is that this wine won't oxidize. A half-filled gallon jug, on the other hand, won't keep very well. (Nor would you like a spare jug taking up so much space in your refrigerator.)

The English call it **plonk**—cheap, undrinkable wine. The word may be a corruption of the French *vin blanc* ("white wine"). Mass-produced inexpensive wines of today, while cheap, are hardly plonk.

The Australians are big on this bag-in-the-box concept. And I must admit, it's a great way to ship these inexpensive, mass-produced wines. But today, you'll see mostly California wines in these packages. Some names I've noted are Franzia, Inglenook, Almaden, Peter Vella, and Summit.

The price? $9 to $14 a box. This works out to between $1.35 and $2.10 a bottle! This is a high-tech manufactured product in a high-tech package. These wines are not horribly bad, though they offer only a few of those things we treasure in better wines. Compared with the cheapest products of 20 years ago, these wines are much better and more consistent in quality. And they're cheaper. Not a bad deal.

And for a Little More

Cheap is a relative term. We've looked here at wines that sell for less than $5 a bottle—sometimes a lot less. But it's remarkable what a few dollars more can buy.

The countries are the same. But the packaging is different. Here's where we leave behind the bag-in-the-box, the jug, and even the magnum. (To be sure, some very fine wines sometimes are bottled in magnums, but not in this chapter.) These will be individual glass bottles of standard 750 ml size. And they'll all have corks.

Instead of less than $5 a bottle, we're moving up to $6 to $7. For these few dollars more, you will get a little more body. You actually will detect some texture and finish. And you will note the beginning of wine complexity. Some of these wines can provide enough of the wine experience to make them genuine everyday partners—even if you own a connoisseur's cellar (see Chapter 31, "From Cellar to Centerpiece").

And for a few dollars more? As we move up to $8 to $10, we get, generally, a little more of everything. I say *generally* because in this price category, as in all wine price ranges, cost is not a sure indicator of quality.

Tasting Tip

I remember once I needed a wine with little or no character. I had wanted to demonstrate the differences between cheap wines and those of moderate price. So I spent four bucks on a bottle of Dao (a wine region of Portugal). We pulled the cork, and you know what? It wasn't bad!

A Little Reverse Snobbery

In the broadest terms; there are two kinds of wine drinkers: those who take most of their pleasure from the prestige of label, scarcity, and price; and those who take it from the wine itself through the experience of sipping.

I think an occasional excursion into everyday wines helps us maintain our appreciation of the basic product of grape fermentation. (And if we happen to find something less expensive that seems a good value, we shouldn't hesitate to enjoy it and to share it.)

Heard It Through the Grapevine

To many people, the dividing line between good wine and the rest is the use of a cork instead of a screw cap. The fact is, corks do not guarantee quality. And screw caps are not an inferior bottle closure. The modern screw cap is an interesting bit of technology. It's actually formed from aluminum in-place right on the threads of the bottle neck. A bit of plastic underneath ensures an airtight seal, at least until it's opened.

I really think wine snobbism works two ways: If we adopt snooty attitudes around others, we make ourselves vulnerable to the dictates of other snobs. And then we will have forsaken our wine pleasures to pursue others of a less substantial kind.

Never, never forget: The appreciation of wine is a personal experience. That experience can range from the mildly pleasant to the ecstatically sublime. But all that enjoyment, in whatever degree, is legitimate.

Where Does It Come From?

Everyday wines are produced everywhere wine is produced. Wine is an important beverage in many cultures, and its importance continues to grow in North America.

Only a very few vineyards can produce a noble wine, no matter how hard others might try. But viticulture is a big and important industry in France, Italy, Spain, Portugal, Germany, Australia, Argentina, and Chile. And let's not forget California, a country in its own right. Add to that New York. The quantities of grapes and of finished wines are enormous, and these find their ways into world markets, sometimes at remarkably low prices.

The Least You Need to Know

➤ The least expensive wines are both better and cheaper than ever before.

➤ The bigger the package, the better the bargain.

➤ All major wine-producing countries are represented in the low-price market.

Attending a Winetasting

You've heard of winetastings, haven't you? Men and women in evening dress, social register all, tasting and talking in discreet tones at some fabulous house in the Hamptons. Right? Not quite.

Winetastings are a growing phenomenon in the U.S. (as is the enjoyment of fine wines). There are no class boundaries. You don't even need to be on someone's invitation list. They're everywhere, and usually, the price is right.

What's a Winetasting?

A winetasting is a gathering of people for the purpose of tasting and comparing wines. This can be serious, or it can be laid-back fun. There are all kinds.

Professional winetastings exist for people in the wine trade. But there are plenty of consumer winetastings meant for your amusement, entertainment, and education. You really ought to try one. (Or several.) I don't know a quicker or more economical way to advance your wine knowledge and experience.

But don't you have to be something of an expert first? Nope! People attend wine-tastings who never had experienced anything beyond a glass of chilled rosé from a gallon jug at someone's summer get-together. And among the kinds of people who attend most winetastings, there's very little snobbery.

If I went to one, what wines would a winetasting taste? And how many? The answer lies at the furthest reaches of your host's imagination. But here are some samples:

➤ A tasting of Chardonnays

➤ A tasting of Bordeaux

➤ A tasting of different wines from the same vintage

➤ A tasting of wines selected within a specified price range

Or how about this idea? A certain number of red (or white) wines from different regions or countries to explore geographic differences. Or maybe a focus on wines from some emerging wine country or region. Or maybe the theme merely is variety, with wines of all colors, prices, and origins.

Now let's look at a few types of winetastings.

Tasting Tip

A little economics: Let's say you want to sample 12 wines, Premier Cru White Burgundies. At $40 a bottle, that's about $500, if you did it alone. But let's say you're one of 12 people bringing just one bottle to a winetasting. Those 12 bottles are enough for all of you, with everyone getting about two ounces, which is enough to do the job.

Stand-Up Tastings

Expect a table. Or maybe several tables. There's no need to worry about seating. There isn't any—not at the tables, anyway. So there'll be no name cards, none of that boy-girl-boy-girl business. Just a table, or several, with lots (you hope) of bottles of wine.

The tablecloth will be white, of course, the better to assess the color of your wines. It might be linen. Or it might be paper. It depends on who's hosting and how much you paid (if you had to pay at all).

Of course, there will be glasses! Expect at least two per person. Real wineglasses, you hope, with lots of room for your nose. And you'll see something else, most likely. Spittoons. Not the sort found in old-time bar-bershops. Perhaps only a few little buckets at table height. More on spitting later. (You can't wait, I'll bet!)

You can expect good lighting, preferably bright incandescent. Flourescents, even the "daylight" sort, cannot give you a reliable color reading.

There may be chairs or sofas in the room. But around the wine tables, just free floor space. This is the setup for the standup winetasting.

Now's your chance to learn about a lot of wines—at your own pace. You'll visit each bottle, pour an 1$\frac{1}{2}$ or 2 ounces into your wineglass. And you'll taste at your own leisure. But you need not swallow. In fact, if you arrived by car, you shouldn't swallow. That's the reason for the spittoons. But more on that later.

Sit-Down Tastings

You've been invited to (or invited yourself to) a sit-down winetasting. Yes, it's a bit more formal, a bit more structured, but there's no need for panic.

The seating may be fixed by your host, or it may be seat-yourself. Either way, you will be seated.

In front of you, there will be several clean glasses, perhaps three or four. And somewhere beside you, something in which to discard the contents of your glass or mouth.

Instead of your going to the wines, the wines come to you—three or more at a time. These are called *flights*. The wines in each flight will have something in common. And they will have features that distinguish them. It's easier to understand, perhaps, if I give you a few examples:

Let's say you are attending a sit-down Bordeaux tasting:

➤ **First flight**   Three from the Cru Bourgeous Petit Château.

➤ **Second flight**   Third and fourth growths, Cru Classé from the Médoc.

➤ **Third flight**   Second growth Cru Classé from the Médoc.

➤ **Fourth flight**   First growth Cru Classé from the Médoc.

Pretty neat, huh? And it's very scientific. You get to compare wines within a quality tier, and you get to compare wines of differing qualities. Are the differences greater within a tier? Or from tier-to-tier? These are important questions. And I know no other way to answer them apart from a full-blown winetasting (short of springing for 12 or 16 bottles of Bordeaux).

How about another example? Let's say your host has decided to compare Chardonnays from California, France, and Australia. This time, we'll use six glasses per person:

➤ **First flight**   Two wines from each country, under $8 each.

➤ **Second flight**   Same, but priced at about $15.

➤ **Third flight**   Same, but $25 to $35. For instance, you might compare a Premier Cru Meursault with a Premier Cru Chassagne Montrachet, along with the two wines each from California and Australia.

In engineering testing labs, this is called balanced-block experimental design. In a winetasting room, you can call it fun as you engage in what amounts to a real scientific investigation.

Heard It Through the Grapevine

Winetastings can be vertical or horizontal. Please! No jokes about "being on the floor!" A *vertical* tasting is one that features several vintages of the same wine (for example, Château Palmer in each vintage from 1979 to 1991). A *horizontal* tasting features wines of a single vintage from several different properties, usually of a similar type, such as 1993 California Chardonnay.

Brown Bag

Now we really get scientific—with blind tasting. That is, you will sample wines from bottles that have their labels hidden. Better still, from unmarked decanters. Regardless of one's experience and professed impartiality, we all know that seeing a label can influence judgment.

It's our human nature. All our lives, we've learned to discern and remember patterns, and to use them to develop expectations. That protects us when we want to cross a busy street. But prior knowledge inevitably will color our taste perceptions of wine.

Let's say you know the wine you are going to taste is very expensive or very highly regarded. Or maybe it's an old friend, a wine you have served yourself many times. Do you really believe you could be impartial?

The Sommelier Says

The worst possible thing to happen at a blind tasting is for the host to lose track of which wine went into which decanters. I've known this to happen at more than one private tasting.

You'll probably know it's a blind tasting before you go. But if not, you'll know when you see your host has covered all the labels. I use those slender paper bags from the wine or liquor stores. Aluminum foil works well, too, but it reveals the bottle's shape, and you want to eliminate all clues. Decanters are best. Apart from color, aroma, bouquet, and taste, no clues are allowed.

After a time, your interest in winetasting may develop to a point where you'll want to discover more than which wines appeal to you. You can make the tastings more interesting and concentrate on fine-tuning your abilities through blind tastings. This learning process proceeds on its own. No need for a teacher or a syllabus.

Heard It Through the Grapevine

You can tune up your palette with these blind tasting tests:

➤ A triangulation test is easy. All you need are two wines and three glasses, tagged with some sort of identifier. Have someone pour one of the wines into two glasses and the other wine into a single glass, recording which went where. Your task is to pick the two glasses filled from the same bottle. Piece of cake, right? It's harder than it sounds, even for experienced tasters.

➤ Another test is working with pairs. Have your friend pour two wines with some dissimilarity into four glasses. You have to match pairs.

In time, you'll find yourself guessing a wine's origin, vintage, region, winemaking style, and even brand. Winetasting is like listening to music. Can you tell Beethoven from Bebop? How about Brahms from Bartok? Maybe even Bach from Buxtehude? You may not realize it at first, but your unconscious mind is filing and processing information: composer, period, style, and so on. You'll get there!

Blind winetastings are a great way for you to test your developing expertise and avoid developing prejudices or a smug sense of certainty. A blind winetasting may be a chance for you to show off, but as happens more often than not, it can also be a humbling experience. The blind test is the Test of Truth.

The important thing is not to make tasting a chore. Think of the test as a game of knowledge and sensory skill. But don't take tasting so seriously that you wind up ruining your enjoyment.

To Eat or Not to Eat

Standup or sit-down, there's going to be food. Your host will have been very careful in its selection. And if you're serious about getting the most out of your winetasting experience, you'll be careful about your eating, too.

Tasting Tip

In the beginning, testing is easier if you taste wines that are substantially different. As your palate develops, choose wines that are increasingly similar.

Maybe the invitation or advertisement reads "Wine and Cheese." That's reasonable. Everybody knows wine and cheese go together. But in this instance, your host will have selected rather bland, neutral cheeses. Cheese with big flavors or aromas can interfere seriously with your tasting. You won't find any blue-veined Roquefort or runny Camembert. (Or you shouldn't.)

Heard It Through the Grapevine

The best way to clean your mouth between tastings? Water. I prefer a neutral or mineral water because it cleans the palate without adding any taste. Some city water is over-treated with chemicals, and that can affect your ability to taste. Likewise, some of the alkaline hard water common in parts of the Midwest and Southwest will interfere with your sense of taste.

Also, your host will make sure there aren't any distinct cooking odors from food being prepared in the kitchen next door. Yes, food and wine do go together, but not at a winetasting! The ideal time to serve food is after the tasting is complete. For eating during the tasting, I recommend nothing fancier than some plain bread or unsalted crackers. But I recommend not eating at all. A glass of plain water is best.

Theme Tastings

Every winetasting will have a theme, even if it's "Let's use up all this leftover wine from that wedding I catered!" Most themes, of course, are a lot more structured.

The theme could be the wines of the Southern Hemisphere. Or Gewürztraminers from around the world. Or vintage comparisons. Or maybe different treatments of the Merlot grape. Themes add fun and intrigue. They also help guide us in our continuing wine education.

Etiquette Tips

As I've tried to point out here, you don't have to know much about wines to attend a winetasting. These are an effective and economical way to expand on your wine education, no matter how far you have come. But it does help to know just a few points of winetasting etiquette.

It might seem obvious, but I feel I must mention it: Don't be a hog. Your host probably has allocated a bottle of each wine for each 10 to 15 people. If you go through the line three times at a standup winetasting, there's a chance someone else will miss out altogether.

You don't need a large amount of wine to assess its properties. Two ounces would be plenty. It's inconsiderate to pour too much. And it's unnecessary.

To Spit or Not to Spit

Okay. I've put this one off as long as I could. But we need to talk. Spitting is okay. At least, it's okay at a winetasting.

Outside the winetasting room, spitting would be bad manners. Inside, its perfectly okay. Taking too much alcohol to make good tasting evaluations is not okay. Taking too much alcohol if you intend to drive is worse than not okay.

Dress for Tasting Success

There's no special uniform for winetasting. As with any social occasion, there will be appropriate dress.

Sometimes the invitation or announcement will stipulate dress. If not, use common sense. If it's a hotel meeting room at 8 P.M., wear business attire. If it's in the basement of the fire hall on Saturday afternoon, jeans and a tee-shirt might be fine.

> **Tasting Tip**
>
> At the very least, your host will have provided some sort of container into which you can dump the remaining contents of your glass. Most will provide buckets, generally tabletop height, for spitting the contents of your mouth. If not, it's okay to spit into your glass and to dump from that.

Who Gives Winetastings?

Winetastings no longer are the province of the rich and the famous. Many people, old and young, well off and not so, attend winetastings. If no one's invited you to one yet, maybe it's time for you to look around. Believe me, you won't have to look far. Check your local newspaper for announcements, or call the paper's food editor (or wine editor, if it has one) for information.

Wineries Woo You

Visit a winery! Tastings there generally are free. And if you find something you like (that's what they hope), you can buy it right there. (In some states, you can save some money, too.)

The Sommelier Says

Of course, when you do your winetasting at a winery, everything you sample will come from that winery. You won't have the variety of experience that many other tastings afford. But you will have an opportunity to sample the winery's line of goods. And to learn a bit about that winery's vinification process.

Plan your next summer vacation, home or abroad, around winery visits. Imagine a winetasting a day! Two, maybe! And (mostly) free, too!

Restaurants Reach Out

There's money in winetastings. For the cost of an average bottle of wine and a meal, a restaurant can hold a tasting (or a monthly tasting night), charge you $50 or a $100, and make a profit. And maybe get a new customer, too. And if you get to taste 8 or 10 wines and eat a meal, too, that's not a bad deal!

How good are these? It depends a lot on that restaurant's own wine knowledge. This is something you can ascertain when you attend its tastings. It's good to know in advance who's good with wine and who isn't.

Everyone Benefits

If there's profit in winetastings for restaurants, there's profit for charities, too. For a fee, service clubs, nonprofit groups, and special fundraisers can engage a professional wine expert who will set up and run a winetasting to help raise money.

What about some organizations you are involved with? Does that give you any ideas?

Don't Forget Your Friends

You want to taste wine? All you need are two things: wine and people. How many friends and business colleagues do you have? How many would like to learn more about wine? Maybe you'd like to host a winetasting in your own home? (See the section on having your own winetasting in Chapter 31, "From Cellar to Centerpiece.")

Tasting Notes

What did you eat for lunch the Thursday before last? What was the headline at the top of last Saturday's newspaper? Let me ask you one more question: Do you really think you'll be able to recall all your winetasting experiences?

It's never too early to begin keeping tasting notes. It's never too late, either. Your impressions will never be keener than when they are fresh. While you wouldn't take out a notebook at a formal banquet or in fancy restaurants, it wouldn't make much sense to attend a winetasting without something to record your impressions.

Join a Wine Club!

Most large cities and many smaller ones have wine clubs. Most of these, actually, are organized specifically to hold winetastings. There's no profit motive here, so these provide terrific value to their members (and lucky guests).

Ask about local wine clubs at your wine dealer. If yours is the right kind of shop (see Chapter 26, "Swimming in the Wine Market"), the local club might buy its wines from that very store.

Or check at your local library. The reference desk can help you track down most local organizations. (Maybe they even meet at your library.)

The Least You Need to Know

➤ You don't need to know a lot about wine to attend a winetasting.

➤ Winetastings are a sure and economical way to develop your palate and your wine knowledge.

➤ Blind tastings are tough, but they keep you honest.

➤ Opportunities for attending winetastings are numerous.

Part 5
Wine à la Maison

In this part, we bring it all home—as you bring wine into your own home. This is where we look more closely at storing your collection, whether it's only a few bottles or a valuable connoisseur's cellar. You'll become comfortable with serving wine to your guests and even consider holding your own winetastings.

Then we'll look seriously at matching wines with foods, with a few basics and a few not-so-basics that will allow you to break the rules now and then—successfully. After wines with foods, we'll explore wine in foods, with enough recipes to earn you a reputation for gustatory savvy.

Finally, we'll examine whether all this attention to wine is good for you. Recent medical research suggests there may be quite a bit of truth to that expression "To your health!" We'll see that we can learn a few things from the French and Italians about longevity and robust health.

Chapter 31

From Cellar to Centerpiece

In This Chapter

➤ Storing your own wine

➤ Stocking your wine cellar

➤ Entertaining with wine

➤ Keeping records

It started simply the day you bought two bottles, drank one, and kept the second for another day. And then the day came when you noticed you had accumulated five bottles. Then 10. Then …

Is it time to give up this new wine hobby, the one that threatens perpetual clutter? Not at all! You deserve to keep wine at home, as much as you like. Your wine deserves good treatment. And your hobby deserves good records. That's what this chapter is all about.

Storing Your Wine at Home

You might want to look back at Chapter 3, "Sensory Sipping and Sensible Storage." That's where we discussed choosing the perfect wine rack or climate-controlled home storage unit. Numerous models are available, and new models seem to come out every week.

Your taste in decor may be traditional, contemporary, or eclectic. Your budget may be tight or limitless. No problem. With a little looking, you're sure to find a storage unit to suit your needs and taste. (And if you're handy with tools, you might be able to combine two hobbies and build your own.)

Forget the Real Estate section of your paper. You won't find too many castles for sale, or even for rent. But you can dream, huh? Imagine: Great hillside location; spacious; airy; with deep, dark cellar for storing wine. Okay. Dream over!

Lacking a natural storage cellar, most of us need to be resourceful or clever. Let's review and expand a bit on some of the things we discussed in Chapter 3.

Keep It Dark

Your wine is maturing. It's not hibernating. Those bottles don't need to be kept in total darkness, but they do need a place away from direct sunlight.

Sunlight is rich in ultraviolet light. That's the part of the light spectrum that does the damage, by changing molecules from one form into another and by hastening certain destructive processes, like oxidation. A moderate amount of artificial light won't harm your wine. Neither will indirect daylight, if not too strong. But when in doubt, darker is better.

The Sommelier Says

When it comes to wine storage, vibration is bad news. Excess vibration can cause uneven maturation. Keep your wine rack away from nearby foot traffic. A rack mounted to the back of a closet door is a bad idea.

Keep It Cool

Prolonged storage in very warm or hot conditions will damage your wine—seriously damage it. Extreme heat causes wine to mature precociously. It goes from adolescence to senility without even passing through a golden middle age.

The best temperature? I recommend 55 degrees Fahrenheit. But anything between 50 and 60 degrees Fahrenheit is excellent. (For you metric folks, that's between 10 and 15.6 degrees Celsius.)

Keep It Humid

Wines like humidity even if you don't. Too dry, and your corks may lose their grip. That would be a disaster for those bottles of vintage Bordeaux you had laid up for your grandchildren.

Try to keep your wine cellar between 75 and 90 percent relative humidity. Humidity above 95 percent encourages mold.

If the air is dry, your wine can seep into and through a too-dry cork. This is a very slow process, but so is maturation of some fine wines. The resulting condition is called *ullage*, a word we also use to denote the empty space between the wine and the cork.

When you lose wine through ullage, it's replaced by air. And air contains oxygen, which is poison to wines. Oxidation is the last thing you want for your valuable collection.

You should buy a *hygrometer*, an inexpensive instrument used to measure *relative humidity*. You can find several specially designed for wine storage areas.

Some hygrometers are single units. Others are mounted with a thermometer (a great idea). You can find these quality-control instruments in wine accessories catalogs and at some better retailers.

> **Vino Vocab**
>
> A **hygrometer** measures **relative humidity**. The amount of moisture air can hold increases with temperature. But drying out depends only on moisture *relative* to the maximum air can hold. That's why wine cellars need hygrometers.

How Important Is Temperature?

The ideal of a constant 55-degree Fahrenheit temperature is a good goal when you select your storage space. But remember, we live in a less-than-ideal world. Unless you have a very deep basement, it's unlikely you have such a spot in your house.

Don't despair. Uniformity of temperature is more important than absolute temperature. Avoid any area with sudden temperature fluctuations over a short period of time. Slow, gradual changes, free of extremes, offer no threat. Let's say you have a typical basement (not all of us do, of course), and its temperature varies from about 50 degrees in winter to about 70 degrees in summer. No problem. If you can keep it steady and less than 70 degrees, don't worry at all.

Starting Your Own Wine Cellar

The idea either excites you or terrifies you: keeping your own wine cellar, just like Dom Pérignon. Let's face it: Some people are not comfortable with that kind of responsibility—providing a controlled environment over the course of years. Decades, maybe. How you feel about this aspect of wine collecting is a big consideration when it comes to choosing how, where... or how many.

> **Tasting Tip**
>
> Do you want to make a decorating statement with your wine rack? You can, of course. There are some beautiful wine racks out there, even of very modest size. But think: The best place for your wine might be in a closet or in the corner of your basement. It's better to purchase wine for its drinking potential than for its decorating promise.

How Many Bottles Should I Keep?

Perhaps your needs are modest: a ready bottle for casual drinking or an emergency stash for unexpected visitors. You'll be happiest with a small rack (many hold 10 to 15 bottles) or even with the case in which your wine arrived.

If you're starting to feel the collector's urge, especially if you're thinking of buying long-aging wines as an investment, just remember you do need to put some effort into upkeep. A bit of honest introspection should give you the answer to how much wine you ultimately will need to store.

What's in a Basic Cellar?

A basic cellar should include a diverse collection for everyday drinking, as well as wine for special events. For your everyday collection, select the styles you prefer in your usual price range for everyday wines. Then supplement this group with a few bottles of better-quality wines for when the occasion demands something extra. Non-vintage Champagnes and good-quality sparkling wines also fall into the special-occasion category.

Then for those momentous occasions, keep a bottle or two of tête de cuvée (best of the lot) Champagne on hand. For occasions when bubbly may not be appropriate, some excellent choices are a Premier or Grand Cru Burgundy, or a Cru Classé Bordeaux from vintages that are ready to drink.

The Thousand-Dollar Cellar

You can create a serious collection from a thousand-dollar investment. This cellar includes the basic selections just mentioned, with a few additions. Here's where you add to the ready-to-drink Premier and Grand Crus Burgundies and Cru Classés Bordeaux a few of their less-mature cousins. These should be a few years away from drinking—not decades.

Include some white Bordeaux, a selection of German wines, and Burgundies—red and white. And do a little shopping from the U.S., with some California Cabernet, Chardonnay, and Zinfandel.

And for Two-and-a-Half Grand?

Now we're getting into some long-term commitment on your part. You will graft this cellar onto the $1,000 cellar. You will add a case of Cru Classé Bordeaux, some red and white Burgundies, and some of the California reds that need five to 10 years of aging.

Heard It Through the Grapevine

Isn't $2,500 too much to spend for wine? If you haven't taken the time to develop your palate and to learn about and experience the world's better wines, any investment might be excessive. But once you have decided an appreciation of wine in all its nuances is a part of your life, it's not so much.

A collection of 200 CDs isn't extraordinary. Neither is owning eight place settings of fine china. Yes, you actually consume your wine collection. But you were going to drink wine anyway, collection or not. Right? So you simply replace what you drink, and enjoy the knowledge that your maturing vintages are a living asset.

Now include several bottles of mature, ready-to-drink vintage Port; mature, ready-to-drink Sauternes; and a few bottles of German late-harvest wines. This collection becomes the core of the connoisseur's cellar.

The Connoisseur's Cellar

The connoisseur's cellar is what you wish every restaurant or hotel maintained. (Many of them wish they could, too.) This collection includes a good selection of wines for everyday drinking, while it houses noble and rare wines of the utmost breed and finesse. Lay down your Bordeaux, Burgundies, California agers, and vintage ports for joyous future consumption.

The connoisseur's cellar also should include some esoteric wines, like vintage Madeiras, high-quality Sherries, and perhaps a curiosity or two. Try Hungarian Tokay. Follow your fancy!

Should You Insure Your Wine?

Home insurance policies generally insure the furnishings and other contents of your house for up

Tasting Tip

If you enjoy the world's more distinguished sweet wines, by all means, bring in several of the sweet Sauternes and the German Beerenauslese and Trockenbeerenauslese. If yours is a connoisseur's cellar, these may belong there. This is your cellar, remember, which must reflect your taste and preferences.

to half the value of the policy. Policies for renters also cover furnishings and such things as a television or two, audio equipment, camera gear, and a personal computer system. However, insurance underwriters don't expect wine cellars.

Very few regular homeowners' policies cover wine in case of fire, theft, breakage, or other damage. (Actually, some policies will cover up to a few thousand dollars.) To be certain your collection is covered, you need to purchase a "rider" on your home- or rental-insurance policy. I recommend the all-risk rider. It won't cost much more. Then you're covered even if your home air-conditioning or your wine refrigeration unit fails and your wine cooks. Figure the cost of wine insurance to be about 40 to 50 cents per $100, per year. For instance, if your wine inventory is worth $75,000, your annual premium might be about $350.

Heard It Through the Grapevine

You can appraise your own wine collection. It's tedious, but not hard. For your younger wines, check current catalog prices. For your older wines, you need to research recent auction sales.

If your appraisal is for insurance purposes, however, you'd better get a professional appraisal. That way, you avoid contention with the insurer in case of loss. I recommend Roger Livdahl (323-460-6999), a well-respected certified appraiser, or William Edgerton (203-655-0566), founder of the *Wine Price File*, a book listing 70,000 recent sale prices of thousands of fine and rare wines.

Two major insurers with experience in wine coverage are the Chubb Group of Insurance Companies and Sedgewick James.

One thing you need to make clear on your policy is that your wine will be insured for its replacement cost, not for what you paid for it. Consider that vintage bottle you purchased for $50 twenty years ago. Today it's worth $500. How much will you recover if you lose it? You need to know.

Another thing you'll need to do is keep good records—of your purchases and of current prices. Insurance claim adjusters are paid to save their companies money. They're fair but tough.

Entertaining with Wine

Every wine enthusiast looks forward to social opportunities to serve wine. Wine lovers like to share their appreciation of fine wines. I feel it enhances the wine experience to know that others are sharing in the colors, aromas, mouthfeel, taste, and aftertaste. The following few guidelines can help you plan events with confidence—verve, even, not apprehension.

Which Wines Should You Serve?

Different occasions and different folks in different numbers suggest different selections of wines. The people and the occasion will determine the overall atmosphere much more than the wines you select. For example, you can't create an upscale impression serving vintage Bordeaux or Burgundy to a disco crowd. (Besides, they'll beg for Gatorade to replace all that disco sweat.) And despite its association with gaiety and festivity, Champagne is not always the right choice. For a less-formal party, I suggest understatement.

At a formal dinner party, it's traditional to serve a wine with each course. (Some more elegant dinners serve two wines with each course.) If you own different glasses for different wines, make sure to wash them carefully (no trace of detergent!) and bring them out. If not, you don't need to go buy them. The basic styles are fine (see the section on wineglass choices in Chapter 2, "Savvy Serving").

The rules for choosing your sequence of wines are

➤ Light wine before heavy wine

➤ White wine before red wine

➤ Dry wine before sweet wine

➤ Simple wine before complex wine

Tasting Tip

For a party where food is incidental (traditional snack foods: a plate of crudités here, a Chinese entrée there), it's best to stick with wines that may be drunk easily without culinary accompaniment. I recommend an inexpensive California Chardonnay. This wine is fruity, refreshing, and very popular. For a red wine, choose a Beaujolais. If it's holiday season, Beaujolais Nouveau is perfect.

Of course, there are always conditions where one rule says one thing and another something else. For instance, if you are serving a light red wine and a rich, full-bodied white, you need to be colorblind and use the "light before heavy" rule. When in doubt, follow your instincts. Once you know your wines, these generally will be sound.

As your guests arrive, you'll want to offer them an apéritif. A white wine, sparkling wine, or Champagne—usually inexpensive to moderately priced—is the ideal ice-breaker. If the party is especially elegant, add a few extra dollars to your bottle. Just don't get carried away. The apéritif is the opening act, not the headliner.

Now your guests are sitting at the table. This is your chance to show how skillfully you marry wine with cuisine. But don't worry about this! Choosing wines is not an esoteric practice like yogi breathing. (For a full discussion on matching wine with food, see Chapter 32, "The Match Game.")

Heard It Through the Grapevine

Each guest should have a fresh glass for each wine. This enables them to savor fully the flavors of each and to drink at their own pace. The glasses don't need to be of different or "correct" styles. An ample supply of the basic wine glass will do the job nicely.

On the subject of glasses, don't forget the water! We drink wine because it's a noble sensory experience, not because it contains water. Healthy dining requires ample libation. Make sure there is plenty of chilled water on hand and that your guests can refill their water glasses easily.

How Much Wine Do You Need?

There are no hard-and-fast rules regarding quantity. The amount of wine you serve depends on the type of party, the preferences of your guests, the number of wines served, the pace of service, and the number of hours you expect the party to last. Here are two suggestions that might make your decisions easier:

1. For an informal party, figure two-thirds of a bottle of wine per guest, which I find is an average by party's end.

2. For a formal dinner party, the simplest rule is a full bottle of wine per guest. If you think this amount will leave your guests weaving their way home, don't worry. You are gearing your service to a leisurely pace, integrating wine consumption with several courses of food.

Popping the Cork

For too long, Champagne (or any sparkling wine) has been surrounded by silly ritual and needless pomp. The occasion may be special, but opening the bottle should be no more ceremonious than opening any other type of wine. Be cautious, however. The contents are under tremendous pressure. Forget the rituals and misconceptions, and keep it safe.

Treat an unopened Champagne bottle with the same respect as a loaded gun. Never point the bottle in anyone's direction, including your own. Hold the bottle at a 45-degree angle away from everyone. Because a sudden temperature change could cause a bottle to fracture, take special care when handling iced or overchilled Champagne. (I know. Some people like it that way.) Use these simple guidelines:

The Sommelier Says

Glass is a very strong material. Without glass bottles, Champagne would never have survived its discovery. But glass with scratches is very vulnerable to fracture. (Engineers tell us scratches concentrate stresses.) Always handle your Champagne purchases with great care.

➤ Always inspect a Champagne bottle for deep scratches or nicks. A badly scratched bottle has the potential to explode.

➤ Never chill Champagne below 45 degrees. Colder temperatures increase the risk of a bursting bottle if it has deep scratches.

➤ When removing the wire cage around the cork, always place your palm over the cork to prevent its shooting out of the bottle.

➤ Always point the neck of the bottle away from yourself and others. A flying Champagne cork works only in the movies. In real life, you run the risk of hurting someone.

➤ Remove the cork with a gentle twisting motion with your palm over the cork. When the edge of the cork clears the neck, you will hear a subtle "poof" and maybe see a wisp of "smoke." Loud pops and gushing foam are vulgar—and an awful waste of good wine.

➤ If the cork is difficult, push gently on alternate sides with your thumbs. When the cork begins to move, cover it immediately with your palm.

Host Your Own Winetasting

You may have the impression that winetastings are undertaken only by those who are deemed (or who deem themselves) wine experts. This is nonsense. You're learning more about wine each day, and your collection is growing. There's no reason why you shouldn't consider a winetasting party of your own. Your guests will never forget the experience. (See Chapter 30, "Attending a Winetasting.")

Vino Vocab

There are no hard and fast rules for describing a wine. Ultimately, your own **perception** is what counts; so the terminology you use should be your own, not that of some expert.

Keeping Notes

Whether you're a novice *oenophile* (wine lover) or you can boast of notches on your taste buds, recalling from memory the details and nuances of a particular wine can be challenging. It's impossible, actually.

Many wine enthusiasts keep notes, not only from organized tastings, but from social occasions that feature wines worth noting. (Do not, however, sit at a formal dinner party with a notepad—not if you want to be invited back.) You can write your notes in detail or abbreviate them with terse symbols. Tasting notes are an invaluable aid, both to help you remember your perception of a wine and as a record of your winetasting education.

You should describe your wine experiences in your own words, but there are certain things you should not neglect:

➤ **Olfactory and taste perceptions**   Aroma, bouquet, fruitiness, and so on

➤ **Structure**   Balance of alcohol/sweetness/tannins/acidity

➤ **Texture**   The feel of the wine in your mouth

You'll also want to chronicle the development of your tasting experience from the first impression to the lingering aftertaste. (See Chapter 3, "Sensory Sipping and Sensible Storage.")

Your Wine Journal

There is no single or best way to organize your tasting notes. Some people love index cards. Others prefer blank notebooks that they can label and file. Still others prefer special wine journals created for this purpose. If you're a fan of electronic organizing, you can find software (check wine-accessory catalogs), or create your own using a database package.

If you have a large, established cellar or even if you are a beginning collector, a cellar log is a useful tool. This log enables you to chart the development of your wines from their date of purchase (don't forget price) through the first sampling (with a note of when to sample next). Even record a lingering, distant impression or two long after you have consumed the very last. As with your wine journal, you can set up your own cellar log or purchase a formatted journal or software.

Scoring Systems

Once you become really serious about wines (it happens), you will want to develop a scoring system for your tastings. This is a good way to catalog particular favorites. Professionals and advanced wine buffs use several systems, but these tend to be unnecessarily complicated. My advice: Keep it simple.

You can use the traditional star system, giving a wine five stars (or three, and so on). You can use a letter system (A, B, C, D, F), though that may seem too much like a report card. Choose your own symbols: smiley/frowny faces, little bottles, say. Just don't get too cutesy. A page covered with pictures of grapevines or corkscrews over time may discourage you from reviewing your own ratings.

Heard It Through the Grapevine

Never downplay the importance of your personal preferences when you rate your wine. After all, wine evaluation is a personal matter. There are no right or wrong ways to respond. Our impressions boil down to two things: what we perceive and what we like.

We may easily perceive a wine's high acidity or residual sugar, or its light or heavy body. But these are separate from what we like. One doesn't matter without the other.

Comparing your own evaluations with those of others is the best way to learn about wine and also about how your perceptions and preferences differ. Understanding why another taster's preference is different from yours is more important in terms of learning about wine than knowing which wine is the better one. The best wine for you is the one you prefer. Knowing why you prefer one wine over another is the essential point.

As you develop more experience, your preferences will change. This is common when you share your tasting experience with someone whose palate and expertise are more sophisticated than yours. Your "wine mentor" can help you to isolate subtle sensations you may have missed. Or your mentor may help you articulate those nuances that you know but can't pin down. A word of caution: Not every experienced wine-taster is a good wine teacher. Above all, never feel that you must adjust your preferences because one wine buff prefers a wine you don't.

The Least You Need to Know

➤ Keep your wine storage area dark, cool, humid, and away from rapid temperature change and vibration.

➤ Holding your own winetastings is one way to learn more about wine.

➤ A wine journal is a good way to remember what wines you tasted and what you thought of them.

Chapter 32

The Match Game

Let's start with a premise: Certain wines and foods go very well together, while certain wines and foods clash. Okay?

I'll bet you've already had some success matching wine with food. Maybe you've said to yourself, "I'm having filet of flounder, so I'll have a light white wine to go with it." Or perhaps something spontaneous, like, "Serving this Beaujolais at brunch with eggs Florentine was a brilliant idea! Who would ever have thought it would work?"

On the other hand, you've probably experienced a little failure, too. Perhaps you chose a Salade Nicoise with vinaigrette, only to have a friend arrive with a bottle of full-bodied red wine. Or maybe you've absent-mindedly munched smoked almonds as you've sipped a light, young wine. What harm could they possibly do? Read on ....

Wine and Food Basics

Some wines and foods simply are not compatible. For example, a very dry wine with a sweet dessert. Try that, and you can chalk up another faux pas learning experience.

Tasting Tip

All wine lovers agree that wine is the natural accompaniment to a meal. A meal without wine is a meal without salt and pepper. But would you put salt on a wedge of Camembert or pepper on chocolate ice cream? Matching wine with food is like adding condiments to a dish. Your aim is to bring out the product's full potential, not to alter or mask its distinction.

Matching a wine with the wrong food (or vice versa) can make both taste bad. Bone-dry wine and the pastry torte? As we say in New York: Fuhgeddaboudit! The wine destroys the dessert's essential sweetness. Sometimes food can neutralize your wine's flavor. Let's say you expect subtle complexities, a symphony of finesse. You intend to show off your noble wine at its peak. But with the wrong food, what did you taste? A very, very expensive jug wine!

Perfect wine and food matching is rare. Success requires knowledge of food and a lot of good luck. Even the greatest chefs don't make a dish exactly the same on each occasion. (Maybe that's what makes them great chefs.) Just a smidgen extra of this or a dollop of that is enough to mar—or if luck is smiling, enhance—the intended combination. Wine can be quirky too, as you've gathered, already. It may not be quite as full or as fruity as you had thought, or those tannins may not have settled.

A Few General Rules

To understand the rules of this game firsthand, experience is definitely required. You may study art history diligently, but your experience of reading about van Gogh's brushstrokes will differ greatly from that of seeing the master's *Sunflowers* up close. Despite all the great things you've read, you may or may not like the painting, depending on (guess what?) your personal preferences. Just as in art, it's your taste preference and, ultimately, your own judgment that counts in wine matching.

The trick is to trigger your wine an food memory and play a matching game. Whenever you taste a wine, think of what flavors go with it to build in your taste memory. This may seem strange at first. I mean, what type of food goes with a wine that evokes tar? But the idea's not really that strange when you think of the terms we use to describe wines—fruity, herbaceous, creamy, tart.

Immediately, certain foods come to mind that have these same qualities. These similarities do not mean that wine and food need to have the same traits! You can work two rather different ways: You can match wine with foods that have similar characteristics; or you can decide that opposites attract. (It's similar to decorating color schemes, isn't it?)

Use these three basic categories as your guide:

1. **Components**   Sugar, acid, bitterness, sourness, and so on.
2. **Flavors**   Peachy, berry-like, herbal, buttery, minty, vanilla, and so on.
3. **Texture**   Medium-bodied, thin, velvety, viscous, and so on.

Heard It Through the Grapevine

To hone your wine-matching skills, you need to develop a taste memory for wine. You already have a taste memory for food. Think of a pear ... Now a banana ... Rib roast ... Your favorite flavor of ice cream ... Good. Chances are you can recall coffee, cola, or orange juice in a flash. Good.

Now try this test with wine: Imagine Beaujolais ... Cabernet Sauvignon ... Chardonnay ... Any other wine ... What? Not so good? Here's a tip: Visualizing the wine first may help. Here's another: Associate wine with some particular occasion, particularly one where it went well with the food. Better, huh?

The first category, Components, is the trickiest. These elements directly affect our taste buds. The components of both food and wine stir the sensory buds in these areas:

Tasting Tip

Your taste buds are specialists that do their things on different parts of your tongue. Sweetness is perceived at the tip of the tongue, sourness along the sides, saltiness in the middle, and bitterness at the back of the tongue.

➤ **Sweetness**   This one is easy. Sweetness is residual sugar in wine, natural or added sugar in food.

➤ **Saltiness**   Some foods are naturally salty (briny oysters or mussels), but most have some added salt. Saltiness rarely is associated with wine. (However, Manzanilla Sherry is said to have the tang of the salty air.)

➤ **Sourness**   Sourness in food is related to high levels of acidity, which can be natural (lemons, limes) or added (salad dressings). In wine, sourness is directly related to acidity.

➤ **Bitterness**   Bitterness is a component you want to taste only sparingly in food or wine. Strong coffee and tea are pleasantly bitter. In wine, a bitter taste or finish can mean a winemaking flaw, such as too much tannin. But the right amount of tannins can afford an interesting bitterness—as with fine espresso.

Keep in mind a few essentials when you are matching, either by contrast or similarity:

➤ Acidic foods are a good combination with acidic wines.

➤ Acidic wines go well with salty foods.

➤ Acidic foods can overpower low-acid wines.

➤ Salty food and high-alcohol wine taste bitter in combination.

➤ Salty food and sweet wine are a good match.

➤ Sweet wine and sweet food go well together. (The preferable way is a sweeter wine and a less sweet dessert.)

➤ Bitter food with bitter wine is just plain bitter.

Heard It Through the Grapevine

You need to remain alert to the possible similarities and contrasts in wines and foods. After a while you'll develop an instinct for what wines go with what foods. Generally, your decision will be based on a flavor, texture, or some other attribute of the food. Singling out some dominant element is an important aspect of choosing wines for a dish.

After you have your components in mind (and palate), pay attention to similarities and contrasts. Ultimately, the judgment is yours, but you might appreciate a few suggestions:

➤ When thinking of flavor similarity, use your taste memory to evoke each specific flavor. For example, Gewürztraminer is usually characterized as a spicy wine, but not in the hot-spicy way. Spicy foods, however, can be anything from curries to cardamom. When it comes to flavors, we can't generalize.

➤ Food and wine that trigger similar flavor sensations probably will go well together—like almonds and Fino Sherry.

➤ Some foods have no real similarities. After all, no wine tastes like fish, garlic, or pork. Adding condiments, fruits, cream sauce, or tomato sauce to such foods, however, may give you matching cues.

White or Red—Any Rules?

As with all conventions, the "white with fish, red with meat" rule originated from the best intent. Meat is heavier than fish, after all, so a meat dish needs a robust wine that can stand up to it. And light, acidic white wine is similar to the lemon juice we squeeze on fish. Also, tannins can mingle unpleasantly with fish and leave a metallic finish.

So this old concept is not just blind tradition. It has some sense of logic. However, these rules go back to the last century, and our wines and eating habits have changed. (And how! Have you ever seen a Victorian-era cookbook? Twenty ways to eat yourself into a heart attack!)

A century ago, the only whites that could hold their own with red meat were the big white Burgundies—an expensive addition to any meal. For most people then, white wine meant light wine. Moreover, reds were robust, full-bodied, and rich. Always. Rhônes were as much in fashion as Bordeaux, and Bordeaux was heavier than it is today. People also drank Port with dinner. And red Burgundy of last century was beefed up with heavier southern reds (a practice that no longer is legal).

Now that we have a selection of New World wines, we have relatively inexpensive alternatives to white Burgundy, such as Chardonnay from California or Australia. And the reds have gotten lighter, too. Connoisseurs have discovered a range of light, red wines like Chinon, Barbera, and Rioja. Just as many other rules of late have changed, so have the rules of wine matching.

The rule of "white wine with fish and red wine with meat" is a good general rule—as far as general rules go. But as we all know, following rules all the time is no fun.

Consider the rule of serving white wine with white meat. Here is one variation that works well and is not too radical:

➤ White meat, white sauce: white wine

➤ White meat, brown sauce: red wine

Some people don't follow color-coding (or rules) at all. Certain red wines are excellent with fish, and some whites are great with meat. You might consider these pairings and their variants:

➤ Serve red meats rare (broil, grill, sauté) with red wine.

➤ Cook red meats rare but with unusual spices or methods (like deep frying) and serve with white wine.

➤ Red meats cooked for a long time can work with either red or white wine.

Tasting Tip

American diets have changed greatly, especially over the past few decades. Cooks today are experimenting with sauces for fish or chicken, some of which seem quite amenable to red wines. And in these health-conscious times, beef dishes have gotten lighter.

405

White Before Red?

The traditional order of serving white wine before red is subject to modification, too. Again, this theory goes back to the light-and-heavy distinctions appropriate to older wines.

White wine usually is lighter. However, a light-bodied red certainly should precede a full-bodied white. Rosés generally are the lightest of all, so if a rosé is on your table, open it first.

Heard It Through the Grapevine

The rule of dry wine before sweet wine has had great staying power. And it is hard to challenge. Occasionally you may find an iconoclastic chef who serves a sweet Sauternes with an appetizer, followed by a medium-dry, full-bodied, low-acid wine. This actually can work. But in general, dry before sweet is one rule your taste buds will not readily forego.

Another traditional rule is to serve young wines before old. This rule may be based more on the vintage mystique than on real sensory experience. The fact is, you may be able to better appreciate the subtle nuances and complexity of an older wine early in the dinner, before your palate has been assaulted by those fruity and tannic youngsters.

On the other hand, if your vintage item is a Port or Madeira, absolutely nothing can follow those acts! (Not even another Port or Madeira.) I'd say the same for a rich, intense, aged Bordeaux. Serve the younger, lighter wines first.

From the Deep

Just as there are light, delicate wines and robust, full-bodied wines, so there are light, delicate fish and robust, full-bodied fish. There are quite a few viscous fish too (though *oily* is a more suitable word). Then there are shellfish: lobster, shrimp, clams, oysters, and mussels. In each group, certain wine pairings work, while certain others do not.

Here are a few suggestions to help you match wine with fish:

➤ If you serve red wine with fish, choose one that is young and fruity.

➤ Choose a high-acid wine, either white or red.

➤ Stay away from oaky whites and tannic reds.

➤ Simple fish dishes work with light whites and light reds.

➤ Use only very light reds with shellfish. (Better yet, follow the rules and serve white.)

➤ Avoid red wines with fishy or oily fish.

Don't turn your nose up at people who insist on drinking or serving white wine with fish dishes. They may be following advice from a book by an author who is not enlightened enough to realize that many red wines go perfectly with fish. Try to educate them to the fact that there is a world of wine possibilities that go well with fish.

Light and Delicate Fish

Fish like sole and flounder are delicate in taste and texture. These most definitely are white-wine fish! The only red that should come anywhere near these fish is a light Beaujolais. Rosés usually are light and may be enjoyable, especially with a summer meal.

Salmon and Other Big Guys

It's no coincidence that the menu often reads "salmon steak." Or sometimes, "tuna steak." They have similar qualities. Both are robust, oily, and substantial in body. These fish easily can overpower many whites. White Burgundy or full-bodied California Chardonnay are your best white matches. Fish in this category can even stand up to red Burgundy or similar wines.

Tasting Tip

Bluefish, mackerel, anchovies, sardines, or herring—oily, all—are best kept with acidic white wines like a French Muscadet or Chablis.

Lobster, Shrimp, and Crabs

These tender shellfish deserve something special—and it's generally white. The succulent and delicate meal of lobster calls for a big white Burgundy or a California Chardonnay. Fine Champagne works well, too. Lobster Newburg goes well with a French Chablis, a white Burgundy, a white Rhône wine, or a California Chardonnay.

Grilled prawns or scampi go well with Californian or Australian Chardonnays or with big white Burgundies, like Meursault. Curried shrimp calls for a spicy wine, say an Alsatian Gewürztraminer.

Soft-shell crabs go nicely with a French white Bordeaux or a California Sauvignon Blanc. For crab cakes, try a California Sauvignon Blanc, Chenin Blanc, or Italian Pinot Grigio. For steamed crabs, like the Dungeness, try a German Riesling Kabinett from the Mosel, a Washington Dry White Riesling, or a French Vouvray.

The rich and delicate meat of the Alaskan king crab calls for a white wine with considerable finesse, such as a French Puligny-Montrachet from Burgundy or a Premier Cru Chablis.

Clams, Oysters, and Other Delights

Oysters and Chablis are a traditional combination. The flinty, acidic flavor of a young, simple Chablis perfectly offsets the briny mineral taste of the oyster. So does a light and crisp Muscadet, particularly one that is *sur lie*.

Speaking of delights from the sea, what better match for caviar than Champagne? If you opt for the real caviar (which includes beluga, the most expensive, or sevruga or osetra), go for real Champagne. The perfect match for caviar is a crisp, bone-dry French Champagne. (At the risk of being called a wine traitor, I consider another perfect match for caviar to be chilled vodka.)

The Sommelier Says

Any restaurateur who serves one of the more expensive caviars will suggest a fine champagne as accompaniment. Just a gimmick to get you to max out your credit card? Unfortunately, no. The two go together. Perfectly. This is what I would call expensive good taste, not snobbism.

Fowl, Domestic and Wild

With fowl you get white wine. Most reds overpower broiled or grilled dishes. However, this is another instance where the sauce or spices can help you get it just right—if you're not afraid to experiment.

With roasted or broiled chicken, you might try a California dry Chenin Blanc (white) or a simple (non-reserva) Spanish Rioja (red). With fried chicken, a red Italian Chianti or simple Spanish Rioja is a good choice. Coq au vin goes well with a Côte de Rhône or a Gigondas, both red. For chicken pot pie, consider an Italian Orvieto (white) or a French Beaujolais-Villages (red).

Chicken Kiev, with its rich buttery interior, calls for a good French white Burgundy or California Chardonnay. Roasted game hens go well with an Italian Chianti or a simple French Burgundy. What you drink with roasted turkey depends on the stuffing, but a California Chardonnay or French white Burgundy usually is a safe bet. For an apple or prune stuffing, you may want to consider a California dry Chenin Blanc, White Riesling, or French Vouvray.

Pasta and Casseroles

For pasta dishes, "going ethnic" with wine is always tempting. Pasta is Italian, so the wine should be Italian, too. Right? Maybe.

If you're trying to create an atmosphere where your guests can imagine they see Mount Vesuvius over the horizon, by all means bring out the Chianti or Orvieto. But like everything else, pasta dishes have changed. Today we eat cold pasta with cherries. We mix all shapes of pasta with our favorite vegetables, some of which are more typical of California than of Calabria. What to do? I'd match California veggies with a California wine. (Next question: California red or white?)

For pasta casserole (or any other), break it down into components. Does the dish contain beef, lamb, chicken, fish, or pork? Is it vegetarian or encased in thick cheese? What type of sauce? What types of herbs and spices?

> **Tasting Tip**
>
> Do you prefer poultry stuffings that are a little out of the ordinary? Then complement them with the right wine selection. A Sauvignon Blanc from California goes well with an oyster stuffing. For a chestnut or walnut stuffing, try an Alsatian Riesling, a California Pinot Noir, or a French Beaujolais-Villages. A California Zinfandel is a nice match for a sausage stuffing.

With lasagna, you may want to go with the Italian Chianti. With ravioli, select a white Italian Pinot Grigio or an Italian Dolcetto d'Alba or similar light red wine. With a meat sauce, try an Italian Montepulciano d'Abruzzo or an Italian Chianti. With a rich alfredo sauce, an Italian Pinot Bianco or Vernaccia is a worthy choice. Italian Orvieto (white) or an Italian Chianti (red) goes well with carbonara sauce. For clam sauce, try an Italian Gavi or Soave. Finally (and important to know), Italian Verdicchio goes well with a pesto sauce.

Picnics and Other Diversions

Some people think of rosés as picnic wines. They're light and outdoorsy and perfect for summer refreshment. Paté goes well with a simple Bourgogne Blanc or Rouge or a sweet wine like a Sauternes. But then, you may have some bold, full-flavored dishes on your picnic table. If a barbecue grill is in the picture, the complexion changes entirely. Try a California Zinfandel or an Australian Shiraz.

Heard It Through the Grapevine

Salads are great picnic foods. Traditional wisdom says never serve wine with a salad. The dressing will ruin any good wine. Contemporary thinking suggests that's not always so. You can match wine and salad and enjoy both. Just observe a few basics:

➤ Always serve an acidic wine.

➤ Stick with light-bodied wines.

➤ If the salad has something sweet, try a wine with mild sweetness.

➤ Avoid complex or subtle wines.

They tell us we never should serve eggs with wine. (Of course, honoring this rule would ruin the pricey Sunday brunches at many trendy restaurants.) Frankly, I don't like mimosas with my omelet. But I can suggest a few options:

➤ Low-alcohol wines, like a Riesling from Germany, go best with eggs.

➤ Use the ingredients with which you prepare the eggs (cheese, meats, spices) as your flavor guide.

➤ Beaujolais can be a very good complement to egg dishes.

Finally, we have cheese—a great picnic food. And a course favored by wine lovers as an essential part of any complete meal. Red wine with your cheese is the maxim, and among the red wines, Burgundy is my favorite with cheese. But be careful:

➤ Firm, dry cheeses go very well with red wine. So does chevre (goat cheese), although to my taste, the tang of a chevre is not compatible with any wine. I find it makes the wine taste of the cheese.

➤ Smelly cheeses overwhelm red wine.

➤ Salty cheeses, particularly blue-veined types, can overpower red wines. These are best served with a Port or similar wine.

➤ Soft or double- and triple-cream cheeses can go well with a red wine like a Burgundy or a white wine like a Chardonnay or Pinot Grigio.

The Least You Need to Know

➤ The old maxim "red with meat and white with fish" is a good guide to simple wine-food matching.

➤ Some red wines can go with fish and white meats.

➤ Some white wines can go with light-colored meats, like veal or pork.

➤ Oysters go well with a Chablis or Muscadet.

➤ You can become your own wine-with-food matching expert by developing a taste memory.

Cooking with Wine

Let's look through your kitchen. Yes, you have salt and pepper. Likely you have onions and garlic, too. Then, perhaps, celery and chives, caraway and anise, cinnamon and nutmeg. And let's not forget parsley, sage, rosemary, and thyme! We use all these (and many more) to season our foods.

So why not season your sauces and broths with wine? After all, wine is the source of the most wonderful flavors found in nature. Why not, indeed!

This chapter contains some wine-cooking basics and a few basic recipes. These will get you started with using wine in your kitchen.

Making It Thick

Wine flavors can run from simple to complex, delicate to authoritative. Wine, as I've said many times, offers flavors found nowhere else in nature. But wine is more than flavor and bouquet, it's liquid. Sometimes you need the flavor but not all the liquid. After all, you don't want to dilute your sauce or gravy too much.

Tasting Tip

What about serving wine cooking to those who cannot take alcohol—for reasons of health, religion, or choice? With most wine recipes, that's no problem. Just bring your wine sauce or any other wine component to a boil. Because of its lower boiling point, all the alcohol will evaporate long before any liquid bubbles. This guarantees an alcohol-free dish.

The Sommelier Says

Cooking with Sherry? Well, don't use "cooking sherry!"

To render Sherry legal for sale as a food, it's heavily salted to make it unpalatable as a beverage. That takes too much of the seasoning control out of your hands—not a good idea. Also, these special "cooking" wines are more expensive than the real thing and are inferior in quality.

It's easy to concentrate the flavors of any wine. You reduce it. There are two ways to reduce wine. You can do it directly by boiling away some of the liquid. Or you can do it indirectly by adding unboiled wine to your gravy or sauce that you have made thicker than you want.

Usually you will use the direct method, simply boiling off some of the water. All you need is a small saucepan and a range top. Reducing the volume by half is common. But I don't think of this so much as a reduction in volume as a concentration in flavor.

That flavor won't survive cooking unchanged, of course. Some of wine's subtleties come from lighter, more volatile compounds. But the essential flavor and bouquet will remain, even after reduction. Don't rush this process! Low to moderate on your burner is best.

Of course, the alcohol won't survive reduction in any wine recipe. That's because alcohol boils at 172 degrees Fahrenheit, 40 degrees cooler than water's 212 degrees F. (These are sea-level temperatures. Both become lower at high altitudes.)

You can store your reduced wine in your refrigerator for use as needed over a few days' time.

The indirect method is somewhat easier. Instead of reducing the wine, you just reduce the sauce you're using it in, and then you add the wine at the end, bringing it back to the right consistency. But let it cook a little to boil off the alcohol.

Marinade Aid

There are two good reasons to marinate your meat, poultry, or fish:

1. Flavoring
2. Tenderizing

A wine-based marinade will add to the flavor of anything that once was hoofed, feathered, or finned. Here the "white with white, red with red" rule has a very practical basis. Red wine will darken the color of anything you marinate with it. The appearance of food influences our taste perceptions. Pink perch or blushing chicken breast may not do well, however good it might taste. (Of course, in a thick sauce, that's less important.)

The acids in wine will tenderize your dish. That's why vinegar is the basis of most marinades. The virtue of a wine marinade is that it won't leave behind any sourness. So wine's not right for Sauerbraten, but for many other dishes, I can't think of anything better.

How long should you marinate? Four or five hours is good for most meat and poultry. Two hours does the job for fish. Longer times add little, if anything. A word of caution, though: You don't want to leave poultry or fish at room temperature any longer than necessary. Let your marinade do its work inside your refrigerator.

Here's a recipe for a simple, all-purpose marinade, one that you can modify to reflect your own preferences. I leave the choice of wine up to you.

(Of course, I'm always happy to make suggestions. If your main interest is tenderizing, choose a white wine, perhaps a Sauvignon Blanc. If you're looking to enhance the flavor of a red-meat dish, start out with a Cabernet Sauvignon.)

Basic Wine Marinade

The character changes with choice of wine.

1 carrot, sliced thinly	1 bay leaf
1 large onion, sliced	8 peppercorns
2 garlic cloves, crushed	1 whole clove
1 sprig of parsley, snipped	$2^{1}/_{2}$ cups of wine, your choice

Pinch of thyme for red meat, marjoram for white

Mix the ingredients thoroughly, as you would a salad dressing. Place whatever you want to marinate into a dish deep enough to allow you to cover it, preferably one in which things can be a little crowded. Add enough marinade to cover, just barely. Then place it in your refrigerator for the desired time. Use paper towels to blot what you've marinated before you cook.

Here's an alternative to that deep dish: Marinate inside a plastic freezer bag. You can cover more food with less marinade, and it's a bit neater.

There's no need to discard your marinade after using. Just strain it and keep it in your refrigerator in a closed jar. You can thicken it for use as a sauce. Or you can add a little butter and use it for basting.

Recipes! Yum!

Remember when you were little and got your first box of eight wax crayons? Good. Now think back to how you felt the first time you saw one of those boxes of 64! You got it. That's how I feel about wine as a cooking ingredient. Wine offers us a variety of flavors and bouquets that's endless in its possibilities. In this section, I'll share a few wine recipes. There's no shortage of such dishes in the vast literature of cooking.

Beef Bourguignon

Call it what you like: Beef Bourguignon, or go all the way with Boeuf Bourguignon. It's still Beef Burgundy, a very popular (and easy) dish.

Beef Bourguignon

Serve with French bread and greens.

3 lb. lean stewing beef, in 2-inch cubes	³/₄ cup sliced carrots
¹/₂ cup flour	2 TB. minced parsley
¹/₂ tsp. salt	1 bay leaf
¹/₈ tsp. black pepper	¹/₂ tsp. thyme
2 TB. olive oil	12 pearl onions
3 TB. butter	2 TB. butter
¹/₄ cup brandy, warmed	1 tsp. sugar
2 cups onion, diced	24 firm white mushroom caps
3 cups California Pinot Noir (real Burgundy is too expensive for this dish)	1 TB. butter

Season the flour with the salt and pepper, and roll the beef cubes in it. In a skillet, brown the beef on all sides using the olive oil and 3 TB. of butter. Place in a casserole dish. Pour the brandy over the beef.

In a skillet, sauté the onions and carrots until limp. Add these to the casserole, along with the parsley, bay leaf, thyme, and wine. Cover and place in the oven at 325 degrees.

When 30 minutes remain, sauté the pearl onions with 2 TB. of butter and the sugar until just a little browned. Then add them to the casserole.

With 5 minutes remaining, sauté the mushrooms in 1 TB. butter and add just before serving.

Serves 6 to 8.

Coq au Vin

If someone knows only one dish prepared with wine, this is it! Even if your French education ended with oui-oui and merci, you know that *au vin* means "with wine."

This is French cooking at its most basic. Variations of this well-known dish are served in country houses throughout France.

Coq au Vin

Serve with rice.

3-lb. chicken, cut up	2 garlic cloves
1 TB. butter	1 bay leaf
3 TB. brandy, lukewarm	2 TB. minced parsley
1 kitchen match	$^1/_4$ tsp. thyme
1 Vidalia onion	Salt and pepper, to taste
1 TB. flour	$^1/_2$ lb. mushrooms
2 TB. tomato paste	1 TB. butter

3 cups French Bordeaux or California Cabernet Sauvignon

Sauté the chicken in 1 TB. butter until it's well browned. Add the warmed brandy and ignite it immediately. Shake the skillet until the flame goes out. Remove the chicken, but keep it warm.

Use the same pan to sauté the onion until it's translucent. Stir in the flour and cook for 1 minute before adding the tomato paste, wine, garlic, and herbs. Season to taste with salt and pepper. When the mixture boils, add the chicken and reduce the heat. Allow it to simmer for 1 hour, turning the pieces several times.

Remove the chicken to a warming platter. Turn up the heat under your skillet a little, and reduce the sauce to about 3 cups. In another skillet, sauté the mushrooms in 1 TB. butter. Return the chicken to the sauce and add the mushrooms. Serve from the skillet.

Serves 4.

Veal Marsala

This Old World dish takes its name and flavor from one of the world's oldest wines.

Veal Marsala

Serve over a bed of linguini.

1 lb. boneless veal leg top round steak	$1/2$ cup chicken stock
3 TB. butter	1 TB. snipped parsley
1 cup sliced fresh mushrooms	$1/4$ cup Marsala (ambro, if you can find it)

Cut the veal into four pieces. Use your meat mallet to pound each piece to $1/8$-inch thickness. Season to taste with salt and pepper.

Melt 1 TB. butter in a large skillet. Cook half the veal over medium-high heat for 1 to 2 minutes on each side until done. Remove from the skillet, but keep it warm. Repeat with the remaining veal and 1 TB. butter.

Cook the mushrooms in 1 TB. butter until tender. Stir in the chicken stock and Marsala. Boil rapidly for 3 to 4 minutes. (This should reduce to about $1/3$ cup.) Stir in the parsley, and pour the sauce over the veal.

Serves 4.

Turkey au Chardonnay

This is my personal favorite. And I don't mind telling you, I developed this one myself. The Chardonnay in the stuffing suffuses the meat from the inside with compatible wine flavors. I hope you enjoy it as much as I do.

Turkey au Chardonnay

Serve with normal turkey dinner accompaniments.

The turkey:

1 young turkey, 14 to 16 lb.	3 TB. butter, softened

The stuffing:

$2^{1}/_{2}$ lb. fresh, whole chestnuts	4 TB. unsalted butter
1 bottle full-body, richly oaked, vintage California Chardonnay ($20 – $30), less 12 oz. (Have a second bottle handy.)	1 TB. salt

continues

Turkey au Chardonnay, continued

The sauce:

12 oz. Chardonnay

2 cups turkey drippings

$^1/_2$ lb. unsalted butter

Remove the neck and giblets; discard or save them for other use. Dry the body cavity. From inside, pierce between the ribs several places using a sharp knife, being careful not to break the skin.

For the stuffing, cut an X into the flat sides of each chestnut and simmer in boiling water until tender, about 15 to 20 minutes. Shell and skin the chestnuts. Mash them, but make sure there is still some texture.

Melt 4 TB. butter, add the Chardonnay, and heat through. Work this mixture into the chestnuts, adding additional Chardonnay as needed—up to 2 cups—until you get the consistency of porridge. Allow it to cool. (You can do everything up to this point ahead of time.)

Preheat your oven to 450 degrees. Stuff the turkey, and lace the openings tightly to hold its moisture. Place additional stuffing (if any) in a separate casserole, covered with foil, and roast it along with the turkey during the last 40 minutes of cooking.

Brush the turkey with the 3 TB. of softened butter, and place the turkey directly on the bottom of a large roasting pan. Roast at 450 degrees for 15 minutes. Reduce temperature to 325 degrees, and cover your turkey with a foil tent.

Roast at 325 degrees for about 4 hours, without basting, until a meat thermometer inserted into the thickest part of the thigh reads 170 degrees Fahrenheit. At intervals during roasting, add warm water, up to 2 cups, to the pan to keep the drippings from burning.

Remove the foil from the turkey and continue roasting an additional 30 to 45 minutes, basting frequently with the drippings, until the meat thermometer reads 180 degrees F. Remove the turkey from the oven and allow it to stand 20 minutes before carving.

To make the sauce, reduce 12 oz. of Chardonnay by half over medium-high heat, until the wine has the consistency of light syrup. Pour the pan drippings into a bowl, skimming and removing the clear fat. Measure 2 cups of the drippings. Add them to the reduced wine, cooking over medium-high heat, until the mixture thickens. Remove from heat.

Whisk in the unsalted butter, a few tablespoons. at a time, allowing it to emulsify completely after each addition. The sauce should be very glossy and light in color and texture when done. Serve with the turkey. (You can hold this sauce up to an hour, covered in the top of a double boiler.)

Serves 8 to 10.

The Best Fondue

This is a dish that evokes the romance of an Alpine chalet, a log fire caressing the room in its warm glow, and someone you love. *Fondu* is the French word for "melted." Sometimes it's hearts that melt, no less than the cheeses.

The Best Fondue

Serve with French bread chunks (and love).

¹/₂ lb. aged Emmenthaler cheese, shredded	1 clove garlic, cut in halves
¹/₂ lb. Gruyère cheese, shredded	¹/₄ tsp. dry mustard
3 TB. kirsch (colorless cherry brandy)	1 TB. cornstarch
1 cup German Riesling, Kabinett (either Rhine or Mosel)	

Toss the cheeses with the cornstarch until they are coated. Rub the inside of a heavy saucepan (or double boiler pan) thoroughly with the garlic. Add the wine, and bring it almost to a boil. (Those first bubbles you see are the alcohol boiling off.) If you aren't using a double boiler, keep the heat low.

Add the cheese in small amounts, stirring each time until the sauce has no lumps. When all the cheese is in the mixture, add the kirsch and the mustard, stirring well. Then transfer to your earthenware fondue dish, which you'll keep warm.

Your fondue should seem a little thin so it will penetrate the bread. If it gets too thick, add a little wine.

Serve with day-old French bread, torn into chunks, each containing a bit of crust. Stick fondue forks through the crusts and swirl in the cheese mixture with a figure-eight pattern.

Serves 2.

Wine Desserts

Until the 1970s, Americans drank more dessert wines than table wines. And I wouldn't argue with anyone over wine's suitability as a dessert. A rich Sauternes, a vintage Port, a well-aged Sherry. But I promised you recipes, and here's one I selected because it combines a bit of the new and the old—fresh fruit with a sweet, rich zabaglione.

Nectarines with Zabaglione

Don't tell your doctor!

4 egg yolks	1 cup heavy cream, whipped
2/3 cup sugar	12 nectarines, pitted and sliced
2/3 cup fino Sherry	

In a double boiler top, whisk the egg yolks until they're thick. Add the sugar gradually while whipping. Stir in the Sherry. Place the pan over hot, but not boiling, water. Cook until thickened, stirring constantly—about 15 to 20 minutes. Remove from heat. Cool slightly. Stir in whipped cream.

Spoon the fruit into dessert glasses and top with the zabaglione.

Serves 4.

The Least You Need to Know

➤ Most dishes that involve cooking and wine contain no alcohol.

➤ Wine is an excellent substitute for vinegar in marinades.

➤ Wine adds flavor versatility to any kitchen.

To Your Health!

They call it the French Paradox. According to much of what we may know about heart disease, France should be one big coronary ward. Look at the French diet (it has its good points): the fat equivalent of a Big Mac. And cigarette use: five times that of the U.S., per-capita (those foul-smelling Galois, at that). And the rate of heart attacks? About 40 percent lower than that of the U.S., with a life span 2^1/$_2$ years greater!

Why? Could it be the consequence of French friendliness toward foreigners? *Au contraire*. Many researchers say it's due to the traditional French practice of enjoying red wine at mealtime.

Wine? Good for us? But wine is an alcoholic beverage, right? Yes, these health claims are as controversial as they are surprising. Even potential supporters want to see more evidence. But that evidence continues to come in from Mediterranean France, Italy, Spain, Greece, Scandinavia, the Netherlands, the U.K.—and from the home of the skeptics, the good old United States.

Daily Wine and the M.D.

If you grew up in the U.S., you must be aware that our culture regards alcohol as a dangerous drug. And indeed, it can be. But for the first time, doctors and others are speaking and writing about some of alcohol's benefits. For example, the latest version of the federal government's "Dietary Guidelines for Americans" gives a thumbs-up to light-to-moderate consumption.

This must play alongside those many messages—from governments and from private organizations—about the dangers of alcohol abuse. I feel we need some of each, the good news and the bad, to ensure we all make informed choices. But I do have some trouble with those messages that suggest an all-or-nothing approach. What's wrong with moderation?

Heard It Through the Grapevine

According to the French National Institute of Health and Medical Research, a moderate intake of alcohol cuts the risk of coronary heart disease by as much as 50 percent. This study has another angle. In addition to the French having far fewer deaths from heart attacks, their death rate from atherosclerotic cardiovascular disease (hardening of the arteries) is roughly half that of the U.S.

What's the reason for this amazing phenomenon? Many experts believe it's the moderate consumption of alcohol, specifically red wine. More recent research has identified important antioxidant effects from certain compounds unique to red wine.

Cultural messages seem to imply that we are incapable of moderation. Slogans like "Just Say No," the youth-oriented message that lumps alcohol in with hard drugs, makes it seem as though there's only one reason to drink: to get drunk. Unfortunately, the slogan works well as a self-fulfilling prophecy and disregards the fact that few wine drinkers drink to drunkenness.

In the countries of Mediterranean Europe—France, Italy, Greece, and Spain—wine is an integral part of the family meal. Children who grow up consuming wine with their parents hardly regard it as some kind of forbidden fruit. Where's the thrill in sipping from a glass poured by your mother? With their parents and other adults as models, young people learn that a glass or two of wine is as natural as oil and vinegar on salad.

These European children learn another important health lesson: the value of leisurely dining. Can you imagine a Spaniard or a Greek standing at the table, briefcase in hand, shoveling in a few bites and then saying, "Gotta run. I'm outa here!"?

Combined with vino, the relaxed atmosphere of the Mediterranean dinner table has a dual effect:

Tasting Tip

The tradition of wine with food says a lot about the personality of wine drinkers. This is noted by Dr. Arthur Klatsky, writing in the *American Journal of Cardiology*. He found that people who pre-fer their alcohol in the form of wine tend to be the most mod-erate and responsible drinkers.

➤ It acts as a stress-reducer, which not only makes you feel good but has a positive effect on the cardiovascular system. Stress can raise your blood pressure by constricting your arteries. Also, it can make blood more likely to clot and raise levels of LDL ("bad") cholesterol.

➤ The longer mealtime may affect the absorp-tion and metabolism of fats. (Remember, the French diet is no lower in fats than our own.) It can mitigate the effects of fat on blood clotting, stabilize insulin levels, and moderate the absorption of alcohol itself.

Provided that you enjoy the company, a slow-paced meal is more than nutrition. It's one of life's greater pleasures. Add a bottle of your favorite wine, and you and your bloodstream will both be happier.

Heard It Through the Grapevine

We all know alcohol soothes feelings of stress. Alcohol acts as a vasodilator, enhancing blood flow by relaxing the muscle tissue of arteries. Alcohol decreases the potential for blood clotting in coronary arteries and increases the level of HDL ("good") cholesterol.

Good food and wine, consumed slowly and leisurely and in the presence of good com-pany, work as a powerful (and very pleasant) stress-reducing trio. You don't have to con-sult your doctor for that. Just refer to your own experience.

Drinking wine with a meal may provide you with alcohol at just the right time: when you need wine's beneficial properties to counteract the effect of the fats you take in. Drinking with dinner ensures the protective effects of alcohol are strongest in the evening, when fatty foods are making their way through your bloodstream. This protective effect lingers into the next morning, the time when most heart attacks take place.

Wine and Heart Disease

Certain positive effects on the heart and cardiovascular system are associated with all alcoholic consumption, wine or otherwise. Moderate drinking may be good for you because it tends to

➤ Decrease levels of bad cholesterol and raise the level of good cholesterol.

➤ Reduce the tendency of blood to clot in arteries and increase the ability to dissolve clots after they have formed.

➤ Moderate the tendency of arteries to constrict during stress.

➤ Lower blood pressure.

➤ Increase coronary artery diameter and blood flow.

In Vino Longevity?

I've already discussed the complexity, the multidimensionality, the breed, the bouquet, and all those other factors that distinguish wine from other beverages. Now wine can take credit for something else. Some of the components in wine are part of a group chemists call phenols, which have antioxidant properties. Phenolic compounds exist in grape skins and seeds, and they contribute to wine's subtle nuances of flavor, aroma, texture, and color.

Fermentation makes these nifty phenolic compounds far more prevalent in wine than in fruits or fruit juices. For example, red wines have about five times higher phenolic levels than fresh grapes. The compounds tend to concentrate in the plant seeds, skins, and stems, parts that are discarded in the making of most juices.

In winemaking, however, these parts are fermented along with the juice, especially in making red wine. This helps explain why red wines tend to be more beneficial than white. But don't despair if you prefer white wine: Both red- and white-wine drinkers reap the cardiovascular benefits of the vinified grape.

I saw one study that identified specific phenolic compounds as the ingredients that inhibit the oxidation of the harmful LDL cholesterol. One of these antioxidants is quercetin. This one may be anticarcinogenic, also. Quercitin is in onions and garlic, as well as in wine, and it may inhibit the action of a cancer gene.

As I understand it, quercetin is inactive in food, but it's stimulated into cancer-fighting action by fermentation or by certain bacteria in the intestinal tract. Studies show that high consumption of quercetin-containing foods lowers the incidence of digestive (stomach, intestinal) and other cancers.

In fact, alcohol is responsible for barely 3 percent of all cancers in the United States, and in many cases, other factors are involved. Even where alcohol in the form of beer and spirits is implicated, wine still appears to come out the good guy. Indeed, wine may have a protective effect on health and longevity, in addition to flavor and fragrance, balance and breed, and just plain old-fashioned enjoyment.

The Sommelier Says

Few public health officials seem to endorse wine for its likely cancer-fighting benefits. Instead, they remain quick to indict alcohol—if not as a major player, then at least as a conspirator—in various cancer risks. The government neglects to inform us, however, that these particular risks are associated only with heavy drinking.

Good Things in Moderation

Moderate consumption usually is defined as 25 grams (about an ounce) of alcohol per day. That's the vinous equivalent of two to two-and-a-half 4-ounce glasses of wine. Some sources will accept a higher level as moderate. A consensus seems to lie between $1^1/_2$ and $3^1/_2$ glasses a day. Fifty grams (five glasses) on a daily basis, however, generally is considered heavy drinking. Thus, two regular servings of wine a day is fine for most people.

The rate of alcohol metabolism varies from one person to another and affects the daily level of consumption that's moderate for you. Body weight is important, too. More weight means more blood, which means lower blood-alcohol levels.

In general, women weigh less than men, with a greater proportion of fat. (Of course, exceptions exist, especially in the fashion industry.) If you're not sure of your body composition or weight, you can get on a scale, take a pinch test, or look in the mirror.

My best advice is simply to recognize that the ability to metabolize alcohol varies a great deal among individuals. So "know thyself." The lower your weight, the lower your consumption should be. The following table shows how long it takes people of varying weights (with average lean body mass) to metabolize different quantities of alcohol.

Before you start thinking that maybe those extra pounds you had planned to shed now have a useful purpose, forget it! Body composition also is a factor. Lean body weight is what assists in the metabolism of alcohol. Body fluids exist in inverse proportion to body fat.

The more lean body mass you have, the higher the percentage of fluids. The more fat you have, the less fluid. Alcohol seeks out bodily fluids. So concentrations of alcohol will be weaker (more diluted) in a person with less fat. (Got that?)

How Long Your Body Takes to Metabolize Alcohol

Body Wt. (lbs.)	1 drink	2 drinks	3 drinks	4 drinks	5 drinks	6 drinks
100-119	0 hours	3 hours	3 hours	6 hours	13 hours	16 hours
120-139	0 hours	2 hours	2 hours	5 hours	10 hours	12 hours
140-159	0 hours	2 hours	2 hours	4 hours	8 hours	10 hours
160-179	0 hours	1 hour	1 hour	3 hours	7 hours	9 hours
180-199	0 hours	0 hours	0 hours	2 hours	6 hours	7 hours
200-219	0 hours	0 hours	0 hours	2 hours	5 hours	6 hours
More than 220	0 hours	0 hours	0 hours	1 hour	4 hours	6 hours

Benefits of Moderate Consumption

Evidence continues to come in—and most of it reflects favorably on wine drinking. Studies continue to show that regular moderate alcohol consumption reduces the risk of heart disease in some people by 25 to 45 percent and overall mortality rates by 10 percent. What's more, the benefits are greater for wine drinkers.

If you're worried about liver cirrhosis, the scourge of alcoholics, remember that the people who experience liver damage are very heavy drinkers. Regions of France with the highest wine consumption happen to have the lowest rates of cirrhosis, lower than figures from the U.S.

I have more for you: Wine drinkers have even been found to age more gracefully than nondrinkers. Perhaps you've heard that old joke about how giving up alcohol doesn't really make you live longer .... It just feels that way. Well, it's not a joke. Keep up the wine drinking, and you may live longer—and happier.

Heeding the Cautions

With all the warnings proclaimed by the antialcohol crowd, it's difficult to tell which requires more caution: these voices of temperance or the wine itself.

Essentially, warnings about alcohol are based on the effects of heavy consumption—of wine or any other alcoholic beverage. One notable example is the label warning for pregnant women:

> Fetal Alcohol Syndrome (FAS) is an unfortunate and avoidable condition that can result in profound mental and growth retardation resulting from a pregnant mother's alcohol consumption.

Guess what? We're not talking about the effects of a few daily glasses of wine, but about heavy drinking and the entire alcoholic lifestyle: low socioeconomic status, poor prenatal care, cigarette smoking, and poor overall health, all significant cofactors with alcohol.

Does this situation really merit such drastic warnings and scare tactics? Many women say no, and so do a growing number of physicians. Let's go back to those Mediterraneans for a moment. French and Italian women read no such warnings on their wine bottles. They continue drinking mealtime wine with no ill effects.

We wine drinkers aren't the irresponsible revelers the voices of temperance may suggest. American wine drinkers are a moderate lot. Statistics reveal the average wine drinker consumes three to five glasses of wine per week, and usually no more than $1^1/_2$ glasses on any given occasion. Additionally, we tend to lead healthy lives. Very few wine drinkers smoke, for instance. (Cigarette smoke ruins the taste and aroma of wine.) And many wine drinkers exercise regularly and consume a produce-rich diet—habits we have in common with those robust Mediterraneans.

Wine drinkers may like to jog or hike, but we also drive cars. So let me close on a note of caution. Wine has been implicated in 2 percent of all arrests for drunken driving. I'd like to do my part to bring that figure down to zero.

The Sommelier Says

Don't get the idea I am recommending daily wine to pregnant women. I'm just a wine expert. I'm not competent to make health decisions for anyone. All I care about is that we all make our own decisions, decisions grounded in fact.

Regardless of what beverage you enjoy, accidents caused by drunk driving are tragic and avoidable. Legal intoxication is usually set at a 0.08 or 0.10 blood-alcohol level (or blood-alcohol content, BAC). However, coordination and judgment are impaired well before that. Use your judgment before you lose it.

Wine affords many pleasures, but they are not free of all care. I advise you to consider the following, what I call The Wine Drinker's Commandments:

➤ Don't operate a vehicle just after drinking: cars, bicycles, motorcycles, boats, airplanes ... anything that moves. (In England, which has a very tough drunk-driving law, some people visit pubs on horseback.)

➤ Don't swim, surf, or water ski when drinking.

➤ Don't participate in athletic activities that require balance and perception, land or water, while drinking. These include in-line skating, skateboarding, skiing, gymnastics, and others.

➤ Don't use firearms or other weapons if you've been drinking.

➤ Don't use power tools, particularly saws, mowers, drills, or the like, after drinking.

➤ Don't drink wine with antihistamines or similar medication. Drowsiness may result. For any other medicines, prescription or over the counter, check the label for guidelines. Or seek advice from your doctor or pharmacist.

➤ Don't drink under a physician's care except with explicit permission.

➤ Finally, don't ever let your guests drive home even a little bit tipsy. A responsible host will phone a cab or make other, safer arrangements.

Official DWI Chart

Body Weight (lbs.)	No. of Drinks in one Hour to .4BAC (Impaired)	No. of Drinks in One Hour to .1BAC (Drunk)
100	2.5	4.0
120	2.5	4.5
140	3.0	5.0
160	3.5	5.5
180	3.5	6.0
200	4.0	7.0
220	4.5	7.5
240	5.0	8.0

The Least You Need to Know

➤ A glass or two of wine each day can be good for your health.

➤ Consumption of red wine may improve your levels of "good" cholesterol.

➤ Don't drive, swim, use power tools, or take antihistamines when you drink alcoholic beverages.

➤ Be a good party host and arrange a ride for any of your guests who have had too much to drink.

Recommended Wines

The following lists are my recommendations of wines that are nationally distributed and that represent consistent quality and good value. The wine region follows the wine name in parentheses. Prices are for regular 750 ml bottles, unless otherwise indicated. Prices are full markup retail prices—you should find these wines at lower prices at discount stores.

Recommended Red Wines Under $9

Banrock Station Shiraz-Cabernet Sauvignon (Australia) $5.99

Barone Ricasoli Chianti (Italy) $8.99

Belle Jour (France) $7.99 (1.5L)

Beringer Gamay Beaujolais (California) $6.99

Bersano Barbera (Italy—Piemonte) $6.99

Bodega Nekeas Cabernet Sauvignon-Tempranillo (Spain) $6.99

Bodegas Montecillo (Spain—Rioja) $7.50

Bogle Petite Sirah (California) $8.99

Bolla Valpolicella (Italy) $7.99

Buena Vista Zinfandel (California) $8.99

Calina Cabernet Sauvignon (Chile—Valle del Rapel) $8.99

Canyon Road Cabernet Sauvignon (California) $7.99

Casa de Santar Dao Reserva (Portugal) $8.99

Casal Thaulero Montepulciano D'Abruzzo (Italy) $7.99 (1.5L)

Castello di Gabbiano Chianti Classico (Italy) $7.99

Chateau Bonnet (France—Bordeaux) $7.99

Chateau de Flaugergues (France—Coteaux du Languedoc) $8.99

Chââteau Gourgazaud (France—Minervois) $7.50

Chateau La Joya Cabernet Sauvignon (Chile) $7.99

Chââteau Pitray (France—Bordeaux) $7.99

Cockatoo Ridge Grenache-Shiraz (Australia) $8.99

Concha y Toro Cabernet Sauvignon/Merlot (Chile) $7.99 (1.5L)

Concha y Toro Merlot (Chile) $8.99

Delicato Zinfandel (California) $5.99

Dessilani Spanna (Italy—Piedmonte) $7.99

Domaine Berthet-Rayne Cotes du Rhone-Villages (France—Rhone) $8.99

Domaine La Tuiliere (France—Cotes du Ventoux) $6.99

Errazuriz Cabernet Sauvignon (Chile) $8.99

Fetzer Valley Oaks Cabernet Sauvignon (California) $7.50

Folonari Merlot-Sangiovese (Italy) $6.99

Georges Duboeuf Beaujolais-Villages (France—Beaujolais) $6.99

Georges Duboeuf Julienas (France—Beaujolais) $8.99

Grand Cru Vineyards Merlot (California) $7.99

Hardys Nottage Hill Shiraz (Australia) $7.99

Hogue Cabernet-Merlot (Washington) $8.99

Jean-Claude Boisset Cabernet-Merlot (Washington—Columbia Valley) $6.99

La Vieille Ferme (France—Côtes du Ventoux) $7.99

Lindemans Shiraz (Australia) $7.99

Los Vascos Cabernet Sauvignon (Chile) $6.99

Louis Jadot Beaujolais-Villages (France—Beaujolais) $8.99

Masi Valpolicella Classico (Italy) $7.99

Michel Bernard Cotes du Rhone-Villages (France—Rhone) $7.99

Michel Torino Malbec (Argentina) $6.99

Miguel Torres Cabernet Sauvignon (Chile) $8.99

Mommessin Beaujolais-Villages (France—Beaujolais) $7.99

Monte Antico (Italy—Tuscany) $7.99

Montevina Zinfandel (California) $6.99

Napa Ridge Winery Cabernet Sauvignon (California) $7.99

Napa Ridge Zinfandel (California) $8.99

Penfolds Shiraz-Cabernet Sauvignon (Australia) $8.99

Pepperwood Grove Zinfandel (California) $6.99

Rabbit Ridge Zinfandel (California) $8.99

Redbank Shiraz (Australia) $8.99

Rosemount Estate Shiraz/Cabernet Sauvignon (Australia) $6.99

Rosemount Grenache-Shiraz (Australia) $7.99

Rosemount Shiraz-Cabernet (Australia) $8.99

Santa Rita Merlot (Chile) $7.99

Santa Sofia Valpolicella Classico (Italy) $8.99

Seaview Cabernet Sauvignon (Australia) $8.99

Serradayres (Portugal) $5.99

Spalletti Chianti (Italy) $8.99

Straccali Chianti (Italy) $5.99

Sutter Home Pinot Noir (California) $5.99

Turning Leaf Zinfandel (California) $7.99

Tyrrell's Long Flat Red (Australia) $7.99

Vendange Cabernet Sauvignon (California) $7.99 (1.5L)

Vina Santa Carolina Cabernet Sauvignon (Chile) $7.99

Recommended White Wines Under $9

Alianca Vinho Verde (Portugal) $5.99

Alice White Chardonnay (Australia) $6.99

Banrock Station Semillon-Chardonnay (Australia) $5.99

Baron Herzog Chenin Blanc (California) $6.99

Boucheron Blanc de Blanc (France) $6.99 (1.5L)

Buena Vista Sauvignon Blanc (California) $8.99

Callaway Chenin Blanc (California) $7.99

Callaway Sauvignon Blanc (California) $7.99

Canyon Road Chardonnay (California) $7.99

Canyon Road Sauvignon Blanc (California) $6.99

Casa Lapostolle Sauvignon Blanc (Chile) $6.50

Castello Banfi Pinot Grigio (Italy) $8.99

Château Bonnet Blanc (France—Bordeaux) $6.99

Château du Cleray Muscadet (France) $8.99

Chateau Souverain Sauvignon Blanc (California) $8.99

Chateau St. Jean Fume Blanc (California) $8.99

Cielo Pinot Grigio (Italy) $5.99

Clos du Bois Sauvignon Blanc (California) $8.99

Columbia Crest Chardonnay (Washington) $8.99

Concha y Toro Chardonnay (Chile) $8.99

Concha y Toro Sauvignon/Semillon (Chile) $6.99 (1.5L)

Covey Run Riesling (Washington) $5.99

Domaine de Pouy (France) $5.99

Fetzer Sundial Chardonnay (California) $7.99

Folonari Pinot Grigio (Italy) $6.99

Georges Duboeuf Macon-Villages (France—Beaujolais) $7.99

Geyser Peak Sauvignon Blanc (California) $8.99

Hardys Chardonnay (Australia) $8.99

Hogue Chardonnay (Washington) $8.99

Hogue Fumé Blanc (Washington) $7.99

Joseph Brigl Pinot Grigio (Italy) $6.99

La Vieille Ferme Blanc (France) $6.99

Lindemans Chardonnay (Australia) $7.99

Louis Latour Chardonnay (France) $6.99

Moreau Blanc (France) $7.49 (1.5L)

Napa Ridge Chardonnay (California) $8.99

Redbank Chardonnay (Australia) $8.99

Rosemount Estate Semillon/Chardonnay (Australia) $7.99

Rosemount Semillon (Australia) $8.99

Rosemount Traminer-Riesling (Australia) $7.99

Ruffino Pinot Grigio (Italy) $8.99

Santa Rita Chardonnay (Chile) $7.99

Seaview Chardonnay (Australia) $8.99

Vendange Chardonnay (California) $7.99 (1.5L)

Vina Santa Carolina Chardonnay (Chile) $7.99

Wente Sauvignon Blanc (California) $7.99

Recommended Red Wines $10–$15

Burgess Zinfandel (California—Napa Valley) $14.99

Carmen Merlot Reserve (Chile—Rapel Valley) $13.99

Ceretto Dolcetto D'Alba (Italy—Piedmont) $13.99

Chateau d'Oupia (France—Minervois) $9.99

Chateau de Chantegrive (France—Graves) $13.99

Chateau du Glana (France—St.-Julien) $13.99

Chateau La Cardonne (France—Medoc) $12.99

Chateau La Joya Cabernet Sauvignon Gran Reserva (Chile—Colchagua Valley) $11.99

Chateau La Tourette (France—Pauillac) $14.99

Chateau Malescasse (France—Haut-Medoc) $14.99

Château Meyney (France—St. Estèphe) $14.99

Chateau Patache d'Aux (France—Medoc) $13.99

Chateau Souverain Zinfandel (California—Dry Creek Valley) $11.99

Cispiano Chianti Classico (Italy—Tuscany) $13.99

Columbia Crest Merlot (Washington—Columbia Valley) $11.99

David Bruce Petite Sirah (California—Central Coast) $14.99

Delas Crozes-Hermitage Les Launes (France—Rhone) $12.99

Domaine Brusset Cotes du Rhone-Villages (France—Rhone) $12.99

Domaine des Murettes (France—Minervois) $10.99

Domaine Sorin (France—Côtes-de-Provence) $10.99

Filliatreau "Grand Vignolle" Saumur-Champigny (France—Loire) $13.99

Georges Duboeuf Morgon (France—Beaujolais) $9.99

Geyser Peak Cabernet Sauvignon (California—Sonoma County) $13.99

La Rioja Alta Vina Alberdi Reserva (Spain—Rioja) $12.99

Louis Latour Côte-de-Beaune-Villages (France—Burgundy) $12.99

McDowell Syrah (California—Mendocino) $9.99

Melini Borghi D'Elsa Chianti (Italy) $10.99 (1.5L)

Meridian Syrah (California—Paso Robles) $13.99

Mommessin Moulin-a-Vent (France—Beaujolais) $13.99

The Monterey Vineyard Classic Cabernet Sauvignon (California) 10.99 (1.5L)

Mouton Cadet Rouge (France—Bordeaux) $14.99 (1.5L)

Paul Jaboulet Aine Cotes du Rhone Parallele 45 (France—Rhone) $9.99

Penfold's Bin 389 Cabernet Sauvignon/Shiraz (Australia) $14.99

Prunotto Barbera d'Asti (Italy—Piedmont) $10.99

Rabbit Ridge Zinfandel (California—Amador County) $11.99

Robert Mondavi "Woodbridge" Cabernet Sauvignon (California) $12.99 (1.5L)

Saintsbury Pinot Noir (California—Carneros) $14.99

Seghesio Zinfandel Sonoma County (California—Sonoma) $13.99

Recommended White Wines $10–15

Alderbrook Sonoma Chardonnay (California—Dry Creek Valley) $13.99

Beaulieu Vineyard Chardonnay (California—Carneros) $12.99

Beringer Chardonnay Napa Valley (California) $11.99

Beringer Sauvignon Blanc (California) $8.99

Cakebread Sauvignon Blanc (California—Napa Valley) $14.99

Caymus Sauvignon Blanc (California—Napa Valley) $13.99

Chartron-Trebuchet Rully "La Chaume" (France—Burgundy) $14.99

Château Cruzeau Blanc (France—Graves) $10.99

Chateau Souverain Chardonnay (California—Sonoma County) $12.99

Concannon Chardonnay (California—Central Coast) $10.99

De Loach Chardonnay Sonoma County (California—Sonoma Cuvee) $12.99

Domaine Aubuisiers Vouvray Sec "Le Marigny" (France—Loire) $12.99

Egon Muller Forster Mariengarten Riesling Kabinett (Germany—Pfalz) $9.99

Fernand Girard Sancerre "La Garenne" (France) $12.99

Ferrari-Carano Fume Blanc (California—Sonoma County) $11.99

Firestone Chardonnay (California—Santa Ynez Valley) $11.99

Gallo of Sonoma Chardonnay (California—Russian River Valley) $11.99

Georges Duboeuf Pouilly-Fuisse (France) $12.99

Groth Sauvignon Blanc (California—Napa Valley) $13.99

Hugel Pinot Blanc Cuvee Les Amours (France—Alsace) $12.99

Kenwood Chardonnay (California—Sonoma County) $14.99

Korbel Chardonnay Heck Family Cellar Selection (California—Russian River Valley) $14.99

Livio Felluga Pinot Grigio (Italy) $12.99

Longridge Chardonnay Hawkes Bay (New Zealand) $9.99

Louis M. Martini Chardonnay (California—North Coast) $9.99

Markham Chardonnay (California—Napa Valley) $14.99

Meridian Chardonnay Edna Valley (California—Coastal Reserve) $14.99

Mirassou Pinot Blanc (California—Monterey County) $10.99

Paul Pernot Bourgogne Blanc (France—Burgundy) $13.99

Pazo de Villarei Albarino (Spain) $13.99

Pierre Sparr Gewurztraminer (France—Alsace) $11.99

Raymond Sauvignon Blanc Reserve (California—Napa Valley) $10.99

Robert Mondavi Fume Blanc (California—Napa Valley) $12.99

Rosemount Chardonnay "Show Reserve" (Australia) $13.99

Sauvion & Fils Muscadet de Sevre et Maine (France—Loire) $9.99

Seven Peaks Chardonnay (California—Central Coast) $13.99

Silverado Vineyards Sauvignon Blanc (California—Napa Valley) $11.99

St. Supery Sauvignon Blanc (California—Napa Valley) $11.99

Sterling Chardonnay (California—Napa Valley) $14.99

Trimbach Riesling (France—Alsace) $13.99

Turning Leaf Sonoma Reserve Zinfandel (California) $13.99

Von Simmern Eltviller Sonnenberg Kabinett (Germany) $13.99

Wente Sauvignon Blanc (California—Livermore Valley) $9.99

Zaca Mesa Chardonnay (California—Santa Barbara County) $13.99

France: Recommended Wine Producers (Châteaux) of Bordeaux, Red Wines

In this section, the Château name is followed by the district in parentheses.

Andron-Blanquet (St.-Estèphe)

Ausone (St.-Emilion)

Batailley (Pauillac)

Beau-Site (St.-Estèphe)

Beausé jour-Duffau (St.-Emilion)

Bon Pasteur (Pomerol)

Branaire-Ducru (St.-Julien)

Calon-Sé gur (St.-Estèphe)

Canon (St.-Emilion)

Canon-La-Gaffelière (St.-Emilion)

Capbern-Gasqueton (St.-Estèphe)

Caronne-St.-Gemme (St.-Estèphe)

Certan de May (Pomerol)

Chasse-Spleen (Moulis)

Cissac (Cissac)

Citran (Avensan)

Clerc-Milon (Pauillac)

Clinet (Pomerol)

Cos d'Estournel (St.-Estèphe)

Cos Labory (St.-Estèphe)

D'Agassac (Ludon)

d'Angludet (Margaux)

Daugay (St.-Emilion)

de Fieuzal (Graves)

De Marbuzet (St.-Estèphe)

Domaine de Chevalier (Graves)

Du Glana (St.-Julien)

Ducru-Beaucaillou (St.-Julien)

Duhart-Milon-Rothschild (Pauillac)

Dutruch Grand-Poujeaux (Moulis)

Ferrand-Lartique (St.-Emilion)

Figeac (St.-Emilion)

Fourcas-Dupré (Listrac)

Fourcas-Hosten (Listrac)

Gazin (Pomerol)

Giscours (Margaux)

Gloria (St.-Julien)

Grand-Mayne (St.-Emilion)

Grand-Puy-Ducasse (Pauillac)

Grand-Puy-Lacoste (Pauillac)

Gruaud-Larose (St.-Julien)

Haut-Bages-Libéral (Pauillac)

Haut-Bailly (Graves)

Haut-Batailley (Pauillac)

Haut-Brion (Graves)

Haut-Marbuzet (St.-Estèphe)

L'Angélus (St.-Emilion)

L'Arrosée (St.-Emilion)

L'Eglise-Clinet (Pomerol)

L'Evangile (Pomerol)

439

La Conseillante (Pomerol)

La Dominique (St.-Emilion)

La Fleur de Gay (Pomerol)

La Fleur Pétrus (Pomerol)

La Lagune (Ludon)

La Louvière (Graves)

La Mission-Haut-Brion (Graves)

Lafite-Rothschild (Pauillac)

Lafleur (Pomerol)

Lafon-Rochet (St.-Estèphe)

Lagrange (St.-Julien)

Langoa-Barton (St.-Julien)

Latour (Pauillac)

Latour à Pomerol (Pomerol)

Le Crock (St.-Estèphe)

Le Pin (Pomerol)

Le Tertre-Roteboeuf (St.-Emilion)

Léoville-Barton (St.-Julien)

Léoville-Las-Cases (St.-Julien)

Léoville-Poyferré (St.-Julien)

Les-Ormes-de-Pez (St.-Estèphe)

Lynch-Bages (Pauillac)

Margaux (Margaux)

Meyney (St.-Estèphe)

Montrose (St.-Estèphe)

Moulin-Pey-Labrie (Canon-Fronsac)

Mouton-Rothschild (Pauillac)

Palmer (Margaux)

Pape-Clément (Graves)

Pavie-Macquin (St.-Emilion)

Petit-Village (Pomerol)

Pétrus (Pomerol)

Phélan-Ségur (St.-Estèphe)

Pichon-Longueville Baron (Pauillac)

Pichon-Longueville-Comtesse de Lalande (Pauillac)

Pontet-Canet (Pauillac)

Poujeaux (Moulis)

Prieuré-Lichine (Margaux)

Rausan-Séglas (Margaux)

Smith-Haut-Lafite (Graves)

Talbot (St.-Julien)

Troplong-Mondot (St.-Emilion)

Trotanoy (Pomerol)

Valandraud (St.-Emilion)

Vieux Chateau Certan (Pomerol)

France: Recommended Wine Producers (Châteaux) of Bordeaux, White Wines

In this section, the Château name is followed by the district in parentheses.

Bonnet (Entre-Deux-Mers)

Bouscaut (Graves)

Bouscaut (Pessac-Leognan)

Carbonnieux (Graves)

Clos Floridène (Graves)

Coucheroy (Pessac-Leognan)

Couhins-Lurton (Graves)

de Fieuzal (Graves)

de Malle (Graves)

Doisy-Daeëne (Bordeaux)

Domaine de Chevalier (Graves)

Haut-Brion Blanc (Graves)

La Louvière (Graves)

La Louviere (Pessac-Leognan)

La Tour-Martillac (Graves)

Larrivet-Haut-Brion (Pessac-Leognan)

Laville Haut Brion (Graves)

Loudenne (Bordeaux)

Olivier (Pessac-Leognan)

Pape-Clément (Graves)

Pavillon Blanc de Château Margaux (Bordeaux)

R de Rieussec (Graves)

Respide (Graves)

Smith-Haut-Lafitte (Graves)

France: Recommended Wine Producers (Châteaux) of Bordeaux—Sauternes/Barsac

In this section, the Château name is followed by the district in parentheses.

Caillou (Barsac)

Climens (Barsac)

Clos Haut-Peyraguey (Sauternes)

Coutet (Barsac)

de Fargues (Sauternes)

Doisy-Daëne (Barsac)

Doisy-Dubroca (Barsac)

Filhot (Sauternes)

Gilette (Sauternes)

Guiraud (Sauternes)

La Tour Blanche (Sauternes)

Lafaurie-Peyraguey (Sauternes)

Rabaud-Promis (Sauternes)

Raymond-Lafon (Sauternes)

Rayne-Vigneau (Sauternes)

Rieussec (Sauternes)

Sigalas Rabaud (Sauternes)

Suduiraut (Sauternes)

France: Recommended Wine Producers of Burgundy, Red Wines

Alain Hudelot-Noëllat

Armand Rousseau

Barthod-Noellat

Bernard Dugat

Bernard Morey

Bertrand Ambroise

Bouchard Père et Fils

Bouré Père et Fils

Bourée-Noellat

Bruno Clair

Chanson Père et Fils

Claude Dugat

Claude et Maurice Dugat

Comte de Vougäé

Comte Lafon

Daniel Chopin-Groffier

Daniel Rion

de l'Arlot

Denis Mortet

Domaine d'Auvenay

Domaine de la Romanée-Conti

Domaine des Lambres

Dominique Laurent

Dujac

Faiveley

George et Chistophe Roumier

Georges Roumier

Haegelen-Jayer

Henri Gouges

Henri Jayer

Hospices de Beaune

Hubert Lignier

J. Confuron-Cotetidot

J. F. Coche-Dury

Jacques Prieur

Jean Chauvenet

Jean et J. L. Trapet

Jean Grivot

Jean Gros

Joseph Drouhin

Labouré-Roi

Lecheneaut

Leroy

Louis Jadot

Louis Latour

Louis Trapet

Marquis d'Angerville

Meo-Camuzet

Michel Chevillon

Michel Lafarge

Michel Prunier

Mongeard-Mugneret

Philippe Leclerc

Pierre Gelin

Ponsot

Ramonet

Remoissenet Père et Fils

René Engel

René Leclerc

Robert Arnoux

Robert Chevillon

Robert Groffier

Robert Jayer-Gilles

France: Recommended Wine Producers of Burgundy, White Wines

Albert Grivault

Antonin Rodet

Ballot-Millot et Fils

Bernard Morey

Blain-Gagnard

Bonneau du Martray

Bouchard Père et Fils

Bruno Clair

Château de Meursault

Château de Puligny-Montrachet

Colin-Dé lé ger

Comte Lafon

Domaine d'Auvenay

Domaine de l'Arlot

Domaine de la Romanée-Conti

Domaine des Comtes Lafon

Domaine du Chateau de Puligny-Montrachet

Domaine Leflaive

Etienne Sauzet

Faiveley

Francois et Jean-Marie Raveneau

Francois Jobard

Georges Dé léger

Guy Amiot

Guy Roulot

J. Moreau et Fils

J. F. Coche-Dury

Jacques Prieur

Jacques Thevenot-Machal

Jean Chartron

Jean Dauvissat

Jean-Marc Boillot

Jean-Marc Morey

Jean-Noel Gagnard

Jean-Philippe Fichet

Joseph Drouhin

Laleure-Piot

Larue

Latour-Giraud

Leflaive

Leroy

Louis Carillon

Louis Jadot

Louis Latour

Marc Colin

Marc Morey

Michel Colin-Deleger

Michel Niellon

Michelot-Buisson

Olivier Leflaive Freres

Patrick Javillier

Philippe Testut	René et Vincent Dauvissat
Pierre Boillot	Roger Caillot
Ponsot	Thierry Matrot
Prieur-Brunet	Tollot-Beaut & Fils
Ramonet	Verget
Remi Jobard	Vincent Girardin
Remoissenet Pere et Fils	

France: The Wines of Bordeaux, the 1855 Classification of Great Growths of the Médoc (Grand Cru Classé)

Following is a list of the wines of Bordeaux.

First Growths (Premiers Crus) Château Haut-Brion[1] (Pessac, Graves)

Château Lafite-Rothschild (Pauillac)

Château Latour (Pauillac)

Château Margaux (Margaux)

Château Mouton-Rothschild (Pauillac)

1 This wine, although a Graves, is classified as one of the five First Growths of the Médoc in recognition of outstanding quality.

Second Growths (Deuxièmes Crus)

Château Brane-Cantenac (Cantenac-Margaux)

Château Cos d'Estournel (St.-Estèphe)

Château Ducru-Beaucaillou (St.-Julien)

Château Durfort-Vivens (Cantenac-Margaux)

Château Gruaud-Larose (St.-Julien)

Château Lascombes (Margaux)

Château Léoville-Barton (St.-Julien)

Château Léoville-Las Cases (St.-Julien)

Château Léoville-Poyferré (St.-Julien)

Château Montrose (St.-Estèphe)

Château Pichon-Lalande (Pauillac)

Château Pichon-Longueville-Baron (Pauillac)

Château Rauzan-Gassies (Margaux)

Château Rausan-Ségla (Margaux)

Third Growths (Troisièmes Crus)

Château Boyd-Cantenac (Cantenac-Margaux)

Château Calon-Ségur (St.-Estèphe)

Château Cantenac-Brown (Cantenac-Margaux)

Château d'Issan (Cantenac-Margaux)

Château Desmirail (Margaux)

Château Ferrière (Margaux)

Château Giscours (Labarde-Margaux)

Château Kirwan (Cantenac-Margaux)

Château La Lagune (Ludon)

Château Lagrange (St.-Julien)

Château Langoa-Barton (St.-Julien)

Château Malescot-St.-Exupéry (Margaux)

Château Marquis d'Alesme-Becker (Margaux)

Château Palmer (Cantenac-Margaux)

Fourth Growths (Quatrièmes Crus)

Château Beychevelle (St.-Julien)

Château Branaire (St.-Julien)

Château Duhart-Milon-Rothschild (Pauillac)

Château La Tour-Carnet (St.-Laurent)

Château Lafon-Rochet (St.-Estèphe)

Château Marquis-de-Terme (Margaux)

Château Pouget (Cantenac-Margaux)

Château Prieuré-Lichine (Cantenac-Margaux)

Château St.-Pierre (St.-Julien)

Château Talbot (St.-Julien)

Fifth Growths (Cinquièmes Crus)

Château Batailley (Pauillac)

Château Belgrave (St.-Laurent)

Château Camensac (St.-Laurent)

Château Cantemerle (Macau)

Château Clerc-Milon-Rothschild (Pauillac)

Château Cos Labory (St.-Estèphe)

Château Croizet-Bages (Pauillac)

Château Dauzac-Lynch (Labarde-Margaux)

Château du Tertre (Arsac-Margaux)

Château Grand-Puy-Ducasse (Pauillac)

Château Grand-Puy-Lacoste (Pauillac)

Château Haut-Bages-Libéral (Pauillac)

Château Haut-Batailley (Pauillac)

Château Lynch-Bages (Pauillac)

Château Lynch-Moussas (Pauillac)

Château Mouton-Baronne Pauline (Pauillac) (formerly known as Mouton-Baron Philippe)

Château Pédesclaux (Pauillac)

Château Pontet-Canet (Pauillac)

445

Italy: Recommended Wine Producers of Piedmont

Albino Rocca	Domenico Clerico
Aldo & Ricardo Seghesio	Enrico Scavino
Aldo Conterno	Fontanafredda
Alfiero Boffa	Francesco Rinaldi
Alfredo & Giovanni Roagna	G.D. Vajra
Alfredo Prunotto	Giacomo Ascheri
Angelo Gaja	Giacomo Bologna
Antoniolo	Giacomo Conterno
Armando Parusso	Giovanni Viberti
Azelia	Guiseppe Mascarello
Bartolomeo	Luciano Sandrone
Batasiolo	Manzone
Beni di Batasiolo	Marcarini
Bersano	Marchese di Gresy
Bertelli	Marchesi di Barolo
Bruno Ceretto	Moccagatta
Bruno Giacosa	Paolo Conterno
Cascina Bongiovanni	Paolo Scavino
Ceretto	Pio Cesare
Cerutti	Poderi Rocche Manzoni Valentino
Ciabot Berton	Produttori di Barbaresco
Cigliuti	Punset
Clerico	Renato Corino
Conterno-Fantino	Renato Ratti
Coppo	Roberto Voerzio
Cordero di Montezemolo	Vietti

Italy: Recommended Wine Producers of Tuscany

Altesino

Ambra

Antico Podere Gagliole

Argiano

Azienda Agricola La Torre

Badia a Coltibuono

Barbi

Biondi-Santi

Caparzo

Carpineto

Case Basse

Castell'In Villa

Castellare di Castellina

Castello Banfi

Castello dei Rampolla Sammarco

Castello di Ama

Castello di Gabbiano

Castello di Querceto

Ciacci Piccolomini d'Aragona

Col d'Orcia

Costanti

Dei

Eredi Fuligni

Fattoria di Felsina

Fattoria di Manzano

Fattoria Le Pupille

Felsina Berardenga

Fontodi

Frescobaldi

Il Poggione

Isole e Olena Collezione de Marchi l'Ermo

L. Antinori

Lisini

Melini

Monsanto

Monte Vertine

Nozzole

Ornellaia

P. Antinori

Pertimali

Podere Il Palazzino

Podere Poggio Scalette

Poderi Boscarelli

Poggerino

Poggio Antico

Ruffino

San Felice

San Giusto a Rententano

Selvapiana

Soldera

Tenuta dell'Ornellaia

Villa Cafaggio

Germany: Recommended Wine Producers

Alfred Merkelbach (Mosel)

August Eser (Rheingau)

Christian Karp-Schreiber (Mosel)

Dr. Burklin-Wolf (Pfalz)

Dr. Loosen-St.-Johannishof (Mosel)

Dr. Thanisch (Mosel)

E. Jakoby-Mathy (Mosel)

Egon Müller (Saar)

F. W. Gymnasium (Mosel)

Freiherr von Heddesdorf (Mosel)

Freiherr zu Knyphausen (Rheingau)

Fritz Haag (Mosel)

H. & R. Lingenfelder (Rheinpfalz)

Heribert Kerpen (Mosel)

Immich-Batterieberg (Mosel)

J. F. Kimich (Rheinpfalz)

J. J. Christoffel (Mosel)

J. J. Prüm (Mosel)

Josef Deinhart (Mosel)

Klaus Neckerauer (Rheinpfalz)

Koehler-Ruprecht (Rheingau)

Konigin Victoria Berg-Deinhard (Rheingau)

Kurt Darting (Rheinpfalz)

Mönchhof (Mosel)

Schloss Schönborn (Rheingau)

Selbach-Oster (Mosel)

von Brentano (Rheingau)

von Kesselstatt (Mosel)

von Simmern (Rheingau)

Weingut Karlsmuhle (Mosel)

Willi Schaefer (Mosel)

Spain: Recommended Table Wine Producers

Bodega S. Arroyo

Bodegas Alejandro Fernandez

Bodegas Arzuaga

Bodegas Hnos. Perez Pascuas

Bodegas Ismael Arroyo

Bodegas Muga

Bodegas Reyes

Bodegas y Vinedos Alion

Condado de Haza

Costers del Siurana

CVNE

Domecq

Frederico Paternina

Hacienda Monasterio

Hijos de Antonio Barcelo

Jean Léon

La Rioja Alta

Marqués de Caceres

Marqués de Grinon
Marqués de Murrieta
Marqués de Riscal
Miguel Torres
Montecillo

Pesquera
René Barbier
Rioja Santiago
Senorio de San Vicente
Vega Sicilia

Spain: Recommended Sherry Producers

Emilio Lustau
Gonzalez Byass
Osborne

Pedro Domecq
Sandeman
Vinicola Hidalgo

Portugal: Recommended Porto Producers

Churchill
Cockburn
Croft
Delaforce
Dow
Ferreria
Fonseca
Graham's

Niepoort
Offley
Quinta do Noval
Ramos-Pinto
Sandeman
Smith-Woodhouse
Taylor Fladgate
Warre

Portugal: Recommended Table Wine Producers

Carvalho, Ribeiro, Ferreira
Casal de Valle Pradinhos
Caves do Barrocào
Caves Dom Teodosio
Caves Sao Joào
Caves Velhas
Conde de Santar

Ferreira
J. M. Da Fonseca
Joào Pires
Luis Pato
Porta dos Cavalheiros
Quinta da Cismeira
Quinta da Lagoalva de Cima

Quinta de la Rosa

Quinta do Carmo

Quinta do Confradeiro

Quinta do Cotto

Sogrape

Tuella

Vasconcellos

Australia: Recommended Australian Wine Producers

Allanmere

Barossa Valley Estate

Berry Estates

Bridgewater Mill

Browen Estate

Brown Brothers

Chateau Reynella

Château Tahbilk

Evans Wine Company

Goundrey

Haselgrove

Hungerford

Leasingham

Lindemans

Maglieri

Mildara

Mitchelton

Orlando

Penfolds

Petaluma

Peter Lehmann

Pikes

Plantagenet

Redbank

Rosemount

Rothbury Estate

Scotchmans Hill

Seppelt

Shaw & Smith

St. Hurbert

Taltarni

Tyrells

Wolf Blass

Wyndham Estates

Wynns

Yalumba

Yarra Ridge

Yarra Yering

California, Oregon, and Washington State: Recommended Cabernet Sauvignon Producers

Ariel	Dry Creek
Arrowood	Duckhorn
Atlas Peak	Dunnewood
Beaulieu	Estancia
Benziger	Far Neinte
Beringer	Ferrari-Carano
Boeger	Fetzer
Burgess	Fife
Cain Cellars	Flora Springs
Cakebread	Forrest Glen
Callaway	ForrestVille
Canyon Road	Franciscan
Cardinale	Gallo—Sonoma
Caymus	Geyser Peak
Château Montelena	Glen Ellen
Château Potelle	Gossamer Bay
Clos du Bois	Grace Family
Château Souverain	Guenoc
Château St. Jean	Hacienda Wine Cellars
Clos du Val	Hawk Crest
Columbia Crest	Heitz
Cuvaison	Hess Collection
Dalla Valle	Husch
De Loach	Inglenook
Dehlinger	J. Lohr
Delicato	Joseph Phelps

Justin	Seaview
Kendall-Jackson	Sebastiani
Kenwood	Seven Peaks
Lolonis	Shafer
Louis M. Martini	Shenandoah
Martin Ray	Silverado
Meridian	Simi
Monterey Vineyard	Smith & Hook
Mount Veeder	Spring Mountain
Napa Ridge	St. Supery
Newton	Stag's Leap
Oakford	Staton Hills
Opus One	Steele
Paradigm	Sterling
R.H. Phillips	Stonehedge
Renaissance	Sutter Home
Ridge	Talus
Robert Mondavi	Turning Leaf
Robert Pecota	Van Asperen
Rodney Strong	Vichon
Round Hill	Villa Mt. Eden
S. Anderson	Wente
Sea Ridge	ZD

California, Oregon, and Washington State: Recommended Merlot Producers

Arrowood	Cain Cellars
Benziger	Cakebread
Beringer	Chappellet

Charles Krug	Markham
Château Souverain	Matanzas Creek
Château St. Jean	Neyers
Chateau Ste. Michelle	Niebaum-Coppola
Columbia Crest	Pine Ridge
Cuvaison	Rabbit Ridge
Duckhorn	Robert Keenan
Ferrari-Carano	Robert Mondavi
Freemark Abbey	Robert Pecota
Frog's Leap	Rutherford Hill
Gary Farrel	Seven Hills
Joseph Phelps	St. Francis
Kenwood	Sterling
Leonetti	Swanson
Lockwood	Whitehall Lane

California, Oregon, and Washington State: Recommended Pinot Noir Producers

Acacia	Chalone
Adelsheim	Château Souverain
Au Bon Climat	Conn Valley
Beaulieu	Cuvaison
Beaux Freres	David Bruce
Benziger	De Loach
Bouchaine	Dehlinger
Byron	Domaine Carneros
Calera	Domaine Drouhin
Carneros Creek	Etude
Caymus	Gary Farrell

453

Kendall-Jackson

Marimar Torres

Meridian

Robert Mondavi

Robert Sinskey

Robert Stemmler

Rochioli

Saintsbury

Sanford

Santa Cruz Mountain

Steele

Villa Mt. Eden

Wild Horse

Williams-Selyem

ZD

California, Oregon, and Washington State: Recommended Zinfandel Producers

A. Rafanelli

Beaulieu Vineyard

Benziger

Beringer

Buehler

Caymus

Château Montelena

Château Potelle

Château Souverain

Cline

De Loach

Dry Creek

Ferrari-Carano

Fetzer

Franciscan

Frick

Gallo—Sonoma

Gary Farrell

Green & Red

Grgich Hills

Guenoc

Gundlach-Bundschu

Hidden Cellars

Hop Kiln

Kenwood

Lolonis

Lytton Springs

Niebaum-Coppola

Quivira

Rabbit Ridge

Ravenswood

Ridge

Robert Mondavi

Rombauer

Rosenblum

Seghesio

St. Francis

Sutter Home

Topolos

Turley

Villa Mt. Eden

Wild Horse

California, Oregon, and Washington State: Recommended Chardonnay Producers

Acacia

Arrowood

Au Bon Climat

Bargetto

Beaulieu Vineyard

Benziger

Beringer

Bouchaine

Buehler

Burgess Cellars

Cakebread

Calera

Carmenet

Carneros Creek

Chalk Hill

Chalone

Chappellet

Château Montelena

Château Souverain

Château St. Jean

Château Ste. Michelle

Château Woltner

Clos du Bois

Cronin

Cuvaison

De Loach

Dehlinger

Ferrari-Carano

Flora Springs

Franciscan

Freemark Abby

Gabrielli

Gainey

Gallo—Sonoma

Girard

Gloria Ferrer

Grgich Hills

Guenoc

Hanzell

Hess Collection

Iron Horse

J. Lohr

Joseph Phelps

Kendall-Jackson

Kenwood

Kistler

Landmark	S. Anderson
Matanzas Creek	Saintsbury
Meridian	Sanford
Mirassou	Shafer
Murphy-Goode	Simi
Napa Ridge	Sonoma Cutrer
Newton	Sonoma-Loeb
Pahlmeyer	Stag's Leap Wine Cellars
Peter Michael	Talbott
Qupé	Truchard
Rabbit Ridge	Vichon
Ridge	Villa Mt. Eden
Robert Mondavi	Williams-Selyem
Robert Sinskey	ZD
Rombauer	

California, Oregon, and Washington State: Recommended Sauvignon Blanc Producers

Adler Fels	Château Potelle
Araujo Estate	Château St. Jean
Babcock	De Loach
Benziger	Dry Creek
Beringer	Duckhorn
Bernardus	Ferrari-Carano
Boeger	Fetzer
Cain	Flora Springs
Cakebread	Geyser Peak
Caymus	Grgich Hills
Chalk Hill	Guenoc Winery

Iron Horse

Kendall-Jackson

Kenwood

Markham

Matanzas Creek

Murphy-Goode

Napa Ridge

Navarro

Preston

Quivira

Robert Mondavi

Robert Pepi

Rochioli

Seghesio

Selene

Silverado Vineyards

Simi

Spottswoode

St. Supery

Stag's Leap Wine Cellars

Vichon

California, Oregon, and Washington State: Recommended Sparkling Wine Producers

Codorniu

Culbertson

Domaine Carneros

Domaine Chandon

Domaine Ste. Michelle

Gloria Ferrer

Handley

Iron Horse

Korbel

Maison Deutz

Mirassou

Monticello

Mumm Napa

Piper Sonoma

Roederer Estate

S. Anderson

Schramsberg

Canada: Recommended Wine Producers

Alderlea Vineyards (B.C.—Vancouver Island)

Andrés Wines (B.C.—Fraser Valley)

Andrés Wines (Ontario—The Niagara Peninsula)

Belle Vista Vineyards (B.C.—Okanagan Valley)

Blue Grouse Vineyards (B.C.—Vancouver Island)

Calona Wines (B.C.—Okanagan Valley)

457

Carriage House Wines (B.C.—Okanagan Valley)

Cave Springs Cellars (Ontario—The Niagara Peninsula)

Cedar Creek Estate Winery (B.C.—Okanagan Valley)

Château de Charmes Wines (Ontario—The Niagara Peninsula)

Château Wolff (B.C.—Vancouver Island)

Cherry Point Vineyards (B.C.—Vancouver Island)

Colio Estate Wines (Ontario—Lake Erie North Shore)

Crowsnest Vineyards (B.C.—Simulkameen Valley)

D'Angelo Estate Winery (Ontario—Lake Erie North Shore)

Domaine de Chaberton (B.C.—Fraser Valley)

First Estate Cellars (B.C.—Okanagan Valley)

Gehringer Brothers Estate Winery (B.C.—Okanagan Valley)

Gersighel Wineberg (B.C.—Okanagan Valley)

Golden Mile Cellars (B.C.—Okanagan Valley)

Gray Monk Estate Winery (B.C.—Okanagan Valley)

Hainle Vineyards (B.C.—Okanagan Valley)

Hawthorne Mountain Vineyards (B.C.—Okanagan Valley)

Henry of Pelham Family Estate Winery (Ontario—The Niagara Peninsula)

Herdner Estate Wines (Ontario—The Niagara Peninsula)

Hester Creek Estate Winery (B.C.—Okanagan Valley)

Hillebrand Estates Winery (Ontario—The Niagara Peninsula)

Hillside Cellars (B.C.—Okanagan Valley)

House of Rose Vineyards (B.C.—Okanagan Valley)

Inniskillin Okanagan Vineyards (B.C.—Okanagan Valley)

Inniskillin Wines (Ontario—The Niagara Peninsula)

Jackson Triggs Vintners (B.C.—Okanagan Valley)

Joseph's Estate Wines (Ontario—The Niagara Peninsula)

Kettle Valley Vineyards (B.C.—Okanagan Valley)

Kittling Ridge Estate Wines (Ontario—The Niagara Peninsula)

Lake Breeze Cellars (B.C.—Okanagan Valley)

Lakeview Cellars Estate Winery (Ontario—The Niagara Peninsula)

Lang Vineyards (B.C.—Okanagan Valley)

Larch Hills Winery (B.C.—Okanagan Valley)

Magnotta Cellars (Ontario—The Niagara Peninsula)

Maplegrove Vinoteca Estate Winery (Ontario—The Niagara Peninsula)

Marynissen Estates (Ontario—The Niagara Peninsula)

Mission Hill Wines (B.C.—Okanagan Valley)

Nichol Vineyard (B.C.—Okanagan Valley)

Pelee Island Wine Pavilion (Ontario—Pelee Island)

Pelee Island Winery (Ontario—Lake Erie North Shore)

Pillitteri Estates Winery (Ontario—The Niagara Peninsula)

Pinot Reach Cellars (B.C.—Okanagan Valley)

Poplar Grove (B.C.—Okanagan Valley)

Quails' Gate Estate Winery (B.C.—Okanagan Valley)

Recline Ridge Winery (B.C.—Okanagan Valley)

Red Rooster Winery (B.C.—Okanagan Valley)

Reif Estate Winery (Ontario—The Niagara Peninsula)

Scherzinger Vineyards (B.C.—Okanagan Valley)

Slamka Cellars (B.C.—Okanagan Valley)

St. Hubertus Estate Winery (B.C.—Okanagan Valley)

Stag's Hollow Winery and Vineyard (B.C.—Okanagan Valley)

Stonechurch Vineyards (Ontario—The Niagara Peninsula)

Stoney Ridge Cellars (Ontario—The Niagara Peninsula)

Strewn (Ontario—The Niagara Peninsula)

Sumac Ridge Estate Winery (B.C.—Okanagan Valley)

Summerhill Estate Winery (B.C.—Okanagan Valley)

Sunnybrook Farm Estate Winery (Ontario—The Niagara Peninsula)

Thirty Bench Wines (Ontario—The Niagara Peninsula)

Tinhorn Creek Vineyards (B.C.—Okanagan Valley)

V.P. Cellars Estate Winery (Ontario—The Niagara Peninsula)

Venturi-Schultze Vineyards (B.C.—Vancouver Island)

Vigneti Zamatta Vineyards (B.C.—Vancouver Island)

Vincor-Niagara Cellars (Ontario—The Niagara Peninsula)

Vineland Estates Winery (Ontario—The Niagara Peninsula)

Walters Estates (Ontario—The Niagara Peninsula)

459

The Best-Known Grosslage Wines of Germany

These wines are from the large Grosslage districts; however, they have generic names that appear to be a single vineyard name (einzellage). These wines are mostly simple everyday wines and should be inexpensive. Don't confuse these names with single vineyard names.

Mosel-Saar-Ruwer

Bernkasteler Badstube

Bernkasteler Kurfärstlay

Erdener Schwarzlay

Graacher Munzlay

Krover Nacktarsch

Piesporter Michelsberg

Trierer Romerley

Wiltinger Scharzberg

Zeller Schwarzer Katz

The Nahe

Kreuznacher Kronenberg

Neiderhausener Burgweg

Rudesheimer Rosengarten

Rheingau

Hattenheimer-Deutelsberg

Hochheimer Daubhaus

Johannisberger Erntebringer

Rauenthaler Steinmacher

Rudesheim Burgweg

Rheinhessen

Bingener Sankt-Rochuskapelle

Niersteiner Gutes Domtal

Niersteiner Rehbach

Niersteiner Spiegelberg

Oppenheimmer-Guldenmorgen

Oppenheimer-Krotenbrunnen

Rheinphalz (Palatinate)

Bockenheimer Grafenstuck

Deiderheimer Hofstuck

Durkheimer Hochmess

Foster Mariengarten

Wachenheimer Schenkenbohl

Kosher Wines: Recommended Wine Producers

Following is a list of recommended producers of kosher wines (To learn more about kosher wines, refer to Chapter 24, "Kosher Wine").

White Wines

Chardonnay, Baron Herzog (California)

Chardonnay, Carmel Private Collection (Israel)

Chardonnay, Fortant de France (France)

Chardonnay, Hagafen (California)

Chardonnay, Herzog Selection (France)

Chardonnay Russian River Special Reserve, Baron Herzog (California)

Chardonnay Special Reserve, Hagafen (California)

Chenin Blanc, Baron Herzog (California)

Gavi, Bartenura (Italy)

Johannisberg Riesling, Hagafen (California)

Johannisberg Riesling Late Harvest, Baron Herzog (California)

Macon-Villages, Bokobsa (France)

Minervois Blanc, Chateau La Reze (France)

Moscato d'Asti (5.5% Alc.), Rashi (Italy)

Pinot Grigio, Bartenura (Italy)

Rose d'Anjou, Remy Pannier (France)

Sauvignon Blanc, Golan (Israel)

Sauvignon Blanc, Weinstock (California)

White Merlot, Abarbanel (France)

White Zinfandel, Baron Herzog (California)

White Zinfandel, Carmel (Israel)

Red Wines

Barbera d'Asti, Barteanura (Italy)

Bordeaux, De La Grave (France)

Bordeaux, La Plaisance de Lafite Montell (France)

Cabernet Franc, Hagafen (California)

Cabernet Sauvignon, Baron Herzog (California)

Cabernet Sauvignon Special Edition, Baron Herzog (California)

Cabernet Sauvignon Special Reserve Alexander Valley, Baron Herzog (California)

Cabernet Sauvignon Special Reserve Napa Valley, Baron Herzog (California)

Cabernet Sauvignon, Abarbanel (France)

Cabernet Sauvignon, Carmel (Israel)

Cabernet Sauvignon, Hagafen (California)

Cabernet Sauvignon, JP Chenet (France)

Chianti Classico, Bartenura (Italy)

461

Chinon, Moulin des Sablons (France)

Emerald Hill Cabernet, Gamla (Israel)

Gamay, Baron Herzog (California)

Merlot, Baron Herzog (France—Bordeaux)

Merlot, Carmel (Israel)

Merlot, Herzog Selection (France)

Merlot, JP Chenet (France)

Minervois, Chateau de Paraza (France)

Minervois, Chateau La Reze (France)

Pinot Noir, Hagafen (California)

Shiraz, Carmel (Israel)

Syrah, Abarbanel (France)

Valflore, Herzog Selection (France)

Zinfandel, Baron Herzog (California)

Sparkling Wines

Asti Spumante, Bartenura (Italy)

Asti Spumante (7.5% Alc.), Rashi (Italy)

Blanc de Blancs, Bartenura (Italy)

Brut, Baron Herzog (California)

Cremant d'Alsace, Abarbanel (France)

Cremant d'Alsace, Royale (France)

Star of Abraham (New York)

Organic Wines: Recommended Wines

Badger Mountain Cabernet Franc (Washington)

Badger Mountain Chardonnay (Washington)

Badger Mountain Johannisberg Riesliing (Washington)

Bernard Delmas Blanquette de Limoux NV (France)

Casina di Cornia "Amaranto" Cabernet Sauvignon (Italy)

Casina di Cornia Chianti Classico (Italy)

Casina di Cornia Chianti Classico Riserva (Italy)

Chateau Bousquette St. Chinian Rouge (France)

Chateau de Boisfranc Beaujolais (France)

Chateau Méric Graves Blanc (France)

Chateau Méric Graves Rouge (France)

Chateau Veronique Coteaux de Languedoc (France)

Domaine de Picheral Vin de Pays d'Oc Merlot (France)

Domaine Delmas Chardonnay (France)

Domaine des Cèdres Cotes du Rhone (France)

Domaine du Bourdieu Entre-Deux-Mers (France)

Domaine La Batteuse Chardonnay 1998 Vin de Pays d'Oc (France)

Domaine Pierre André Chateauneuf du Pape (France)

Domaine St. Anne Bordeaux Blanc (France)

Domaine St. Anne Bordeaux Rouge (France)

Frey Vineyards Cabernet Sauvignon (California)

Frey Vineyards Chardonnay (California)

Frey Vineyards Merlot (California)

Frey Vineyards Pitite Sirah (California)

Frey Vineyards Sauvignon Blanc (California)

Guy Bossard Cabernet Franc de Bretagne (France)

Guy Bossard Methode Champenoise NV Brut (France)

Guy Bossard Muscadet Sèvre et Maine sur lie (France)

Guy Chaumont Bourgogne Chardonnay (France)

Guy Chaumont Bourgogne Pinot Noir (France)

Jacques Frelin Cotes du Rhone (France)

Jacques Frelin Crozes-Hermitage 1997 (France)

Jacques Frelin Vin de Pays d'Oc Rouge (France)

Kawarau Estate Sauvignon Blanc (New Zealand)

La Rocca Vineyards Cabernet Sauvignon (California)

La Rocca Vineyards Merlot (California)

La Rocca Vineyards Zinfandel (California)

Les Romarins Cotes du Ventoux (France)

Mario Torelli Moscato d'Asti "San Grod" (5% alc.) (Italy)

Mas Coutelou Vin de Pays d'Oc Syrah (France)

Nevada County Wine Guild Chardonnay (California)

Nevada County Wine Guild Merlot (California)

Nouva Cappelletta Barbera del Monferrato (Italy)

Nouva Cappelletta Barbera "Minola" del Monferrato (Italy)

Nouva Cappelletta Grignolino del Monferrato Casalese (Italy)

Nouva Cappelletta Piemonte Chardonnay (Italy)

Octopus Mountain Cellars Chardonnay (California)

Orleans Hill White Zinfandel (California)

Orleans Hill Zinfandel (California)

San Vito Chianti (Italy)

San Vito Chianti DOCG (Italy)

Serge Faust Carte d'Or NV Brut Champagne (France)

Serge Faust Cuvée Reserve NV Brut Champagne (France)

Terres Blanches Aix-en-Provence Les Baux Rouge (France)

Terres Blanches Aix-en-Provence Rosé (France)

Wine Words

acidic   A description of wine with a total acidity that is so high it imparts a sharp feel or sour taste in the mouth.

acidity   The nonvolatile acids in a wine, principally tartaric, malic, and citric. These acids provide a sense of freshness and an impression of balance to a wine. Excessive acidity provides a sharp or sour taste; too little results in a flat or flabby character.

aftertaste   The impression of a wine after it is swallowed. It is usually described as the "finish" of a wine. It ranges from short to lingering. A lingering aftertaste is a characteristic indicator of quality.

aged   Describes a wine that has been cellared either in cask or bottle long enough to have developed or improved. As a tasting term, it describes the characteristic scent and taste of a wine that has so developed while in its bottle.

American Viticultural Area (AVA)   Official place-name designation for American vintners.

Amontillado (aw-MOHN-tee-YAW-doh)   A dry Sherry of the fino type, but darker, fuller, with a nutty flavor.

Année (aw-NAY)   Vintage.

Apéritif (aw-PEH-ri-TEEF)   A dry before-dinner beverage.

Appellation d'Origine Côntrolée or AOC or AC (aw-peh-law-see-OHN daw-ree-ZHEEN caw-troh-LAY)   The top category in the official French system of quality assurance. It means "Appellation of Controlled Origin."

aroma   The basic olfactory elements present in a wine, generally the fruity smell characteristic of the varietal.

Asti   Town in the Piedmont region of Italy, famed for sweet, sparkling Spumante.

astringent   A puckering, tactile sensation imparted to the wine by its tannins. A puckering quality adds to the total sense of the wine, giving it a sense of structure, style, and vitality. Tannins are an essential component in red wines, which are made to improve with age while in the bottle. Red wines lacking in tannins are generally dull and uninteresting. Wines vinified for prolonged aging are harshly tannic when young, but mellow when the wines age and the tannins precipitate to form a sediment in the bottle.

Auslese (OWSS-lay-zeh)   Literally, "picked out" (for example, selected). Under the new German wine law, Auslese wine is subject to all regulations included in Qualitätswein mit Prädikat (quality wine with special attributes). Auslese wine is made entirely from selected, fully ripe grapes, with all unripe and diseased grapes removed. No sugar may be added. The wine is especially full, rich, and somewhat sweet.

balance   The proportion of the various elements of a wine: acid against sweetness, fruit flavors against wood, and tannic alcohol against acid and flavor.

balthazar   Large bottle, equal to 16 standard bottles or 12 liters.

Barbera (bar-BARE-aw)   Red wine grape grown in northern Italy and parts of California.

barrel-fermented   The fermentation of a wine in a small oak cask as opposed to a large tank or vat.

Beaujolais (BOW-zhoh-lay)   An early-maturing red wine from the southern Burgundy district in France.

Beaune (bohn)   Small medieval city in Côte d'Or, headquarters of French Burgundy wine trade.

Beerenauslese (BEAR-en-OWSS-lay-zeh)   "Berry-selected," for example, individual grape berries picked out (by order of ripeness) at harvest for their sugar content, quality, and the amount of Edelfaule (noble rot).

Bereich (beh-RYSH)   A geographic region for German wine classification.

blanc (blawk)   French for "white."

Blanc de Blancs (blawk-duh-BLAWK)   Describes a white wine made from white grapes. The term refers to both still table and sparkling wines. The words "Blanc de Blancs" do not signify a quality better than other white wines.

Blanc de Noir (blawk-duh-NWAWR)   White wine made from black (red) grapes. Champagne made 100 percent from Pinot Noir grapes.

blanco (BLAWN-koh)   Italian for "white."

Blauburgunder (BLOU-BOOR-goon-dehr)   German for the Pinot Noir grape.

bodega   In the Spanish wine trade, a wine house, wine company, wine cellar, or even wine shop.

body   The tactile impression of fullness on the palate caused by the alcohol, glycerin, and residual sugar in a wine. The extremes of "body" are full and thin.

Bordeaux (bor-DOH)   Important seaport city in southwestern France, where the Garonne River empties into the Gironde estuary. The heart of the Bordeaux wine-growing region. Many wine dealers are located there.

Botrytis cinerea   A species of mold that attacks grapes grown in moist conditions. It is undesirable for most grape varieties, or when it infects a vineyard prior to the grapes reaching full maturity. Vineyards are treated to prevent its occurrence. When it attacks fully mature grapes, it causes them to shrivel, concentrating both the acidity and the sugar, and resulting in an intensified flavor and a desired sweetness balanced by acidity. This is beneficial and highly desirable for white varieties such as the Johannisberg Riesling, Sauvignon Blanc, Semillon, and Chenin Blanc, from which unctuous, luscious, and complex white wines are made in various wine regions of the world.

bouquet   The scent of a mature wine, the complex mix of smells developed through fermentation and aging.

Bourgogne (boor-GOH-nyeh)   French for Burgundy, the region or its wine.

breed   A term used to describe the loveliest, most harmonious, and refined wines that achieve what is called "classical proportions." The term is elusive to definition, but wines that deserve such acclaim are unmistakable when encountered.

Brix   Specific gravity method used in the U.S. to ascertain the sugar content of grape must. Named for German chemist Adolf Brix.

Brut (broot)   French for "raw, unrefined." Applied to driest Champagnes.

Bureau of Alcohol, Tobacco, and Firearms (BATF)   Part of the U.S. Treasury Department responsible for setting and enforcing labeling standards for alcoholic beverages, including wine.

Burgundy   Region in eastern France. Several wine districts growing red and white wines, some renowned and expensive. Applies to any wine from that region or, generically, to many red wines.

Cabernet Franc (KAB-air-nay FRAWK)   Fine red grape varietal, grown widely in the Bordeaux region of France.

Cabernet Sauvignon (KAB-air-nay SOH-vinn-yawn)   Premium red grape grown widely in the finest wine regions of Bordeaux.

cask   Cylindrical vessel of wood or stainless steel in which wine is fermented or aged. Ranges in size from 135 to 2,475 liters, depending on country and locale.

centrifuge   Modern machine that uses forces generated by rotation to separate wine from its solid impurities.

Chablis (shaw-BLEE)   Small town in the north of the Burgundy region. A source of fine, rare white wine. Used generically to describe lesser white wines.

chai (shay)   Above-ground winemaking and storage facility at French wine estates.

Champagne   Sparkling wine from a small, controlled region in eastern France, south of Reims. In the U.S. some sparkling wines are called "champagne."

chaptalization (shawp-TAW-lee-ZHAW-see-ohn)   The addition of sugar to the must to increase alcohol formation through fermentation.

Chardonnay (SHAR-doh-nay)   White wine grape used in finest white wines from Burgundy and elsewhere throughout the world.

charmat process   Also called "bulk process." Hastens second fermentation process for creating sparkling wines in large, pressurized tanks.

Château   French for "castle." A French wine estate or the wine itself. Plural, châteaux.

Chianti (kee-YAWN-tee)   Famous red wine of the Tuscany region of Italy.

claret   Generic term used by the English to denote light red wines in the Bordeaux style.

classico (KLAW-see-koh)   Italian for "classic." Smaller defined areas within a designated wine region of Italy.

Cliquot (klee-KOH)   Madame Cliquot was a wine merchant's widow in early nineteenth-century France who developed and promoted the local Champagnes. Her cellar master developed the modern Champagne cork.

clone   A grape variety developed through cutting or grafting to create new characteristics.

cooperage   Wooden barrels and tanks used for aging wines.

corkiness   Wine fault caused by a faulty cork. Odor that suggests putrefaction.

Côte de Beaune (koht-deh-BOHN)   Southern half of Burgundy's Côte d'Or, home to noble red and white wines.

Côte de Nuits (koht-deh-NWEE)   Northern half of Burgundy's Côte d'Or, source of superb red wines based on Pinot Noir.

cotto (KOT-toh)   Italian for "cooked." The process of adding caramelized must to some Marsala wines.

cru (kroo)   French for "growth." Applied to a vineyard and the wine it produces.

Cru Bourgeois   Refers to red Bordeaux wines from the Haut-Médoc that rank just below the Grande Cru Classé wines of the 1855 Bordeaux classification.

Cru Classé   "Classified growth." Refers to those wines originally classified as Grand Cru Classé in the 1855 Bordeaux classification.

crush   Commonly used to refer to the grape harvest or vintage. Most specifically the breaking of the grape stems, which begins a fermentation process.

crust   Sediment deposited on insides of bottles as wines age. Generally applied to old Ports.

cuve   A large vat, usually made of wood, used for the fermentation of grape juice into wine.

cuvée   The contents of a wine vat. More loosely used to refer to all the wine made at one time or under similar conditions. Sometimes a specific pressing or batch of wine. Sometimes used as part of a brand name or trademark, or as wine; label nomenclature to refer to a batch of wine.

decant   To transfer wine from one container to another.

dégorgement   Process of removing sediment from second bottle fermentation of Champagne.

Denominacion de Origin Calificada, DOCa (day-noh-mee-nawth-YOHN deh oh-REE-hen kaw-lee-fee-KAW-daw)   Highest designation used in labeling Spanish wines.

Denominazione di Origine Controllata, DOC (deh-NOH-mee-naw-tsee-OH-neh dee oh-REE-jee-nee kon-troh-LAW-taw)   Controlled denomination of origin, the Italian law for specifying place names for wines.

Denominazione di Origine Controllata e Garantita, DOCG (deh-NOH-mee-naw-tsee-OH-neh dee oh-REE-jee-nee kon-troh-LAW-taw eh gaw-ren-TEE-taw)   Italian quality designation above DOC.

Dom Pérignon   Monk at Reims who developed controlled process for making Champagne in the early eighteenth century.

domaine   The French term applied to wine estates in Burgundy.

dosage (doh-SAWZH)   A small amount of sugar, Champagne, and brandy that is added to Champagne right after dégorgement. The final sweetness of the wine is determined by this step.

doux (doo)   French for "sweet." Applied to the sweetest Champagnes.

Einzellage (EYN-tsel-law-geh)   Under German wine law, an individual vineyard or estate.

469

Eiswein (EYSS-veyn)   Intensely sweet and rich German wine made from frozen Beerenauslese harvest, where freezing concentrates the must. Rarely made.

éleveur (eh-leh-VEHR)   A wine firm that cares for wines in its barrels and bottles them, frequently blending to provide better structure and balance. Often this firm is also a négociant or shipper.

estate-bottled   A wine that has been bottled at the vineyard or winery in which it was made. Has legal significance in several countries, particularly France, Germany, and Italy, but is not controlled in others. Basically it connotes wine that was under the control of the winemaker from vineyard to bottle. It does not ensure the excellence of a wine, although it once did, as a general rule, many years ago.

fass (fuss)   German for "oaken barrel" or "cask."

fermentation   The process of converting sugar into alcohol, usually by the action of yeast on the juice of fruit, such as grapes. It is a complex process in which the yeast produces enzymes that convert the sugar into alcohol, carbon dioxide, and heat.

fiasco (FYAH-skoh)   Old style of Italian wine bottle, bulbous and covered with woven straw.

finesse   A quality of elegance that separates a fine wine from a wine that is simply good. It is a harmony of flavors and components rarely found in wine. The term is hard to define, but a wine with finesse is unmistakable when encountered.

fining   A clarifying technique that introduces an electrolytic agent, such as egg white, powdered milk, blood, diatomaceous earth (bentonite), or gelatin, to attract the solids and settle them to the bottom of a cask. Beaten egg whites or bentonite are the most frequently used agents.

finish   The aftertaste of a wine when it has been swallowed. Usually consists of both flavor and tactile sensations from the acidity, alcohol, and tannins of the wine.

fino (FEE-noh)   Spanish for "fine." The palest and driest Sherry.

flor   A film of yeast or bacteria, usually in the cask on top of a wine, but also found in unhygienically bottled wines. In Spain, it is a specific yeast that grows in Jerez and imparts a delicate, nutty quality to its wines. When Sherry is affected by this yeast, called *Saccharomyces fermentati*, it is called *fino*.

fortified   A wine to which alcohol has been added to raise its alcoholic strength. These wines usually range from 15 to 21 percent alcohol.

free-run juice   The juice that is released from the grape as it is being crushed, before the pulp and skins are pressed. This juice, generally less harsh than press wine, is used for the finest wines. Free-run accounts for about 60 percent of the juice available from the grapes for fine wine. This juice is separated immediately from the skins for white wine but is combined with the skins and pulp for reds. It is drained off the solids prior to the pressing of the remaining grape material.

French oak   The wood from the great oak forests of France, particularly from Nevers and Limousin, which impart a distinctive and mellow character to wine aged in barrels made from them. Also used as a term to describe the flavor imparted to wine by barrels made from this oak.

Fuder (FOO-d'r)   Large German barrel, usually 1,000 liters.

Gamay (GAH-may)   Red wine grape grown extensively in the Beaujolais district of France.

generic wine   A broadly used wine term signifying a wine type, as opposed to a more specific name, such as a grape variety or the actual region of production. Such names have frequently been employed on American wines using famous European place-names such as Chablis, Burgundy, Rhine, Champagne, or European wine types such as claret or Sherry.

Gewu[um]rztraminer (guh-VERTS-trah-mee-ner)   White-wine grape grown in Germany, Alsace, France, and elsewhere. The name means "spicy Traminer."

Gironde (zhee-ROHND)   Large estuary emptying into the Atlantic. The finest wine districts of Bordeaux lie along its western bank.

Goût de Terroir (GOO deh ter-WAH)   The specific taste characteristic imparted from the soil of a particular wine district.

Goût de Vieux (GOO deh VYOO)   The distinctive taste of an old wine.

Grand Cru (graw KROO)   "Great growth." A classification of French wines considered to be superior in quality. Used in Bordeaux, Burgundy, and Alsace.

gravelly   Term that describes wine with a clean, earthy taste.

Graves (grawv)   District in France's Bordeaux region, a source of superb red wines. The name means "gravel," after the soil type.

Grenache (greh-NAWSH)   A sweet pink grape used as a blend in France, Spain, and California.

Grosslage (GROHSS-law-geh)   Under German wine law, a region intermediate between the large Bereich and the vineyard-sized Einzellage.

halbtrocken (hawlp-TRAWK-en)   German for "half-dry" or "Semisweet."

Haut-Médoc (OH may-DAWK)   Wine region of Bordeaux responsible for its best wines.

hock   Older generic English word denoting German white wines.

hybrids   New grape varieties genetically produced from two or more different varieties—usually defined as varieties from different species, although the term is loosely used to include vines "crossed" within the same species.

hydrogen sulfide   A chemical compound that is a natural by-product of fermentation and imparts the smell of rotten eggs. With proper handling, it dissipates prior to the finishing of a wine but remains in poorly handled wines.

Jerez (hayr-ETH)   Spanish city, the wines of which have been called Sherry for hundreds of years.

jeroboam   A large wine bottle. In Champagne, four standard bottles (3 liters). In Bordeaux, six standard bottles (4.5 liters).

jug wines   Refers to inexpensive, everyday drinking wines, usually bottled in large bottles known as *jug bottles*. Most wines in this category are generics, but occasionally varietals also appear in jug bottles.

Kabinett (kaw-bee-NET)   A legally defined quality level of German wines that is governed by the German government. Kabinett wines are the lowest rank of Qualitätswein mit Prädikat wines, stringently defined as to geographical region of origin, natural sugar content, and other attributes.

Keller   German for "wine cellar."

kosher wine   Any wine made under strict rabbinical supervision, suitable for Jewish observance.

lambrusca   Grape species, *Vitis lambrusca*, native to North America. Generally not suitable for making fine wines.

Landwein (LAWNT-veyn)   German for "regional wine."

late-harvest   A type of wine made from overripe grapes with a high sugar content. Generally, late-harvest wines have been made from grapes deliberately left on the vine to achieve high sugars and concentrated flavors. White wine grapes are frequently affected by *Botrytis cinerea*, the noble mold, which further concentrates the grape and imparts its own unique, honeyed character. Most late-harvest wines are unctuously sweet, luscious in flavor, and are meant to be drunk with dessert or by themselves rather than with a meal.

lees   The sediment that results from clarifying a wine following fermentation in casks or tanks after separation from the skins and pulps. Usually consists of dead yeast cells and proteins. Wines are left on their lees to gain character and complexity; improper procedures can result in wines with unattractive flavors.

legs   The "tears," or streams of wine, that cling to the glass after a wine is swirled. Legs are usually a sign of a wine with body and quality and are caused by the differences in evaporation rates of alcohol and other liquids in the wine.

Liebfraumilch (LEEP-frouw-meelsh)   Literally, "Milk of the Blessed Virgin." A trade name for a blend of white wines, widely exported.

Limousin (lee-moo-ZAN)   The great white oak of the Limoges Forest in France, which is considered to be among the finest oak for aging wines and brandies. It imparts a mellow, complex vanilla character, with subtle nuances particular to its species that add complexity and elegance to a wine aged in casks made from it.

Loire (lwawr)   Major river in France. Wines, red and white, of all qualities are grown along this large wine region.

Maceration Carbonique   The whole-berry, intercellular fermentation by bacterial, rather than yeast, action on the grapes in an airtight container. Imparts a fresh, fruity, jam-like quality to wines so treated, which are light in body and meant to be consumed when young.

Madeira   Portuguese island in the Atlantic, off the coast of Morocco, long-time origin of famous fortified wines.

maderized   A wine that has lost its freshness or has spoiled due to oxidation in the bottle, either from storage in an excessively warm area or simply because of overaging. Maderized wines tend to smell like the wines from Madeira, hence the term. They have a sharp yet sweet caramelized character that is not attractive. Maderized white wines darken in color to amber or brown.

magnum   A large wine bottle, equivalent to two standard bottles.

Maître de Chai (MAY-truh duh SHAY)   In France, a winery's cellar master, who is charged with tending the maturing casks of wine. Frequently he or she is also the winemaker. This position is the most important in a winery.

Malbec (MAL-bek)   Red wine grape grown extensively in Bordeaux.

malolactic fermentation   The secondary fermentation that occurs in some wines due to the action of certain bacteria on the wine that transform the hard malic acid to softer lactic acid. It also imparts new subtle flavors that, depending on the wine type, may or may not be wanted. It is usually undesirable in white wines, which require malic acid for freshness.

Margaux (mar-GOH)   Bordeaux district along Gironde that produces superb wines.

Marsala   Famous fortified wine of Italy, from the Island of Sicily.

Médoc (meh-DAWK)   The heart of France's world-famous Bordeaux wine region.

mercaptans (mer-KAP-tens)   Odorous compounds resulting from hydrogen sulfide, indicating faulty winemaking or storage.

Merlot (mehr-LOH)   Famous red grape variety grown in many parts of France's Bordeaux region and elsewhere throughout the world.

Méthode Champenoise   The traditional method of making sparkling wine and the only one permitted in the French district of Champagne where it was invented. It is the most labor-intensive and costly way to produce sparkling wine but also imparts a character and refinement not obtainable with other methods, particularly with regard

473

to the quality of the bubbles produced. A shortcut to the Méthode Champenoise is called the *transfer process*, which eliminates the riddling and dègorgement steps, which are the most costly and time-consuming and produce wines that are sometimes indistinguishable from the more complicated method.

Meursault (mehr-SOH)   Region of France famous for its white wines.

mevushal (MEH-voo-shawl)   A term applied to wine that's kosher by reason of having been pasteurized.

middle body   The part of the taste sensation that is experienced after the initial taste impact on the palate. It provides the core of the taste on which assessments are usually based. The first, or entry, taste and finish should both be in harmony with the middle body. A wine with a weak middle body generally gives the impression of being incomplete.

Mis en Bouteilles Sur Lie (MEEZ ahn boo-TEH-yah soor LEE)   "Put in bottles on its lees," the practice of bottling a wine directly from the barrel, immediately after fermentation without racking. The wine (almost always white) retains a fresh, lively quality, often with a slight petillance due to carbon dioxide absorbed during fermentation that had not completely dissipated when bottled. "Sur lie" wines often experience a malolactic fermentation in the bottle, which also contributes to the petillance or "coming alive" in the bottle in the year after bottling.

Mosel-Saar-Ruwer (MOH-zl zawr ROO-vehr)   German winegrowing region just west of the Rhine regions.

mousseux (moo-SUHR)   French term that means "foamy," applied to sparkling wines that aren't Champagne.

mouthfeel   Wine textures, apart from taste, detected in the mouth.

Mu[m]ller-Thurgau (MUH-lerr TOOR-gouw)   A Riesling-Silvaner hybrid that is the most widely grown grape in Germany. It's planted elsewhere throughout the world.

Muscadet (mis-kaw-DEY)   A popular, light, dry wine from France's Loire Valley.

Muscatel   Any wine made from the Muscat grape. In California, the term is applied to certain fortified wines of low quality.

must   The unfermented grape juice produced by crushing the grapes. It is a loosely defined word and equally defines grape juice, crushed grapes, or the juice after pressing.

must weight   The number of grams above 1,000 of a liter of grape juice; a reliable indicator of sugar content because sugar is denser than water.

nebuchadnezzar   The largest Champagne bottle, rarely used, containing 20 standard bottles (15 liters).

Négociant (nay-goh-SYAWN)   The person who sells or ships wine as a wholesaler.

nero (NAY-roh)   Italian for "black." Any red grape variety.

noble rot   Common term for the fungi of genus *Botrytis* that infect grape skins, sometimes contributing to the complexity of a finished wine.

nutty   A wine flavor attribute, generally associated with Sherry or tawny Port.

oaky   A wine flavor attribute that is toasty and reminiscent of vanilla.

Oechsle (ERKS-leh)   A scale used in Germany and Switzerland for ascertaining sugar from must weight.

oenology   The study of wine. (Sometimes spelled *enology*.)

oenophile   A wine lover. (Also, *enophile*.)

Oporto   Portuguese city famed for shipping Porto (formerly Port) wines.

Organic Grapes into Wine Alliance, OGWA   An association of U.S. organic growers and vintners.

overripe   Wines with more sugar, less acidity, because of extended ripening. If out of balance, may be a wine fault.

oxidation   The process of oxygen from the air combining with some wine compounds to form new compounds, which usually detract from the wine's quality. Oxidized wine is said to be *maderized*.

Pauillac (Poh-YAK)   Bordeaux district along Gironde that produces superb wines.

phenolic compounds   Compounds occurring naturally in skins, seeds, and oak barrels, which contribute astringency, flavor, and color to wine.

Pinot Blanc (PEE-noh Blawk)   A white wine grape that is part of the Pinot family, distinct from the Chardonnay.

Pinot Gris (PEE-noh GREE)   Grey-colored member of the Pinot family of wine grapes.

Pinot Noir (PEE-noh NWAH)   The most important red grape of France's Burgundy region.

plonk   Any wine so lacking in character and quality as to render it unsuitable for any reader of this book.

Pouilly-Fuissé (poo-YEE fwee-SAY)   Distinguished white whine from southern Burgundy region.

Prüfungsnummer (PREE-foongz-noo-mer)   Registration number appearing on German wine labels, indicating the wine has been inspected and certified.

Qualitätswein (kwaw-li-TAYTS-veyn)   Literally "quality wine," which, under the German wine law, is one grade above Tafelwein ("table wine") and one grade below Qualitätswein mit Prädikat (quality wine with special attributes). Quality wine must come from a single district, and among other qualifications, must be of a minimum alcoholic strength.

racking   The traditional way of clarifying a wine by transferring it from one cask to another and leaving the precipitated solids behind.

raisiny   A wine flavor attribute suggesting raisins, characteristic of late-harvest wines.

rehoboam   A Champagne bottle containing six standard bottles (4.5 liters).

reserva (ray-ZEHR-vah)   Spanish quality designation for good wines that have met aging requirements.

residual sugar   The unfermented sugar remaining in a wine. It is usually described in terms of the percentage by weight and is detectable when it exceeds 0.75 percent. Above 2 percent tastes quite sweet.

Retsina (ray-TSEE-nah)   Greek wine made in ancient manner, with added pine-tree resins.

Rheingau (REYN-gouw)   One of Germany's finest wine regions, planted widely in the Riesling grape.

Rheinhessen (REYNN-hess-en)   Germany's largest wine region.

Riesling (REEZ-ling)   Germany's most distinguished grape, producing that country's greatest white wines. Grown widely elsewhere.

Rioja (ree-OH-hah)   Red wine from a designated region in the north of Spain.

Riserva (ree-ZEHR-vah)   Italian for "reserve," applied to DOC and DOCa wines that have been aged.

robe   The color of a wine in general and, more specifically, the wine's color when the glass is tipped at an angle.

Rosé (roh-ZEY)   French for "pink." Applied to wines lightly colored.

Rosso (RAWS-soh)   Italian for "red," applied to red wines made from approved varietals.

Rotwein (ROHT-veyn)   German for "red wine."

Saint-Estèphe   Bordeaux district along Gironde that produces superb wines.

Saint-Julien   Bordeaux district along Gironde that produces superb wines.

salmanazar   Large Champagne bottle, 12 standard bottles (9 liters).

Sauternes (soh-TEHRN)   A Bordeaux appellation from which come some of the world's greatest sweet white wines.

Sauvignon Blanc (SOH-veen-yawn Blawn)   White wine grape widely cultivated in France and California.

Schloss (shlohss)   German for "castle." A wine estate.

sec   French; literally means "dry," and a dry wine. Its use is not legally defined, and it frequently appears on wine labels of wines that are off-dry or even somewhat sweet.

seco (SEH-koh)   Spanish for "dry."

sediment   The deposit precipitated by a wine that has aged in the bottle.

Sekt (Zekt)   German sparkling wine.

Semillon (seh-mee-YOHN)   White wine grape planted around the world.

Sherry   A fortified wine made in the Jerez DO of Spain.

Shiraz   Australian name for the Syrah grape.

Silvaner   White wine grape once the most prevalent in Germany. (Also spelled *Sylvaner*.)

solera (soh-LEH-rah)   The traditional Spanish blending system used in making Sherry. The solera itself is a series of Sherry casks containing wines of various ages that are fractionally blended by transferring part of the contents of a younger cask into an older one.

sommelier (soh-meh-lee-EH)   Wine steward.

sparkling   A wine that, under pressure, has absorbed sufficient carbon dioxide to bubble, or "sparkle" when poured into a glass.

Spatburgunder (SHPAYT-boor-GOON-der)   German name for Pinot Noir.

Spätlese   In German nomenclature, a wine made from fully ripe grapes.

Spumante   Refers to Italian sparkling wines.

still wine   Any wine that has no bubbles.

sulfites   A class of compounds created from sulfurous acid, the result of contact with sulfur dioxide gas, which is used widely in winegrowing and winemaking. Some individuals may be sensitive to these compounds.

sur lie (soor LEE)   French term applied to wines aged "on the lees." Believed to add complexity.

Süss (Zeess)   German for "sweet."

Syrah   The red grape favored in France's Rhône region. In Australia, called *Shiraz*.

Tafelwein (TAH-fel-veyn)   German for "table wine."

tannin   An astringent acid, derived from the skins, seeds, and wooden casks, that causes a puckering sensation in the mouth. Tannin is an essential preservative for quality wines. A moderate puckering sensation caused by the tannins adds to the pleasurable character of a red wine.

tawny   The dark, oxidized color characteristic of aged Port wine.

terroir (tehr-WAHR)   French term referring to the unique combination of soils and microclimate that distinguish one fine wine from another.

tinto (TEEN-toh)   Spanish word meaning "red" when applied to wine.

Tokay (toh-KAY)   The great, sweet white wine from Hungary.

tonneau   A Bordeaux measure of wine equivalent to four barrel or 100 cases of wine.

transfer process   A shortcut method of making bottle-fermented champagne. In this process, the wine is filtered rather than riddled and disgorged.

trocken   German word for "dry."

Trockenbeerenauslese   The highest Prädikat a German wine can carry. It signifies that the wine is made entirely from late-picked, individually selected grape berries that have been allowed to shrivel on the vine, usually after being attacked by the *Botrytis cinerea*, the noble rot, which imparts a special quality to the finished wine.

ullage (oo-LEEZH)   The empty space at the tops of bottles and casks, sometimes applied to loss of liquid through faulty storage or container.

unfiltered   A wine that has been bottled without being clarified or stabilized by filtration. When bottled without any cellar treatment, such a wine is labeled as "Unfiltered and Unfined."

unfined   A wine that has not been fined as part of its cellar treatment. Also implies that the wine has not been filtered and has received a minimum of treatment.

varietal   Refers either to a wine named after a grape variety or one that is made entirely from a single grape variety. As legally defined, such a wine need be made only from 75 percent of the named grape.

varietal character   The recognizable flavor and structure of a wine made from a particular variety of grape.

vin (van)   French for "wine."

Vin Délimité de Qualité Supérieure, VDQS (VAN dee-lee-mee-TAY deh kaw-lee-TAY soo-pehr-YOOR)   Delimited wine of superior quality, the French quality classification just below AOC.

vinho (VEE-nyoo)   Portuguese for "wine."

vinifera, Vitis vinifera   The species of grape varieties known as "the wine bearers," which are responsible for all the finer wines of the world.

vinify   To turn grapes into wine.

vino (VEE-noh)   Italian for "wine."

vinosity   The characteristic flavor of a wine as a result of fermented grape juice. It is distinct from any other flavors such as those of the unfermented grape, oak cask, or other flavor components.

viticultural area   A delimited region in which common geographic or climatic attributes contribute to the definable characteristic of a wine. Although it is called by different names in various countries, it is usually referred to as an *Appellation of Origin*. In the United States, such an appellation is called a *viticultural area* and is defined by geography alone, as opposed to requirements regulating the varieties of grapes grown, yield, or nature of wine produced.

viticulture   Grape-growing, particularly for wine.

Vitis vinifera   The species of grape that accounts for all the world's best wines. Indigenous to central Asia and Europe.

volatile acid   The acid component of a wine that can be detected in the aroma. In wine this is acetic acid, the acid of vinegar. It is always present in wine, usually undetectable or at low levels that add to the complexity and appeal of a wine. When excessive, it is an undesirable defect.

Wein (veyn)   German for "wine."

Weisswein (VEYSS-veyn)   German for "white wine." (In the German alphabet, this is written *Weißwein*.)

yeast   The single-celled microorganism, reproducing by budding, responsible for fermentation of grapes and other liquids containing sugars.

Recommended Books for Further Reading

1855: A History of the Bordeaux Classification. Dewey Markham, Jr. 1998. 535 pp. Hard. $69.95

A Companion to California Wine: An Encyclopedia of Wine and Winemaking from the Mission Period to the Present. Charles L. Sullivan. 1998. 368 pp. Hard. $39.95

A Passion for Piedmont: Italy's Most Glorious Regional Table. Matt Kramer. 1997. 336 pp. Hard. $28

Alaska Backyard Wines. Jan O'Mears. 1988. 60 pp. Soft. $7.95

American Winescapes: The Cultural Landscapes of America's Wine Country. Gary L. Peters. 1997. 176 pp. Soft. $18

Australian Wine: A Pictorial Guide. Thomas Hardy and Milan Roden. 1995. 352 pp. Hard. $34.95

Austria: New Wines from the Old World. Giles MacDonough. 1998. Hard. $35

Beyond the Grapes, an Inside Look at Napa Valley. Richard Paul Hinkle and Dan Berger. 1991. 256 pp. Hard. $39.95

Bollinger: Tradition of a Champagne Family. Cyril Ray. Hard. $30

Bordeaux, second edition. David Peppercorn. 1991. 720 pp. Hard, $49.95; Soft $42.95

Bordeaux: A Comprehensive Guide to the Wines Produced from 1961 to 1997. Robert M. Parker Jr. 1998. 1,200 pp. Hard. $50

Bordeaux: A Legendary Wine. Michel Dovaz. 1998. 268 pp. Hard. $75

Burgundy. Anthony Hanson. 1995. Soft. $33.95

Burgundy: A Comprehensive Guide to the Producers, Appellations, and Wines. Robert M. Parker, Jr. 1990. 1,051 pp. Hard. $39.95

Cabernet Sauvignon. Harry Eyres. 1992. Hard. $20

California Wine Winners 1999: The Best of the 1998 Judgings. Trudy Ahlstrom and J. T. Devine. Soft. $8.95

Champagne and Sparkling Wines. Michael Edwards. 1998. 240 pp. Soft. $14.95

Chardonnay, Your International Guide. Alan Young. 1991. 182 pp. Hard. $26.95

Château Latour: The History of a Great Vineyard: 1331[em]1992. Charles Higounet. 1993. 572 pp. Hard. $225

Chianti and the Wines of Tuscany. Rosemary George. 1990. 200 pp. Hard. $39.95

Christie's World Encyclopedia of Champagne & Sparking Wine. Tom Stevenson. 1998. 320 pp. Hard. $50

Clarke & Spurrier's Fine Wine Guide: A Connoiseur's Bible. Oz Clarke and Steven Spurrier. 1998. 320 pp. Soft. $30

Côte d'Or: A Celebration of the Great Wines of Burgundy. Clive Coates. 1997. 1,008 pp. Hard. $55

Discovering Wine. Joanna Simon. 1994. 157 pp. Soft. $18

Enjoying American Wines. Jay Harlow. 1986. 128 pp. Soft. $9.95

Food & Wine Magazine's Official Wine Guide 1999: How to Buy, Enjoy, Collect and Even Pronounce Your Favorite Wines. Stephen Tanzer. 1998. 240 pp. Soft. $9.95

Gourmets' Guide to Northwest Wines and Wineries. Chuck Hill. 1998. 280 pp. Soft. $16.95

Grands Crus of Bordeaux. Hans Walraven. 1995. 267 pp. Soft. $19.95

Grands Vins: The Finest Châteaux of Bordeaux and Their Wines. Clive Coates. 1995. Hard. $55

Harvests of Joy: My Life, My Way. Robert Mondavi. 1998. 368 pp. Hard. $27

Haut-Brion. Asa Briggs. 1994. Hard, $24.95; Soft, $14.95

Hugh Johnson's How to Enjoy Wine. Hugh Johnson. 1985. 144 pp. Soft. $11

Hugh Johnson's Modern Encyclopedia of Wine. Hugh Johnson. 576 pp. Hard. $40

Hugh Johnson's Pocket Encyclopedia of Wine, 1999. 280 pp. Soft. $13

Italian Wines 1998. Gambero Rosso. 600 pp. Soft. $24.95

Jancis Robinson's Guide to Wine Grapes. Jancis Robinson. 1996. Hard. $13.95

King Tut's Wine Cellar. Leonard H. Lesko. 1977. 50 pp. Soft. $5.95

Larousse Encyclopedia of Wine. C. Foulkes and C. Segrave, ed. 1994. 608 pp. Hard. $40

Larousse Pocket Encyclopedia of Wine. C. Foulkes. 1996. 256 pp. Soft. $11.95

Loire Valley & Its Wines. James Seely. 1990. 168 pp. Hard. $24.95

Making Sense of Wine. Matt Kramer. 1989. 208 pp. Soft. $15

Making Sense of Wine: A Study in Sensory Perception, fourth edition. Alan Young. 1995. 167 pp. Soft. $17.99

Margaux. Bernard Ginestet. 200 pp. Hard. $19.95

Margaux. Nicholas Faith. 1991. 215 pp. Hard. $50

Mendocino: The Ultimate Wine & Food Lover's Guide. Heidi Haughy Cusick. 1997. 120 pp. Soft. $19.95

Michael Broadbent's Pocket Guide to Wine Tasting. Michael Broadbent. 1995. Hard. $17

Michael Broadbent's Wine Vintages. Michael Broadbent. 1998. 208 pp. Soft. $14.95

Millennium Champagne and Sparking Wine Guide. Tom Stevenson. 1998. 224 pp. Soft. $19.95

Napa Valley: The Ultimate Winery Guide, revised. Antonio Allegra. 1997. 118 pp. Soft. $19.95

Northwest Wines: A Pocket Guide to the Wines of Washington, Oregon and Idaho, second edition. Paul Gregutt, Jeff Prather, Dan McCarthy. 1996. 208 pp. Soft. $11.95

Oz Clarke's Pocket Wine Guide 1999. Oz Clarke. 1998. 304 pp. Soft. $12

Oz Clarke's Wine Atlas: Wines and Wine Regions of the World. Oz Clarke. 1995. $60

Parker's Wine Buyer's Guide, fourth edition. Robert M. Parker, Jr. 1995. 1,200 pp. Soft. $25

Passions: The Wines and Travels of Thomas Jefferson. James M. Gabler. 1995. Hard. $29.95

Pauillac: The Wines and Estates of a Renowned Bordeaux Commune. Stephen Brook. 1998. 192 pp. Hard. $45

Pictorial Atlas of North American Wines. Thomas K. Hardy and Milan Roden. 360 pp. Hard. $39.95

Plain Talk About Fine Wine. Justin Meyer. 1989. 200 pp. Soft. $9.95

Port Wine Quintas of the Douro. Alex Liddell and Janet Price. 1992. 280 pp. Hard. $39.95

Portugal's Wines and Winemakers: Port, Madeira and Regional Wines. Richard Mayson. 1997. 224 pp. Hard. $34.95

Puligny-Montrachet: Journal of a Village in Burgundy. Simon Loftus. 1992. 308 pp. Soft. $14.95

Rhône Renaissance. Remington Norman. $50

Romanée-Conti. Richard Olney. 1995. Hard. $35

Sauternes: A Study of the Great Sweet Wines of Bordeaux. Jeffrey Benson and Allistair MacKenzie. 1990. 184 pp. Hard. $39.95

Sauternes and Other Sweet Wines of Bordeaux. Stephen Brook. 1995. 192 pp. Hard. $24.95; Soft, $15.95

Sauvignon Blanc and Semillon. Stephen Brook. 1992. 255 pp. Hard. $20

Seasons of the Vineyard. Robert Mondavi, Margrit Biever Mondavi and Carolyn Dille. 1996. 224 pp. Hard. $40

Sherry, fourth edition. Julian Jeffs. 1992. 320 pp. Hard, $29.95; Soft, $14.95

Sherry and the Sherry Bodagas. Jan Read. 1988. 192 pp. Hard. $45

Sonoma: The Ultimate Winery Guide. Heidi Haughy Cusick. 1995. 120 pp. Soft. $18.95

Sparkling Harvest. Jamie Davies and Jack Davies. 1997. 140 pp. Hard. $45

St.-Emilion. Bernard Ginestet. 200 pp. Hard. $19.95

St.-Julien. Bernard Ginestet. 200 pp. Hard. $19.95

Story of Champagne: The History and Pleasures of the Most Celebrated of Wines. Nicholas Faith. 1989. 246 pp. Hard. $21.95

The Bordeaux Atlas. Michael Broadbent and Hubrecht Duijker. 1997. 400 pp. Hard. $50

The Commonsense Book of Wine. Leon D. Adams. 1991. 168 pp. Soft. $8.95

The Connoisseurs' Handbook of the Wines of California and the Pacific Northwest, fourth edition. Norman S. Roby and Charles E. Olken. 1998. 448 pp. Soft. $19.95

The Country Wines of Burgundy and Beaujolais. Patrick Delaforce. 1989. 192 pp. Soft. $12.95

The Essential Wine Book: An Indispensable Guide to Wines of the World. Oz Clarke. 1997. 300 pp. Soft. $21

The Great Domaines of Burgundy: A Guide to the Finest Wine Producers of the Côte d'Or, second edition. Remington Norman. 1996. 288 pp. Hard. $45

The Great Wine Blight. George Ordish. 1987. 246 pp. Hard. $25

The Instant Wine Connoisseur: A Practical Guide to Tasting, Buying and Cooking with Wine. Mervyn L. Hecht. 1997. 146 pp. Soft. $9.95

The New Sotheby's Wine Encyclopedia. Tom Stevenson. 1997. 600 pp. Hard. $50

The New Spain: The First Complete Guide to Contemporary Spanish Wine. John Radford. 1998. 224 pp. Hard. $40

The Origins and Ancient History of Wine. Patrick McGovern, Stuart Fleming and Solomon Katz, eds. 1995. 528 pp. Hard, $85; Soft, $45

The Oxford Companion to Wine. Jancis Robinson, ed. 1994. Hard. $60

The Port Companion: A Connoiseur's Guide. Godfrey Spence. 1997. 224 pp. Hard. $23.95

The Simon and Schuster Guide to the Wines of Germany. Ian Jamieson. 1992. 318 pp. Soft. $13

The Simon and Schuster Guide to the Wines of Spain. Jan Read. 1992. 288 pp. Soft. $13

The Taste of Wine, second edition: The Art and Science of Wine Appreciation. Émile Peynaud. 1996. 346 pp. Hard. $60.50

The University Wine Course, second edition. Marian W. Baldy, Ph.D. 1994. Soft. $35

The Wild Bunch: Great Wines from Small Producers. Patrick Matthews. 1997. 288 pp. Soft. $13.95

The Wine Atlas of France. Hubrecht Duijker. 1997. 264 pp. Hard. $45

The Wine Project: Washington State's Winemaking History. Ronald Irvine. 1997. 456 pp. Soft. $29.95

The Wine Routes of Argentina. Alan Young. 1997. 176 pp. Hard. $29.95

The Wines of Alsace. Tom Stevenson. 1994. Soft. $24.95

The Wines of Bordeaux and Western France. John J. Baxevanis. 1987. 288 p. Hard. $45

The Wines of Chablis. Rosemary George. 216 pp. Hard. $29.95

The Wines of France, New Revised Edition. Clive Coates. 1998. 436 pp. Hard. $50

The Wines of Germany. Andrew Jefford. 1994. 100 pp. Hard. $10

The Wines of Italy. Burton Anderson. 1990. 320 pp. Hard. $45

The Wines of New Zealand. Rosemary George. 1996. 330 pp. Hard, $33.95; Soft, $16.95

The Wines of South Africa. James Seely. 1997. 320 pp. Hard, $32.95; Soft, 18.95

The Wines of the Rhône, third edition. John Livingstone-Learmonth. 1992. Soft. $28.95

The Wines of the Rhône Valley. Robert M. Parker, Jr. 1997. 464 pp. Hard. $40

The Zinfandel Trail. Ian Huton. 1998. $27

Toasting Temecula Wines. Vic Knight, Jr. 1996. 109 pp. Soft. $12.95

University of California Sotheby Book of California Wine. Doris Muscatine et al., ed. 1984. 640 pp. Hard. $50

Vines, Grapes & Wine: The Winedrinker's Guide to Grape Varieties. Jancis Robinson. 1986. 272 pp. Soft. $27.95

Vineyard: A Year in the Life of California's Wine Country. Joy Sterling and Andy Katz. 1998. 96 pp. $25

Vintage Feasting: A Vintner's Year of Fine Wines, Good Times, and Gifts from Nature's Garden. Joy Sterling. 1996. 240 pp. Hard. $22

Vintage Talk: Conversations with California's New Winemakers. Dennis Schaefer. 1994. 203 pp. Soft. $15.95

White Burgundy. Christopher Fielden. 1988. 160 pp. Hard. $24.95

Windows on the World Complete Wine Course 1999. Kevin Zrarly. Hard. $24.95

Wine. Hugh Johnson. 1974. 260 pp. Soft. $18.95

Wine Appreciation, second edition. Richard P. Vine. 1997. 480 pp. Hard. $65.95

Wine Lover's Companion. Ron Herbst and Sharon Tyler Herbst. 1995. 644 pp. Soft. $12.95

Wine Price File, 12th edition. William Edgerton. 1998. 651 pp. Soft, $45; disk, $95

Wine Regions of the Southern Hemisphere. Harm J. De Blij. 1985. 272 pp. Hard. $45

Wine with Food. Joanna Simon. 1996. 160 pp. Hard. $25

Winequest: The Wine Dictionary. Ted Grudzinski. 1985. 469 pp. Hard. $28

Wines & Vines of California. Gary L. Peters. 1989. 184 pp. Soft. $16.95

Wines from Chile. Jurgen Matthis. 1997. 144 pp. Hard. $24.95

Wines of Burgundy. Serena Sutcliffe. 1998. 170 pp. Soft. $14.95

Wines of Spain, second edition. Jan Read. 1986. 272 pp. Soft. $13.95

Wines of the Graves. Pamela V. Price. 1988. 387 pp. Hard. $45

Wines of the Loire. Roger Vos. 1995. Hard, $29.95; Soft. $16.95

Wines of the Rioja. Jan Read. 1984. 170 pp. Hard. $35

World Atlas of Wine, fourth edition. Hugh Johnson. 1994. Hard. $50

Zinfandel: A Reference Guide to California Zinfandel. Cathleen Francisco. 1998. 274 pp. Soft. $24.95

Wine Toasts

Among Friends

Friends and colleagues, here we meet.
First a toast, before we eat!

May the quiet opulence of this rare wine bring us, also, peace and plenty.

The wine is dear; our fellowship, priceless.

Let us praise sparkling wine and sparkling wit!

To food, to fellowship, and wine
And all those other things as fine!

May our hearts remain as true as this wine is red!

Age before beauty, they say. Okay. To old wine! Now to new friendship!

Let us experience the warmth of our camaraderie in the warmth of our wine.

Wine Lovers

May the sunshine of Bordeaux infuse our spirits!

To sun, to rain, to grape, to all
That brought this wine into our hall!

And here's to Bacchus, but for whom this toast would not be possible!

A glass of Rhine let's lift on high,
As we the bonds of friendship tie!

Business and Politics

With wine of noble appellation,
Let us honor our great nation!

May our blue-chip friendship forever pay dividends!

A glass of wine to tinge our cheeks:
Now we toast him; then he speaks.

Champagne now we all must tally,
As we to our party rally!

The soup is hot; the wine is cold:
Let us begin our venture bold!

Lift high your glasses, as high as your hopes.

Humor

A fine white wine, and not too chilled,
Now let's all drink it, 'fore it's spilled.

Doctor, dentist, lawyer, thirst:
Which do you think we'll pay first?

Champagne for my real friends! (Real pain for my sham friends.)

In wine there is truth. May the truth ever be in us!

T'ain't Champagne; I've got to warn ya:
This here wine's from California!

Special Events

With this wine of flavors supple,
Let us toast the happy couple!

A toast, a cheer! To couple's love, to families united!

A vintage year, this glass of wine,
To toast our guest before we dine!

Old wine in new glasses. To old love and new dreams!

Wine to lips around this room
As we toast our bride and groom!

Toast him now! Let's toast him doubly!
Elevate your flutes of bubbly!

Sparkling wine to toast the product of that spark of love!

Wine Accessories

Bonsai Grapevine A real miniature grapevine that goes through all the natural seasonal changes of branching, budding, fruit bearing, and dormancy. Produces real grapes. About $75.

Champagne Key A special device to grip the cork and make removal a breeze. Chrome or gold-plated. About $9.

Cork Retriever Cork pushed into the bottle. Retrieve it with this nifty device. About $10.

Grapevine Coffee Table Glass-top coffee table with a base made out of the trunks of very old grapevines. Quite attractive. About $200.

LCD Wine Thermometer Clamp this unit onto your bottle and read the temperature from a large LCD display. About $20.

Monopoly—Napa Valley Edition America's best-loved board game in the wine-lover's edition. Own vineyards and wineries. Become a wine baron. $35.

Riedel Wineglasses Crystal wine glasses from this German manufacturer are considered the very best. They come in many shapes and sizes. Starting at about $35 for a set of four.

Stemware Washing Brush A dishwashing brush designed especially for wine glasses. About $8.

Terra Cotta Wine Cooler This unique cooler will maintain your wine's temperature for hours. About $30.

Vinocave Cellars Handsome temperature-controlled wine storage units range in capacity from 140 to 630 bottles. Start at $1,250.

Wine Apron An attractive plastic apron covered with wine bottles, wine corks, corkscrews, and the like. About $20.

Wine Credenza Elegant handcrafted furniture pieces that hold from 90 to 270 bottles. Will enhance any room. Starts at $1,950.

Wine Decanters A beautiful way to serve your wine. Essential for older wines. Many styles and sizes. Start at $25.

Wine Luggage Protect your wine while traveling. Models from one bottle to six. Two bottle bag $40.

Wine Rack Coffee Table Glass-top coffee table with a wrought-iron wine rack base that holds 24 bottles. About $200.

Wine Tags Write the name of your wine on these nifty reusable plastic tags and hang them from the neck of the bottle. You will no longer have to pull your wine out of the rack to determine what it is. About $10 for 50 tags.

Wine Ties Imagine your silk tie with a wine motif. Several styles showing wine labels, wine bottles, or corks. About $35.

Wrought Iron Wine Racks These attractive wine racks come with a curved top. Sizes range from 12 bottles to 72 bottles. 72-bottle unit is about $150.

Wines for All Occasions

Wedding

French Champagne

California sparkling wine

Moderately priced red wine such as a French Beaujolais

Moderately priced white wine such as a California Chenin Blanc

Bar Mitzvah

Old-style Concord grape kosher wine

Modern-style kosher wines from California or France, such as a Merlot or Cabernet Sauvignon

Anniversary

A fine Bordeaux or Burgundy from the year of your marriage

A high-quality French Champagne

First Date

Good-quality Bordeaux or Burgundy

A reserve California Cabernet Sauvignon or Pinot Noir

A high-quality California sparkling wine

Marriage Proposal

The best French Champagne you can afford

Birthday

A wine from the year of birth

Wine Faux Pas

Don't store wine in hot places.

Don't keep wine in the trunk of your car.

Don't shake an old bottle of wine.

Don't store your wine standing up.

Don't keep a wine past its prime.

Don't store wine in the sunlight.

Don't store wine around strong odors.

Don't store a wine around vibration.

Don't order expensive wine storage equipment from someone you don't know.

Don't let your guests drive home inebriated.

Don't let your Champagne bottles get scratched.

Don't push the cork into the wine bottle.

Don't serve wine in unwashed glasses.

Don't serve wine in musty glasses.

Don't fill a wineglass more than halfway.

Don't pop the Champagne cork.

Don't aim the Champagne bottle at anyone.

Don't use saucer or hollow-stemmed Champagne glasses.

Don't use wineglasses with hollow stems.

Don't serve maderized wine.

Don't serve a white wine too cold.

Don't put ice cubes in a glass of wine.

Don't use stemware that's too fragile.

Don't buy wine from the store window.

Don't patronize a wine store with a bad attitude.

Don't patronize a wine store with unknowledgeable clerks.

Don't give too much attention to wine snobs.

Don't assume a cork in a bottle is a sign of quality.

Don't assume a vintage date means good quality.

Don't fail to ask when you don't understand wine terminology.

Don't take 100-point rating systems too seriously.

Don't confuse the Silvaner or Grey Riesling with the noble Johannesburg Riesling.

Don't confuse wines made from the Muscat grape with "Muscatel."

Don't confuse the Bordeaux Grand Cru Classé with Burgundy's Grand Cru.

Don't assume "Estate-bottled" or "Grown, produced, and bottled by" are indicators of quality in California wines.

Don't assume all Napa Valley wines are superior.

Don't assume Australian "Rieslings" are made from the Riesling grape.

Don't assume all champagne is Champagne.

Don't confuse "fermented in *the* bottle" with "fermented in *this* bottle."

Don't pour bottle-aged wines in haste.

Don't assume all wine labeled "Port" is real Porto wine.

Don't assume all wine labeled "Sherry" is real Sherry.

Don't assume the words "reserve" or "classic" on a U.S. wine label have any significance.

Don't assume all bottle-aged wines in a single case will be of the same quality.

Don't neglect to note mouthfeel when you drink wine.

Don't use "cooking wines" sold in supermarkets.

Don't let the sommelier intimidate you.

Don't accept a faulty wine in a restaurant.

Don't accept a bottle in a restaurant that hasn't been opened at your table.

Wine on the Internet

Resource Sites

Africus Rex
www.cyberus.ca/~chorniak/

Billed as the world's smallest vineyard and winery, this site shows what can be done to grow grapes in your own backyard and produce wine from a basement winery.

Auctionvine
www.auctionvine.com

This site conducts wine auctions for several auction houses and well-known wine retailers. It is worth visiting if you buy wine at auction. All wines purchased carry a money-back guarantee.

Australian Wine Online
www.winetitles.com.au/wineonline.html

Information resource for Australian wines, wineries, industry suppliers, articles, databases, and more.

BC Wine Information Centre
www.bcwineinfo.com

Information about the British Columbia wine industry, the wineries, and the VQA Vintners Quality Alliance (VQA) program.

Bureau Interprofessional des Vins de Bourgogne
www.bivb.com

French and English versions. Information about the Burgundy region of France, the appellations, news, events, and more.

Champagne France

www.champagnes.com

Presented by the Champagne Wine Information Bureau. History, regional information, winemaking, food pairing, and more.

German Wine

www.germanwine.de/english/dwi/index.htm

A bilingual language site. Wine information, food pairings, grape varieties, online shopping, etc. Hosted by the German Wine Institute.

Greek Wine

www.greekwine.gr/frames/index.html

Although some parts of this site are incomplete, there is still good information about the wine-producing regions of Greece, the varietals, appellation designations, and more.

Homearts.com Wine Navigator

http://homearts.com/helpers/winenav/wine.htm

The main feature of this site, which is part of a larger Web site, is the food- and wine-matching function. You also can search for wines by style and price.

Interwines Guide to Spain (Guia Internet de Los Vinos de Espana)

www.filewine.es

Spanish- and English-language versions. This site is updated weekly and features information about the various regions, producers, and grape varieties.

Into Wine

www.intowine.com

Good information about wine in general. Plus vintage charts for a number of regions, serving temperature guide for wines, wine storage, and a few other wine-related sections.

Mike L's Guide to Washington Wineries

http://vintners.net/wawine/

A good resource site for discovering the wineries of Washington State. Maps of various regions and brief winery description pages.

New Zealand Wines Online

www.nzwine.com

A virtual tour of New Zealand and its wines. Includes some winery information, food and wine, wine regions, and a video tour.

Oregon Wine

www.oregonwine.org

A good starting point to learn about Oregon wines, the appellations, history, wineries, events, and more.

The Origins and Ancient History of Wine
www.upenn.edu/museum/Wine/wineintro.html

A look at the history of wine, presented by the University of Pennsylvania Museum of Archeology and Anthropology.

Port Wine
www.wildfire.com/~ag/portwine/

A good source for learning about Port wines. History, production, storing, and vintage chart (up to 1994).

Riedel Crystal
www.riedelcrystal.com

Bilingual (German & English). Information at this site includes competitions, tastings, news, and a wine search facility to identify the most suitable glass for any wine.

Robin Garr's Wine Lovers' Page
www.wine-lovers-page.com

One of the best "personal" wine sites on the Internet originating in the U.S.A. Great educational resource, lots of tasting notes, a weekly newsletter, and a very active discussion forum. Continually updated.

South African Wine
www.wine.co.za

South African wine directory, news, and information on the wine industry. Brief information is given for a lot of wineries and their wine lists.

Spanish Wine Page
http://vino.eunet.es/vino/index.html

Everything you want to know about Spanish wine. Regions, grape varieties, wineries, food, news and events, tasting notes, tours, and more.

Strat's Place
www.stratsplace.com

Started out as a small site about gardening, the arts, and wine labels and has expanded into a "wine" community. Many sections in the wine area including pronunciation of wine terms, cellar pictures, food pairings, columns, tasting notes, and much more.

Tastings.com
www.tastings.com

This site is operated by the Beverage Testing Institute in Chicago, Illinois, which founded the World Wine Championships. It reviews more than 5,000 wines each year and maintains a searchable database where you can view tasting notes and scores along with a list of producers it recommends.

Terroirs Bourguignons
www.terroirs-b.com

A multilanguage site. Information about the Burgundy region in France, including news, events, selected wineries, gastronomy, tourism in the region, and more.

Tom Cannavan's Wine Pages
www.wine-pages.com

Another one of the best "personal" wine sites originating in the United Kingdom. Personal tasting notes, regional guides to wine-producing regions, an online wine course, and more. Updated continually.

Unusual Wines
www.geocities.com/Heartland/Fields/7246/

This site features unusual wines, unusual varieties, wines from unusual places, and wines with weird or funny labels.

Victoria Wineries Home Page
www.wineries.tourism.vic.gov.au

Wine information about the Australian state of Victoria. Includes winery information, events, news, and tours. Two presentation versions: plain and Shockwave.

Vine2Wine.com
www.vine2wine.com

A comprehensive directory of links to wine sites on the Internet. More than 2,000 links to wineries, educational resources, clubs, publications, and more. Listings are grouped into categories and listed in alphabetical order. Majority of Web sites are rated for quantity of content.

Vineyards of England and Wales
http://sol.brunel.ac.uk/~richards/wine/start.htm

Yes, there are wineries in the British Isles, and if you want to know more about the history of winemaking and the wines of England and Wales, this is the place to start.

Vins "Cotes du Rhone" Wines
www.rhone-wines.com

Bilingual. Regional information, winery information, wine notes, and news. Site appears to have some dated information.

Vinternet
www.vinternet.net

A bilingual-language site offering information about a number of French wineries. Site has links to wineries and other information, such as winemaking, online forum for discussions, and so on. If your browser supports Shockwave, select that option.

Wine Education Site
www.wineeducation.com

Presented by Buyers and Cellars Wine Consultants. Information about wine, from beginner to advanced.

Wine of the Week
www.nettivuori.com/weeklywine/

Personal tasting notes organized by date and region with some very appealing and interesting photographs accompanying the prose.

Wine Place
www.wineplace.nu

Personal Web pages offering information about wine, tasting notes, a forum, and local events in Singapore.

The Wineries and Vineyards of Idaho
www.idahowine.com

All about the wine industry in Idaho, including news, events, winery information, food and wine pairing, and recipes. Online ordering available.

Wines from Austria
www.austrian.wine.co.at/wine/eindex.htm

Multilingual site with information about wineries, wines, vintages, history, events, and more.

Wines of Jumilla
www.jumillawine.com

Bilingual. Official Web site of the Wine Council in Jumilla, Spain. Regional background and history, wine, producers, and news.

Wines on the Internet
www.wines.com

Billed as the Cyberspace Guide to Wine and Wineries. Features a searchable database, articles, reviews, plus Jerry Mead's column, "Mead on Wine," and "Wine Tributaries," featuring news and events from Sonoma.

Wines Online—The Wines of Italy
www.agriline.it/wol/wol_eng/Default.htm

Multilingual site with extensive information, including searches within the site itself.

Winetasting Journeys in the Loire Valley and Alsace
http://members.aol.com/melroche/fr/vacation.html

Personal pages by a Brooklyn couple about traveling through the two regions during 1997 and 1998. Travel information, winery information, and tasting notes.

Wineward
www.wineward.com

Information about the wineries of the Niagara Peninsula of Ontario, Canada. Tour information and places to stay.

The Zin Zealot
http://home.earthlink.net/~nagyv/

If you want to learn about Zinfandel from Sonoma County, here is a place to start.

Online E-Zines and Magazines

Bung! The Wine Brats
www.wine.brats.org

The online publication from the Wine Brats. Assorted topics, food and wine, and more.

Christoph's Quarterly & Wine Reviews
www.christophs.org

E-zine from *Philidelphia Sun* wine critic Justin Christoph. Online resource for a quarterly magazine featuring wine, cigar, dining, and art reviews.

Food & Wine
www.pathfinder.com/@@0jGsoQUA6hmjeu7o/FoodWine/

E-zine operated by American Express. Features a section called "The Wine Guide," which has some good pages about selecting wines, pairing wine with food, and other useful wine-related information.

The Home Winemakers Manual
http://home.att.net/~lumeisenman/

An online book on home winemaking by Lum Eisenman. Twenty chapters covering all aspects of home winemaking. Read online, material is copyrighted but available free of charge.

James Halliday, Wine on the Web
www.jameshalliday.com.au

Web site for renowned Australian wine writer. Reviews, articles, wine forum, and newsletter. A good source of Australian wine information.

Wine & Dine E-Zine
www.winedine.co.uk

Wine reviews, news, and more. Monthly publication.

The Wine Authority
www.wineauthority.com/welcome.html

An online journal updated almost every day with reviews and articles about the California wine industry. Archived newsletter, national retailer directory, and other information.

Wine Enthusiast
www.winemag.com

E-zine. Daily articles, vintage charts, wine and cigar buying information, etc.

Wine-People
www.wine-people.com/wine-people/index.htm

To quote from the front page: "Wine interviews, reviews, rants and a torrent of other wine wisdom to impress other wine geeks, bore your spouse and alienate your friends ..." But don't let that put you off!

The Wine Spectator
www.winespectator.com

Online edition of the popular printed magazine. Reviews, articles, food and wine, reviews, tasting notes, and more.

Winetoday.com
www.winetoday.com

Online magazine with articles about the California wine industry. Information about California wineries plus links where available.

Winery Sites

Bava—Italy
www.bava.com

Beringer Vineyards—USA
www.beringer.com/index.html

Blue Mountain Vineyards—USA
www.bmvc.com

Bodegas Torres—Spain
www.torres.es/idiomas.htm

Bolla—Italy
www.bolla.com

Bouchard Pere et Fils—France
www.bouchardpere.com/bouchard/

Carmel Mizrachi—Israel
www.carmelwines.co.il

Castello Banfi—Italy
www.castellobanfi.com

Castello di Monterinaldi—Italy
www.intervos.com/monterinaldi/

Château d'Yquem—France
www.chateau-yquem.fr

Chateau des Charmes Wines—Canada
www.chateaudescharmes.com

Château Figeac—France
www.vinternet.net/Figeac/

Château Haut-Brion—France
http://haut-brion.com

Château Lafite Rothschild—France
www.lafite.com

Château Margaux—France
www.chateau-margaux.com

Chateau Musar—Lebanon
www.chateaumusar.com.lb

Chateau St. Michelle Vineyards & Winery—USA
www.ste-michelle.com

Clos Du Val Winery—USA
www.closduval.com

Coldstream Hill Winery—Australia
www.coldstreamhills.com.au

Corbans—New Zealand
www.corbans.co.nz

Couly-Dutheil—France
www.coulydutheil-chinon.com

Croft Port—Portugal
www.croft.com

David Coffaro Vineyard & Winery—USA
www.coffaro.com

Domaine Carneros by Taittinger—USA
www.domaine.com

Domaine E. de Montmollin Fils—Switzerland
www.montmollinwine.ch

El Coto de Rioja—Spain
www.elcoto.com/ingles/index.html

Fortant de France—France
www.fortant.com

Gruppo Italiano Vini—Italy
www.giv.it

Hainle Vineyards—Canada
www.hainle.com

Husch Vineyards—USA
www.huschvineyards.com

Jordan and Jordan—Germany
www.saarwein.com/e_index.htm

Joseph Drouhin—France
www.drouhin.com

Joseph Phelps Vineyards—USA
www.jpvwines.com

Kendall Jackson Winery—USA
www.kj.com

King Estate—USA
www.kingestate.com

KWV—South Africa
www.kwv.co.za/index.htm

L'Ecole No 41—USA
www.lecole.com

La Rioja Alta—Spain
www.riojalta.com

Le Comte (Hawthorne Mountain)—Canada
www.hmvineyard.com

Lingenfelder Estate—Germany
www.lingenfelder.com

Louis Latour—France
www.LouisLatour.com

Marchesi Antinori—Italy
www.antinori.it

Marsovin Group—Malta
www.marsovin.com.mt

McWilliam's Wines—Australia
www.mcwilliams.com.au

Merlen Estate—New Zealand
www.nzwine.com/merlen/index.html

Mildara Blass Wines—Australia
www.worldwidewines.com/homepage2.html

Moet & Chandon—France
www.moet.com

Morgenhof Wines—South Africa
www.morgenhof.com

Pellegrini Winery & Vineyard—USA
http://pellegrinivineyards.com

Quivira Vineyards—USA
www.quivirawine.com

Real Companhia Velha—Portugal
www.realcompanhiavelha.pt

Ridge Vineyards—USA
www.ridgewine.com/ridge/

Robert Mondavi—USA
www.robertmondavi.com/index.html

SARAfIN—Turkey
www.sarafin.com/Engl/home_e.htm

Schlumberger AG—Austria
www.schlumberger.co.at

Schug Carneros Estate Winery—USA
www.schugwinery.com

Simonsig—South Africa
www.simonsig.co.za

Sumac Ridge Estate Winery—Canada
www.sumacridge.com

Vina Santa Carolina—South America
www.santacarolina.com

Vina Santa Rita—South America
www.santarita.com

Viña Viu Manent—South America
www.chilevinos.cl/viumanent/

Wynns Coonwarra Estate—Australia
www.wynns.com.au/index.asp

Wine Magazines, Newsletters, and Catalogs

Wine Magazines

Decanter. Published in London. Monthly, $80 a year. Telephone (USA): 1-800-875-2997.

Vintage Magazine. 8 issues a year, $19.95 a year. Telephone: 212-369-8358

Wine & Spirits. 8 issues a year, $22 a year. Telephone: 212-695-4660.

The Wine News. Bimonthly, $24 a year. Telephone: 305-444-7250.

Wine Spectator. 18 issues, $40 a year. Telephone: 1-800-752-7799.

Newsletters

Connoisseur's Guide to California Wine. Monthly, $50 a year. Telephone: 510-865-3150.

Stephen Tanzer's International Wine Cellar. Bimonthly, $48 a year. Telephone: 1-800-946-3505.

The Vine (Clive Coates). Monthly, $120 per year. www.clive-coates.co.uk.

The Wine Advocate (Robert Parker). Bimonthly, $45 a year. Telephone: 410-329-6477.

The Wine Reporter. Weekly, $29.95 a year. Telephone: 1-800-332-0278.

Catalogs

Kellgren's Wine Book Catalog (Specialty Books Company). Telephone: 1-800-274-4816.

Wine & All That Jazz. Telephone: 1-800-610-7731.

Index

C

515

519